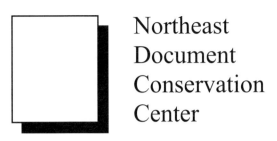

Northeast
Document
Conservation
Center

PRESERVATION

OF LIBRARY

& ARCHIVAL

MATERIALS:

A MANUAL

Third Edition

Revised and Expanded

Edited by Sherelyn Ogden

Northeast Document Conservation Center, Andover, Massachusetts 1999

The Institute of Museum and Library Services, a federal agency that fosters innovation, leadership, and a lifetime of learning, supported the publication of this manual, *Preservation of Library & Archival Materials: A Manual,* Third Edition, Revised and Expanded, by the Northeast Document Conservation Center.

The National Endowment for the Humanities, an independent grant-making agency of the federal government, funded the creation of many of the individual technical leaflets published here. NEH continues to support the Field Service Program of the Northeast Document Conservation Center.

The opinions expressed by individual authors in the book are their own, and are not taken as representing the views of any institution or organization, including NEDCC. NEDCC does not warrant that the information contained herein is complete or accurate, and does not assume, and hereby disclaims any liability to any person for any loss or damage caused by errors or omissions in *Preservation of Library & Archival Materials: A Manual,* whether such errors or omission result from negligence, accident or other cause.

Library of Congress Cataloging Number
ISBN No. 0-963-4685-2-9

This publication is printed on paper that meets the requirements of American National Standard for Information Sciences—Permanence of Paper for Printed Library Materials, ANSI Z39.48-1992.

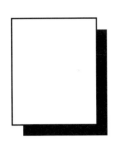

Northeast Document
Conservation Center
100 Brickstone Square
Andover, MA 01810-1494
www.nedcc.org
Tel: (978) 470-1010
Fax: (978) 475-6021

PRESERVATION OF LIBRARY & ARCHIVAL MATERIALS: A MANUAL

TABLE OF CONTENTS

EMERGENCY MANAGEMENT

STORAGE AND HANDLING

REFORMATTING

CONSERVATION PROCEDURES

Northeast Document
Conservation Center
100 Brickstone Square
Andover, MA 01810-1494
www.nedcc.org
Tel: (978) 470-1010
Fax: (978) 475-6021

PREFACE

I am pleased and proud to present this updated third edition of the manual to the professional community. When the Northeast Document Conservation Center (NEDCC) published the original manual in 1992, we had no idea that demand for it would be as great as it proved to be. Nearly 6,000 copies have been sold or distributed in the intervening years, and the reviews have been consistently laudatory. Many colleagues have used it as a text for courses and workshops. It has been translated into Spanish, Portuguese, and Russian. The publication's ability to serve as an authoritative reference source and translate up-to-date scientific research into layman's language has motivated us to expand it. The new edition incorporates much new information, including new sections on digital format conversion.

NEDCC, a nonprofit service organization devoted to the preservation of library and archival materials, has had a strong commitment to the dissemination of information since its founding. This manual, which represents the expertise of NEDCC staff and colleagues, was produced in the spirit of this commitment. NEDCC hopes that the manual will prove useful to the field and will lead to improvements in the condition of library and archival collections. I am grateful to the editor of the manual, Sherelyn Ogden, who also served as editor of the first two editions; to Steve Dalton, NEDCC's Field Service Director, who served as project manager; and to Kim O'Leary who served as Webmaster. I would like especially to thank the Institute of Museum and Library Services for their kind support of the electronic publication of the manual, which will make the information available at no cost to an enormous new audience. I would also like to thank the National Endowment for the Humanities for its generous support of NEDCC's Field Service office.

Ann Russell
Executive Director
NEDCC
September 1999

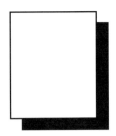

Northeast Document
Conservation Center
100 Brickstone Square
Andover, MA 01810-1494
www.nedcc.org
Tel: (978) 470-1010
Fax: (978) 475-6021

ACKNOWLEDGEMENTS

The success of this manual is due to the many people who have contributed to it from the beginning. For this reason, those who were instrumental in producing the first two editions as well as those who contributed to this third edition are gratefully acknowledged here.

The information in this manual reflects the collective experience and knowledge of the staff, both past and present, of Northeast Document Conservation Center (NEDCC). Although these staff members are too numerous to cite individually, two former staff members should be recognized. They are the late George Cunha, former Director of NEDCC, and Mildred O'Connell, former Director of Field Service, who prepared many of NEDCC's first technical leaflets.

I would like to thank the authors who contributed to the manual. Those who are currently members of NEDCC's staff or who were on the staff when they wrote their leaflets are: Gary Albright, Senior Conservator; Karen E. Brown, Field Service Representative; Steve Dalton, Director of Field Service; Mary Todd Glaser, Director of Paper Conservation; Karen Motylewski, formerly Director of Field Service; Beth Lindblom Patkus, formerly Field Service Representative; and Debra Saryan, Librarian, who also assisted with copyright procedures. Other contributing authors are: Nick Artim, Director, Fire Safety Network, Middlebury, VM; Sally A. Buchanan, Associate Professor, School of Information Science, University of Pittsburgh, Pittsburgh, PA; Dr. Margaret Child, Preservation Consultant, Washington, D.C.; Christopher Clarkson, Conservator, Oxford, England; Paul Conway, Head, Preservation Department, Yale University, New Haven, CT; Rebecca Thatcher Ellis, Mechanical Engineer, Orr, Schelen, Mayeron and Associates, Inc., Minneapolis, MN; Richard Horton, Conservator, Bridgeport National Bindery, Agawam, MA; Peter Jermann, Preservation Officer, St. Bonaventure University, St. Bonaventure, NY; and Jan Paris, Conservator for the Academic Affairs Library, University of North Carolina at Chapel Hill, Chapel Hill, NC. I am very grateful to all these colleagues who generously wrote, revised, or updated technical leaflets. Their contributions are invaluable. Steve Dalton served most ably as Project Manager as well as author. I am grateful for his assistance.

I would like to thank Margaret R. Brown, Special Assistant and Registrar, Library of Congress Preservation Directorate, Washington, D.C., whose fine illustrations greatly enhance the text. The sound technical assistance of Patricia McCarthy, formerly Administrative Assistant, Field Service, NEDCC, in the production of the technical leaflets in the first two editions is appreciated. The competence and expertise of Kim O'Leary, Webmaster, NEDCC in converting the third edition to electronic format as well as in preparation of this edition for publication in print form is very gratefully acknowledged.

Thanks to the following organizations for permission to reprint material that they had published: Southeastern Library Network, Inc., Atlanta, GA, for permission to reprint *Choosing and Working with a Conservator*; the American Association for State and Local History, Nashville, TN, for permission to reprint *Disaster Planning for Cultural Institutions*; the American Association of Museums, Washington, D.C., for permission to use parts of *Preservation Planning: Guidelines for Writing A Long-Range Plan*; and to Butterworth Heinemann, Oxford, England, for permission to use material in the upcoming book *Conservation of Works of Art on Paper*. I also would like to thank Betty Walsh, Conservator, British Columbia Information Management Services, Victoria, British Columbia, Canada, for assistance as well as permission to link to the electronic version of this book article "Salvage Operations for Water Damaged Archival Collections: A Second Glance."

I am very grateful to the following for professional advice, assistance, and discussion: Jennifer Banks, Preservation and Collections Librarian, Massachusetts Institute of Technology, Boston, MA; Robert de Candido, Automation Specialist for Preservation, New York Public Library, New York, NY; Mary-Lou Florian, Conservation Scientist, Victoria, British Columbia, Canada; B.W. Golden, Vice President, Engineering, Interior Steel, Cleveland, Ohio; Pamela Hatchfield, Associate Conservator, Museum of Fine Arts, Boston, MA; Jan Merrill-Oldham, Malloy-Rabinowitz Preservation Librarian, Harvard University Library Preservation Center, Cambridge, MA; Robert Mottice, Mottice Micrographics, Manchester, MI; Paul Parisi, President, Acme Bookbinding Company, Charlestown, MA; Nicholas Pickwoad, Conservator, Norwich, England; Steven Puglia, Photographic Preservation Specialist, National Archives, Special Media Preservation Branch, College Park, MD; and Deborah Wender, Director of Book Conservation, NEDCC. The assistance of Gay Tracy, Public Relations Coordinator, NEDCC with publication procedures is gratefully acknowledged. The suggestions and design work of Steve Sakowich, Sakowich Design, Lincoln, MA, are appreciated.

Sincere thanks are also due to Dr. Michèle V. Cloonan, Chair and Associate Professor, University of California at Los Angeles and to Dr. Sidney E. Berger, Head of Special Collections, University of California at Riverside, for their valuable assistance proofreading all three editions of the manual. Their knowledge and skill are greatly appreciated. Thanks also go to Paul Hudon, freelance writer, Lowell, MA, and to Diane Barrie, Archivist, Ronald Reagan Presidential Library, Simi Valley, California, for checking references and procedural descriptions for accuracy in the first edition. Of course, I accept responsibility for any errors. I am very grateful to Dr. Josephine Fang, Professor Emerita, Simmons College, Boston, MA, for encouragement, advice, and practical help. Allan Thenen, Paper Conservator, St. Paul, MN, deserves special acknowledgement and thanks for his suggestions and assistance. His support is deeply appreciated.

Most notable thanks go to Dr. Ann Russell, Executive Director, NEDCC, who secured the financial assistance that made this project possible. Without her faith in the project and significant efforts to obtain funding, not one edition of the manual would have been possible. I would also like to thank all my colleagues at NEDCC for their assistance and support. Finally, I would like to thank the Institute of Museum and Library Services for generously supporting the development and production of this third edition of the manual, and the National Endowment for the Humanities for its kind support of NEDCC's field service office.

Sherelyn Ogden

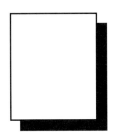

Northeast Document Conservation Center
100 Brickstone Square
Andover, MA 01810-1494
www.nedcc.org
Tel: (978) 470-1010
Fax: (978) 475-6021

INTRODUCTION

Libraries and archives are threatened by a massive problem of deterioration and loss of the collections they contain. Many collections are becoming increasingly fragile, and some are in danger of being lost forever. The problem of deterioration has several interrelated causes: inherent chemical instability of the components of library and archival materials; unsuitable environmental conditions in areas where collections are stored; inappropriate storage and handling practices; natural disasters; and theft and vandalism. For most libraries and archives, professional conservation treatment as a way to rectify the problem is, and always will be, prohibitively expensive. Adequate preventive care for collections, however, including proper storage, handling, and security, is not an unrealistic goal.

The term *preservation* as it is used in this manual refers to the "activities associated with maintaining library, archival, or museum materials for use, either in original physical form or in some other format."[1] This definition, suggested by the American Library Association (ALA), broadly includes a number of procedures from control of the environment to conservation treatment. *Conservation,* again according to ALA, refers to "the treatment of library or archive materials, works of art, or museum objects to stabilize them physically, sustaining their survival as long as possible in their original form."[2]

The purpose of this manual is to provide the basic, practical information needed to enable nonconservator staff of libraries and archives to plan and implement sound collections care programs or to incorporate preservation principles into existing collections care programs. The manual is not intended to answer all questions related to preservation or collections management. Instead, it aims to provide direction or guidance on preservation issues. The focus of the manual is on preventing or, more accurately, retarding the deterioration of paperbased library and archival materials (deterioration cannot be stopped; it can only be slowed down). For the most part, the manual emphasizes preservation of entire collections rather than that of single objects. The information it contains is introductory in nature. It is intended to be used by staff who have little or no professional training or experience in preservation of collections, but who want to upgrade standards of care in order to better preserve materials. It is also intended for those who cannot avoid making decisions that affect preservation of collections, such as the selection of storage enclosures or the specification of storage locations and methods. If readers of the manual have questions about application of the information to their particular situation, they should contact the staff at Northeast Document Conservation Center (NEDCC) or other preservation professionals.

Since its founding in 1973, NEDCC has issued leaflets in response to specific requests from clients for information. Because of the high number of such requests, it was decided to make the information available in an organized format. All existing leaflets were updated and revised. New leaflets were written to provide any information that was lacking, so that a body of basic introductory information would be produced for this manual, which was first published in 1992.

Increasingly NEDCC's clients have been asking that preservation information be made available to them in electronic format. This manual is well suited to electronic distribution, being made up of individual leaflets that can be searched quickly by subject. In response to this request, NEDCC decided to produce this third edition for distribution electronically, making it available to cultural institutions worldwide at no cost. This electronic version of the manual will be updated on a regular basis. Users are encouraged to download single copies of leaflets freely.

Several of NEDCC's clients requested that a printed version of the manual be made available along with the electronic one. This printed book was published in response to those requests. The book was produced from the electronic version of the manual, and its content and layout are the same. Because many of the leaflets were intended to stand alone electronically rather than be used as part of a printed book, information is repeated from one leaflet to another. The printed version does not contain an index in order to keep the purchase price of the book as low as possible. It is hoped that the table of contents and the explanatory title of the leaflets will provide adequate assistance in locating information. The search engine for the electronic version also is available to provide assistance.

Every leaflet in the third edition has again been reviewed and updated or revised as required to reflect new information and changing opinions. Recently published references have been added to the bibliographies and new products and sources have been added to supply lists. All addresses and phone and fax numbers have been checked and updated as needed. Many leaflets were expanded and several new leaflets were written, totaling approximately 100 pages of new information in this edition.

A manual such as this can never be complete. It will always be expanding to meet the evolving needs of NEDCC's clients and to reflect the ongoing issues in the field. Updates and revisions will be made and additional leaflets are expected. Suggestions for topics for new leaflets and any comments are invited. Thus, we hope that the manual will continue to be a useful tool for improvement in the care of library and archival materials and will serve as a catalyst for concentrating more resources on the preservation of these materials.

[1] *ALCTS Newsletter, "Glossary of Selected Preservation Terms," ALCTS Newsletter 1.2 (1990): 15.*
[2] *ALCTS Newsletter, p.14.*

Sherelyn Ogden
Editor
June 1999

Sherelyn Ogden was Director of Book Conservation at the Northeast Document Conservation Center for seventeen years. During that time she edited the first two editions of *Preservation of Library and Archival Materials: A Manual.* She is the author of *Preservation Planning: Guidelines for Writing a Long-Range Plan*, which was published by the Northeast Document Conservation Center and The American Association of Museums in 1997. She was Director of Field Services at the Upper Midwest Conservation Association for two years and is now Head of Conservation at the Minnesota Historical Society.

PLANNING AND PRIORITIZING

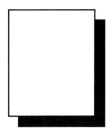

Northeast Document
Conservation Center
100 Brickstone Square
Andover, MA 01810-1494
www.nedcc.org
Tel: (978) 470-1010
Fax: (978) 475-6021

**PLANNING &
PRIORITIZING**

Section 1, Leaflet 1

WHAT IS PRESERVATION PLANNING?

**by Sherelyn Ogden
Head of Conservation
Minnesota Historical Society**

Libraries, archives, museums, and historical societies are responsible not only for collecting, interpreting, and exhibiting significant materials that document history, but also for the long-term preservation, security, and accessibility of these materials. The American Association of Museums recognizes this responsibility. It states in its *Code of Ethics for Museums* that a museum must insure that the "collections in its custody are protected, secure, unencumbered, cared for, and preserved."[1] Preservation is an integral part of a cultural institution's mission, and preservation planning should be part of its overall strategic plan.

- Preservation planning is a process by which the general and specific needs for the care of collections are determined, priorities are established, and resources for implementation are identified.

- Its main purpose is to define a course of action that will allow an institution to set its present and future preservation agendas.

- In addition, it identifies the actions an institution will take and those it probably will never take so that resources can be allocated appropriately.

THE LONG-RANGE PRESERVATION PLAN

The result of the planning process is the formulation of a written, long-range preservation plan. This is an important document for an institution to have.

- A long-range preservation plan delineates an institution's preservation needs and charts a course of action to meet these needs for its collections.

- It provides the framework for carrying out established goals and priorities in a logical, efficient, and effective manner; it is a working tool for achieving agreed-upon priorities over a set period of time. It helps maintain continuity and consistency in a preservation program over time.

- A plan validates the role and importance of preservation, helping to make preservation an equal partner with acquisitions and interpretation.

- It is an important aid in securing necessary resources to assist with implementation of recommendations.

- It records the past and current preservation activities and shapes the future efforts of an institution.

A preservation plan must dovetail with other key management tools in the institution, such as the collections management policy. The preservation plan cannot be drafted in isolation but needs to be composed within the same frame of reference that is used for all collections' policies and plans. This frame of reference is the institution's mission statement. All policies and management documents should flow from the mission statement and be understood and implemented within its parameters.

A preservation plan needs to be comprehensive and include all of an institution's collections. The integration of all collections into a plan is vital for developing a complete understanding of long-term preservation priorities. Also, such integration will allow for the linkage of preservation activities with other strategic planning agendas. A good preservation plan is realistic and practical. A document that is outside the ability of an institution to implement and support is not useful. While the plan must recognize all preservation needs, it should focus on those steps that can be accomplished with existing or obtainable resources (e.g., through grants or fundraising).

Every institutional plan is different. Some are long, complex, and detailed while others are short and simple. They all, however, flow from and are based on the needs assessment survey(s) the institution has done.

THE NEEDS ASSESSMENT SURVEY

Needs assessment surveys are essential to preservation planning and must be carried out before a plan is drafted. A preservation plan is based on the needs of an institution and the actions required to meet these needs. This information is provided in the reports of the surveys. Many institutions have only one survey that considers the needs of all the collections in general terms. For some institutions with numerous diverse collections and complex planning needs, additional surveys that address particular problems or the needs of specific collections or types of materials may be required.

Since surveys are the foundation of preservation planning, having a survey that meets the institution's planning needs is critical.

- A survey must evaluate the policies, practices, and conditions in an institution that affect the preservation of all the collections.
- It must address the general state of all the collections, what is needed to improve that state, and how to preserve the collections long-term.
- It must identify specific preservation needs, recommend actions to meet those needs, and prioritize the recommended actions.

A survey covers the entire building in which collections are housed. Hazards to collections are identified, considering such factors as environment, storage, security and access, housekeeping, conservation treatment, and policies and practices. It is important to note that the building in which collections are housed is often itself a part of the collections. This is the case with a historic or architecturally significant structure. In this instance, the actions required to preserve the building as well as the collections it houses must be considered.

All this information should be recorded in a formal survey report, written in clear direct language and formatted in such a way that information can be easily located and extracted from it. The report is the tool for drafting the preservation plan; it must contain information in plain language and in an easily accessible form.

ASSISTANCE IS AVAILABLE

Regional field services programs are available to assist cultural institutions in all aspects of preservation planning. They sponsor workshops, conduct general needs assessment and item-specific surveys, and provide guidance to institutional staff who are conducting in-house surveys. For more information, contact a conservation center for information on local field services programs.

NOTE

[1] American Association of Museums, *Code of Ethics for Museums*, revised and adapted 1993 (Washington, D.C.: American Association of Museums, 1994), 8.

Acknowledgements

This technical leaflet is from *Preservation Planning: Guidelines for Writing A Long-Range Plan*, by Sherelyn Ogden, produced by NEDCC with the assistance of the Institute of Museum and Library Services. It is available from the American Association of Museums.

Northeast Document
Conservation Center
100 Brickstone Square
Andover, MA 01810-1494
www.nedcc.org
Tel: (978) 470-1010
Fax: (978) 475-6021

PRESERVATION ASSESSMENT AND PLANNING

by Dr. Margaret Child
formerly Preservation Consultant
Washington, DC

Designing a preservation program should not be viewed as an arcane process requiring technical expertise in paper chemistry or hands-on conservation skills. It is instead much like other management decision-making: a process for allocating available resources to activities and functions important to carrying out an institution's mission. Indeed, in order to demystify preservation decision-making, we should think about preservation as an aspect of collection management.

Like other institutional programs, the goals and priorities of a preservation program should be firmly rooted in the institutional mission statement. They should also be based on a coherent, well defined collection policy. If either the mission statement or the collection policy is too general and vague to serve as the basis for planning, it should be rewritten so that it reflects the actual goals of the repository and shows clearly how the collections support these goals.

Preservation of a repository's holdings can be divided into two categories. The first is preventive preservation, which usually focuses on preventing deterioration of the collections as a whole. The second is remedial preservation measures to correct physical or chemical deterioration. Remedial preservation is labor intensive and often requires highly trained professionals to carry it out. Consequently it is expensive and so is often limited to selected portions of the total collection. Any planning process must be structured to produce a program that will incorporate both categories of activity.

PLANNING METHODOLOGIES

A standard strategic planning methodology can be applied to preservation planning. Also, a number of specialized tools have been developed to help librarians, archivists, and curators assess their preservation needs and decide on priorities for addressing them. The Northeast Document Conservation Center's workbook *Preservation Planning: Guidelines for Writing a Long-Range Plan* is intended to assist institutions that have completed needs assessments in drafting a long-range planning document. The Association of Research Libraries offers a *Preservation Planning Program* that, although targeted at large research libraries and intended to be carried out with the assistance of an experienced preservation administrator as a consultant, can provide a useful outline of and information for evaluating the issues that must be considered by any repository. *CALIPR* is a computer software package that assists all types of California repositories to carry out a simple preservation needs assessment. These tools, as well as others in the field, help the administrator evaluate basic components of preservation planning: the extent to which the collections are at risk from a number of factors; the portions of collections of greatest enduring value; the availability of resources in terms of staff time, technical expertise, and financial resources; and the political feasibility of particular actions. The results of these assessments must be combined to produce a list of priorities.

CALCULATING RISK

Reliable data on the dimensions of the preservation problem within the repository are needed in order to begin to set institutional preservation priorities. Information should be collected on the extent and kinds of deterioration present, on the environmental conditions in which materials are stored and used, and on systems and policies, such as fire detection and suppression and security measures, that protect the collections from damage or loss.

Condition Surveys

Many major research libraries have conducted intensive condition surveys of their holdings during the past 15 years. These have produced reliable data on the proportion of acidic paper, the extent of embrittlement and of incomplete textblocks, deterioration of the text or image, and the percentage of damaged bindings or the lack of protective enclosures. There is a considerable literature available on the topic. Most of these surveys show much the same pattern of deterioration, so that it is probably no longer necessary for any institution to do an intensive quantitative survey unless it has idiosyncratic holdings or has housed them in exceptionally poor environments. It is, however, useful to have at least a small sampling of one's own collections both to verify that they conform to national patterns and to use as illustrative material in making a budget case or preparing a grant proposal.

Environmental Surveys

To obtain data for planning purposes on the environment in which the collections are stored and used, one must measure and record temperature and relative humidity in order to obtain a profile of their fluctuations around the clock and throughout the year. Assistance in setting up a monitoring program can be obtained from regional preservation field service programs, from state libraries with a preservation program, or from a helpful, nearby university library with a preservation administrator. Assistance from a consultant is often needed to interpret accurately the data collected and to identify options for remedial action.

How extensively to monitor the variety of climates that may exist within a repository is a management issue that depends on local conditions and on the extent of the resources available to the repository to conduct such a survey. In a survey of a repository's environmental conditions, attention should be paid to sources of potential damage from exposure to light from windows or light fixtures. Ideally, pollution levels would also be evaluated, but realistically most pollution problems must wait for a comprehensive renovation or replacement of an HVAC system.

Surveys of Protective Systems and Practices

In addition, effective planning for a preservation program requires a repository to review the various systems and policies intended to prevent damage to the collections from storage, use, and handling as well as from disasters, vandalism, and theft. Ascertaining the extent to which protective procedures, systems, and policies are in place allows an assessment of the degree to which collections are exposed to future deterioration and sudden damage or loss.

The building fabric should be surveyed to identify possible problems such as leaks or fire hazards. Fire detection and suppression systems should also be assessed. Security systems, both mechanical and procedural, and disaster planning should be evaluated. It is also essential to examine staff and user training in the care and handling of collections, and to evaluate storage furniture, binding and preservation microfilm contracts, and the storage enclosures and materials used to protect or repair collections. It may be helpful to track a number of items or collections from acquisition through binding or boxing and foldering, cataloging, shelving, circulation, and inter-library loan in order to identify all the points at which existing procedures and practices might endanger an item. Such an exercise will point up the potentially damaging effects of common practices.

DETERMINING VALUE

Repository staff attempting to develop a strategic plan for a preservation program must also assess the breadth and depth of various portions of the collection in order to determine their intellectual value. In libraries, the *Research Libraries Group Conspectus* has proved to be a useful tool for this purpose. *CALIPR,* mentioned earlier, offers four simple questions intended to estimate book collection value within the context of a state's total library resources.

If the repository chooses not to use one of the tools cited above, these following questions will help to establish the enduring research or educational value of a collection or a publication in terms of institutional priorities and the overall documentation available on the topic covered:

1. What is the importance of the topic documented by this collection or this publication? Is its primary significance local, statewide, regional, national, or international?

2. How does this collection or this publication relate to other holdings at your repository that document the same topic?

3. How does it relate to materials on the same topic held by other repositories?

4. Is the information it contains unique or does it duplicate information contained in records, publications, or other sources held by other repositories?

5. Is the repository committed to continuing to document this topic?

6. Why would it be better to spend funds on the preservation of this material than to acquire new material?

7. What impact would the destruction of this material have on the documentation and understanding of the topic?

In going through this process, it is helpful to recognize that for most repositories, the great majority of their holdings are not of enduring value. These holdings are, however, of current interest and should therefore be protected against deterioration and damage so that they can be used for as long as possible.

The evaluator should also establish whether or not the collection or item has intrinsic value by determining its artifactual, monetary, associational, or symbolic value. Intrinsic value will affect priority for preservation. It will often also determine whether or not it is acceptable to reformat materials or to choose among the appropriate conservation treatments.

AVAILABLE RESOURCES

The information gathered on the condition of the collections, environmental conditions, other factors related to their housing, and estimates of their value all eventually have to be weighed against the resources that can be mobilized by the institution and the technical abilities of the staff available to address the needs identified. At this point the planning process moves into the realm of practice and must identify those actions that it may actually be possible to undertake.

Planners should be aware that some initiatives that will contribute significantly to extending the life of collections can be undertaken without adding new budget lines or substantially increasing existing ones. For example, training staff and users in care and handling, revising the binding contract to follow recommendations of the Library Binding Institute *Standard for Library Binding*, carrying out systematic holdings and stack maintenance, preparing a disaster plan, following preservation criteria when buying storage furniture and supplies, working with plant managers to stabilize temperature and humidity, and incorporating preservation considerations into all policies and procedures can often be accomplished with existing personnel and budget allocations. This is not a comprehensive list, but a sample of improvements that can be achieved by changing existing practice to respect preservation concerns.

In contrast, budget increases are usually required for such options as replacing significant quantities of storage furniture or preservation enclosures, upgrading poor environmental conditions by renovating a building or installing a new climate control system, setting up a systematic reformatting program, and providing conservation treatment either in-house or on contract. Moreover, the last three activities demand a level of staff expertise in preservation management and conservation issues over and beyond that which can be obtained from a workshop or other short training course, even if the work is ultimately contracted out.

POLITICAL ISSUES

Any planning process must take into account the political environment within which the program it hopes to implement will be carried out. It is therefore necessary to be as alert to possible political obstacles as to technical deficiencies or lack of resources. Much of the success of a preservation program will depend on the willingness of the repository's administration to support the changes recommended. That support should be clearly evident from the start of the planning process and should be continually nourished by regular reports on progress and checks that emerging recommendations will be approved. It is also important to make sure on a continuing basis that at least some of the resources that will be needed, be it staff time or the ability to redirect certain budget lines or even new money, will be forthcoming. This may mean keeping senior or parent institution administrators involved in and supportive of the process.

Much also depends on the cooperation of other staff in the repository. To the greatest extent possible, planning should forestall turf wars by involving all staff whose functions may eventually be affected and convincing them of the importance of any changes recommended. Similarly, parts of an effective preservation program may necessitate working with staff outside the repository such as building managers or plant engineers. Again, it is important to educate them about the importance of upgrading building systems or making repairs to the survival of the collections.

In all instances, it is wise to come armed with reliable data about the effects of failing to change, including if possible the dollar costs of remedying damage and deterioration, as well as solid estimates of the costs of the changes being sought. It is also wise to present the program as a series of goals to be accomplished in stages so that each problem is clearly defined rather than limitless, and so that the various resources needed can be sought over a period of several years or stages.

PREVENTIVE PRESERVATION

In the move from collecting information and planning for a preservation program to setting priorities and implementation, it is helpful to keep in mind that an administrator's first responsibility is to ensure the longest possible useful life for the entire collection. This is true if for no other reason than to protect the institution's capital investment in those materials. It is also important to recognize that the most cost-effective method of extending longevity is to prevent deterioration to the greatest extent possible. Preventive preservation plays much the same role with respect to library and archival materials as do public health and preventive medicine for people. Most of the activities that can be grouped under the heading of *preventive preservation* are things that the institution does normally: acquisitions, binding, processing non-print materials, shelving, circulation, cleaning both library facilities and the collections, photocopying, minor repair, and deaccessioning. However, as components in an integrated preservation program, they will now be done with a new awareness of their effect on the long-term survival of the collections and in accordance with current preservation standards and guidelines. Thus, a preventive preservation program should not be viewed as an add-on but rather as an integral component of the day-to-day operations and responsibilities of the repository.

This is not to say that implementing a preservation program will be cost free. Indeed, its most important component, a climate-control system that can provide a stable environment day and night and throughout the year within the fairly narrow ranges prescribed by national standards for various types of media, can be very expensive. As a preservation plan is developed, the costs of providing an optimum environment for all or part of a repository's collections must therefore be carefully balanced against the costs of failing to do so. In particular, in setting priorities, it should be understood that appropriate environmental control is the foundation on which all other preservation and conservation activities rest. Everything else that a repository may do to prevent deterioration of its holdings or to repair the effects of physical or chemical damage will be undermined if the materials continue to be housed under poor environmental conditions. It is therefore extremely important that every repository holding documentary resources of enduring value integrate preservation into its entire range of operations. It is equally important to achieve the best environments with existing systems while making the highest preservation priority the effort to upgrade the environments for collections storage to conform to national standards.

REMEDIAL PRESERVATION

At present, there are limited options available to custodians of documentary resources who wish to extend the life of portions of their collections. If they are dealing with acidic paper, it can be deacidified either item-by-item or by sending it to a vendor of a mass deacidification treatment. Mass deacidification has yet to materialize as a practical option. It may still become an effective treatment that will substantially slow the chemical deterioration of paper. It should, however, be remembered that mass deacidification is not a strengthening process, and that is it does not restore flexibility or strength to paper that is already seriously brittle. It is most effective when applied to relatively new acidic paper before the process of embrittlement has begun.

Another option is to reformat a document or book to capture as much as possible of the information that it contains. This is most often done by microfilming or photocopying onto alkaline paper. There also is an increasing number of model projects experimenting with digitization. Several caveats must be kept in mind regarding all such projects. Generally accepted technical standards govern archival photocopying, and any repository embarking on such a project should follow the standards carefully. Filming must also be done in accordance with existing national standards and the archival negative must be stored under carefully controlled environmental conditions if the product is to be considered a true preservation microfilm. It takes a substantial amount of knowledge to manage a preservation filming project, and it is advisable to seek the assistance of a knowledgeable consultant when setting up and monitoring such a project. Finally, it is premature for any except the most sophisticated repositories with highly trained personnel to consider digitization. While much has been learned by several projects embarked upon, too little is known about archiving costs, transferability of data, and other factors to make it a practicable option for the ordinary repository.

Finally, there is conservation treatment. This encompasses a variety of procedures that should be carried out only by a professional conservator. A few large research libraries and museums have a conservation laboratory and trained conservators in-house. Most repositories contract for conservation treatment with either a regional laboratory or a conservator in private practice.

In general, when considering preservation treatments of any kind, the preservation manager should first of all be sufficiently informed about the nature of the deterioration to be remedied and the character of the material to be treated to know what cannot be done with the level of expertise available locally. To put it another way, it is important to recognize that volunteers trained by a skilled preservation professional to do basic repairs on a circulating collection should not be allowed to work on materials of enduring value. In addition, a preservation manager should be sufficiently knowledgeable to choose the appropriate option for treatment, that is, to know when an item should be photocopied rather than filmed or when reformatting should not be used because it will result in a loss of information.

Designing a preservation program requires a great deal of decision making. The decisions are often not easy to make, and it may be necessary to seek professional assistance from a consultant. It may help to bear in mind that by sound preservation planning you are providing the endangered portions of your collections of enduring value with the best medical advice available in order to try to keep them alive.

SUGGESTED FURTHER READING

American Library Association, Subcommittee on Guidelines for Collection Development. *Guide for Written Collection Policy Statements.* Bonita Bryant, ed. Collection Management & Development Guides, no. 3. Chicago: American Library Association, 1989, 32 pp.

American Library Association, Subcommittee on Guidelines for Collection Development. *Guide to the Evaluation of Library Collections.* Barbara Lockett, ed. Collection Management & Development Guides, no. 2. Chicago: American Library Association, 1989, 25 pp.

Atkinson, Ross. *"Selection for Preservation: A Materialistic Approach." Library Resources & Technical Services* 30 (Oct./Dec. 1986): 344-53.

Calmes, Alan, Ralph Schofer, and Keith R. Eberhardt. "Theory and Practice of Paper Preservation for Archives." *Restaurator 9* (1988): 96-111.

Child, Margaret S. "Further Thoughts on Selection for Preservation: A Materialistic Approach." *Library Resources & Technical Services* 30 (Oct./Dec. 1986): 354-62.

Cloonan, Michèle. *Organizing Preservation Activities.* Association of Research Libraries Resource Guide. Washington, DC: Association of Research Libraries, 1993, 98 pp.

Cox, Richard J. "Selecting Historical Records for Microfilming: Some Suggested Procedures for Repositories." *Library and Archival Security 9.2* (1989): 21-41.

Darling, Pamela W., and Wesley Boomgaarden, comps. *Preservation Planning Program Resource Notebook.* Washington, DC: Association of Research Libraries, Office of Management Studies, 1987, 719 pp.

Darling, Pamela W., with Duane E. Webster. Preservation Planning Program: An Assisted Self-Study Manual for Libraries. Expanded ed. Washington, DC: Association of Research Libraries, Office of Management Studies, 1987, 156 pp.

Drott, M. Carl. "Random Sampling: A Tool for Library Research." *College & Research Libraries* (March 1969): 119-25.

Gwinn, Nancy E., and Paul H. Mosher. "Coordinating Collection Development: The RLG Conspectus." *College & Research Libraries* 43 (March 1983): 128-40.

Merrill-Oldham, Jan, and Paul Parisi. *Guide to the Library Binding Institute Standard for Library Binding.* Chicago: American Library Association, 1990, 60 pp.

Motylewski, Karen. "What an Institution Can Do to Survey Its Own Preservation Needs." In *Collection Maintenance and Improvement.* Sherry Byrne, ed. Washington, DC: Association of Research Libraries, 1993.

Ogden, Barclay. *On the Preservation of Books and Documents in Original Form.* Washington, DC: The Commission on Preservation and Access, 1989, 5 pp.

Ogden, Barclay, and Maralyn Jones. *CALIPR.* Sacramento, CA: The California State Library, 1997. [An automated tool to assess preservation needs. Available from the California State Library Foundation, P.O. Box 942837, Sacramento, CA 94237-0001.], http://sunsite.berkeley.edu/CALIPR/.

Ogden, Sherelyn. *Preservation Planning: Guidelines for Writing a Long-Range Plan.* Washington, DC.: American Association of Museums and Northeast Document Conservation Center, 1997.

Parisi, Paul A., and Jan Merrill-Oldham, eds. *Standard for Library Binding.* 8th ed. Rochester, NY: Library Binding Institute, 1990, 17 pp.

Paskoff, Beth, and Anna H. Perrault. "A Tool for Comparative Collection Analysis: Conducting a Shelflist Sample to Construct a Collection Profile." *Library Resources & Technical Services* 34 (April 1990): 199-215.

RLG Preservation Needs Assessment Package (PreNAP). Mountain View, CA: Research Libraries Group, 1991. [An automated tool to assess preservation needs. Available from Preservation Publication Coordinator, RLG, 1200 Villa Street, Mountain View, CA 94041-1100.]

Walker, Gay. "Notes on Research and Operations: Assessing Preservation Needs." *Library Resources & Technical Services* 33 (Oct. 1989): 414-19.

Walker, Gay, Jane Greenfield, John Fox, and Jeffrey S. Simonoff. "The Yale Survey: A Large-Scale Study of Book Deterioration in the Yale University Library." *College & Research Libraries* 46 (March 1985): 111-32.

Waters, Peter. "Phased Preservation: A Philosophical Concept and Practical Approach to Preservation." *Special Libraries* (Winter 1990): 35-43.

Northeast Document
Conservation Center
100 Brickstone Square
Andover, MA 01810-1494
www.nedcc.org
Tel: (978) 470-1010
Fax: (978) 475-6021

THE NEEDS ASSESSMENT SURVEY

**by Sherelyn Ogden
Head of Conservation
Minnesota Historical Society**

Needs assessment surveys are essential to preservation planning. A preservation plan is based on the needs of an institution and the actions required to meet these needs. This information is provided in the reports of the surveys. Many institutions have only one survey that considers the needs of all the collections in general terms. For some institutions with numerous diverse collections and complex planning needs, additional surveys that address particular problems or the needs of specific collections or types of materials may be required.

Since surveys are the foundation of preservation planning, having a survey that meets the institution's planning needs is critical.

- A survey must evaluate the policies, practices, and conditions in an institution that affect the preservation of all the collections.

- It must address the general state of all the collections, what is needed to improve that state, and how to preserve the collections long-term.

- It must identify specific preservation needs, recommend actions to meet those needs, and prioritize the recommended actions.

A survey covers the entire building in which collections are housed. Hazards to collections are identified, considering such factors as environment, storage, security and access, housekeeping, conservation treatment, and policies and practices. It is important to note that the building in which collections are housed is often itself a part of the collections. This is the case with an historic or architecturally significant structure. In this instance, the actions required to preserve the building as well as the collections it houses must be considered.

All this information should be recorded in a formal survey report. The report should be written in clear direct language and should be formatted in such a way that information can be easily located and extracted from it. The report is the tool you will use when drafting your preservation plan; it must contain the information you need in plain language and in an easily accessible form.

A needs assessment survey can be conducted by an outside consultant or by qualified in-house staff. There are advantages and disadvantages to both, which should be considered before a decision is made to hire an outside surveyor or to begin the process in-house. If contracting an outside person, be certain to check the credentials and experience of the surveyor. Ask for and check references before hiring.

OUTSIDE SURVEYOR VERSUS IN-HOUSE STAFF

Outside Surveyor/Advantages

1) An outside surveyor may be more experienced than anyone in your institution. A consultant from the outside may have done more surveys, may be more familiar with the survey process, and may have dealt with more diverse situations. Also, an outside consultant may be more aware of outside resources that would enable projects to be accomplished. This gives the surveyor a broader, more comprehensive base for making recommendations.

2) The surveyor may be a specialist in a particular area or type of collection. This is also useful in making recommendations.

3) An outside consultant comes without preconceptions and biases and can usually see situations objectively.

4) An outside surveyor can say things that may be interpreted as critical without fear of being penalized. Thus a consultant is more likely to point out situations that need to be changed even if the change is an unpopular one. Likewise a consultant is not limited or hampered by the political situation of an institution.

5) Often an outside surveyor has more credibility with the staff and administration, even if this is not justified. The surveyor is viewed as an authority.

6) Perhaps the greatest advantage to using an outside surveyor is that this person has the time to do the job. A consultant can be scheduled to come at a certain time and be expected to complete the survey and produce a written report by a specific date.

Outside Surveyor/Disadvantages

1) An outside surveyor does not know the history or institutional framework in which situations exist. A consultant is unfamiliar with institutional traditions and idiosyncrasies and, as a result, may make recommendations that are unrealistic or out of scope for a particular institution.

2) Hiring an outside consultant requires an outlay of money for consulting fees. This money may not be available. This makes the surveyor seem more expensive even though in reality an in-house survey may cost as much, or even more, in staff time.

In-House Staff/Advantages

1) An in-house surveyor knows an institution's values and functions and understands the institutional framework and background of existing situations. For this reason a staff member may be able to make more realistic recommendations than can an outside person.

2) An in-house surveyor tends to know where all the collections are housed, the peculiarities of the storage spaces, and how the facilities work. This enables the surveyor to work faster, and to make more appropriate recommendations.

3) An in-house surveyor may be more thorough, if there are no limitations on the staff member's time, compared to the outside consultant whose time is limited.

4) Using in-house staff avoids an additional cash expense; an outlay of money is not required. This makes the survey seem less expensive, although it may actually cost more in staff time.

In-House Staff/Disadvantages

1) In-house staff come with their own prejudices and agendas, which may cloud their interpretation of situations and influence their recommendations.

2) It is harder for an in-house person to be an instrument of change than it is for an outsider. In-house staff may be reluctant to recommend certain changes because of the negative impact this may have on themselves or others. Also, they may be reluctant to recommend a change because they assume, based on previous experience, that changes will not be made.

3) In-house staff may take longer than an outside consultant to conduct a survey and produce a report, because they must carry out their regular job responsibilities while doing the survey.

4) An in-house person may be viewed by the administration and other staff as not having the same level of expertise and knowledge as an outside consultant, even if this is not true. A staff member may not have as much credibility.

SOURCES OF HELP

Outside Consultants

Funding for surveys is available from state and federal agencies. To obtain the names and addresses of appropriate state agencies, contact local cultural institutions and preservation organizations. Federal funding for surveys is available through the following:

> Conservation Assessment Program
> Heritage Preservation
> 1730 K Street, NW
> Suite 566
> Washington, DC 20006
> Telephone: (202) 634-1422
>
> MAP II: Collections Management Assessment
> American Association of Museums
> Museum Assessment Program
> 1575 Eye Street, NW, Suite 400
> Washington, DC 20005
> Telephone: (202) 289-9118
>
> Institute of Museum and Library Services
> 1100 Pennsylvania Ave. NW, Suite 510
> Washington, DC 20506
> Telephone: (202) 606-8536

Referrals for consultants who provide surveys can be obtained from:

> American Institute for Conservation of Historic
>   and Artistic Works
> 1717 K Street, NW, Suite 301
> Washington, DC 20006
> Telephone: (202) 452-9545

In-House Surveys

For assistance in doing an in-house survey, obtain a copy of the publication *The Conservation Assessment/A Tool For Planning, Implementing, And Fundraising,* 2nd. ed., edited by Sara Wolf Green, and published in 1991 by the National Institute for the Conservation of Cultural Property (now Heritage Preservation) and The Getty Conservation Institute. The publication is available from either organization at the following addresses:

> Heritage Preservation
> 1730 K Street, NW
> Suite 566
> Washington, DC 20006
> Telephone: (202) 634-1422

> Getty Conservation Institute
> 1200 Getty Center Drive
> Suite 700
> Los Angeles, CA 90049-1684
> Telephone: (310) 440-7325

For assistance in surveying archival collections, obtain a copy of the publication *The Conservation Assessment For Archives,* published in 1995 by the Canadian Council of Archives. It is available from:

> Canadian Council of Archives
> 344 Wellington
> Ottawa, Ontario, Canada
> Telephone: (613) 996-6445

For surveying library and archival collections, contact the Northeast Document Conservation Center (NEDCC) for a copy of the self-survey guide *What An Institution Can Do To Survey Its Own Preservation Needs* by Karen Motylewski. This guide provides an outline of the information gathered in a survey, along with basic information needed to interpret observations and find solutions. It draws on a number of sources, including the 1982 edition of *Conservation Survey Manual,* the survey protocol designed by George Cunha when he was the Director of the NEDCC, writings on the subject of library binding by Jan Merrill-Oldham, and the experience of the NEDCC and Southeastern Library Network (SOLINET) survey programs under the direction of Mildred O'Connell, Karen Motylewski, and Lisa Fox. The address to contact is:

> Northeast Document Conservation Center
> 100 Brickstone Square
> Andover, MA 01810
> Telephone: (978) 470-1010

Automated needs assessment tools have been developed for library and archival collections. One, *CALIPR,* recently became available at no charge over the World Wide Web. It is available at:

> http://sunsite.berkeley.edu/CALIPR/

Additional publications that may prove helpful are the *Standard Practices Handbook For Museums* (1990) and the *Self-Evaluation Checklist* (1991), both published by the Alberta Museums Association. These are available from:

Alberta Museums Association
9829 103 St.
Edmonton, Alberta, Canada T5K 0X9
Telephone: (403) 424-2626

A publication that is part of the Museum Assessment Program that may be useful is *Shaping the Museum: The MAP Institutional Planning Guide* (1993), produced by the American Association of Museums (AAM). This publication is available from:

American Association of Museums
1575 Eye Street, NW
Suite 400
Washington, DC 20005
Telephone: (202) 289-9127

Another useful publication is *A Preventive Conservation Calendar for the Smaller Museum,* published in 1997 by the International Centre for the Preservation and Restoration of Cultural Property. It can be obtained from:

International Centre for the Preservation and Restoration of
Cultural Property
Via di San Michele 13
1-00153 Rome, Italy

Acknowledgements

This technical leaflet is from *Preservation Planning: Guidelines for Writing A Long-Range Plan,* by Sherelyn Ogden, produced by NEDCC with the assistance of the Institute of Museum and Library Services. It is available from the American Association of Museums.

Northeast Document
Conservation Center
100 Brickstone Square
Andover, MA 01810-1494
www.nedcc.org
Tel: (978) 470-1010
Fax: (978) 475-6021

CONSIDERATIONS FOR PRIORITIZING

by Sherelyn Ogden
Head of Conservation
Minnesota Historical Society

Most institutions have many preservation needs that require a variety of actions to meet. Resources in an institution are always limited and every action cannot be accomplished. It is crucial to determine which actions are the most important so that those receive consideration first.

- Prioritizing is the process of deciding which actions will have the most significant impact, which are the most important, and which are the most feasible.

Systems of risk assessment and management are being developed.[1] These offer a highly pragmatic approach as is required by the large and diverse natural history collections for which they were first developed. These are geared toward setting collections care priorities and, when coupled with the complementary systems of collection profiles and categories of specimens, show promise for prioritizing actions.[2] Training in this methodology is available from the Canadian Museum of Nature in the form of interactive one- and two-day workshops for institutions, groups of institutions, and organizations.[3]

Presently the easiest way for staff of most institutions, especially smaller ones, to prioritize preservation actions is by carefully considering specific criteria, weighing appropriate collections-related factors, and making informed value judgments before reaching a decision.

CRITERIA FOR PRIORITIZING

It is helpful to consider three criteria when prioritizing preservation actions.

- The first is impact, the extent to which an action will improve the preservation of the institution's collections. In her manual on preservation planning for libraries, Pamela Darling describes high impact actions as "…those that will result in dramatic improvement in the present condition of materials, substantial decrease in the rate of deterioration, substantial increase in efficiency of current preservation activities, or considerable savings of time, energy or money."[4] To evaluate impact, consider the following questions. To what extent will implementing a specific action improve preservation of the collections? How great is the immediate impact and what is the potential impact of implementing this action? The greater the impact of an action, the higher its priority.

- The feasibility of implementing an action should also be considered. Actions vary in the amount of time and resources required to implement them. Some are easy to implement, while others are impossible. Factors to look at include staffing levels and expertise (availability of technical and management capability), financial implications (capital outlays, expenditures for materials and services, ongoing operating costs, fundraising potential), and policy and procedural changes (if these are required and who can make them). The political feasibility of various actions must also be realistically evaluated. If it is not likely that you can implement an action, it may be given a low priority even if its impact is high.

- Another criterion to consider is urgency of an action. Darling explains that an action can be regarded as urgent if waiting to implement it would cause further problems or would mean bypassing an opportunity.[5] All other factors being equal, those actions requiring immediate implementation would be given highest priority.

FACTORS INFLUENTIAL IN PRIORITIZING

The use, storage, condition, and value of the materials in the collections are influential in prioritizing actions and are important to consider.

- The amount and type of use items receive is significant. Items on permanent exhibition have different needs from those in storage. Items that are used frequently for research purposes have different needs from those that are consulted only infrequently. Items that are used heavily or in a damaging way are at higher risk and in more urgent need of attention.

- Housing of collections is important. Materials that are stored under poor environmental conditions or in harmful containers, or are susceptible to theft, vandalism, fire, or other disasters, also are at higher risk.

- Those problems are particularly threatening to materials in poor or fragile condition, making the risk factor even greater for those vulnerable items. Actions that would mitigate those risks may be a high priority for implementation.

- Yet another factor to consider is the value of the materials. The nature of the value of items (monetary, intrinsic, associational, bibliographic), their rarity, their provenance, and their significance to the institution need to be considered.

- For how long materials need to be preserved and in what form they need to be preserved are additional important considerations.

IMPLEMENTATION PRIORITIES

The implementation priorities for an institution are the most important priorities. They are the high-priority actions that are *achievable*. To determine these, it is helpful to consider the criteria of impact and feasibility together for each action. A device that is useful for this is a grid developed by Pamela Darling, which is shown here in a modified form. The impact and feasibility of each action are plotted on the grid shown on the following page.

Darling explains that those actions that are of high impact and can be implemented with little difficulty are placed in box #1. Those actions that have high impact but are difficult to implement go into box #3.

Those actions that are not difficult to implement but will have little impact go into box #2. Those actions that are difficult to implement and have little impact go into box #4.

Darling explains that the actions in box #1 probably deserve highest priority, since they can be easily accomplished and will have significant impact. Those in box #4 can often be postponed or even disregarded because they achieve little while requiring great effort. Many of those in box #2 can also be eliminated because they accomplish little, though some may be worthwhile because they are easy to do. Box #3 items need careful consideration: despite their difficulty, they deserve implementation because of their high impact.[6]

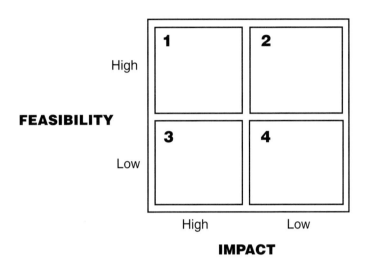

REMEMBER

One of the most difficult aspects of preservation planning is prioritizing. Planning requires significant people skills and an understanding of the organizational dynamics of the institution. Nowhere is this more evident than in prioritizing. You need to bring all your interpersonal skills to bear on discussions of priorities with your colleagues. You need to listen to what the issues of other departments are and be able to focus on what best serves the needs of the institution as a whole rather than just on the needs of your particular department or area of expertise. In the long run, this will best serve your needs as well. At the same time, you need to be a skillful negotiator and a good sales person. As with most other dealings with people, a good sense of humor will ease the process.

NOTES

[1] Robert Waller, "Conservation Risk Assessment: A Strategy For Managing Resources For Preventive Conservation," in *Preprints of the Contributions to the Ottawa Congress, 12-16 September 1994, Preventive Conservation: Practice, Theory and Research*, eds. A. Roy and P. Smith (London: International Institute for Conservation of Historic and Artistic Works, 1994).

Stefan Michalski, "A Systematic Approach to Preservation: Description and Integration with Other Museum Activities," in *Preprints of the Contributions to the Ottawa Congress, 12-16 September 1994, Preventive Conservation: Practice, Theory and Research*, eds. A. Roy and P. Smith (London: International Institute for Conservation of Historic and Artistic Works, 1994.

[2] J. McGinley, "Where's the Management in Collections Management: Planning for the Improved Care, Greater Use, and Growth of Collections," in *Current Issues, Initiatives, and Future Directions for the Preservation and Conservation of Natural History Collections*, ed. C.L. Rose et al. (Madrid: Consejeria de Educacion y Cultura, Comunidad de Madrid, Direccion General de Bellas Artes y Archivos, Ministerio de Cultura, 1993), 309-38.

J.C. Price and G.R. Fitzgerald, in "Categories of Specimens: A Collection Management Tool," *Collection Forum* 12, no. 1 (1996), 8-13.

Robert Waller, "Preventive Conservation Planning for Large and Diverse Collections," in *Preprints of the June 10-11, 1996 Workshop Preservation of Collections Assessment, Evaluation, and Mitigation Strategies* (Washington, D.C.: American Institute for Conservation of Artistic and Historic Works, 1996), 1-9.

[3] Canadian Museum of Nature, "Assessing and Managing Risks to Your Collections" (brochure, 1994).

[4] Pamela W. Darling with Duane E. Webster, *Preservation Planning Program, An Assisted Self-Study Manual For Libraries*, expanded 1987 edition (Washington, D.C.: Association of Research Libraries, Office of Management Studies, 1987), 29.

[5] Darling and Webster

[6] Darling and Webster, 30.

Acknowledgements

The grid was adapted and reproduced with the kind permission of the Association of Research Libraries. This technical leaflet is from *Preservation Planning: Guidelines for Writing a Long-Range Plan,* by Sherelyn Ogden, produced by NEDCC with the assistance of the Institute of Museum and Library Services. It is available from the American Association of Museums.

Northeast Document
Conservation Center
100 Brickstone Square
Andover, MA 01810-1494
www.nedcc.org
Tel: (978) 470-1010
Fax: (978) 475-6021

COLLECTIONS POLICIES AND PRESERVATION

by Dr. Margaret Child
formerly Preservation Consultant
Washington, DC

"Every library collection is established for one or more definite purposes. A collection development and management program organizes and directs the processes of acquiring materials, integrating them into coherent collections, managing their growth and maintenance, and deselecting them when appropriate in a cost- and user-beneficial way."[1] A coherent collection policy also establishes the parameters within which a systematic preservation program operates. The collection policy is based on the institutional mission statement, which enunciates the goals that the collections are to achieve. The collecting priorities that the collection policy establishes help to focus preservation activity on the most important parts of the collections. To put it colloquially, the mission statement tells you where you are going; the collection policy gives you the details of how you will get there; and the preservation policy makes sure that at least the most valuable portions of the baggage do not fall apart en route.

Collection policies define the scope of current collections and indicate areas in which future collections may be developed. By specifying the subjects and formats to be included in or excluded from the collections, the policy encourages consistency in selection of new materials and deselection of those that no longer serve institutional goals. Because it deals with the full range of a library's collections, the policy makes selectors or bibliographers aware of the breadth and variety of materials being collected and thus helps them to see the collections as a whole rather than focus on just those portions for which they are responsible. It thereby encourages communication and cooperation, identifies areas of weakness, and helps to determine priorities for other library functions such as cataloging and preservation.

A collection policy also looks outward, if only by implication. This means that it takes into consideration the holdings of other repositories, especially in subjects of relatively esoteric research interest. Until recently, this has in most cases meant repositories located fairly nearby which could and would provide convenient access. The advent of the photocopy machine, the growth of automated ILL systems, the steadily increasing number of preservation microfilms of important research collections, and now the ability to digitize on demand information for electronic transmission have steadily expanded the geographic range from which materials can be obtained with relative ease. As a result, collection policies and preservation programs tend to place a higher priority on materials of particular importance to the institution's programs that cannot be readily obtained elsewhere.

It is not possible to develop a successful preservation program without a clear mission statement and a comprehensive collection policy. Ultimately, preservation is about setting priorities because not even the richest institutions are able or willing to preserve everything they have collected for all time. The collection policy helps to determine preservation priorities because it states the level at which the institution collects in any given subject. That level is in turn usually determined by the importance of a given collection to the institution's programs and ultimately to its mission. An objective methodology for determining collection level by measuring the quantity and types of materials in it is often used by collection managers and preservation administrators. "The RLG Conspectus is a collection assessment method that maps subjects' strengths and weaknesses within an individual library, a consortium of libraries, or a geographical region using standardized criteria and descriptions."[2] The Conspectus uses a numerical scale with standard definitions to describe the types of client activities supported by the collection. These are, in descending order: comprehensive (5), research (4), intermediate (3), basic (2), minimal (1), and out of scope (0). Levels (1) and (2) are subdivided into two levels and (3) into three levels to provide finer distinctions that are useful in describing smaller collections. The ALA *Guide for Written Collection Policy Statements* cited in note 1 provides further information on the use of the Conspectus in collection policies.

Collection level is not, however, the only criterion to be noted in determining a collection's importance to an institution as a factor in establishing its priority for preservation. Another important feature is whether or not it contains materials that are artifactually valuable or have a significant associational value for the institution. In dealing with archival materials, one should also consider evidential value. Such value pertains to materials needed because of their legal, administrative, and/or fiscal significance to an organization.

If well thought-out and comprehensive, collection policies provide a vital point of reference for making preservation decisions. Preservation considerations must also inform a collection policy if it is to serve as a reliable guide to the development and management of collections. "All collection management decisions, made from the time of acquisition of an item, are embodied in that item's physical deterioration and its ultimate need for preservation intervention."[3] Thus, at each stage of the process of acquiring, processing, housing, providing access to, maintaining, and eventually deselecting materials, all library staff, and especially those directly involved in collection development and management, should have clearly in mind the preservation implications of their decisions and actions.

Acquisitions decisions should consider not just the importance of a title to a subject area or whether it should be acquired in hard copy, microformat, or electronically to serve user needs best, but also the long-term preservation requirements of those formats. If a title is printed on acidic paper or if experience has shown that a serial is particularly apt to be stolen or have articles cut out of it, it may be preferable to acquire it right at the start in a film or electronic format to achieve either greater physical longevity or better security.

It is particularly important to look gift horses in the mouth by asking how a collection has been stored in the past and checking its current condition. A wise collection manager examines any prospective collection carefully for signs of embrittlement, defacement or physical damage, deteriorating bindings, mildew, and insect infestation. Donor forms should state clearly that the library may choose to deaccession items from the collection not just because they are out of scope or duplicate existing holdings, but also because the costs of preservation outweigh their intellectual value to the institution.

Once materials have been acquired, sound collection management includes measures to prevent future deterioration. For example, decisions to provide certain kinds of materials with commercial library binding demonstrate an awareness that bindings that meet current national standards provide excellent long-term protection. Indeed, they are the most cost-effective step a library can take to preserve items that are intended to be permanent additions to the collections. Similarly, archival and manuscript collections should be given the protection of alkaline folders and boxes as they are accessioned.

Collection managers should be active partners with preservation administrators in working to insure the best possible environment for housing collections of permanent value. Research done at the Library of Congress and the Image Permanence Institute has proven beyond any doubt that the life expectancies of collections that have enjoyed stable, moderate temperature and humidity are dramatically extended. In these days of sharply declining book budgets, Collections managers are becoming increasingly aware that the fewer replacements that have to be bought, the more funds there are for new acquisitions.

When a volume has deteriorated beyond repair, selectors and preservation staff can cooperate in making the wisest possible decision about whether or not to replace it and if so, with what. For example, in most cases it makes little sense to acquire another copy of an edition that has deteriorated because it was printed on highly acidic paper and shoddily bound. If and how it should be reformatted should be decided by a bibliographer knowledgeable about the relative merits, defects, and costs of the several available reformatting options: filming, photocopying, digitizing.

In addition, a number of leading research libraries such as those at Harvard and the University of Texas have recently constructed remote cold storage facilities. These have been carefully planned, not just to relieve overcrowding in the on-campus stacks, but to provide preservation environments with stable, low temperatures and low humidity to extend the life of older paper- and film-based collections. Collection managers and preservation administrators are working together to identify those collections that will benefit most by removal to such protected environments.

One sign of the increasing symbiosis of collection management and preservation in American libraries is the changing character of needs assessments. In the 1970s and early 1980s when preservation programs were first being developed, collection surveys were used simply to determine physical condition. Today they also collect data on storage environments, fire protection, disaster preparedness, level of use, and value. The two latter factors fall into the traditional domain of collection management.

There is a historical reason for this change. The preservation movement in this country began primarily as a response to the growing amount of deteriorating acidic paper in the stacks of American research libraries. This mushrooming crisis had clearly outstripped the traditional solutions of replacement or repair which were essentially ad hoc remedies designed to deal with a single volume, a set, or a small group of manuscripts or records. By the mid-1970s it was apparent that more massive and all-encompassing solutions were needed. Initially, the panacea of choice was microfilming, especially of large, important subject collections in research libraries, the so-called "Great Collections" approach to salvaging essential components of our intellectual heritage.

Inevitably, as the preservation movement grew, it evolved. More and more professional preservation administrators gained hands-on experience in addressing the full range of their institutions' preservation needs. Training programs were developed that encouraged analysis of those needs and generated new ideas for solutions. Regional preservation services provided training and consulting expertise to a broader range of types of institutions, many of which were not large enough to justify a full-time preservation administrator but combined preservation with other responsibilities. Scientific investigations to determine the causes of deterioration of paper and film led to recommendations for ways to prolong life, methods that were best applied to whole collections and even entire repositories.

One of the most striking features of the evolution that has occurred over the past 20 years is that the focus of preservation has increasingly shifted from response to prevention. It is no longer chiefly a rescue mission to save information with significant research value from imminent destruction. Today, preservation programs are wide-reaching efforts to prevent or at least slow down the deterioration of the full range of library and archival materials. As a result, preservation has become an integral component of collection management, and collection management for its part has become increasingly concerned with maintaining collection strength over time, not just for the present.

NOTES

[1] Bonita Bryant, ed., *Guide for Written Collection Policy Statements.* Collection Management and Development Guides. (Chicago and London: American Library Association, 1989).

[2] Larry R. Oberg, "Evaluating the Conspectus Approach for Smaller Library Collections," *College & Research Libraries* 49.3 (May 1988): 187-96.

[3] Ellen Cunningham-Kruppa, "The Preservation Officer's Role in Collection Development," *Wilson Library Bulletin* (November 1992): 27.

Northeast Document
Conservation Center
100 Brickstone Square
Andover, MA 01810-1494
www.nedcc.org
Tel: (978) 470-1010
Fax: (978) 475-6021

PRESERVATION PLANNING: SELECT BIBLIOGRAPHY

by Debra Saryan
Librarian
Northeast Document Conservation Center

This short bibliography is intended to assist managers of collections of library, museum, and archives collections in the development of their preservation program. It provides a range of sound, specialized information to help in the assessment of preservation needs, and in deciding priorities for addressing them. Collections managers should also consult the literature on standard strategic planning methodologies to further support this planning process.

Annotations have been provided for most of the references listed. These come courtesy of NEDCC staff, from published reviews, or *A Core Collection in Preservation* [1st ed., by Lisa L. Fox (1988); 2nd ed. by Don K. Thompson and Joan Ten Hoor (1993): Chicago: American Library Association]. The Society of American Archivists (SAA), Education Committee of the Preservation Section, issues annual updates of their "Selected Readings in Preservation," an excellent review resource of the archives preservation literature.

A list of serials and periodicals is given at the end of this leaflet as a guide to current literature, which focuses on organizing the various aspects of a preservation program.

Alberta Museums Association. *Self-Evaluation Checklist.* Edmonton, Alberta: Alberta Museums Association, 1991.

Alberta Museums Association. *Standard Practices Handbook for Museums.* Edmonton, Alberta: Alberta Museums Association, 1990.

American Association of Museums. *Shaping the Museum: The MAP Institutional Planning Guide.* 2nd ed. Washington, D.C.: American Association of Museums, 1993.

American Library Association, Subcommittee on Guidelines for Collection Development. *Guide for Written Collection Policy Statements.* Bonita Bryant, ed. Chicago: American Library Association, 1989; Collection Management and Development Guides, No. 3, 32 pp.
This and the following two publications are part of a series of collection development guides produced by ALA. All of their information is simple, straightforward, and readily applicable. They are highly recommended.

American Library Association, Subcommittee on Guidelines for Collection Development. *Guide to the Evaluation of Library Collections.* Barbara Lockett, ed. Chicago: American Library Association, 1989; Collection Management and Development Guides, No. 2, 25 pp.

American Library Association, Subcommittee on Guidelines for Collection Development. *Guide to Review of Library Collections.* Lenore Clark, ed. Chicago: American Library Association, 1991; Collection Management and Development Guides, No. 5, 41 pp.

Association of Research Libraries (ARL). *Preservation Planning Program Resource Guides.* Jutta Reed-Scott, general editor. Washington, D.C.: ARL, 1993, various lengths. *Seven guides, compiled by senior preservation administrators in academic libraries, intended to provide norms against which a library can measure its preservation efforts, enhance existing activities, and develop new initiatives. Titles cover reformatting, conservation/repair, binding, collections maintenance, emergency planning, staff and user training, and preservation management.*

Barry, Bryan W. *Strategic Planning Workbook for Nonprofit Organizations, Revised and Updated.* St. Paul, MN: Amherst H. Wilder Foundation, 1997. *Provides step-by-step guidance and worksheets to develop a plan. Available from http://www.wilder.org.*

Calmes, Alan. "Preservation Planning at the National Archives and Records Adminstration." *The Record* 1. 2 (November 1994): 1.

Cloonan, Michèle V. *Organizing Preservation Activities.* Association of Research Libraries Resource Guide. Washington, D.C.: Association of Research Libraries, 1993, 98 pp.

Darling, Pamela W., and Wesley Boomgaarden, comps. *Preservation Planning Program Resource Notebook.* Washington, D.C.: Association of Research Libraries, Office of Management Studies, 1987, 719 pp. *Excellent source of bibliographies, background and technical readings, and important ephemeral materials useful in library preservation planning and implementation. Developed for use with Darling and Webster's Self-Study Manual (1987)[See next entry].*

Darling, Pamela W., with Duane E. Webster. *Preservation Planning Program: An Assisted Self-Study Manual for Libraries.* Edited and revised by J. Merrill-Oldham and J. Reed-Scott. Washington, D.C.: Association of Research Libraries Office of Management Studies (OMS), 1993. *Developed to help libraries plan and implement preservation programs by a process that educates and involves a large number of staff members. Outlines a self-study process for assessing needs, setting priorities, and planning a condition survey of the collection, organization and staffing, disaster control, education of staff and users, and inter-institutional cooperation. Augmented by Darling and Boomgaarden's Resource Notebook (1987) and seven new ARL Preservation Planning Program Resource Guides (1993). Final reports of institutions that have completed the formal self-study are also available from OMS.*

DeCandido, Robert, and Cheryl Shackleton. *Who Ya Gonna Call? A Preservation Services Sourcebook for Libraries and Archives.* New York: The New York Metropolitan Reference and Research Library Agency (METRO), 1992, 132 pp. Available from the New York State Library, Division of Library Development, Cultural Education Center, Albany, NY 12230. *Provides listings for sources of various preservation services, including preservation surveys, microfilming, flat paper treatment, bookbinding, library binding, and sources of supplies. Covers an area bounded by Washington, DC; Philadelphia; and Boston; but also includes more distant institutions that are able to provide services within that area.*

Drewes, Jeanne M., and Julie Page, eds. and comps. *Promoting Preservation Awareness in Libraries: A Sourcebook for Academic, Public, School, and Special Collections.* Westport, CT: Greenwood Press, 1997.

One of the comprehensive reviews of library user preservation education programs for personnel in school, public, academic, and special collections. Provides practical examples on how institutions can educate and inform their staff and users. Concludes with useful appendixes on effective graphics for displays, bibliographies, and audiovisual lists.

Ellis, Judith, ed. *Keeping Archives.* 2nd ed. Sydney, Australia: D.W. Thorpe with Australian Society of Archivists, 1993, 512 pp.
A one-stop guide. Covers every aspect of archives management, including preservation, in simple, practical language. Excellent for introduction, review, or reference; provides breadth rather than depth. Available from Society of American Archivists.

Gallery Association. *Insurance and Risk Management for Museums and Historical Societies.* Hamilton, NY: Gallery Association, 1985, 96 pp.
Examines basic risk management concerns and insurance options for museums; information transferable to other cultural collections and institutions. Available from American Association of Museums, Washington, D.C. 20005.

Green, Sara Wolf, ed. *The Conservation Assessment. A Tool For Planning, Implementing, and Fundraising.* 2nd ed. Marina del Ray, CA, and Washington, D.C.: Getty Conservation Institute and National Institute for the Conservation of Cultural Property, 1991.

Harvey, Douglas R., ed. "Developing a Library Preservation Program." Chap. 10 in *Preservation in Libraries: A Reader.* New York: Bowker-Saur, 1993.
Outlines four models of integrating preservation into libraries: small specialized libraries, high-use collections, lower-use retrospective collections, and collections of national importance. Available from Bowker-Saur, 121 Chanlon Rd. New Providence, NJ 07974. 1-800-521-811.

Hoagland, K. Elaine, ed. *Guidelines for Institutional Policies & Planning in Natural History Collections.* Washington, D.C.: Association of Systematics Collections, 1994.

Jones, Maralyn, comp. *Collection Conservation Treatment: A Resource Manual for Program Development and Conservation Technician Training.* Berkeley: Conservation Department, Library, University of California, 1993, 451 pp.
Material (book repair procedures, work space organization, decision trees, etc.) from the Berkeley conference on repair-technician training, 1992. Offers alternatives for common procedures for large-scale book repair programs. Available from Association of Research Libraries, Washington, D.C. 20036.

Lusenet, Yola De. *Choosing to Preserve: Towards a Cooperative Strategy for Long-Term Access to the Intellectual Heritage.* Papers of the International Conference. European Commission on Preservation and Access, Amsterdam, Netherlands, 1997, 165 pp. http://www.knaw.nl/ecpa.

Managing Preservation: A Guidebook. Columbus, Ohio: State Library of Ohio and the Ohio Preservation Council, 1995. Available from Clara Ireland, State Library of Ohio, 65 S. Front Street, Columbus, Ohio.
A manual for the new and the experienced preservation manager.

McCord, Margaret, and Catherine Antomarchi. *A Preventive Conservation Calendar for the Smaller Museum.* Rome: International Centre for the Preservation and Restoration of Cultural Property, 1997.

Merrill-Oldham, Jan, Carolyn Clark Morrow, and Mark Roosa. *Preservation Program Models: A Study Project and Report.* Association of Research Libraries, Committee on Preservation of Research Library Materials. Washington, D.C.: Association of Research Libraries, 1991, 54 pp.
Intended to provide library administrators with guidelines for assessing preservation programs; divides ARL libraries into four groups by size, and within each group assesses program maturity with benchmarks for personnel, production, and budget. Discusses ten components of a comprehensive preservation program. A useful model regardless of library size or mission.

Mibach, Lisa. *Collections Care: What to Do When You Can't Afford to Do Anything.* Oberlin, Ohio: Mibach & Associates, Collection Conservation.

Motylewski, Karen. "What an Institution Can Do to Survey Its Own Preservation Needs." In *Collection Maintenance and Improvement.* Sherry Byrne, ed. Washington, D.C.: Association of Research Libraries, 1993.

National Association of Government Archives & Records Administrators. *NAGARA Guide and Resources for Archival Strategic Planning.* Albany, NY: National Association of Government Archives & Records Administrators, 1991.
Consists of three tools: a computer-assisted self-study program that employs artificial intelligence to derive and report goals, objectives, and priorities tailored to the institution; a manual on planning strategies; and a 700-page "Resource Compendium" with published and unpublished readings. Society of American Archivists, 600 South Federal, Suite 504, Chicago, IL 60605. Telephone: (312) 922-0140, ext. 21, E-mail: info@archivists.org, http://www.archivists.org/publications/catalog/catalog.html.

New York State Archives and Records Administration. *Guidelines for Arrangement and Description of Archives and Manuscripts: A Manual for Historical Records Programs in New York State.* Albany, NY: New York State Archives and Records Administration, 1991, 35 pp. Available from Documentary Heritage Program, State Archives and Records Administration, New York State Education Department, Room 9B44 Cultural Education Center, Albany, NY 12230.
A simple introduction to archival theory and the MARC format, applicable to any institution entrusted with historical materials. Provides an excellent overview of accepted archival procedures for arrangement and description, and includes a short bibliography, which lists the basic tools and manuals widely used in archival description. An ideal starting place for small organizations and untrained archivists.

Ogden, Barclay, and Maralyn Jones. *CALIPR.* Sacramento, CA: The California State Library, 1997.
PC-based software (with accompanying manual) that provides an automated tool to assess preservation needs of book and document collections based on a 100-item random sample. Available from the California State Library Foundation, P.O. Box 942837, Sacramento, CA 94237-0001 or can be downloaded at no charge directly from the Berkeley Library Digital Sunsite http://sunsite.berkeley.edu/CALIPR/.

Ogden, Sherelyn. *Preservation Planning: Guidelines for Writing a Long-Range Plan.* Washington, D.C.: American Association of Museums and Northeast Document Conservation Center; 1997.
Assists in writing a long-range preservation plan for collections care. Provides extensive worksheets in both print and electronic format: IBM-compatible disk.

Pickett, A.G., and M.M. Lemcoe. *Preservation and Storage of Sound Recordings.* (Rpt. of 1959 Library of Congress publication.) Silver Springs, MD: Association for Recorded Sound Collections, 1991, 75 pp. Available from Society of American Archivists, Chicago, IL.

Commonly recommended as essential reading for managers of sound collections. Surprisingly current; most recommendations for storage are still valid. Predates digital technology.

RLG Preservation Needs Assessment Package (PreNAP). Mountain View, CA: Research Libraries Group, 1991.
An automated tool to assess preservation needs. Available from Preservation Publication Coordinator, RLG, 1200 Villa Street, Mountain View, CA 94041-1100.

Reed-Scott, Jutta, ed. *Preservation Planning Program.* Washington, D.C.: Association of Research Libraries, 1993.
An excellent series of seven resource guides offering comprehensive and easy-to-use reprints of articles, documents, and bibliographies concerning the major components of preservation in libraries. Developed primarily for use with the PPP Assisted Self-Study Manual. Series includes: 1. Options for Replacing and Reformatting Deteriorated Materials (Jennifer Banks, ed.); 2. Staff Training and User Awareness in Preservation Management (Wesley Boomgaarden, ed.); 3. Disaster Preparedness (Constance Brooks, ed.); 4.Collection Maintenance and Improvement (Sherry Byrne, ed.); 5. Collections Conservation (Robert DeCandido, ed.); 6. Managing a Library Binding Program (Jan Merrill-Oldham, ed.); 7. Organizing Preservation Activities (Michèle V. Cloonan, ed.). Association of Research Libraries, 21 Dupont Circle, N.W., Suite 800, Washington, DC, 20036. (202) 296-2296, E-mail: pubs@arl.org, http://www.arl.org/pubscat/index.html.

Ritzenthaler, Mary Lynn. *Preserving Archives and Manuscripts.* Chicago: Society of American Archivists, 1993; SAA Archival Fundamentals Series. 232 pp.
A comprehensive and important guide for preservation of archives and manuscripts.

Thompson, Don, and Joan Ten Hoor, eds. *A Core Collection in Preservation.* 2nd ed. Chicago: American Library Association, 1993, 41 pp.
Excellent bibliography for basic preservation education. See also Lisa Fox, A Core Collection in Preservation. *Chicago: ALA, 1988, 15 pp.*

Tuttle, Craig A. *An Ounce of Preservation: A Guide to the Care of Papers and Photographs.* Danvers, MA: Rainbow Books, 1995, 111 pp.
"The information in this book will prove useful to anyone interested in preserving paper-based items and photographs. Church secretaries, historical society volunteers, veterans, grandparents, geneaologists, historians, librarians, manuscript curators, archivists and collectors will find this book essential" (Intro.).

Waller, Robert. "Preventive Conservation Planning for Large and Diverse Collections." In *Preservation of Collections: Assessment, Evaluation, and Mitigation Strategies.* Preprints of the June 10-11, 1996, Workshop. Washington, D.C.: American Institute for Conservation of Historic and Artistic Works, 1996.

Wolf, Sara J. "Conservation Assessments And Long-Range Planning." In *Current Issues, Initiatives, And Future Directions For The Preservation And Conservation Of Natural History Collections.* Madrid: Consejeria de Educacion y Cultura, Comunidad de Madrid. Direccion General de Bellas Artes y Archivos, Ministerio de Cultura, 1993.

PERIODICAL AND SERIAL PUBLICATIONS

Abbey Newsletter. Ellen McCrady, ed. 7105 Geneva Drive, Austin, TX 78723.
Source of timely information on preservation and conservation subjects, including bookbinding, commercial binding, educational programs, supply sources, and news. Especially useful are book reviews and thorough listings of relevant publications from a wide range of sources. Essential reading for anyone concerned with preservation and conservation issues.

American Association of State and Local History Technical Leaflets. Suite 102, 172 Second Avenue North, Nashville, TN 37201. info@archivists.org,
A series of leaflets providing up-to-date technical information of interest to historical agencies and museums. Covers a wide range of subjects, from general administrative issues to management of local government records, landscaping, care of textiles, and oral history.

Basic Manual Series and ***Archival Fundamentals Series.*** Society of American Archivists, 600 South Federal Street, Suite 504, Chicago, IL 60605, info@archivists.org, http://www.archivists.org/publications/webcat99/index.html
Excellent resources for those with archival responsibilities. The BMS, published in the 1980s, describes and illustrates basic archival functions such as accessioning, appraisal, arrangement and description, reference and access, security, reprography, and conservation. The AFS, in production since 1990, updates and expands upon the earlier series.

CCI Notes. Canadian Conservation Institute, National Museum of Canada, 1030 Innes Road, Ottawa, Ontario K1A 0M5, Canada. www.pch.gc.ca/cci/cci-icc/english/pubs/pubs.htm
Pamphlets which offer practical advice about issues related to the care, handling, and storage of cultural objects.

CLIR Issues. Council on Library and Information Resources, Commission on Preservation and Access, 1755 Massachusetts Avenue, NW, Suite 500, Washington, D.C. 20036-2188, Telephone: (202) 939-4750, info@clir.org, http://www.clir.org.
Includes a section with preservation and access related articles; focus is on digital initiatives. Issues available online.

Conserv-O-Gram Series. National Park Service, Curatorial Services Division, Harpers Ferry, WV 25425.
One- or two-page leaflets designed for use by the staff of national parks and museums provide detailed instruction as opposed to broad guidelines. Address environment, housekeeping, storage and handling, and health and safety, among other subjects. Cover objects of various types, biological specimens, and paper. Issued in 3-ring binder format, and periodically reviewed and updated. Can now be downloaded at no charge directly from their website at http://www.cr.nps.gov/csd/publications/conservogram/conserv.html

Library Resources and Technical Services. Association of Library Collections and Technical Services, American Library Association, 50 East Huron Street, Chicago, IL 60611. Telephone: (800) 545-2433, http://www.ala.org/alcts/lrts/
Provides articles on the latest technical developments, preservation, and other technical services.

National Center for Preservation Technology and Training (NCPTT) Notes. NSU Box 5682, Natchitoches, LA 71497. www.ncptt.npo.gov
Provides information relative to the field of preservation and conservation in technology, education, and training.

Regional Alliance for Preservation (RAP). Published by AMIGOS Bibliographic Council, Inc. 14400 Midway Road, Dallas, TX 75244.
A cooperative project to share preservation training resources. RAP Website, http://www.solinet.net/rap/index.html.

Spec Kits. Systems and Procedures Exchange Center, Association of Research Libraries, Office of Management Studies, 1527 New Hampshire Avenue, NW, Washington, D.C. 20036.
Series devoted to library management issues, many of which relate to preservation. Each kit contains charts and documents gathered from various institutions that deal with the kit topic. Subjects include collection analysis, preservation organization and staffing, and exhibits.

WAAC Newsletter. Western Association for Art Conservation, Publication Order c/o Chris Stavroudis, 1272 North Flores Street, Los Angeles, CA 90069, Telephone: (213) 654-8748, cstavrou@lx.netcom.com, http://palimpsest.stanford.edu/waac/wn/.
Contains feature articles, regional news, technical exchange, event calendar, positions available, and a publication section. WAAC also has a Membership Directory that lists more than 400 manufacturers and suppliers of conservation related materials.

Waters, Peter. "Phased Preservation: A Philosophical Concept and Practical Approach to Preservation." *Special Libraries* 81.1 (December 1990): 35-43.

Acknowledgements

NEDCC gratefully acknowledges the previous work of Karen Motylewski in preparing this technical leaflet.

Northeast Document
Conservation Center

100 Brickstone Square
Andover, MA 01810-1494
www.nedcc.org
Tel: (978) 470-1010
Fax: (978) 475-6021

PRESERVATION CONCERNS IN BUILDING DESIGN: SELECT BIBLIOGRAPHY

**by Karen E. Brown
Field Service Representative
Northeast Document Conservation Center**

A properly designed and constructed building is critical to protecting collections over the long term. Building projects are complex, made even more so for housing cultural collections where strict environmental conditions are required. Preservation knowledge and technology are therefore critical concerns during construction or renovation. It is likely that many preservation issues will be unfamiliar to architects and engineers involved with the process. Cultural institutions must be able to communicate their needs in discussion with a range of professionals, including engineers, architects, and various contractors, if they are to ensure the best design and performance of a facility.

The following bibliography has been compiled to help libraries, archives, and museums with the design and construction of their buildings. In addition to material on planning, there is information on environmental guidelines, security features, disaster prevention, the safe movement of collections, and the use of proper furnishings. Many of the items cited will have their own bibliographies, and can be consulted for further references where more in-depth research is required.

All citations are briefly annotated. The annotation is provided by NEDCC or is preceded by a reference to the source. Full references are listed at the end of this leaflet. The text is broken down into the following:

- Planning, Design, and Construction
- Heating, Ventilation, and Air Conditioning
- Environmental Recommendations and Media-Specific Considerations
- Light
- Environmental Monitoring
- Disaster Prevention and Protection
- Storage and Transportation
- References
- Acknowledgements

PLANNING, DESIGN, AND CONSTRUCTION

Briggs, James R. "Preservation Factors in the Design of New Libraries: A Building Services Engineer's Viewpoint." In *Conservation and Preservation in Small Libraries.* Ed. Nicholas Hadgraft and Katherine Swift. Cambridge, England: Parker Library Publications, 1994,pp. 49-69.

Introduction:
"The objective of this paper is to consider the methods of environmental control at different efficacy and cost to suggest that it may be possible to reduce the installation, energy and maintenance costs without the need for air conditioning or at least without mechanical cooling."

Cohen, Aaron, and Elaine Cohen. *Designing and Space Planning for Libraries: A Behavioral Guide.* New York: Bowker, 1979. Larsen:
"Dated, but still relevant guide to designing libraries from a behavioral standpoint. Excellent chapter on lighting, HVAC and environmental factors."

Conrad, Ernest A. "The Dews and Don'ts of Insulating." *Old House Journal* 24.3 (1996): 36-41. Kerschner & Baker:
"Accurate information on how to safely insulate and ventilate an old house, [including] practical climate control considerations."

Craddock, Ann Brooke. "Control of Temperature and Humidity in Small Collections." In *Conservation Concerns.* Ed. Konstanze Bachmann, pp. 15-22. Washington, D.C.: Smithsonian Institution Press, 1992.
A brief well rounded introduction to climate control.

Dahlgren, Anders C., and Erla P. Heyns. *Planning Library Buildings: A Select Bibliography.* 4th ed. Chicago: American Library Association, June 1995.

Edwards, Heather M. *University Library Building Planning.* Metuchen, NJ: Scarecrow Press, 1990. *Book News, Inc.:*
Edwards (U. of Witwatersrand) provides information and ideas on physical planning for those who are considering building a new library or an extension. She gives an overview of factors influencing change in libraries and looks at the qualities desirable in any good building. A chapter on space standards provides the planner with a useful base from which to develop a program. Case studies of successful library buildings are drawn from the US, the UK, and South Africa. (Annotation copyright Book News, Inc. Portland, OR).

Freifeld, Roberta, and Caryl Masyr. *Space Planning.* Washington, D.C.: Special Libraries Association, 1991.
Although preservation concerns are not well addressed, information on evaluating the existing building prior to renovation will prove useful.

Gibson, Scott. "Air and Vapor Barriers." *Fine Homebuilding* 88 (1994): 48-53. Kerschner & Baker:
"An excellent article explaining how air and vapor barriers work. Most useful for new construction, but important to understanding why a historic building without vapor and air barriers could be harmed by high RH."

Grant, Christopher L. "Construction Instruction." *Museum News* 69.4 (July/August 1990): 55-57.
Simple guidelines for developing a construction contract to help ensure that an institution gets the building it expected when it entered the planning phases of an architectural project. Includes advice on preparing contracts.

Hilberry, John D. "Plan to Expand." *Museum News* 69.4 (July/August 1990): 51-54.
Brief overview of important components in an institution's planning process for building; written by an architect knowledgeable about and sympathetic to the full spectrum of functions of buildings and institutions that hold collections. Applicable to libraries with minor changes of detail.

Hilberry, John D. "Hiring an Architect? Begin By Determining Exactly What Services You Require." *Museum News* 69.4 (July/August 1990): 54.
The author, an architect, offers good advice when choosing architectural services.

Hilberry, John D., and Associates. "Museum Storage Design Checklist." Andover, MA: Northeast Document Conservation Center, 1994.
Available as single leaflets by contacting NEDCC, (978) 470-1010, or via email, nedcc@nedcc.org.

Hilberry, John D. "Architectural Design Considerations." In *Storage of Natural History Collections: A Preventive Conservation Approach.* Vol. I. Eds. Carolyn L. Rose, Catharine A. Hawks, and Hugh H. Genoways, 103-22. Iowa City, Iowa: Society for the Preservation of Natural History Collections, 1995.
This useful discussion should assist in developing appropriate criteria for preservation storage environments, including information on space planning. A useful "Storage Design Checklist" is appended.

Hilberry, John D. "The Building Design and Construction Process." In *Storage of Natural History Collections: A Preventive Conservation Approach.* Vol. I. Eds. Carolyn L. Rose, Catharine A. Hawks, and Hugh H. Genoways. Iowa City, Iowa: Society for the Preservation of Natural History Collections, 1995, pp. 43-49.
Overview of who makes up the project team, and the various stages of a building project.

Hilberry, John D. "What Architects Need to Know, and Don't Want to Hear." *Museum News* 61.5 (June 1983): 54-61. Hilberry: *". . . an article that I wrote some time ago, but that clients and prospective clients have found helpful."*

Hoke, John Ray, Jr., ed. *Architectural Graphic Standards.* New York: John Wiley & Sons, 1994. 9th ed.
1998 Supplement also available. The architect's standard reference for over 60 years, now available in CD-Rom. See especially sections on building types.

Holt, Raymond. *Wisconsin Library Building Project Handbook.* Madison, WI: Wisconsin Department of Public Instruction, 1990. Larsen:
"The standard text for public library planning. Does not cover specific preservation topics, but is an essential tool for good building design. Partially updated by Anders C. Dahlgren with "Public Library Space Needs: A Planning Outline /1998," available at http://www.dpi.state.wi.us/dlcl/pld/plspace.html (March 1998)."

Hookham, Francis. "Preservation Factors in the Design of New Libraries: An Architect's Viewpoint." In *Conservation and Preservation in Small Libraries.* Eds. Nicholas Hadgraft and Katherine Swift. Cambridge, England: Parker Library Publications, 1994, pp. 70-73. Introduction:
"This paper touches on a few factors from the architect's point of view, concerning the [adaptation] of old buildings for library purposes, and the construction of new libraries...."

Leighton, Philip D., and David C. Weber. *Planning Academic and Research Library Buildings*, 2nd ed. Chicago: American Library Association, 1986. Lull:
"Although this book is focused on libraries, the discussions of the planning process are helpful on any project. The book is not organized as a reference so it must be read from cover to cover. This volume contains a good section on lighting. A third edition is expected to be published in 1999."

Leuder, Dianne C., and Sally Webb. *Administrator's Guide to Library Building Maintenance.* Chicago: American Library Association, 1992. Larsen: *"Concise and systematic treatment of all areas of building maintenance including HVAC, lighting, safety, fire detection and suppression, environmental quality, and disaster management. Should be required reading for all library administrators and trustees."*

Lord, Gail Dexter, and Barry Lord, eds. *The Manual of Museum Planning.* London: HMSO, 1991.
An extensive guide to planning and managing design and construction from the museum's point of view. Preservation issues are included; specific climate recommendations need to be adapted to geography, economics, and recent research findings.

Lugano, Fred. "Fixing a Cold, Drafty House." *Fine Homebuilding* 105 (Oct./Nov. 1996): 92-97.
Excellent description of the mechanism of air infiltration, and various options for sealing and insulating existing spaces.

Lushington, Nolan, and James M. Kusack. *The Design and Evaluation of Public Library Buildings.* Hamden, CT: Library Professional Publications, 1990.
Divided into two parts, this volume covers planning and design, as well as postoccupancy evaluation.

Massachusetts Board of Library Commissioners. *Library Construction Program: Selected Bibliography.* Boston, MA: MBLA, June 1998.
To obtain a copy, contact Anne Larsen using the information listed under Consulting and Contract Services at the end of this leaflet. This bibliography is expected to be made available early in 1999 online at The Massachusetts Library and Information Network Web site, http://www.mlin.lib.ma.us/index.htm.

McCarthy, Richard C. *Designing Better Libraries: Selecting and Working with Building Professionals.* Fort Atkinson, WI: Highsmith, 1995. Larsen:
"Provides methods and techniques for evaluating, choosing, and working with architects and contractors. Gives effective communication techniques to ensure library design and construction follow good library and preservation practice."

O'Bright, Alan W. "New Mechanical Systems for Historic Structures." *CRM* 15.6 (1992): 44-46. Kerschner & Baker:
"Excellent article comparing three climate control strategies for three different historic houses."

Oreszczyn, T., M. Cassar, and K. Fernandez. "Comparative Study of Air-Conditioned and Non-Air-Conditioned Museums." In *Preventive Conservation: Practice, Theory, Research.* Preprints of the Contributions to the Ottawa Congress, 12-16 September 1994. London: International Institute for Conservation, 144-48.
A study of the possible problems associated with the installation of air cooling systems in historic buildings.

Rose, William. "Effects of Climate Control on the Museum Building Environment." *Journal of the American Institute for Conservation* 33.2 (Summer 1994): 199-210. Abstract:
"Practical matters presented include: setting upper and lower humidity limits in the exhibition space; temperature and moisture distributions in a space and in a climate control zone; the winter and summer performance of mechanical equipment; instrumentation; and building monitoring. Finally, guidelines for climate control that are aimed at maintaining the museum building envelope are presented."

Thatcher-Ellis, Rebecca. "Getting Function From Design: Making Systems Work." In *Preservation of Library and Archival Materials,* 3rd ed. Revised and expanded; ed. Sherelyn

Odgen. Andover, MA: Northeast Document Conservation Center, 1999.
Detailed explanation of the procedures for start-up/commissioning, and ongoing operation that apply to all building projects. Special attention is paid to components affecting environmental control. Available through the NEDCC Web site, www.nedcc.org.

Thompson, Godfrey. *Planning and Design of Library Buildings*, 3rd ed. London: Butterworths, 1989.
Written for the librarian new at the task of creating or renovating a library. This detailed manual should be read by those involved with building projects.

Trinkley, Michael. *Preservation Concerns in Construction and Remodeling of Libraries: Planning for Preservation.* Columbia, SC: South Carolina State Library, 1992.
This manual will prove an extremely valuable resource for building projects where collection preservation is a concern. The author addresses topics that are often difficult to research, such as proper finishes, roof construction, floors, and the design of book returns. Useful appendices and bibliography. Contact the SC State Library, (803) 734-8666 for ordering information.

Sannwald, William W. *Checklist of Library Building Design Considerations.* 3rd ed. Chicago: American Library Association, 1997. Larsen:
"Although preservation concerns are not handled separately, issues related to proper collection preservation appear throughout this essential planning document."

Weber, Martin E., with F.G. Matero. *Conserving Buildings: Guide to Techniques and Materials.* New York: John Wiley, 1993. Swartzburg:
"A basic text on buildings conservation, with emphasis on assessing old and new technologies to be able to integrate them effectively."

Wilcox, U. Vincent. "Facility Management." In *Storage of Natural History Collections: A Preventive Conservation Approach.* Vol. I. Eds. Carolyn L. Rose, Catharine A. Hawks, and Hugh H. Genoways. Iowa City, Iowa: Society for the Preservation of Natural History Collections, 1995, pp. 29-41.
Good discussion on the need for proper space management in the planning stage of a building project, written from the perspective of a facilities manager. Describes the types of spaces needed in a workplace in terms of physical structure, utilities, cleaning, safety, security services, and pest control.

HEATING, VENTILATION AND AIR CONDITIONING

American Society of Heating, Refrigeration and Air-Conditioning Engineers. *Ventilation for Acceptable Indoor Air Quality, ASHRAE Standard 62-1989,* 1989. (Supersedes ASHRAE Standard 62-1981). 62a-1990 Addendum to ANSI/ASHRAE 62-1989. Scope:
"This standard applies to all indoor or enclosed spaces that people may occupy, except where other applicable standards and requirements dictate larger amounts of ventilation than this standard."

American Society of Heating, Refrigeration and Air-Conditioning Engineers. *1995 ASHRAE Handbook: HVAC Applications.* Atlanta, GA: ASHRAE, 1995. Scope:
"HVAC requirements for an extensive range of applications are covered, including descriptions of the equipment needed to create a specific condition." A new edition is expected in June 1999.

American Society of Heating, Refrigeration and Air-Conditioning Engineers. *1996 ASHRAE Handbook: HVAC Systems and Equipment.* Atlanta, GA: ASHRAE, 1996. Scope:
"The 1996 HVAC Systems and Equipment Handbook [has] chapters on hydronic heating and

cooling systems design; fans; unit ventilators; unit heaters; makeup air units, humidifiers; desiccant dehumidification and pressure drying equipment, air-heating coils."

American Society of Heating, Refrigeration and Air-Conditioning Engineers.
Humidification and Dehumidification Control Strategies. Atlanta, GA: ASHRAE, 1996. Scope:
"Presents 10 papers from the 1996 ASHRAE Annual Meeting…. Topics include: control options for various humidification technologies; mechanical dehumidification control strategies and psychrometrics; six steps to follow that ensure proper humidification system design and control; field experience in residential humidification control with temperature-compensated automatic humidistats; controlling rotary desiccant wheels for dehumidification and cooling; maintaining temperature and humidity and non-humidity-generating spaces."

American Society of Heating, Refrigeration and Air-Conditioning Engineers. *1997 ASHRAE Handbook: Fundamentals.* Atlanta, GA: ASHRAE, 1997. Scope:
"As the anchor for the Handbook Series, the Fundamentals volume covers the basic principles and data for the entire technology of the industry, including theories, engineering concepts and data on basic working materials. The most popular volume in the series, this edition has new chapters on Energy Resources, Control Fundamentals, and Building Envelopes." Includes new information for controlling humidity based on thirty years of empirical data of peak humidity loads.

Harriman, Lewis G., ed. *The Dehumidification Handbook.* 2nd ed. Amesbury, MA: Munters Cargocaire, 1990. Introduction:
"This handbook explains how and why to dehumidify air. It is written for the engineer who has a basic understanding of building heating and cooling systems, or who operates a building or process which is influenced by atmospheric humidity." Includes good information on basic concepts, use of psychometric charts, and load calculations.

Harriman, Lewis G., Dean Plager, and Douglas Kosar. "Dehumidification and Cooling Loads from Ventilation Air." *ASHRAE Journal* (November 1997): 37-45. Harriman:
"This article quantifies the moisture loads and heat loads from air infiltration over the course of an entire year for 239 locations in the United States. It shows that moisture loads outweigh heat loads by about 4:1 in all but desert and high-altitude climates."

Lafontaine, Raymond H. "Humidistatically Controlled Heating: A New Approach to Relative Humidity Control in Museums Closed for the Winter Season." *Journal of the International Institute for Conservation - Canadian Group* 7.1-2 (Spring 1982): 35-41. Conrad:
"Although dated, it is still good information for low-tech approaches to collections care in historic buildings and non-museum facilities."

Rose, William. "Effects of Climate Control on the Museum Building Envelope." *Journal of the American Institute for Conservation* 33 (1994): 199-210. Kerschner & Baker:
"A technical article analyzing how moisture moves through the building envelope. Humidity control that overrides temperature control during periods of extreme outdoor conditions is recommended to stabilize RH levels for collection artifacts."

Rose, William B., and Anton TenWolde, eds. *Bugs, Mold & Rot II: A Workshop on Control of Humidity for Health, Artifacts, and Buildings,* Nov. 16-17, 1993. Washington, D.C.: National Institute of Building Sciences, 1993. (152 pp., $35 from NIBS, 1202 L. St., NW Suite 400, Washington, D.C., 20005 [202/289-7800]). Ellen McCrady:
"[Papers from a] workshop by the Building Environment and Thermal Envelope Council (BETEC, part of NIBS) and Oak Ridge National Laboratory. The papers are…relevant to [the preservation] world…; some provide crucial, hard-to-find information. Almost all of them are technical and fact filled."

Sebor, Andrew J. "Heating, Ventilating, and Air-Conditioning Systems." In *Storage of Natural History Collections: A Preventive Conservation Approach*. Vol. I. Eds. Carolyn L. Rose, Catharine A. Hawks, and Hugh H. Genoways. Iowa City, Iowa: Society for the Preservation of Natural History Collections, 1995, pp. 135-46. Introduction: *"Critical issues in heating, ventilating, and air-conditioning (HVAC) systems, planning, design, and selection are discussed...." Good overview of types of system components and options.*

Weintraub, Steven, and Sara J. Wolf. "Macro- and Microenvironments." In *Storage of Natural History Collections*: *A Preventive Conservation Approach,* Vol. I. Eds. Carolyn L. Rose, Catharine A. Hawks, and Hugh H. Genoways. Iowa City, Iowa: Society for the Preservation of Natural History Collections, 1995, pp.123-134. Introduction: *"...many methods are available that can provide some level of environmental control, are inexpensive and relatively simple to implement, and are capable of reducing the rate of environmentally induced damage to collections significantly."*

ENVIRONMENTAL RECOMMENDATIONS AND MEDIA SPECIFIC CONSIDERATIONS

ANSI/PIMA IT9.2-998. "Imaging Media—Photographic Processed Films, Plates, and Papers—Filing Enclosures and Storage Containers."
ANSI/PIMA IT9.25-1998. "Imaging Materials—Optical Disc Media—Storage."
ANSI/PIMA IT9.23-1998. "Imaging Materials—Polyester Base Magnetic Tape—Storage."
ISO 5466:1996. "Photography—Processed Safety Photographic Films—Storage Practices."
ANSI/NAPM IT9.16-1993. "Imaging Media—Photographic Activity Test."
These standards should be consulted for information regarding the proper storage of imaging media. Standards can be ordered through the American National Standards Institute Web site, www.ansi.org.

Appelbaum, Barbara. *Guide to Environmental Protection of Collections.* Madison, WI: Sound View Press, 1991.
Basic information for those without technical training in the care of any kind of collection.

Calmes, Alan. "Video Tapes." In *Storage of Natural History Collections*: *A Preventive Conservation Approach*, Vol. I. Eds. Carolyn L. Rose, Catharine A. Hawks, and Hugh H. Genoways. Iowa City, Iowa: Society for the Preservation of Natural History Collections, 1995, pp. 395-400.
Describes the manufacture and proper care of valued videorecordings.

Carmody, John, and Peter H. Herzog. *Energy-Efficient Operation of Commercial Buildings: Redefining the Energy Manager's Job.* New York: McGraw Hill, 1997.
Provides practical methods for achieving energy efficiency, and introduces the basic concepts of building operation and performance.

Canadian Conservation Institute. "Storing Works on Paper." *CCI Notes* 11/2. Ottawa, ON: CCI, 1995. NLC:
"Covers preparation for storage, and optimum environmental conditions." To order, contact CCI, 1030 Innes Road, Ottawa, ON Canada, TK1A 0M5, tel. (613) 998-3721, fax (613) 998-4721.

Cassar, May. *Environmental Management.* London: Routledge, 1995. NLC:
"Provides guidelines for [a] strategic approach to environmental management. Includes select bibliography and list of sources to other information."

Christensen, Carol. "Environmental Standards: Looking Beyond Flatlining?" *AIC News* 20.5 (1995): 1-2, 4-8.
A full discussion of new standards for storing collections, based on research at the Smithsonian's Conservation Analytical Laboratory (CAL), allowing a wider range of relative humidity than previously recommended.

Conrad, Ernest A. "Balancing Environmental Needs of The Building, The Collection, and the User." In *Abstracts of Papers Presented at the Twenty-Fourth Annual Meeting, Norfolk, Virginia, June 10-16, 1996, by the American Institute for Conservation.* Washington, DC: AIC, 1996, pp. 15-18.
A six-part classification system is presented based on three major climate-control categories, including examples of the kinds of collections and/or use which could be considered for each type of space. This system is in wide usage as a tool in the balancing act often needed in historic house museums.

Conrad, Ernest A. "Energy Conservation Issues for Modern Buildings." In *Preserving the Recent Past.* Eds. Deborah Slaton and Rebecca A. Shiffer. Washington, DC: Historic Preservation Education Foundation, 1995, pp. 137-140.
Considers energy conservation in recent historic buildings. Relates building structures and systems to a range of twentieth-century influences and issues. Includes practical heating and ventilation tips.

Druzik, James, and Paul Banks. "Appropriate Standards for the Indoor Environment." *Conservation Administration News* 62/63 (1995): 1, 3-8.
Further discussion on CAL's environmental specifications.

Erhardt, David, and Marion Mecklenberg. "Relative Humidity Re-Examined." In *Preventive Conservation: Practice, Theory, Research.* Preprints of the Contributions to the Ottawa Congress, 12-16 September 1994. London: International Institute for Conservation, 1994, pp. 32-38. Kerschner & Baker:
"This paper presents results of materials research on museum objects conducted by the authors that leads them to the conclusion that many museum artifacts can safely withstand wider fluctuations in relative humidity than previously accepted by many conservators."

Foot, Mirjam M. "Housing Our Collections: Environment and Storage for Libraries and Archives." *IFLA Journal* 22 (1996): 110-14.
Good general discussion on the importance of a good environment, and the importance of balancing use of collections with preferred storage conditions.

Hansen, Eric F., Steven N. Lee, and Harry Sobel. "The Effects of Relative Humidity on Some Physical Properties of Modern Vellum: Implications for the Optimum Relative Humidity for the Display and Storage of Parchment." *Journal of the American Institute for Conservation* 31 (1992): 325-42.
Research results on the effects of different relative humidities on the physical properties of parchment. Abstract: "…a relative humidity of 30% seems optimum for such objects. At 30% RH, a cyclic variation of ±5% can be permitted with minimal effects of swelling and shrinkage."

Kerschner, Richard L. "A Practical Approach to Environmental Requirements for Collections in Historic Buildings." *Journal of the American Institute for Conservation* 31 (1992): 65-76. Scope:
"Ideal environmental conditions for the preservation of artifacts housed in a historic structure often differ from the ideal conditions for the preservation of the structure itself. It is important to consider carefully the preservation requirements of both the collection and the building when setting specific temperature and humidity standards and designating climate control systems."

McCormick-Goodhart, Mark H. "The Allowable Temperature and Relative Humidity Range for the Safe Use and Storage of Photographic Materials." *Journal of the Society of Archivists* 17.1 (1996): 7-21.
Describes the research leading to recommendations for cold storage to help ensure the long-term preservation of photographs.

Michalski, Stefan. "Relative Humidity: A Discussion of Correct/Incorrect Values." In *ICOM Committee for Conservation: 10th Triennial Meeting, Washington, D.C., 22-27 August 1993, Preprints*. Vol. 2. Ed. J. Bridgeland. Paris: ICOM Committee for Conservation, pp. 624-29. Kerschner & Baker:
"An excellent, understandable, detailed explanation of what RH levels are safe and what are not for a variety of materials."

Nugent, William R. "Compact Discs and Other Optical Discs." In *Storage of Natural History Collections: A Preventive Conservation Approach*. Vol. I, Eds. Carolyn L. Rose, Catharine A. Hawks, and Hugh H. Genoways. Iowa City, Iowa: Society for the Preservation of Natural History Collections, 1995, pp. 401-08.
Accurate description of various types of optical discs, including information on proper care and expected longevity. Extensive list of references may be useful for more in-depth research.

Reilly, James M. *IPI Storage Guide for Acetate Film*. Rochester, NY: Image Permanence Institute, Rochester Institute of Technology, 1993. Scope:
"The main purpose of the Guide is to help collection managers evaluate the quality of the storage environment they provide for their film." Includes a booklet, a two-sided Wheel, Time Contours for Vinegar Syndrome, and a "Time Out of Storage" Table. To order copies call (716) 475-5199 or fax (716) 475-7230.

Reilly, James M. *Storage Guide for Color Photographic Materials*. Rochester, NY: Image Permanence Institute, 1998. Scope:
"A 48-page book accompanied by a wheel of environmental conditions (a kind of circular slide rule), explains how and why color images fade, why they need special storage, and what can be done to make them last as long as possible." The cost of this publication is $20.00. Order forms can be found at the New York State Library web site at http://www.nysl.nysed.gov/libdev/storage.htm. Checks must be made payable to The State University of New York. Credit card orders can be placed through the Image Permanence Institute by calling 716-475-5199. The cost through IPI is $25.00 plus $3.00 for postage and shipping.

Reilly, James M., Douglas Nishimura, and Edward Zinn. *New Tools for Preservation: Assessing Long-Term Environmental Effects on Library and Archives Collections*. Washington, D.C.: Commission on Preservation and Access, 1995. NLC:
"Introduces the concept of the Time Weighted Preservation Index (TWPI), a new way to measure how temperature and RH changes affect the preservation quality of storage environments." Available by sending a check for $10 made payable to CLIR to: CLIR Publication Orders, 1755 Massachusetts Avenue, NW, Suite 500, Washington DC, 20036-2124. If you wish to pay by Visa or Mastercard, please contact them by phone (202-939-4750), fax (202-939-4760), or e-mail (info@clir.org).

Roosa, Mark. *Care, Handling, and Storage of Photographs*. International Federation of Library Associations, Core Programme on Preservation and Conservation, 1992.
Concise information on the care of a wide range of photographic materials. Includes an extensive bibliography and a list of applicable standards.

Sebera, Donald K. *Isoperms: An Environmental Management Tool.* Washington, D.C.: Commission on Preservation and Access, 1994. NLC:
"The isoperm method quantifies the effect of temperature and relative humidity on the life expectancy of paper-based collections." Available in full text at http://www.clir.org/pubs/reports/isoperm/is operm.html, or can be ordered by sending a check for $10 made payable to CLIR to: CLIR Publication Orders, 1755 Massachusetts Avenue, NW, Suite 500, Washington DC, 20036-2124. If you wish to pay by Visa or Mastercard, please contact them by phone (202-939-4750), fax (202-939-4760), or e-mail (info@clir.org).

Thomson, Garry. *The Museum Environment.* 2nd ed. Boston: Butterworths, 1994.
A comprehensive, advanced text for conservators and curators concerning the damaging effects on exhibits of light, humidity, and air pollution, and what to do to minimize damage. Available from Butterworth-Heinemann, 225 Wildwood Ave., Woburn, MA 01801, (800) 336-2665 or fax (800) 446-6520. Orders may also be placed through their Web site at http://www.bh.com.

Van Bogart, John W.C. *Magnetic Tape Storage and Handling: A Guide for Libraries and Archives.* Washington, D.C.: The Commission on Preservation and Access, 1995.
Report from the National Media Lab; contains the best and most current information on the long-term storage and care of magnetic materials. Available in full text at http://www.clir.org/pubs/reports/isoperm/isoperm.html, or can be ordered by sending a check for $10 made payable to CLIR to: CLIR Publication Orders, 1755 Massachusetts Avenue, NW, Suite 500, Washington DC, 20036-2124. If you wish to pay by Visa or Mastercard, please contact them by phone (202-939-4750), fax (202-939-4760), or e-mail (info@clir.org).

Vogt-O'Connor, Diane. *Caring for Photographs: General Guidelines.* Conserve O Gram Series No. 14/4. Washington, D.C.: National Park Service, June 1997.
Environmental conditions and recommendations for storage and handling of photographs are succinctly outlined. Available to non-NPS institutions and interested individuals by subscription through the Superintendent of Documents, U.S. Government Printing Office, Washington, DC 20402, fax (202) 512-2250.

Vogt-O'Connor, Diane. *Caring for Photographs: Special Formats.* Conserve O Gram Series No. 14/5. Washington, D.C.: National Park Service, June 1997.
Environmental conditions and recommendations for storage and handling of materials such as cased photographs and glass plate negatives are outlined. See above for ordering information.

Wilhelm, Henry, and Carol Bower. *The Permanence and Care of Color Photographs.* Grinell, IA: Preservation Publishing Company, 1993.
Detailed, specific information on the storage of photographs, including black & white media. One of the best reference books available.

Wilson, William K. *Environmental Guidelines for the Storage of Paper Records.* NISO Technical Report (NISO-TR01-1995). Bethesda, MD: NISO Press, 1995. Scope:
"This report will help librarians, archivists, architects, and building and environmental engineers establish appropriate environmental guidelines for the storage of records in libraries, archives, and other storage facilities. Recommended requirements for specific storage conditions such as temperature, relative humidity, light and air pollutants are given. A detailed review of the technical and scientific literature which led to the conclusions presented by the author is also included." Available from NISO Press, P.O. Box 338, Oxon Hill, MD, 20750-0338; 1-800-282-NISO. This and other publications can also be ordered through their Web site at www.niso.org.

LIGHT

Canadian Conservation Institute. "A Light Damage Slide Rule." *CCI Notes* 2.6. Ottawa, ON: CCI, 1989. NLC:
"Tool to assist with decision-making on lighting of art and artifacts." To order, contact CCI, 1030 Innes Road, Ottawa, ON Canada, TK1A 0M5, (613) 998-3721, fax (613) 998-4721.

Colby, Karen M. "A Suggested Exhibition Policy for Works of Art on Paper." *Journal of the IIC-CG* 17 (1992): 3-17. Also available at http://www.lightresource.com/policy1.html. Abstract:
"This paper examines a new exhibition policy for works of art on paper as developed by the conservation department at the Montreal Museum of Fine Arts in 1991. It focuses specifically on the recommended exposure times to which works can be reasonably subjected in light of the Museum's concurrent but sometimes conflicting mandates of preservation and display. The policy involves 3 sensitivity categories and proposes an annual limit (which can be converted into a bi-annual or tri-annual limit as required). Category lists have been prepared which classify most materials in the works on paper class to assist the conservator with accurate classification of works of art into appropriate categories."

Florentine, Frank A. "The Next Generation of Lights: Electrodeless." *WAAC Newsletter* 17.3 (Sept. 1995): 12-13.
Considers continuing research and design of lights that can be used for exhibition of collections.

Freifeld, Roberta, and Caryl Masyr. *Space Planning.* Washington, D.C.: Special Libraries Association, 1991.
Includes useful information on lighting treatments.

Layman, David. "Lighting Design Terminology: A Mini-Lesson." *Exhibitionist* 13.1 (Spring 1994): 46-47.
Lists the key terms that need to be defined when investigating lighting options.

Lull, William P., with Paul N. Banks. *Conservation Environment Guidelines for Libraries and Archives.* Ottawa, ON: Canadian Council of Archives, 1995.
An excellent resource for specifying environmental conditions for collections care, including information on light sources and treatments. A new edition is planned for 1999 from the New York State Library. Ordering information will be available through their Web site, http://www.nysl.nysed.gov/

Michalski, Stefan. "New Lamps for Museum Lighting." *CCI Newsletter* 17 (March 1996): 7-8. *Explains the new types of lamps manufactured for sale in Canada for improved energy efficiency.*

National Park Service and the American Institute for Conservation. *Museum Exhibit Lighting.* Presession to the AIC 25th Annual Meeting, San Diego, CA, June 9-10, 1997.
Broad range of current, in-depth articles covering visual perception, light sources, lighting treatments, and control of UV energy. To order, contact AIC at 1717 K St. NW, Ste. 301, Washington, D.C. 20006, tel. (202) 452-9545, fax (202) 452-9328, or e-mail InfoAIC@aol.com.

New England Museum Association. *Lighting for Exhibits and Historic Sites.* Boston, MA: NEMA, 1998.
To order contact Katie Hazard at NEMA, Boston National Historic Park, Charlestown Navy Yard, Boston MA 02129, (617) 242-2283, or fax (617) 241-5797. Cost is $3.00 per pamphlet.

Nicholson, Catherine. "What Exhibits Can Do To Your Collection." *Restaurator* 13.3 (1992): 95-113. Scope:
"Possible exhibition-related hazards are discussed including light damage, exposure to gaseous pollutants and increased fluctuation of temperature and relative humidity, and physical damage from handling, inadequate support, vibration and transport. Guidelines are suggested for the safe light exposure of archival and library materials."

Weintraub, Steven. "Creating and Maintaining the Right Environment." In *Caring for Your Collections*. Ed. Harriet Whelchel. New York: Harry N. Abrams, Inc., 1992, pp. 18-29.
A good introductory article on the importance of climate control, including a useful section on lighting.

Weintraub, Steven. "Technics: Natural Light in Museums: An Asset or a Threat." *Progressive Architecture* 5 (1990): 49-54.
Written for the lighting designer; discusses the compromises to be considered when balancing the use of natural light with conservation concerns.

ENVIRONMENTAL MONITORING

EPA and NIOSH. *Building Air Quality: Guide for Building Owners & Facility Managers.* Washington, D.C.: Environmental Protection Agency, 1992. NLC:
"Information on indoor air quality problems and how to correct or prevent them." To order, contact the National Center for Environmental Publications and Information, PO Box 42419, Cincinnati, OH 45242-2419, (800) 490-9198, fax (513) 489-8695. See the EPA Web site for further information, http://www.epa.gov.

Grzywacz, Cecily M. "Air Quality Monitoring." In *Storage of Natural History Collections: A Preventive Conservation Approach*. Vol. I. Eds. Carolyn L. Rose, Catharine A. Hawks, and Hugh H. Genoways. Iowa City, Iowa: Society for the Preservation of Natural History Collections, 1995, pp. 197-209.
Describes methods of detecting pollutants in the museum environment, such as acetic acid and formaldehyde. A list of materials and suppliers is appended.

Leeke, John. "Detecting Moisture." *Old House Journal* 24.3 (1996): 42-45. Kerschner & Baker:
"The basic equipment and techniques used to identify moisture problems in old buildings are discussed."

Lull, William P., with Paul N. Banks. *Conservation Environment Guidelines for Libraries and Archives*. Ottawa, ON: Canadian Council of Archives, 1995.
Specifies environmental conditions for collections care. The monitoring section is the part most often referenced and reproduced. Good section on the design and construction process. Out of print; a new edition is planned for 1999 from the New York State Library. Ordering information will be available through their Web site, http://www.nysl.nysed.gov/.

Weintraub, Steven, and Sara J. Wolf. "Environmental Monitoring." *In Storage of Natural History Collections: A Preventive Conservation Approach*. Vol. I. Eds. Carolyn L. Rose, Catharine A. Hawks, and Hugh H. Genoways. Iowa City, Iowa: Society for the Preservation of Natural History Collections, 1995, pp. 187-96.
Covers monitors such as humidistats, thermostats, and dataloggers; calibration; measuring light levels; and pollutants.

DISASTER PREVENTION AND PROTECTION

Artim, Nick. "An Introduction to Automatic Fire Sprinklers." *WAAC Newsletter* 15.3

(September 1994): 20-27, and 17.2 (May1995): 23-28.
Explains the various types of sprinkler systems and their advantages and disadvantages.

Artim, Nick. "An Introduction to Fire Detection, Alarm, and Automatic Fire Sprinklers." In *Preservation of Library and Archival Materials*, 3rd. ed., revised and expanded. Ed. Sherelyn Ogden. Andover, MA: Northeast Document Conservation Center, 1999.
Available through the NEDCC Web site, http://www.nedcc.org.

Federal Emergency Management Agency/Federal Insurance Administration. "Flood-Resistant Materials Requirements for Buildings Located in Special Flood Hazard Areas." *Technical Bulletin* 2-93. Washington, D.C.: FEMA/FIA, 1993.
For anyone building or renovating in areas at risk of flooding. Prepared in accordance with the National Flood Insurance Program. Available from FEMA/FIA Office of Reduction, Technical Standards Division, 500 C St., SW, Room 417, Washington, D.C., 20472.

Fennelly, Lawrence J., ed. *Effective Physical Security.* 2nd ed. Boston: Butterworth-Heinemann, 1997.
An invaluable resource detailing the essential components of a secure facility, including security hardware and systems.

Fortson, Judith. *Disaster Planning and Recovery: A How-To-Do-It-Manual for Librarians and Archivists.* New York: Neal Schuman Publishers, 1992. How-To-Do-It Manuals for Libraries, No. 21.
Excellent, comprehensive guidance for emergency preparedness, risk prevention, response, and recovery. Includes resource lists, bibliography, and decision tree. [If you can buy only one emergency planning guide, this should be it.]

Frens, Dale H. "Specifying Temporary Protection of Historic Interiors During Construction and Repair." *Preservation Tech Note.* Washington, D.C.: National Park Service. 1993.
A must for anyone considering renovation when buildings and collections are at high risk of fire damage. Copies can be obtained from Heritage Preservation Services Information Desk (2255), National Center for Cultural Resource Stewardship and Partnerships, PO Box 37127, Washington, D.C., 20013-7127, 202-343-9538, or via email hps_info@nps.gov.

Kahn, Miriam. *Disaster Prevention and Response for Special Libraries: An Information Kit.* Washington: Special Libraries Association, 1995. Trinkaus-Randall:
"Includes steps for writing a disaster plan and suggestions on preventing disasters and emergencies, especially for [small] operations."

Kahn, Miriam. *First Steps for Handling & Drying Water-Damaged Materials.* Columbus, OH: MBK Consulting, 1994. Trinkaus-Randall:
"Includes procedures and remedies for dealing with water-damaged materials." Clear, usable graphic format presented in 3-ring binder makes it especially useful during an emergency. For copies, contact MBK Consulting, Miriam B. Kahn, 60 N. Harding Rd., Columbus, OH 43209-1524, (614) 239-8977, or e-mail mbkcons@netexp.net.

Keller, Steve. "Securing Historic Houses and Buildings." Steven R. Keller and Associates, Inc., 1994. http://histhous.txt@www.horizon-usa.com/architect/histhous.txt (August 1998).
Practical advice provided courtesy of a security consulting firm which specializes in museums, cultural institutions, and historic sites. See also the following two articles.

Keller, Steve. "The Most Common Security Mistakes That Most Museums Make." Steven R. Keller and Associates, Inc., 1994. http://www.horizon-usa.com/horizon/common.txt (August 1998).

Keller, Steve. "The Most Common Security Mistakes That Most Museum Architects Make." Steven R. Keller and Associates, 1994. http://histhous.txt@www.horizon-usa.com/horizon/archmst.txt (August 1998).

Liston, David, ed. *Museum Security and Protection.* ICOM and the International Committee on Museum Security. New York: Routledge Inc., 1993.
An essential, detailed tool for protecting any building from threats of theft, vandalism, etc. Detailed lists, checklists, and guidelines throughout.

Motylewski, Karen. "Protecting Collections During Renovation." In *Preservation of Library and Archival Materials.* 3rd ed., rev. and expanded. Ed by Sherelyn Odgen. Andover, MA: Northeast Document Conservation Center, 1999. Online. Available through the NEDCC Web site, http://www.nedcc.org.

National Fire Protection Association. NFPA 909: *Protection of Cultural Resources* (Item No. PY-909-97); NFPA 913: *Protection of Historic Structures and Sites* (Item No. PY-913-92); NFPA 914: *Fire Protection in Historic Structures* (Item No. PY-914-94). Quincy, MA: National Fire Protection Association.
Contact them at 1 Batterymarch Park, Quincy, MA 02269-9101, (617) 770-3000, or order through their Web site, http://www.nfpa.org. These standards discuss the causes, prevention, detection, and suppression of fire in libraries, museums, archives, and historic structures. They contain descriptions and standards for fire detection/suppression equipment, synopsis of the role of the institution's staff in fire protection, and a bibliography of resources. Each includes useful self-inspection checklists.

National Fire Protection Association. *Guide for Fire Protection for Archives and Records Centers.* NFPA 232A. Quincy, MA: National Fire Protection Association, 1995. Scope: "NFPA 232A provides guidelines on fire protection for file rooms exceeding 50,000 cubic feet in volume, as well as all archives and records centers." Contact them at 1 Batterymarch Park, Quincy, MA 02269-9101, (617) 770-3000, or order through their Web site, http://www.nfpa.org.

Trinkaus-Randall, Gregor. *Protecting Your Collections; A Manual of Archival Security.* Chicago: The Society of American Archivists, 1995.
Practical considerations for protecting collections from disaster and theft. Informative section on physical security.

Wilson, J. Andrew. "Fire Protection." In *Storage of Natural History Collections: A Preventive Conservation Approach.* Vol. I. Eds. Carolyn L. Rose, Catharine A. Hawks, and Hugh H. Genoways. Iowa City, Iowa: Society for the Preservation of Natural History Collections, 1995, pp. 57-72
Comprehensive discussion of all aspects of fire protection for cultural institutions, including disaster planning, prevention and reaction to fire, as well as building design considerations.

STORAGE AND TRANSPORTATION

ANSI/NISO Z39.73-1994. *Single-Tier Bracket Shelving.*
Essential information on the specifications and installation of library shelving. Standards can be ordered through the American National Standards Institute Web site, www.ansi.org.

Bright, Franklyn. *Planning for a Movable Compact Shelving System.* Chicago: American Library Association, 1991.
Invaluable advice and technical information regarding the installation of compact shelving.

Brown, Carol R. *Planning Library Interiors: The Selection of Furnishings for the 21st Century.* Phoenix, AZ: Oryx Press, 1995. Oryx:

"The updated and revised edition reveals how to comply with the latest government regulations while creating and furnishing inspiring and practical areas. The author discusses how to plan for electronic equipment and create a goals-and-objectives statement for a library planning project. Other topics covered include creating inviting and suitable children's areas, selecting the proper furniture for work areas and electronic equipment, and coordinating computers with power and data distribution."

Burkhardt, Joanna M. "Do's and Don'ts for Moving a Small Academic Library." *College & Research Libraries News.* 59.7 (July/August 1998): 499-503.
Provides practical suggestions for the planning stages and process of moving a collection.

Hatchfield, Pamela. "Wood and Wood Products." In *Storage of Natural History Collections: A Preventive Conservation Approach.* Vol. I. Eds. Carolyn L. Rose, Catharine A. Hawks, and Hugh H. Genoways. Iowa City, Iowa: Society for the Preservation of Natural History Collections, 1995, pp. 283-89.
Discusses the risks associated with wood, along with options for its use. This should be read by those considering the installation of wooden cabinets or shelving in their repository.

Moore, Barbara P., and Stephen L. Williams. "Storage Equipment." In *Storage of Natural History Collections: A Preventive Conservation Approach.* Vol. I, Eds. Carolyn L. Rose, Catharine A. Hawks, and Hugh H. Genoways. Iowa City, Iowa: Society for the Preservation of Natural History Collections, 1995, pp. 255-67.
Excellent, detailed review of storage systems from a preservation perspective. Has an extensive, useful bibliography.

movlibs-L.
LAMA electronic discussion list provides a forum for those involved in moving libraries, including relocating collections, furniture, equipment, and personnel. Created by the LAMA Moving Libraries Discussion Group, established at the 1998 ALA Midwinter Meeting. To subscribe, send a message to listproc@ala.org (subject line is blank) with the message: subscribe movlibs-L [first name, last name].

Sam, Sherrie, and Jean A. Major. "Compact Shelving of Circulating Collections."*College & Research Libraries News.* 54.1 (Jan. 1993): 11-12.
Brief research article on the effect of compact shelving on use of the collection.

Stolow, Nathan. *Conservation Standards for Works of Art in Transit and on Exhibition.* Paris: UNESCO, 1979.
A standard reference work for the safe movement of collections. Good information on case construction.

Thorpe, Valerie, and Colleen Wilson. "Moving the Collections at the Royal British Columbia Museum." In *Preventive Conservation: Practice, Theory, Research.* Preprints of the Contributions to the Ottawa Congress, September 1994. London: International Institute for Conservation, 1994, pp. 48-52.
Describes how the Royal BC Museum found solutions to moving their collections and permanently upgrading storage enclosures and furnishings. Although specimens and artifacts were involved, the philosophy behind the process makes worthwhile reading.

von Endt, David W., W. David Erhardt, and Walter R. Hopwood. "Evaluating Materials Used for Constructing Storage Cases." In *Storage of Natural History Collections: A Preventive Conservation Approach.* Vol. I. Eds. Carolyn L. Rose, Catharine A. Hawks, and Hugh H. Genoways. Iowa City, Iowa: Society for the Preservation of Natural History Collections, 1995, pp. 269-82.
Concerns choosing finishes for cases or built shelving.

Wells, Mariana S., and Rosemary Young. *Moving and Reorganizing a Library.* Brookfield, VT: Ashgate Publishing Company, 1997. AN:
"Throughout the book, the authors do an excellent job of balancing the quality of information while keeping it brief and concise."

White, Kris A., and Glenn S. Cook. "Round 'Em Up, Move 'Em Out: How to Move & Preserve Archival Materials." *Conservation Administration News* 57 (April 1994): 16-17.
Short report on moving collections describes brief hands-on solutions to transporting collections.

References

Conrad, Ernest A. Landmark Facilities Group, Inc., East Norwalk, CT. All Conrad annotations provided through personal correspondence with NEDCC, November 1998.

Fitzgerald, John D., Jr., "Reviews," *Abbey Newsletter* 22.1 (1998): 10.

Harriman, Lew. Mason-Grant Consulting, Portsmouth, NH. All Harriman annotations provided through personal correspondence with NEDCC, November 1998.

Kerschner, Richard L., and Jennifer Baker, "Practical Climate Control: A Selected, Annotated Bibliography." http://palimpsest.stanford.edu/byauth/kerschner/ccbiblio.html (December 1998). All Kerschner and Baker annotations in this leaflet are taken from this compilation.

Larsen, Anne. Associate Library Building Consultant, Massachusetts Board of Library Commissioners, Boston, MA. All Larsen annotations provided through personal correspondence with NEDCC, November 1998.

Lull, William P., with Paul N. Banks, *Conservation Environment Guidelines for Libraries and Archives.* Ottawa, ON: Canadian Council of Archives, 1995: 96. This annotation is for the work by Leighton only. All other annotations provided through personal correspondence with NEDCC, November 1998.

McCrady, Ellen. "Reviews," *Abbey Newsletter* 18.8 (December 1994): 117.

National Library of Canada (NLC). Chapter 5, "Environmental Control." Revised 1996-12-11. http://www.nlc-bnc.ca/resource/presv/ebibl5.htm (August 1998). All NLC annotations in this leaflet are taken from this bibliography.

Swartzburg, Susan G. *Conservation Administration News* 56 (Jan. 1994): 28.

Trinkaus-Randall, Gregor. Collection Management/Preservation Specialist, Massachusetts Board of Library Commissioners, Boston, MA. All Trinkaus-Randall annotations provided through personal correspondence with NEDCC, November 1998.

Acknowledgements

The author would like to thank Ms. Anne Larsen and Mr. Gregor Trinkaus-Randall, Massachusetts Board of Library Commissioners; Mr. Lew Harriman, Mason-Grant Consulting; Mr. Ernest

Conrad, Landmark Facilities Group, Inc.; Mr. William Lull, Garrison/Lull Inc.; and Mr. John D. Hilberry, John Hilberry Museum Consulting, for their kind assistance and expert advice with preparing this bibliography. NEDCC also gratefully acknowledges the previous work of Ms. Karen Motylewski in preparing this bibliography.

Northeast Document
Conservation Center
100 Brickstone Square
Andover, MA 01810-1494
www.nedcc.org
Tel: (978) 470-1010
Fax: (978) 475-6021

SOURCES OF INFORMATION

This leaflet provides information sources about the following subjects:

- Organizations and Professional Associations with Preservation/Conservation Interests: National
- Organizations and Professional Associations with Preservation/Conservation Interests: International
- Regional Conservation Centers
- Funding Agencies for Preservation/Conservation Activities
- Preservation/Conservation Training
- Information Resources for Preservation/Conservation and Related Concerns

This list is not exhaustive. You should contact cultural institutions or organizations in your area for the names of local sources of information.

Organizations and Professional Associations with
Preservation/Conservation Interests: National

Abbey Publications, Inc.
7105 Geneva Dr.
Austin, TX 78723
Telephone: (512) 929-3992
Fax: (512) 929-3995
E-mail: abbeypub@flash.net
http://palimpsest.stanford.edu/byorg/abbey

American Institute for Conservation of Historic and Artistic Works (AIC)
1717 K Street NW, Suite 301
Washington, DC 20006
Telephone: (202) 452-9545
Fax: (202) 452-9328
E-mail: InfoAic@aol.com
http://palimpsest.stanford.edu/aic

American Association of Museums (AAM)
1575 Eye Street, NW, Suite 400
Washington, DC 20005
Telephone: (202) 289-1818
Fax: (202) 289-6578http://www.aam-us.org

American Association of State and Local History (AASLH)
530 Church Street, Suite 600
Nashville, TN 37219-2325
Telephone: (615) 255-2971
Fax: (615) 255-2979
E-mail: aaslh@aaslh.org
http://www.aaslh.org

American Library Association (ALA)
50 East Huron Street
Chicago, IL 60611
Toll Free: (800) 545-2433
Fax: (312) 440-9374
E-mail: ala@ala.org
http://www.ala.org

The Association for Library Collections & Technical Services (ALA/ALCTS)
Preservation and Reformatting Committee
50 East Huron Street
Chicago, IL 60611
Toll Free: (800) 545-2433
Telephone: (312) 944-6780
Fax: (312) 280-3257
http://www.ala.org/alcts/organization/pars

Association of Moving Image Archivists
8949 Wilshire Boulevard
Beverly Hills, CA 90211
Telephone: (310) 550-1300
Fax: (310) 550-1363
E-mail: amia@ix.netcom.com
http://www.amianet.org

Association of Records Managers and Administrators (ARMA)
4200 Somerset Dr., Suite 215
Prairie Village, KS 66208
Telephone: (913) 341-3808
US and Canada WATS (800) 422-2762
Fax: (913) 341-3742
E-mail: hq@arma.org
http://www.arma.org

Association of Research Libraries (ARL)
21 DuPont Circle NW, Suite 800
Washington, DC 20036
Telephone: (202) 296-2296
Fax: (202) 872-0884
E-mail: arlhq@arl.org
http://arl.cni.org

College Art Association
275 7th Avenue
New York, NY 10001
Telephone: (212) 691-1051
Fax: (212) 627-2381
E-mail: nyoffice@collegeart.org
http://www.collegeart.org

Council on Library and Information Resources (CLIR)
1755 Massachusetts Avenue, NW, Suite 500
Washington, DC 20036-2188
Telephone: (202) 939-4750
Fax: (202) 939-4765
E-mail: info@clir.org
http://www.clir.org

Friends of Dard Hunter
c/o Marion E. Cluff
121 Church Street #17
Lake Oswego, OR 97034
Telephone: (503) 699-8653
Fax: (503) 699-8653
E-mail:
[Information on papermaking and handmade papers]

Guild of Book Workers
521 Fifth Avenue
New York, NY 10175
Telephone: (212) 292-4444
E-mail: Karen Crisalli, President at KarenC5071@aol.com, or
E-mail: Bernadette Callery, Membership Secretary at bcallery@flounder.com
http://palimpsest.stanford.edu/byorg/gbw

Heritage Preservation
1730 K Street, NW
Suite 566
Washington, DC 20006
Telephone: (202) 634-1422
Fax: (202) 634-1435
http://www.heritagepreservation.org

National Trust for Historic Preservation
1785 Mass. Avenue, NW
Washington, DC 20036
Toll Free: (800) 944-6847
Telephone: (202) 588-6000
Fax: (202) 588-6038
http://www.nationaltrust.org

Research Libraries Group, Inc. (RLG)
1200 Villa Street
Mountain View, CA 94041-1100
Toll Free: (800) 537-7546
Telephone: (650) 962-9951
Fax: (650) 964-0943
E-mail: bl.ric@rlg.orghttp://www.rlg.org

Society of American Archivists (SAA)
527 S. Wells, 5th Floor
Chicago, IL 60607
Telephone: (312) 922-0140
Fax: (312) 347-1452
http://www.archivists.org

State Archives and Records Administration (SARA)
New York State Archives, Reference Service
Rm. 11D40 Cultural Education Center
Empire State Plaza
Albany, NY 12230
Telephone: (518) 474-8955
Fax: (518) 473-9985
http://www.sara.nysed.gov

Organizations and Professional Associations with Preservation/Conservation Interests: International

Association for Information and Image Management (AIIM)
1100 Wayne Avenue, Suite 100
Silver Spring, MD 20910
Telephone: (301) 587-8202
Fax: (301) 587-2711
E-mail: aiim@aiim.org
http://www.aiim.org

Association for Preservation Technology International (APT)
PO Box 3511
Williamsburg, VA 23187
Telephone: (540) 373-1621

Australian Institute for Conservation of Cultural Material, Inc.(AICCM)
GPO Box 1638
Canberra, ACT 2601
Australia
Telephone: 06-2434-531
Fax: 06-2417-998
E-mail: gina.drummond@awm.gov.au
http://www.vicnet.au/~conserv/hp.hc.htm

Canadian Association for Conservation of Cultural Property (CAC)
(formerly International Institute for Conservation - Canadian Group)
280 Metcalfe, Suite 400
Ottawa, Ontario Canada K2P 1R7
Telephone: (613) 567-0099
Fax: (613) 233-5438
E-mail: info@museums.ca http://www.cac-accr.ca

Canadian Association of Professional Conservators (CAPC)
PO Box /CP 9195 Terminal
Ottawa, Ontario K1G 3T9
Canada
Telephone/Fax: (819) 684-7460

Canadian Conservation Institute (CCI)
1030 Innes Road
Ottawa, Ontario K1A 0M5
Canada
Telephone: (613) 998-3721
Fax: (613) 998-4721
http://www.pch.gc.ca/cci-icc

The Institute For Paper Conservation (IPC)
Leigh Lodge
Leigh, Worcester WR6 5LB
England
Telephone: +44 1886 832323
Fax: +44 1886 833688
E-mail: clare@ipc.org.uk

**International Centre for the Study of the Preservation
and the Restoration of Cultural Property (ICCROM)**
Via di San Michele 13
00153 Rome, Italy
Telephone: +39-6 585-531
Fax: +39-6 585-3349
E-mail:
http://www.iccrom.org

**International Council of Museums (ICOM) Committee for Conservation
Canadian Conservation Institute**
1030 Innes Road
Ottawa KIA OM5
Canada
Telephone: 613-988-3721
Fax: 613-998-4721

International Council on Archives (ICA)
60 rue des Francs-Bourgeois
75003 Paris, France
Telephone: 33-1-40-27-63-06
Fax: 33-1-42-72-20-65
E-mail: 100640.54@compuserve.com
http://www.archives.ca/ica/index.html

International Federation of Library Associations (IFLA)
P.O.B. 95312
2509 CH The Hague
The Hague, Netherlands
Telephone: +31-70-314-0884
Fax: +31-70-383-4827
E-mail: ifla.hq@ifla.nl
http://www.nlc-bnc.ca/ifla

International Institute for Conservation of Historic & Artistic Works (IIC)
6 Buckingham Street
London WC2N 6BA, England
Telephone: +44 (0)171-839-5975
Fax: +44 (0)171-976-1564
E-mail: iicon@compuserve.com
http://www.natmus.dk/cons/iic

Scottish Society for Conservation and Restoration (SSCR)
The Glasite Meeting House
33 Barony Street
Edinburgh EH3 6NX, Scotland
Telephone: 0131-556-8417
Fax: 0131-557-5977
E-mail: admin@sscr.demon.co.uk

UNESCO-ICOM Information Centre
Maison de l'UNESCO, 1 rue Miollis
F-75732 Paris cedex 15, France
Tel: +33 (0) 47 34 05 00
Fax: (33 1) 43 06 78 62
E-mail: jani@icom.org

United Kingdom Institute for Conservation (UKIC)
6 Whitehorse Mews
Westminster Bridge Road
London SE1 7QD, England
Telephone: 44-171-620-3371
Fax: 44-171-620-3761

Regional Conservation Centers/Organizations

Balboa Art Conservation Center
P.O. Box 3755
San Diego, CA 92163
Telephone: (619) 236-9702
Fax: (619) 236-0141

Bay Area Art Conservation Group
1124 Clelia Court
Petaluma, CA 94954-8694
Telephone: (707) 763-8694

Chicago Area Conservation Group
Deller Conservation Group, Ltd. 2600 Keslinger Road
Geneva, IL 60134
Telephone: (708) 232-1708

Conservation Center for Art and Historic Artifacts
264 South 23rd Street
Philadelphia, PA 19103
Telephone: (215) 545-0613
Fax: (215) 735-9313
http://www.ccaha.org

Gerald R. Ford Conservation Center
1326 South 32nd Street
Omah, NE 68105
Telephone: (402) 595-1180
Fax: (402) 595-1178
E-mail: grfcc@radiks.net
http://www.nebraskahistory.org/sites/ford/index.htm

Intermuseum Conservation Association
Allen Art Building
83 North Main Street
Oberlin, OH 44074-1192
Telephone: (440) 775-7331
Fax: (440) 774-3431

Midwest Regional Conservation Guild
Indiana University Art Museum
Conservation Department
Bloomington, IN 47405
Telephone: (812) 855-1024
Fax: (812) 855-1023

New England Conservation Association
Kathryn Myatt Carey
24 Emery Street
Medford, MA 02155
Telephone: (781) 396-9495

Northeast Document Conservation Center (NEDCC)
100 Brickstone Square
Andover, MA 01810-1494
Telephone: (978) 470-1010
Fax: : (978) 475-6021
E-mail: nedcc@nedcc.org
http://www.nedcc.org

Rocky Mountain Regional Conservation Center
University of Denver
2420 South University Blvd.
Denver, CO 80208
Telephone: (303) 733-2712
Fax: (303) 733-2508
http://www.du.edu/rmcc

Society for Preservation of New England Antiquities Conservation Center
185 Lyman Street
Waltham, MA 02154
Telephone: (617) 891-1985

Straus Center for Conservation
Harvard University Art Museum
32 Quincy Street
Cambridge, MA 02138
Telephone: (617) 495-2392
Fax: (617) 495-0322
http://www.artmuseum.harvard.edu

Textile Conservation Center
American Textile History Museum
491 Dutton Street
Lowell, MA 01854-4221
Telephone: (978) 441-1198
Fax: (978) 441-1412
http://www.athm.org

Upper Midwest Conservation Association (UMCA)
Minneapolis Institute of Arts
2400 3rd Ave. South
Minneapolis, MN 55404
Telephone: (612) 870-3120
Fax: (612) 870-3118
E-mail: umca@mtn.org
http://www.preserveart.org

Virginia Conservation Association
PO Box 4314
Richmond, VA 23220
Telephone: (804) 358-7545
Washington Conservation Guild
PO Box 23364
Washington, DC 20026
Telephone: (301) 238-3700 ext. 178

Western Association for Art Conservation
1272 N. Flores Street
Los Angeles, CA 90069
Telephone: (213) 654-8748
Fax: (213) 656-3220

Western New York Conservation Guild
51 Park Lane
Rochester, NY 14624
Telephone: (716) 248-5307

Williamstown Art Conservation Center
225 South Street
Williamstown, MA 01267
Telephone: (413) 458-5741
Fax: (413) 458-2314
E-mail: wacc@clark.williams.edu
http://wso.williams.edu/~dhodgman/final.htm

Funding Agencies for Preservation/Conservation

Bay Foundation
17 West 94th Street, 1st Floor
New York, NY 10025
Telephone: (212) 663-1115
Fax: (212) 932-0316

The Getty Grant Program
1200 Getty Center Drive
Suite 800
Los Angeles, California 90049-1685
Telephone: (310) 440-7320
Fax: (310) 440-7703
http://www.getty.edu/grant

Institute of Museum & Library Services
1100 Pennsylvania Ave., NW, Room 609
Washington, DC 20506
Telephone: (202) 606-8539
Fax: (202) 606-8591
E-mail: imlsinfo@imls.fed.us
http://www.imls.fed.us

Samuel H. Kress Foundation
174 East 80th Street
New York, NY 10021
Telephone: (212) 861-4993
Fax: (212) 628-3146
http://www.users/interport.net/~kress/

Andrew W. Mellon Foundation
Arts and Cultural Programs
140 East 62nd Street
New York, NY 10021
Telephone: (212) 838-8400
Fax: (212) 223-2778
http://www.mellon.org

Carnegie Mellon Research Institute
Warner Hall
Technology Drive
Pittsburgh, PA 15213
Telephone: (412) 268-3100

National Endowment for the Arts, Museum Program
Creation & Preservation
1100 Pennsylvania Avenue, NW
Washington, DC 20506
Telephone: (202) 682-5452
http://arts.endow.gov

National Endowment for the Humanities
Division of Preservation and Access
1100 Pennsylvania Avenue NW, Rm. 441
Washington, DC 20506
Telephone: (202) 606-8570
Fax: (202) 606-8639
http://www.neh.fed.us

National Historic Publications and Records Commission (NHPRC)
National Archives & Records Administration
NHPRC Room 106
700 Pennsylvania Avenue, NW
Washington, DC 20408-0001
Telephone: (202) 501-5610
Fax: (202) 501-5601
E-mail: nhprc@arch1.nara.gov
http://www.nara.gov/nara/hnprc

Pew Charitable Trusts
1 Commerce Square
2005 Market Street, Suite 1700
Philadelphia, PA 19103-7017
Telephone: (215) 575-9050
Fax: (215) 575-4939
http://www.pewtrusts.com

Preservation/Conservation Training
Buffalo State College
Art Conservation Department
Rockwell Hall 230
1300 Elmwood Avenue
Buffalo, NY 14222-1095
Telephone: (716) 878-5025
Fax: (716) 878-5039
http://www.buffalostate.edu

Campbell Center for Historic Preservation Studies
203 East Seminary
PO Box 66
Mount Carroll, IL 61053
Telephone: (815) 244-1173
Fax: (815) 244-1619

The Conservation Center of the Institute of Fine Arts
New York University
14 East 78th Street
New York, NY 10021
Telephone: (212) 772-5848
Fax: (212) 772-5851
E-mail: conservation.program@nyu.edu
http://www.nyu.edu/gsas/dept/fineart/home.html

George Eastman House, Inc.
900 East Avenue
Rochester, NY 14607
Telephone: (716) 271-3361

National Center for Preservation Technology and Training (NCPTT)
NSU Box 5682
Natchitoches, LA 71497
Telephone: (318) 357-6464
Fax: (318) 357-6421
E-mail: ncptt@ncptt.nps.gov
www.ncptt.nps.gov

North Bennet Street School
39 North Bennet Street
Boston, MA 02113-1998
Telephone: (617) 227-0155
Fax: (617) 227-9292

Queen's University
Art Conservation Programme
Kingston, Ontario K7L 3N6
Canada
Telephone: (613) 545-2156
Fax: (613) 545-6889

Smithsoniam Center for Materials Research and Education
Museum Support Center
Smithsonian Institution
Washington, DC 20560
Telephone: (301) 238-3700
Fax: (301) 238-3709
E-mail: ABN@SCMRE.si.edu
http://www.si.edu/scmre

Straus Center for Conservation
Harvard University Art Museum
32 Quincy Street
Cambridge, MA 02138
Telephone: (617) 495-2392
Fax: (617) 495-0322
http://www.artmuseum.harvard.edu

University of Texas at Austin
Preservation & Conservation Studies Program
Graduate School of Library and Information Science
SZB #564
Austin, TX 78712-1276
Telephone: (512) 471-8290
Fax: (512) 471-8285
E-mail: glabs@utxdp.dp.utexas.edu
http://volvo.gslis.utexas.edu/~pcs/pcshome.html

Winterthur/University of Delaware Program in the Conservation of Historic and Artistic Works
303 Old College
University of Delaware
Newark, DE 19716
Telephone: (302) 831-2479
Fax: (302) 831-4330

Information Resources for Preservation/ Conservation and Related Concerns

American Chemical Society
1155 16th Street, NW
Washington, DC 20036
Telephone: (202) 872-4600
Fax: (202) 872-4615
http://www.acs.org

American National Standards Institute (ANSI)
11 West 42nd Street
New York, NY 10036
Telephone: (212) 642-4900
Fax: (212) 398-0023
http://www.web.ansi.org

American Society of Appraisers
P.O. Box 17265
Washington, DC 20041
Toll Free: (800) 272-8258
Telephone: (703) 478-2228
Fax: (703) 742-8471

AMIGOS Bibliographic Council
12200 Park Central Drive
Suite 500
Dallas, TX 75251
Telephone: (972) 851-8000
Toll Free: (800) 843-8482
Fax: (972) 991-6061
http://www.amigos.org

Arts, Crafts and Theatre Safety
181 Thompson Street, #23
New York, NY 10012-2586
Telephone: (212) 777-0062

Association for Information and Image Management
1100 Wayne Ave., Suite 1100
Silver Springs, MD 20910-5603
Telephone: (301) 587-8202; (888) 839-3165
Fax: (301) 587-2711
http://www.aiim.org

Getty Conservation Institute
1200 Getty Center Drive, Suite 700
Los Angeles, CA 90049-1684
Telephone: (310) 440-7325
Fax: (310) 440-7702
http://www.getty.edu

Image Permanence Institute
Rochester Institute of Technology
Frank E. Gannett Building
70 Lomb Memorial Drive
Rochester, NY 14623-5604
Telephone: (716) 475-5199
Fax: (716) 475-7230

Institute of Paper Science & Technology
500 10th Street, NW
Atlanta, GA 30318-5794
Telephone: (404) 894-5700
Toll Free: (800) 558-6611
Fax: (404) 894-4778
http://www.ipst.edu

Leather Conservation Centre
34 Guildhall Road
Northampton NN1 1EW, England
Telephone: 01604-232723
Fax: 01604-602070

Library Binding Institute
7401 Metro Boulevard, Suite 325
Edina, MN 55439
Telephone: (612) 835-4707
Fax: (612) 835-4780

Library of Congress
Office of the Director for Preservation
Rm. LM-G21
101 Independence Avenue, SE
Washington, DC 20540
Telephone: (202) 707-1840
Fax: (202) 707-3434
http://www.loc.gov

National Archives & Records Administration
Document Conservation Branch
NWTD
9th Street and Pennsylvania Avenue, NW
Washington, DC 20408
Telephone: (202) 501-5360
Fax: (202) 219-9324
http://www.nara.gov

National Center for Film & Video Preservation
American Film Institute
2021 North Western Avenue
Los Angeles, CA 90027
Telephone: (213) 856-7637; (213) 467-4578

National Information Standards Organization (NISO)
4733 Bethesda Avenue, Suite 300
Bethesda, MD 20814
Telephone: (301) 654-2512
Fax: (301) 654-1721
http://www.niso.org
E-mail: nisohq@niso.org

National Media Laboratory
P.O. Box 33015
Saint Paul, MN 55133-3015
Telephone: (612) 733-1110
http://www.mmmg.com

National Park Service
Curatorial Services Division
800 North Capitol Street, NW
P.O. Box 37127
Washington, DC 20002
Telephone: (202) 208-7394
Fax: (202) 343-1767
http://www.nps.gov

National Park Service
Division of Conservation
Harpers Ferry NHP
P.O. Box 65
Harpers Ferry, WV 25425
Telephone: (304) 535-6298
Fax: (304) 535-6055
http://www.nps.gov/hafe

New York State Conservation Consultancy
c/o Textile Conservation Workshop
3 Main Street
South Salem, NY 10590
Telephone: (914) 763-5805
Fax: (914) 763-5549

New York State Office of Parks, Recreation and Historic Preservation
Bureau of Historic Sites
Collections Care Center
Peebles Island, P.O. Box 219
Waterford, NY 12188
Telephone: (518) 237-8643
Fax: (518) 235-4248
http://nysparks.state.ny.us

Professional Picture Framers Association
4305 Sarellen Road
Richmond, VA 23231
Telephone: (804) 226-0430
Fax: (804) 222-2175
http://www.ppfa.com

SOLINET Preservation Program
1438 W. Peachtree Street, NW, Suite 200
Atlanta, GA 30309-2955
Toll Free: (800) 999-8558
Telephone: (404) 892-0943
Fax: (404) 892-7879
http://www.solinet.net

Technical Association of the Pulp and Paper Industry (TAPPI)
Technology Park/Atlanta
P.O. Box 105113
Atlanta, GA 30348-5113
Telephone: (770) 446-1400
Toll Free: (800) 332-8686
Fax: (770) 446-6947
http://www2.empiretappi.org

Transaction Publishers
Dept. NISO Standards
Rutgers University The State Universtiy
35 Berrue Circle
Piscataway, NJ 08854-8042
Telephone: (732) 445-2280
Fax: (732) 445-3138
http://www.transactionpub.com

THE ENVIRONMENT

Northeast Document
Conservation Center
100 Brickstone Square
Andover, MA 01810-1494
www.nedcc.org
Tel: (978) 470-1010
Fax: (978) 475-6021

TEMPERATURE, RELATIVE HUMIDITY, LIGHT, AND AIR QUALITY: BASIC GUIDELINES FOR PRESERVATION

by Sherelyn Ogden
Head of Conservation
Minnesota Historical Society

Control of temperature and relative humidity* is critical in the preservation of library and archival collections because unacceptable levels of these contribute significantly to the breakdown of materials. Heat accelerates deterioration: the rate of most chemical reactions, including deterioration, is approximately doubled with each increase in temperature of 18°F (10°C). High relative humidity provides the moisture necessary to promote harmful chemical reactions in materials and, in combination with high temperature, encourages mold growth and insect activity. Extremely low relative humidity, which can occur in winter in centrally heated buildings, may lead to desiccation and embrittlement of some materials.

Fluctuations in temperature and relative humidity are also damaging. Library and archival materials are hygroscopic, readily absorbing and releasing moisture. They respond to diurnal and seasonal changes in temperature and relative humidity by expanding and contracting. Dimensional changes accelerate deterioration and lead to such visible damage as cockling paper, flaking ink, warped covers on books, and cracked emulsion on photographs. In some situtations, however, materials may be protected from moderate fluctuations. Mild changes appear to be buffered by certain types of storage enclosures and by books being packed closely together.

Installation of adequate climate controls and operation of them to maintain preservation standards will retard the deterioration of materials considerably. Climate control equipment ranges in complexity from a simple room air conditioner, humidifier, and/or dehumidifier to a central, building-wide system that filters, cools, heats, humidifies, and dehumidifies the air. It is always advisable to seek the guidance of an experienced climate control engineer prior to selection and installation of equipment. Additional measures can be taken to control temperature and relative humidity. Buildings should be kept well maintained. Cracks should be sealed as soon as they occur. External doors and windows should have weatherstripping and should be kept closed to prevent exchange of unconditioned outside air. In areas of this

Relative humidity is a ratio (expressed as a percentage) of the amount of water vapor in a specific amount of air compared to how much that same amount of air can hold at the same temperature and pressure. Because relative humidity is dependent upon temperature, these two factors should be considered together.

country that experience cold winter weather, windows can be sealed on the inside with plastic sheets and tape. In storage areas windows can be sealed using both wallboard and plastic.

Authorities disagree on the ideal temperature and relative humidity for library and archival materials. A frequent recommendation is a stable temperature no higher than 70°F and a stable relative humidity between a minimum of 30% and a maximum of 50%. Research indicates that relative humidities at the lower end of this range are preferable since deterioration then progresses at a slower rate. In general, the lower the temperature the better. The temperature recommendations for areas used exclusively for storage are much lower than those for combination user and storage areas. Cold storage with controlled humidity is sometimes advisable for remote storage or little-used materials. When materials are taken out of cold storage, however, the radical, rapid temperature changes they experience may cause condensation on them. In such cases, gradual acclimatization may be required.

Maintaining stable conditions is crucial. An institution should choose a temperature and relative humidity within the recommended ranges that can be maintained twenty-four hours a day, 365 days a year. The climate-control system should never be turned off, and settings should not be lowered at night, on weekends, or at other times when the library or archives is closed. Additional costs incurred by keeping the system in constant operation will be far less than the cost of future conservation treatment to repair damage caused by poor climate.

While these recommendations may be expensive or even impossible to achieve in many libraries and archives, experience and scientific testing indicate that the useful life of materials is significantly extended by maintenance of moderate, stable levels of temperature and relative humidity. Where economics or inadequate mechanical systems make it impossible to maintain ideal conditions year round, less stringent standards may be chosen for summer and winter with gradual changes in temperature and relative humidity permitted between the two seasons. The seasonal standards should be as close to the ideal as possible. It is important to note that temperature and relative humidity requirements of non-paper-based materials in the collections may differ from those of paper-based materials. Also, maintaining the ideal level of temperature and relative humidity may damage the fabric of the building that houses the collections. Difficult choices and compromises may be unavoidable.

Temperature and relative humidity should be systematically measured and recorded. This is important since the data produced 1) documents existing environmental conditions; 2) supports requests to install environmental controls; and 3) indicates whether available climate-control equipment is operating properly and producing the desired conditions. Remember that changing one factor may alter others. If measures are taken without considering the environment as a whole, conditions may worsen rather than improve. It is essential to know (from recorded measurements) what conditions actually are and to seek the advice of an experienced climate-control engineer before making major changes. The importance of continued monitoring after the institution of a change cannot be stressed too much.

LIGHT

Light accelerates deterioration of library and archival materials. It leads to weakening and embrittlement of cellulose fibers and can cause paper to bleach, yellow, or darken. It also causes media and dyes to fade or change color, altering the legibility and/or appearance of documents, photographs, art works, and bindings. Any exposure to light, even for a brief time, is damaging, and the damage is cumulative and irreversible.

Visible light levels are measured in lux (lumens per square meter) or footcandles. One footcandle equals about 11 lux. For many years generally accepted recommendations limited visible light levels for light-sensitive materials, including paper, to 55 lux (5 footcandles), and for less sensitive materials to a maximum of 165 lux (15 footcandles). In recent years these recommendations have been debated, with aesthetic concerns and varying rates of light fading for different media being considered.

Although all wave lengths of light are damaging, ultraviolet (UV) radiation is especially harmful to library and archival materials because of its high level of energy. The standard limit for UV is 75 µW/l . The sun and tungsten-halogen or quartz lamps, mercury or metal halide high intensity discharge lamps, and fluorescent lamps are some of the most damaging sources of light because of the high amounts of UV energy they emit.

Because total damage is a function of both intensity and duration of exposure, illumination should be kept as low as possible (consistent with user comfort) for the briefest amount of time feasible. Ideally materials should be exposed to light only while in use. When not in use, they should be stored in a light-tight container or in a windowless room illuminated only when materials are being retrieved. Illumination should be by incandescent bulbs. When materials are being used, light should be from an incandescent source. It is important to note that incandescent bulbs generate heat and should be kept at a distance from materials. Light levels should be as low as possible, and exposure should be for the shortest time that is feasible.

Windows should be covered by drapes, shades, blinds, or shutters that completely block the sun. This will also aid in temperature control by minimizing heat loss and limiting generation of heat by sunlight during the day. Skylights that allow direct sunlight to shine on collections should be covered to block the sun or painted with titanium dioxide or zinc white pigments, which reflect light and absorb UV radiation. Filters made of special plastics also help control UV radiation. Ultraviolet-filtering plastic films or UV-filtering Plexiglas can be used for windows to lower the amount of UV radiation passing through them. These filters, however, do not provide 100% protection against light damage. Drapes, shades, blinds, or shutters that completely block the light are preferable. Fluorescent tubes should be covered with ultraviolet-filtering sleeves in areas where collections are exposed to light. An alternative is the use of special low-UV fluorescent tubes. Timed switches should be used for lights in storage areas to help limit duration of exposure of materials.

Permanent exhibition of materials should be avoided. Since even slight exposure to light is damaging, permanent exposure is deadly. If materials must be displayed, it should be for the briefest time and at the lowest light levels, with light coming from an incandescent source. Materials should never be displayed where the sun shines directly on them, even if for only a short time and even if the windows are covered with an ultraviolet-filtering plastic.

AIR QUALITY

Pollutants contribute heavily to the deterioration of library and archival materials. The two major types of pollutants are gases and particulates. Gaseous contaminants—especially sulfur dioxide, nitrogen oxides, peroxides, and ozone—catalyze harmful chemical reactions that lead to the formation of acid in materials. This is a serious problem for paper and leather, which are particularly vulnerable to damage caused by acid. Paper becomes discolored and brittle, and leather becomes weak and powdery. Particulates—especially soot—abrade, soil, and disfigure materials.

Controlling air quality is difficult and complex and depends upon several inter-related factors. Various standards for air quality have been suggested. However, until more experience is gained, the most reasonable recommendation is that the amount of pollutants in the air be reduced as much as practicable.

Gaseous contaminants can be removed by chemical filters, wet scrubbers, or a combination of both. Particulate matter can be mechanically filtered. Electrostatic precipitators should not be used because they produce ozone. Equipment varies in size and complexity from individual filters attached to vents, furnaces, or air conditioners to building-wide systems.

Equipment also varies greatly in effectiveness. It is important that the equipment chosen be suited to the institution's needs and the level of pollution in the area where the institution is located. A regular schedule of maintenance and filter replacement should be followed. An experienced environmental engineer should be consulted for recommendations.

There are several additional ways to control air quality. One is the provision of good air exchange in areas where collections are stored or used, with replacement air being as clean as possible. Care should be taken to insure that air intake vents are not located near sources of heavy pollution such as a loading dock where trucks idle. Another measure is keeping exterior windows closed. Yet another measure is storage of library and archival materials in archival-quality enclosures, which may help decrease the effects of pollutants on materials. Newly available enclosures made with molecular traps such as activated carbon or zeolites, which will capture pollutants, appear to be particularly effective in this regard. Finally, origins of pollution should be eliminated as much as possible. Automobiles and industry, major sources of pollution, will probably be beyond control. Other sources, however, may be reduced. These include cigarettes, photocopying machines, certain types of construction materials, paints, sealants, wooden storage/display materials, cleaning compounds, furniture, and carpets.

Temperature, relative humidity, light, and air quality all affect the longevity of library and archival collections. By following the guidelines provided above, one can significantly extend the life of these collections.

SUGGESTED FURTHER READING

Carrier Corporation (CC). *The ABC's of Air Conditioning.* Syracuse, NY: Carrier Corporation, pp. 1-17, 23-24. Available from CC, P.O. Box 4808, Syracuse, NY 13221.

Lull, William P., with the assistance of Paul N. Banks. *Conservation Environment Guidelines for Libraries and Archives.* Ottawa, ON: Canadian Council of Archives, 1995.

Lull, William P., and M.A. Garrison. "Planning and Design of Museum Storage Environments." *Registrar* 5.2 (Spring 1988): 3-13.

Lull, William P., and Linda Merk. "Lighting for Storage of Museum Collections: Developing a System for Safekeeping of Light-Sensitive Materials." *Technology & Conservation* 7.2 (Summer 1982): 20-25.

National Bureau of Standards (NBS). *Air Quality Standards for Storage of Paper-Based Archival Records,* NBSIR 83-2795. Gaithersburg, MD: NBS, 1983, unpaginated, approximately 100 pp.

National Information Standards Organization. *Environmental Guidelines for the Storage of Paper Records.* Technical Report NISO-TR01-1995.

National Research Council. *Preservation of Historical Records.* Washington, DC: National Academy Press, 1986, 108 pp.

Reilly, James M., Douglas W. Nishimura, and Edward Zinn. *New Tools for Preservation/Assessing Long-Term Environmental Effects on Library and ArchivesCollections.* Washington, DC: Commission on Preservation and Access, 1995.

Sebera, Donald. "A Graphical Representation of the Relationship of Environmental Conditions to the Permanence of Hygroscopic Materials and Composites." In *Proceedings of Conservation in Archives International Symposium* (Ottawa, May 10-12, 1988). Ottawa: National Archives of Canada, 1989, pp. 51-75.

Sebera, Donald K. *Isoperms An Environmental Management Tool*. Washington, DC: Commission on Preservation and Access, 1994.

Walch, Victoria Irons. "Checklist of Standards Applicable to the Preservation of Archives and Manuscripts." *American Archivist* 53 (Spring 1990): 324-38.

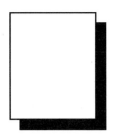

Northeast Document
Conservation Center
100 Brickstone Square
Andover, MA 01810-1494
www.nedcc.org
Tel: (978) 470-1010
Fax: (978) 475-6021

MONITORING TEMPERATURE AND RELATIVE HUMIDITY

by Beth Lindblom Patkus
Preservation Consultant
Walpole, MA

INTRODUCTION

Books, photographs, and other paper-based artifacts are vulnerable to damage from their environment. Heat, moisture, light, and pollutants produce destructive chemical reactions. Warmth and damp promote biological processes like mold and insect infestation. While some materials used to produce books, documents, and art on paper have proven quite durable, others (like ground wood pulp and acidic inks) deteriorate rapidly under adverse conditions. Museums, libraries, and historical societies are subject to the same phenomena as any other buildings, but have an extraordinary responsibility for preserving their collections for future generations.

While we cannot eliminate all of the causes for decay of our cultural records without forfeiting access to our collections, we can greatly slow deterioration by moderating the environment. Control of some factors, such as light, is relatively easy and inexpensive. Controlling the climate (temperature and relative humidity) is a much more difficult task. Monitoring of temperature and relative humidity is essential to the success of climate control. Monitoring can have several purposes: to provide data showing that current climate control is inadequate; to document current conditions in preparation for making changes in equipment; to evaluate the effect of equipment changes that have been made; and/or to guard against any environmental extremes that might occur.

WHY IS CLIMATE CONTROL IMPORTANT?

Climate control is important because inappropriate temperature and relative humidity (RH) can severely limit the lifespan of paper collections. Many people assume that temperature has the greatest effect on collections (as it does on people), but in fact RH is at least as important a contributor to paper deterioration. Most people are aware that high temperature and RH can encourage mold growth and insect infestation, but in reality the effect of the storage climate on collections is much more complex.

It is important to realize that temperature and RH are interrelated—a change in one will bring about a change in the other. Warmer air holds more moisture than cooler air, so if the absolute amount of moisture in a space remains constant, the relative humidity (which represents "the amount of moisture in the air relative to the amount the air is capable of holding, expressed as a percentage"[1]) will fall as the temperature rises, and it will rise as the temperature is lowered (these relationships between temperature and RH can be calculated using a psychometric chart). For example, if a space is at 60° F and 70% RH, the RH will fall to about 40% if the temperature is raised to 75° F. On the other hand, if the temperature is lowered the RH will rise—and when it reaches 100% the air will become saturated and moisture will condense out (this is called the dewpoint). For example, if a space is at 70° F and 50% RH and the temperature suddenly drops to below 50° F, condensation will occur on collections.

Embrittlement of paper (along with many other forms of decay in such organic materials as leather, textiles, and magnetic tape) is an indication of chemical deterioration, and the chemical reactions that govern this process are greatly influenced by the climate. *Temperature* increases the speed of the chemical reactions that cause acidic deterioration. A familiar rule of thumb estimates that chemical reactions double with each 18°F (10°C) increase. In the special case of cellulose, artificial aging tests indicate that each 9°F increase nearly doubles the rate of deterioration, even in the absence of light, pollutants, or other factors. Relative *humidity* provides moisture to fuel these reactions—the higher the humidity, the more quickly deterioration proceeds.

Research models have been developed in the last several years that quantify the effects of temperature and relative humidity on chemical deterioration. The Image Permanence Institute (IPI) at the Rochester Institute of Technology has developed the "Preservation Index," which builds on work done by Donald Sebera, formerly of the Library of Congress. This tool gives a general idea of the length of time it would take paper collections to become noticeably deteriorated at a particular temperature and RH. The model shows that short-lived organic materials stored at 72° F and 50% RH would have an approximate lifetime of 33 years, but if the temperature were lowered to 62° F and the humidity to 40%, such materials would have a lifetime of 88 years. The model also shows that if materials are subjected to high temperatures and humidities (such as 82° F and 75% RH) noticeable deterioration would occur in 9 years or less.[2]

Another interesting aspect of this research is that it demonstrates that the same projected lifespan can be achieved through different combinations of temperature and RH. For example, conditions of 57° F and 50% RH or 62° F and 35%RH would both result in a predicted lifetime of close to 100 years.[3] This has the potential to offer institutions some flexibility in how they control the climate, although extremely high humidities or temperatures must always be avoided due to the danger of mold and insect infestation.

The effects of fluctuations in temperature and RH on collections is another important concern for climate control. Fluctuations in temperature are serious—research done at the Library of Congress has shown that chemical deterioration of paper proceeds more quickly if paper is exposed to temperature fluctuations than if it is stored at a constant temperature. In addition, paper—like many other materials—is hygroscopic, meaning it absorbs and gives off moisture. This means that as the temperature rises and the RH decreases, moisture will migrate from a hygroscopic object to the air as the object tries to maintain equilibrium. As the temperature drops and the RH rises again, moisture will move back into the object. This process can cause physical stress as the changing moisture content causes the material to swell and shrink. It can result in serious damage to composite materials such as furniture and art works, and it can cause cockling and distortion in books and paper (although in some situations books and paper collections are protected from moderate RH fluctuations because RH changes are buffered by storage enclosures or by books being packed closely together[4]).

Finally, collections managers must be aware that while there is no danger associated with low temperature storage (in fact such storage greatly slows deterioration), very low RH can be damaging to some materials. Traditionally there has been concern about paper becoming too brittle to be handled at very low humidities. Research has shown that paper can be safely handled at around 20% RH—or 30% if it is to be folded—so there is no need to store it at

40-50% RH for the purposes of handling. For parchment and photographic materials, lower humidities are being recommended for chemical stability—but these materials should not be stored below 30% RH. Especially in the case of parchment, it is also important not to change the climate rapidly, since this might cause damage.[5]

It seems clear that a significant investment in the acquisition of information, aesthetic artifacts, and cultural records for research, exhibit, and education warrants active protection of the acquired materials. It should be equally clear that the climate of a storage environment will profoundly affect the condition of these objects.

CLIMATE CONTROL IS EXPENSIVE - WHAT IS GOOD ENOUGH?

Although the preservation community has been unable to agree on specific standards for climate control in paper-based collections, authorities do agree on several general conclusions that emanate from research:

- Temperatures above about 70°F and RH above about 55-60% encourage mold and insects.

- Additional damage occurs at climatic extremes: high RH increases acid formation; RH below 30% can embrittle paper, parchment, adhesives, photographic emulsions, and other materials.

- Within these limits, the lower the temperature and RH can be kept, the better—**provided they do not fluctuate.** [6]

As a first step towards limiting deterioration by good climate control, an institution should aim at maintaining stable conditions year round, no higher than 70°F and between 30-50% RH. These are the suggested values given in *Environmental Guidelines for the Storage of Paper Records*, a technical report issued by the National Information Standards Organization. This report is not a standard, but it offers useful guidelines for climate control. The report specifies that one target value within the range of 30-50% should be chosen for relative humidity, depending on what the institution's climate control system can maintain consistently. The report notes that temperature should not vary more than ± 2°F and RH should not vary more than ±3% in any 24-hour period. If fluctuations can be controlled, damage to collections will be significantly slower than it has been under the typical range of storage conditions in many areas of the United States and Canada.

Institutions committed to long-term preservation must be willing to budget for the best achievable climate. At least, where winter-long heating is necessary, temperatures should be kept as low as staff can be persuaded to tolerate (assuming the resulting RH is acceptable). Where summer temperature and RH are high, collections of lasting importance should be air conditioned.

In no case should climate-control equipment be turned off or thermostat settings altered over night, during weekends, or in other periods when the facility is unoccupied. The rapid, repeated changes that result when equipment attempts to bring a building from "closed" conditions to "working" conditions produce significant stress on collections. In some areas, severe weather or economics force institutions to close for the winter. In such situations, it is not cold that is a preservation hazard, but potentially unstable humidity in a building that is inadequately insulated or poorly sealed to prevent air migration. Procedures for winterizing collections have been developed. In addition, it appears that control of winter humidity by low levels of heat in conjunction with humidity sensors may be practical.

If winters are severe, central heating can dramatically lower the RH of a building. Where a humidification system is feasible, it should be steam-based, and the source of the steam should be clean and independent of other systems. Most steam and hot water heating systems use anti-corrosive chemicals to prevent damage to pipes. These chemicals can harm staff and collections if they are injected into the air.

Under prolonged high humidity, conventional air conditioning alone usually will not provide adequate dehumidification. Environments that are air conditioned should therefore be carefully monitored. Chemical desiccants can put damaging abrasives into the air and should be used only in emergencies. Additional refrigeration cooling is preferable.

Maintaining perfect conditions is difficult and expensive, particularly in northern climates subject to both hot, humid summers and cold, dry winters. The NISO guidelines include specifications for allowing the temperature and relative humidity to drift (change gradually in one direction) 3°F or 3% RH each month, following the changes of the seasons. The maximum allowable daily fluctuation would be ±2°F and ±3% RH. Careful monitoring is necessary to track such changes accurately.

HOW CAN YOU TELL IF THE CLIMATE IS OK?

The only way to know what climate exists in your building is to measure and record temperature and RH with instruments designed for that purpose. This should be done systematically wherever collections of permanent value are stored. A concrete, accurate record can move climate control out of the hypothetical realm into a set of practical steps or goals for improving storage or exhibit conditions. It is often helpful in convincing senior decision-makers that concerns about a building's climate are not imaginary.

In addition to documenting existing conditions, a monitoring program can guide and record the effect of changes in the operation of available climate control equipment. Heating, ventilation, and air conditioning (HVAC) systems are seldom optimally used, even when all the components are in place. A building maintenance engineer or the contractor responsible for the HVAC system can often improve its performance, if concrete information is available to show the effect of altered thermostats, filter replacement, or even rearranging furniture to unblock vents.

If climate-control equipment was designed to produce the desired conditions, but problems cannot be solved by simple adjustments and routine maintenance, it may be necessary to have the system professionally rebalanced. Balancing is a process that measures air flow and other characteristics of HVAC systems; it requires the expertise of a professional climate-control engineer.

If conditions cannot be improved with existing equipment, a monitoring program can document the severity of the problem and support the need to add machinery. Under the best circumstances, it will indicate that available climate-control equipment is operating properly and handling the environmental load. It may also identify occasional transient problems.

HOW DO YOU MONITOR CLIMATE?

There are various instruments available to measure temperature and RH. They fall into two categories: those that provide "snapshot" measurements (i.e., a record of conditions at a specific moment) and those that provide a continuous record of climate conditions. Each institution must analyze its own needs and resources to determine which monitoring instrument is most appropriate. The most common instruments are described below.[7]

"Snapshot" monitoring devices:

1. **Thermometers** can provide accurate temperature information for about $10.00. Calibrated thermometers for scientific use are available, but at this level of accuracy, a standard thermometer that measures the entire range of foreseeable conditions in your building is satisfactory. Most instruments that measure RH incorporate a temperature sensor of some sort, since RH is a function of air temperature and the amount of moisture available in the air.

2. **Simple dial-type hygrometers**, available from most hardware stores for $15.00 or less, are an inexpensive way to measure RH, but they are not recommended because they can be inaccurate and most cannot be recalibrated. The only exception are "animal membrane" dial hygrometers, which are more accurate.

3. **Humidity indicator strips or color cards** are another inexpensive (from $1.00 -$5.00 per strip) humidity-monitoring device. Some are reversible and thus can be reused, while others are for one-time use. Humidity indicator strips provide only approximate readings; they have been shown to be reliable for indicating extremely high or low conditions.

4. **Sling psychrometers** (about $100) are the least expensive instrument capable of accurate RH measurements. Two thermometers are mounted side by side. The bulb of one is covered with a wick, which the user wets with distilled water. The instrument is swung, rotating about once per second for several minutes to get an accurate reading. The resulting flow of air over the wet wick cools the second thermometer, and the difference between the dry bulb and wet bulb temperatures is used to calculate the RH.

   While conditions can be recorded using a sling psychrometer (preferably several times per day), accuracy depends on the design of the instrument and the skill of the user. The people responsible for monitoring need to practice until readings are reproducible.

   The major advantages of a sling psychrometer are cost and portability. One instrument can be used in many spaces each day. Disadvantages are inaccuracy in the hands of an inexpert user, problems with reproducible measurements, and the fact that a monitoring program based on spot readings will not provide critical information such as the speed and frequency of variations in each 24-hour period. These instruments provide only a rough picture of the environment, dependent on a human monitor who may not be around to record information at midnight, or over holidays and weekends, when conditions will often reach extremes. For useful comparison, measurements need to be made at the same times and the same locations each day.

5. **Battery-operated (motor-blower) psychrometers** work on the same principle as a sling psychrometer, but use a motor-driven fan to generate the air flow. These are moderately priced (about $150 and up), are less prone to error, and can be conveniently moved to monitor a wide variety of spaces. They too are likely to fail to measure the most extreme conditions and rapid changes in the environment, since they depend on a human user. Replacement batteries should always be on hand.

6. **An electronic temperature/humidity meter** is another hand-held instrument that uses a calibrated sensor to measure RH at a known temperature. Many have liquid crystal displays that give both RH and room temperature. These range from about $300 and up, and also depend on the time and frequency of measurements. While they are capable of great accuracy and are easy to use, some of the more inexpensive models may be accurate only to ±3-5% and may take several minutes to react to changes in RH. These instruments need to be recalibrated periodically as recommended by the manufacturer.

7. **Min/max digital thermohygrometers** are battery-operated instruments that combine temperature and RH sensors with a computer chip that retains a memory of minimum and maximum values until it is manually reset. Like other spot measurement tools, these provide information about conditions at only one moment in time, but they do insure a record of highest and lowest conditions in each interval. A human monitor must record the measurements and reset the meter once a day. Humidity measurements tend to be accurate only to about ±5% (at mid-range temperatures—accuracy may be less at temperature extremes), but these instruments can provide an initial broad outline of climate conditions. These are available at below $70.00 through several vendors.

Continuous monitoring devices:

1. A **recording hygrothermograph** has been the standard choice for monitoring temperature and RH. Features to look for include:

   - The hygrothermograph should use a human hair bundle to measure RH and a bimetallic device to measure temperature.
   - The sensors will be attached to pens that record changes continually on a simple graph—these pens should be an easily replaceable cartridge type.
   - The minimum acceptable variation in accuracy for temperature is ±2°F; minimum RH is ±5% (±3% is preferred). Make sure the instrument will work in the most extreme conditions your building experiences.
   - Hygrothermographs are available with circular charts, but linear charts (also called drum charts) are preferred since they are easier to read.
   - The hygrothermograph should offer variable speed, so that 24-hour, 7-day, or 1- or 2-month charts can be used. While daily or weekly charts provide the most detailed information, monthly charts may be useful if staff cannot change the charts regularly.

   For a recording hygrothermograph with the above features, cost ranges up from about $700 per instrument. If more than one space needs to be monitored, hygrothermographs can be relocated as needed, but should be left in each area for at least a couple of weeks during each season.

   Regular maintenance is essential for recording hygrothermographs. The cover must be used to protect the mechanism from dust, and the instrument should be cleaned periodically following the instructions in its manual. Periodic rehydration of the human hair bundle, perhaps as often as once per year, is necessary. Recording hygrothermographs must also be recalibrated regularly (usually at least once a month and whenever they are moved) using a battery-operated psychrometer or good quality electronic hygrometer. If an instrument is not recalibrated regularly, it can be off by as much as 10-20%. For both rehydration and recalibration it is best to follow the manufacturer's instructions. The human hair bundles also need to be replaced every three to five years—or as often as the manufacturer recommends.

2. **Dataloggers** are battery-powered instruments about the size of an audio cassette. They use electronic sensors and a computer chip to record temperature and RH at intervals determined by the user. Data is transferred between the datalogger and a personal computer by a cable. Once the data has been downloaded, software that comes with the datalogger allows the user to produce customized charts and graphs that illustrate conditions over time. This is an advantage over hygrothermographs, the data from which must be replotted by hand for analysis.

Some issues to consider when purchasing a logger include:

- The frequency you wish to take measurements and how often you wish to download data. A datalogger does not provide continuous monitoring in the way that a recording hygrothermograph does—most loggers can take measurements at intervals ranging from a few seconds to a few hours. More frequent measurements will occupy more memory, require more frequent downloading of data, and add to the staff time required to maintain the logger.

- Real-time display of climate conditions. An increasing number of loggers, but not all, provide this.

- Accuracy of the electronic sensors. Some loggers use sensors that are temperature-compensated—meaning the logger can provide about 3% accuracy for RH over a wide range of temperature and humidity—while others do not. Also, some sensors may have a "time-lag" of 4 or 5 minutes if the humidity is falling—this would be a disadvantage if frequent sampling is required.

Prices vary, but units are available for about $500 and up. The electronic sensors must be recalibrated periodically according to the manufacturer's instructions. Like the traditional recording hygrothermograph, a datalogger can be moved to monitor several locations, but you must keep a careful log of the time of the moves to correlate with the data.

HOW DO YOU DECIDE WHAT INSTRUMENT TO BUY?

Cost may be the major consideration for a small institution. Look at catalogs from a number of suppliers and compare the features and prices of their equipment. If the catalogs do not provide all of the information you need, ask questions. Talk to colleagues who have developed climate-control programs.

The following questions are important to ask in making an informed decision:

1. What do you want the information for? If you are documenting the effect of operating changes for your climate-control equipment, you may need a recording hygrothermograph to continuously document small changes in temperature or RH. If climate control in your building is limited to steam heat during the winter, and you want to prove that conditions in your collection regularly fall outside acceptable limits, a sling psychrometer may be an adequate first step.

2. What range of conditions does the instrument need to measure? If you are monitoring an unheated building through a year on the coast of Maine, temperature may drop below 0°F and rise above 90°F. Relative humidity in a building with heat, but without air conditioning, may range from less than 10% to nearly 100% RH. Will your instrument record the entire predictable range? Does it need to?

3. How exact do your measurements need to be? If you do not have sophisticated climate-control equipment, or if your collections do not include valuable artifacts, less sensitive instruments may be adequate. On the other hand, if you are developing a case for changing equipment or procedures, and increasing expense, you may need to present an extremely accurate record.

4. Do you need to record information when the building is unoccupied? If you are measuring changes in climate due to altered climate-control settings at night and over weekends, an instrument capable of continuous monitoring is necessary.

5. How easy do calibration, operation, and maintenance need to be? Who will be responsible for these tasks, and what skills do they have? Can you afford both a recording instrument and a calibration instrument?

6. How durable does your equipment have to be? Will it be exposed to careless handling or untrained users?

7. What powers the instrument? Can your building provide dependable electricity, or do you need a battery-operated instrument?

8. Will this equipment give you the information you need your monitoring program to provide?

WHAT DO YOU NEED BESIDES INSTRUMENTS?

Monitoring should be the assigned responsibility of a specific person in the institution. A back-up person should be trained to cover during absences and vacations.

A good monitoring program includes a written plan for collecting information and maintaining instruments. This should identify spaces to be monitored, the procedures to be used, and forms for recording desired information.

If monitoring depends on a person rather than an automatic recording instrument, try to sample the widest variation in conditions: take measurements when they can be expected to be at the highest and lowest points. For practical purposes, in most libraries or museums this will be the first thing in the morning, and at noon or 5:00 p.m.

Except for special purposes, it is important to position automatic recording instruments to measure representative conditions. They should be located above floor level, away from air vents, heating/cooling/humidity equipment, and doors and windows.

Records of weather conditions and special events (exhibit openings, for example, where unusual numbers of visitors alter temperature and RH in a space, or a failure of the boiler or air-conditioning system) should be maintained so that changes recorded by the instruments can be interpreted usefully. Regional weather records are available from the National Oceanic and Atmospheric Administration (NOAA), Washington, DC. They may also be available from a local or college weather station or local airport.

If a limited number of recording hygrothermographs or dataloggers is available, a reasonably accurate profile of conditions in several spaces can be developed by leaving an instrument in each area for several weeks in each season. At the end of a year, these records will show typical conditions. The readings should be interpreted by a professional consultant. The most important information will be the extremes of temperature and humidity and the speed and extent of changes in the environment.

Each chart (or form in a manual monitoring program) should be labeled with the location and date of the measurements, the initials of the monitor, and recalibration information (date, time, alteration) if a change is made. Interpretation of the information provided by hygrothermograph charts will be easier if it is transcribed regularly onto a running graph that gives highs and lows, fluctuations, and frequency of fluctuations. This should be done each week (or month) as the chart is changed.

WHAT DO YOU DO ONCE YOU KNOW WHAT YOU HAVE?

Remedial measures to improve environmental conditions for museum, library, and archival collections may include: (1) installation of central environmental controls; (2) use of portable air conditioners, humidifiers, and/or dehumidifiers; (3) removal of collections from attics, which tend to be hot, or basements, which can be damp; (4) creation of compartmentalized storage spaces; and/or (5) improvements in insulation and building seals. It is critical to remember that temperature and RH are intimately related and that the correction of one factor may alter the balance of other important factors (e.g., a dehumidifier may generate enough heat to require additional cooling). If remedial measures are taken without considering all contributors to the environment, conditions may worsen, not improve. It is essential to know (from recorded measurements) what conditions exist and to seek the advice of a climate-control engineer with experience in collections-holding institutions before making major changes. The importance of continued monitoring after the institution of a change cannot be over-emphasized.

In choosing a climate-control consultant, look for someone whose clients include libraries, archives, museums, or other institutions with collections of long-term value. If no one with this specific experience is available in your region, look for an engineer with experience in climate-control of computer facilities, which also have demanding requirements.

For preservation purposes, it is the collections that are important, not the comfort of people, who are much less sensitive. A design that works splendidly for a hotel or shopping mall will not work for 19th-century books, a historic building, or a museum. Ask for references from clients whose needs may have been similar to your own, and talk to those clients about the success or failure of the system designed for them. Make sure your consultant understands what your ideal conditions and minimum requirements will be.

It is important to recognize the limits of a building's tolerance when making climate-control decisions. Here again, the advice of a climate-control engineer or preservation architect who is knowledgeable about collections' needs is indispensable. Uninsulated, historic, and some masonry buildings can be damaged by major changes such as the installation of central heating or humidification systems. Such buildings may need major alterations to be compatible with the needs of their contents; in such a case, it may be necessary to relocate collections to provide conditions suitable for preservation.

A systematic monitoring program properly carried out is one of the best measures of an institution's success in providing conditions favorable to the long-term survival of its collections. It will not, in itself, solve the difficult problem of climate management, but it is the only dependable tool for decision-making.

NOTES

[1] Barbara Appelbaum, *Guide to Environmental Protection of Collections* (Madison, CT: Sound View Press, 1991), p. 25. Appelbaum gives an excellent description of relative humidity, its relationship to temperature, and their effect on collections of all types.

[2] James M. Reilly, Douglas W. Nishimura, and Edward Zinn, *New Tools for Preservation: Assessing Long-Term Environmental Effects on Library and Archives Collections* (Washington, DC: Commission on Preservation and Access, November 1995), p. 7.

[3] Reilly, et al., p. 7.

[4] Reilly, et al., p. 20.

[5] National Information Standards Organization, *Environmental Guidelines for the Storage of Paper Records. Technical Report* NISO-TR01-1995 (Bethesda, MD NISO Press, 1995), p. 1. This report gives a good summary of conclusions drawn from recent research into the effect of temperature and RH on paper-based collections.

[6] In 1994, the Smithsonian Institution issued a controversial press release that appeared to contradict this conclusion. It asserted that research done by scientists in its Conservation Analytical Laboratory indicated that wider fluctuations in temperature and humidity than previously recommended could be tolerated by a wide range of museum collections. However, this research was primarily concerned with mechanical damage to collections–rather than the chemical damage that is the primary cause of paper deterioration—and hence of limited applicability to library and archives collections. Articles providing further information on the Smithsonian controversy are cited at the end of this leaflet.

[7] See "Setting Up an Environmental Monitoring Program," prepared by William P. Lull (Princeton Junction, NJ: Garrison, Lull, Inc., September 1995) as a supplement to the monitoring discussion in *Conservation Environment Guidelines for Libraries and Archives* from which material here was used.

ADDITIONAL READING AND RESOURCES

Erhardt, David, Marion F. Mecklenburg, Charles S. Tumosa, and Mark McCormick-Goodhart. "The Determination of Allowable RH Fluctuations." Online at http://palimpsest.stanford.edu/waac/wn/wn17/wn17-1/wn17-108.html. **Lull, William P.,** "Further Comments on Climate Control Guidelines." Online at http://palimpsest.stanford.edu/waac/wn/wn17/wn17-1/wn17-111.html. **Real, William A.,** "Some Thoughts on the Recent CAL Press Release on Climate Control for Cultural Collections." Online at http://palimpsest.stanford.edu/waac/wn/wn17/wn17-1/wn17-110.html. All in *WAAC Newsletter* 17(1) (January 1995).
The first article provides an overview of the Smithsonian Conservation Analytical Laboratory research on climate control, while the others question recommendations made by a Smithsonian press release describing the research. For further discussion of this controversy, see WAAC Newsletter 18.3 (September 1996). Online at http://palimpsest.stanford.edu/waac/wn/wn18/wn18-3/.

Kerschner, Richard L., and Jennifer Baker. *Practical Climate Control: A Selected, Annotated Bibliography.* Online at: http://palimpsest.stanford.edu/byauth/kerschner/ccbiblio.html.
A good bibliography of alternative strategies to standard heating, ventilation, and air conditioning (HVAC) systems that includes books, conference proceedings, and articles.

Lull, William P., with the assistance of Paul N. Banks. *Conservation Environment Guidelines for Libraries and Archives.* Ottawa, ON: Canadian Council of Archives, 1995. Available from Canadian Council of Archives, 344 Wellington St., Room 1009, Ottawa, ON, K1A 0N3, Canada.
A fundamental and highly recommended guide to criteria, assessment, monitoring, and goals for creating or improving environmental conditions for the preservation of collections. Important reading for library staff, architects, and systems designers prior to the design phase. Discusses building systems, cost trade-offs, responsible compromises, and steps in the planning, design, and construction process. Provides a glossary of common terms used in design and construction of the building systems.

National Information Standards Organization. *Environmental Guidelines for the Storage of Paper Records.* Technical Report NISO-TR01-1995. Bethesda, MD: NISO Press, 1995, p. 1.
Not a standard, but provides guidelines for storage conditions and gives a summary of research into the effect of temperature and RH on paper-based collections. Available for $35 plus $5 shipping from: NISO Press Fulfillment, PO Box 338, Oxon Hill, MD, 20750-0338; 800 282-NISO (6476). http://www.niso.org.

Padfield, Tim. *An Introduction to the Physics of the Museum Environment.* Online at: http://www.natmus.dk/cons/tp/index.htm.
An online book-in-progress, (as of 1999) with various chapters on controlling humidity in museums. Includes a chapter on data loggers and climate sensors.

Reilly, James. *IPI Storage Guide for Acetate Film.* Rochester, NY: Image Permanence Institute (IPI), 1993. 24 pp. Available from IPI, Frank E. Gannett Memorial Building, P.O. Box 9887, Rochester, NY 14623.
Discusses the effect of temperature and relative humidity on acetate film, provides tools to help project the life expectancy of film-based materials, and identifies film preservation strategies.

Reilly, James M., Douglas W. Nishimura, and Edward Zinn. *New Tools for Preservation: Assessing Long-Term Environmental Effects on Library and Archives Collections.* Washington, DC: Commission on Preservation and Access, November 1995. Available for $10 from: CLIR Publication Orders, 1755 Massachusetts Avenue, NW, Suite 500, Washington DC, 20036-2124; (202) 939-4750 or fax (202) 939-4760 or e-mail info@clir.org or http://www.clir.org.*
Describes and explains the Image Permanence Institute's "time-weighted preservation index," a tool that demonstrates the effect of temperature and humidity on the life-expectancy of paper.

Sebera, Donald K. *Isoperms: An Environmental Management Tool.* Washington, DC: Commission on Preservation and Access, June 1994. Online at: http://www.clir.org/pubs/reports/isoperm/isoperm.html.
Detailed explanation of the "isoperm" method for quantifying the effect of temperature and relative humidity on the lifespan of paper collections. The basis for IPI's "Storage Guide for Acetate Film" and "New Tools for Preservation," described above.

Smithsonian Institution Press Office. "Work of Smithsonian Scientists Revises Guidelines for Climate Control in Museums and Archives"; and Ellen McCrady, "Temperature & RH Guidelines Challenged by Smithsonian." Both in *Abbey Newsletter,* 18.4-5 (Aug-Sep 1994) (http://palimpsest.stanford.edu/byorg/abbey/an/an18/an18-4/).
This 1994 Smithsonian press release initiated a controversy over recommendations for temperature and humidity levels in museums, libraries, and archives.

SOURCES OF EQUIPMENT

This list is not exhaustive, nor does it constitute an endorsement of the suppliers listed. We suggest that you obtain information from a number of vendors so that you can make comparisons of cost and assess the full range of available products.

A more complete list of suppliers is available from NEDCC. Consult the Technical Leaflets section of NEDCC's website at www.nedcc.org or contact NEDCC for the most up-to-date version in print.

ACR Systems Inc.
Unit 210-12960 84 Avenue
Surrey, British Columbia, Canada V3W-1K7
Telephone: (604) 591-1128
Toll Free: (800) 663-7845
Fax: (604) 591-2252
E-mail: acr@acrsystems.com
http://www.acrsystems.com
Dataloggers

Dickson Instruments Company
930 South Westwood Avenue
Addison, IL 60101-4917
Telephone: (630) 543-3747
Fax: (630) 543-0498
E-mail: info@dicksonweb.com
http://www.dicksonweb.com
Dataloggers, temperature/humidity chart recorders

Fisher Scientific Company
52 Fadem Road
Springfield, NJ 07081
Toll Free: (800) 766-7000
Fax: (800) 926-1166
http://www.fishersci.com
Temperature/humidity meters

Gaylord Brothers
Box 4901
Syracuse, NY 13221-4901
Toll Free: (800) 448-6160
Toll Free: (800) 428-3631 (Help Line)
Fax: (800) 272-3412
http://www.gaylord.com
Hygrothermographs, min/max thermohygrometer

Herzog/Wheeler & Assoc.
2183 Summit Avenue
St. Paul, MN 55105
Telephone: (651) 647-1035
Fax: (651) 647-1041
Dataloggers

Langan Products, Inc.
2660 California Street
San Francisco, CA 94115
Telephone: (415) 567-8089 (voice/fax)
E-mail: langan@sirius.com
http://www.langan.net/lpi/
Dataloggers

Onset Computer Corporation
PO Box 3450
Pocasset, MA 02559-3450
Telephone: (508) 759-9500
Fax: (508) 759-9100
http://www.onsetcomp.com/
Dataloggers

Preservation Resource Group
P.O. Box 1768
Rockville, MD 20849-1768
Telephone: (301) 309-2222
Fax: (301) 279-7885
http://www.prginc.com
Temperature/humidity meters

Rustrak Ranger
1201 Main Street
Indianapolis, IN 46224
Toll Free: (800) RUSTRAK
Telephone: (317) 244-7611
Toll Free Fax: (800) 899-5160
Fax: (317) 247-4749
http://www.rustrakranger.com
Dataloggers

Scientific Sales, Inc.
P.O. Box 6725
Lawerenceville, N.J. 08648
Telephone: (609) 844-0055
Fax: (609) 844-0466
E-mail: sciensales@aol.com
http://www.scientificsales.com
Hygrothermographs

University Products
517 Main Street
P. O. Box 101
Holyoke, MA 01041
Toll Free: (800) 628-1912
Telephone: (413) 532-3372
Toll Free Fax: (800) 532-9281
Fax: (413) 432-9281
E-mail: info@universityproducts.com
http://www.universityproducts.com
Sling psychrometer, hygrothermographs, dataloggers, temperature/humidity meters, min/max thermohygrometer

VWR Scientific
1310 Goshen Parkway
West Chester, PA 19380
Toll Free: Orders: (800) 932-5000
Telephone: (610) 431-1700
Fax: (610) 429-9340
http://www.vwrsp.com/
Temperature/humidity meters

Robert E. White Instruments, Inc.
34 Commercial Wharf
Boston, MA 02110
Toll Free: (800) 992-3045
http://www.robertwhite.com/
Sling psychrometers, hygrothermographs, temperature/humidity meters, min/max thermohygrometer

Acknowledgements

The author and NEDCC gratefully acknowledge the previous work of Karen Motylewski in preparing this leaflet.

Northeast Document
Conservation Center
100 Brickstone Square
Andover, MA 01810-1494
www.nedcc.org
Tel: (978) 470-1010
Fax: (978) 475-6021

TECHNICAL
LEAFLET

THE
ENVIRONMENT

Section 2, Leaflet 3

GETTING FUNCTION FROM DESIGN:
MAKING SYSTEMS WORK

by Rebecca Thatcher Ellis
Sebasta Blombert & Associates, Inc.
Minneapolis, MN

INTRODUCTION

The following information is based on the assumption that the design of a building's mechanical system is appropriate for the building's specific application and will provide the desired environment if installed as designed, if controlled as designed, and if properly maintained. The people who have the greatest interest in the final outcome of any project, large or small, are those who will depend on the new or renovated systems. Therefore, in addition to being involved in the design process, the institution should become familiar with the procedures for construction, start-up/commissioning, and ongoing operation that apply to all building projects. This is especially true when strict environmental control is a high-priority goal.

The author has gathered the recommendations and information that follow after working through construction, start-up, commissioning, and subsequent problems on many projects with critical goals for temperature and humidity control. The findings may appear to come from a cynical engineer, but it is prudent to expect shortcuts from contractors implementing a professional's design rather than to assume the contractors will perform their jobs exactly as specified.

The suggestions herein are presented as verification tasks the institution will want performed. It is certainly not the institution's responsibility to carry out these tasks, although some may find it easier to do certain things themselves instead of convincing others to perform the tasks for them. Ideally, these tasks would be the direct responsibility of the designer, but it is a rare design team that assumes the level of detail described here.

"Construction Phase" tasks are almost always within the designer's scope of work, and it is safe to assume at least minimal attention will be paid to them. "Start-up/Commissioning" is often neglected, though not necessarily ignored, by the design team. It is not to the design team's advantage to find operational flaws in their system. Given the potential for conflict of interest problems, testing the installed system may be a task for a special consultant, if such a luxury can be afforded. Finally, the tasks under "Normal Operation" are almost never part of the design team's scope of work. Preventive maintenance and monitoring programs are typically the individual institution's responsibility and, unfortunately, are often considered late in the process, e.g., after a few months of operation when the system begins to degrade for lack of attention.

CONSTRUCTION PHASE

The key activity during the construction phase of a project is to insure that the specified equipment is provided and properly installed . If it is not, it is imperative to insure that the items of equipment substituted as "equal" are indeed equivalent in quality and performance to those specified in the design documents.

Typically, "special" equipment that is not usually installed in standard commercial buildings will be provided by the contractor as specified. Humidifiers, dehumidifiers, activated carbon filters, etc. fall into this category.

Contractors will often want to use commonplace system components, such as air handling units, cooling coils, heating coils, fans, pumps, diffusers, dampers, control systems, etc. that differ from those specified. The contractor's motivation is typically economic (i.e., the substituted items are less expensive than the specified items), but it can also be that the contractor has more experience with, and therefore is more comfortable with, the substituted components.

It is usually the designer's responsibility to review the suggested substitutes and determine whether or not they are actually equivalent to the equipment specified. Designers vary widely in the amount of attention they give this task, but in general most are conscientious. The institution should be vigilant when working with design firms that separate the design and construction support functions between different departments. If the person/team reviewing the submitted substitutions is not the same person/team who specified the equipment, there may be a lack of communication regarding what specified characteristics are most important.

Equipment Characteristics

Some key specified equipment characteristics to insist upon are listed below:

Capacity. Will the substituted item provide the pumping, air distribution, heating, cooling, humidifying, dehumidifying, or filtering capability required? Cooling coils are particularly tricky to evaluate because of the differences between total cooling, sensible cooling (cooling with no dehumidification), and latent cooling (cooling with dehumidification) capacities. To insure proper dehumidification, which is often a misunderstood concept, one must see to it that the latent cooling capacity must be equal to or greater than that specified.

Size. Will the substituted item physically fit into the space allotted for it, or will the substitution require rearranging other components of the system?

Noise Levels. A number of different models for rotating equipment (such as fans) can usually perform the specified function. Different models (i.e., sizes) will generate different noise levels. As a rule, the smaller a fan wheel, the faster it must rotate in order to supply the same amount of air; the faster it rotates, the noisier it is. There is clearly a trade-off between size (and initial cost) and noise levels.

Reliability, Serviceability, and Support. It will be beneficial, throughout the life of the system, to consider the intangible characteristics of reliability, serviceability, and on-going support during construction. Beware of "off-brand" equipment manufactured by firms that may not remain in business over the next 20 to 40 years. It is critical to confirm that there are service companies within a reasonable distance of your facility who are familiar with the equipment installed. Otherwise, the equipment will operate as specified only until the first problem.

Equipment Installation. Proper installation of equipment should also be verified by the designers. Depending on the designers' contract, the number of site visits can vary from a total of two or three visits during construction to once a week or more frequently. Between visits construction work continues and is often permanently hidden from view behind walls or above ceilings before the designer returns. The enlightened client, who may be near the job site on a daily basis, will make a point of frequently walking around the site, visually inspecting the installation, and informing the designer of any anomalies discovered. The client will undoubtedly be a nuisance to the designer who is not accustomed to having "help," but the client must live with the system after the designer moves on to other projects.

Installation features requiring verification:

Thermal Insulation and Vapor Barrier Integrity in Walls. The importance of insulation and a complete vapor barrier is indisputable. They must be installed properly to perform their functions. Contractors may take shortcuts, because once the finished wall is up it is extremely difficult to verify the existence of insulation and almost impossible, non-destructively, to verify the existence of a vapor barrier.

Ductwork. Significant deviations from the designer-specified ductwork sizes and routes can affect the capability of a system to function as required. Longer duct runs, smaller ducts, and more turns can all increase the total static pressure of a fan system. As static pressure increases, the amount of air the fan can distribute through the system decreases. As the air flow decreases, the system's ability to heat, cool, humidify, and dehumidify also decreases. Walk-through inspections should compare actual installation with designed installation. Duct sizes are not usually substituted, but note any changes in how the ductwork gets from the fan to the room-supply outlets and return inlets.

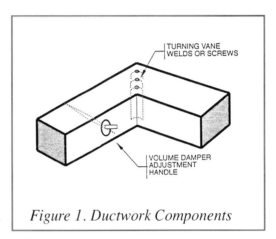

Figure 1. Ductwork Components

Turning Vanes. The absence of turning vanes in elbows will also increase system static pressure. Installation of vanes in 90° elbows is easy to verify from the exterior of the duct before the elbows are hidden above ceilings. The turning vane welds or screws shown in Figure 1 will be visible on both sides of the elbow. In addition to increasing system pressure, the absence of turning vanes will increase "air noise" from the ductwork.

Dampers. Manual volume dampers should be installed in all locations specified in the design. These dampers are used by the air balancer to insure that the proper amounts of air are delivered to each space, thus insuring desired temperature and humidity control. Volume dampers are also easy to identify from the exterior of the ductwork, because they have adjustment handles that protrude from the sheet metal as shown in Figure 1.

Ductwork Lining. Some systems use ductwork lining to serve the dual purpose of thermal insulation (which prevents heat loss and condensation on cold ductwork) and noise suppression. In order to verify that the lining has been installed, one has to actually find an opening in the ductwork. Openings can be found during construction at the ends of incomplete ductwork and in holes cut for supply and return registers.

Ductwork Insulation. If the ductwork is not internally lined, it should be externally wrapped with insulation and covered with an airtight vapor barrier. Verification of the vapor barrier is critical, because if humid air comes into contact with a cold duct, condensation will soak the insulation; this degrades its performance and causes a nasty mess.

Pressure Gauges. Finally, if specified, differential pressure gauges across air filters are important items that are sometimes neglected. These gauges provide a quick way of determining when filters should be changed.

Access Doors. Doors or panels should be installed to provide access to equipment requiring future maintenance or service. Sheet metal doors will be located in ductwork for access to coils, dampers, fans, humidifiers, etc. Architectural access panels should be installed in walls, ceilings, or floors concealing valves, motors, and any other moving equipment. They should also be provided at ductwork access doors.

Piping. Faulty piping is usually not a problem for long, because a leaky pipe will be noticed. Pipe insulation, however, can sometimes be forgotten, especially on pipe fittings such as elbows and valves. Missing insulation on cold pipes can result in condensation, which will drip from the pipes just like a leak.

Coil Monitors. If they are specified, it is important to verify that thermostats and pressure gauges at heating and cooling coils are installed. These items are invaluable when it comes to future trouble-shooting.

Controls. Most control system components are "invisible" to anyone casually inspecting a construction site, but the temperature and humidity sensors for spaces should be self-evident. Sensor locations should be verified and the cleanliness of the sensors protected. Sanding and painting in the vicinity of unprotected sensors should be prohibited, but if this is impossible to enforce, sensors can be temporarily covered with plastic and masking tape when necessary.

Change Orders. A final note of caution for the construction phase of a project has to do with change orders. Changes to a project after the "final" design documents are printed and distributed are expected on every job. Unfortunately, the distribution of change order requirements is often limited and many times the subcontractors actually affected by a change do not receive or properly incorporate the change order into their plans. Change orders are critical to the correct construction of a project (the designer will not take the trouble to issue change orders if they are not), and their implementation should be verified.

START-UP/COMMISSIONING

At the end of the installation stage of a project everyone involved is fatigued and anxious to have it completed. Often there is no more money to spend, the completion is behind schedule, people need to move into the new space, and the designers and contractors want to move on to their next projects. This is exactly the time when a new burst of energy is required of someone, preferably the designer or other consultant familiar with the intended operation of the new system, to insure that the systems function properly.

The job is not complete until the systems are operating on a consistent basis, and it is the contractor's responsibility to make it so. Not many contractors would deliberately install a system which does not work, but many do not take the time at the end of a project to test their handiwork. In the contractor's opinion, there is no reason to believe a system will not function as intended, because the contractor has watched it being constructed day by day. Many an installation has been plagued by complaints from occupants from the day they move in because system verification testing was not performed.

Without verification testing by a professional unrelated to the contractors, the institution may need to call the contractors back frequently to "fix" the new system. The institution that does not know the intricacies of the system will be at the mercy of the contractors, who are not about to find something wrong with their own installation. The designers, probably long gone from the scene, will be blamed for a faulty system that the contractors are "doing their best to make work." The finger pointing will stop only when the institution gives up trying or calls in the designer or another professional consultant, who should have been involved immediately upon completion of the installation.

Historically the most unreliable parts of a new mechanical installation are air and water balancing and the automatic control system. Therefore these elements require the most attention during the start-up/commissioning phase of any project.

BALANCING

Balancers are typically either subcontractors or regular employees of the mechanical contractor, and it is their responsibility to insure that the air supplied by fans is distributed to individual spaces in the quantities and proportions specified in the design. They also insure that water supplied by pumps is distributed to individual pieces of equipment as required to allow for the proper performance of that equipment.

Balancers use special instruments to test and measure air and water flow, and they should be required to submit a report to the designers following completion of the balancing procedures. Sometimes designers review only the report and agree that the flows recorded meet the requirements of the specifications. Designers usually do not consider it their responsibility to verify the results of the report. For this reason balancers have a reputation for recording the airflows required regardless of actual field conditions. This unfairly accuses honest balancers, but one should proceed under the assumption that the balancing reports are not 100% accurate.

Verification testing requires instruments similar to those used by the balancers and therefore requires an investment by the professional performing the tests. An institution can hire an independent balancing contractor with no vested interest in the results to perform verification testing. The results are likely to be much more reliable than the contractor's results.

Spot checking a few air diffusers and registers for comparison to the balancing report should provide an institution with a feel for the accuracy of the entire report. If the random samples agree with the report it is probably not necessary to test each air outlet and inlet. On the other hand, if the random sample results vary widely from the report, it will probably be necessary to check each device and include the new results in a report for presentation to the original balancer. The original balancer will be required to return to the site (at no extra compensation) to rebalance all systems and submit a revised report. It is hoped that the balancer will realize that the institution is "serious" about the balancing report (many institutions are not) and perform the work correctly the second time. The third-party balancer should still be called in to spot check revised reports until the institution is satisfied that the systems are balanced as specified.

The same is true for water balancing, although balancers tend to be conservative in initial water balancing procedures by providing more water to individual pieces of equipment than specified. This is preferable to insufficient flow because the standard use of control valves will automatically modulate the flow of water to equipment as required to achieve the desired environmental conditions. Although a precise water balance is more desirable, the results of an overly conservative balance will not be as detrimental to system performance as a poor air balance.

AUTOMATIC CONTROLS

The brain of any mechanical system is its automatic control system. Testing of the controls, therefore, is critical to insure system conformance to specifications. Unfortunately this is another often neglected task, partly because many people do not adequately understand controls. If a project's designer does not feel comfortable performing the controls verification task, a third-party specialist should be brought in to perform the testing.

Each control system is different, especially with today's computer-based direct digital control (DDC) systems, but the designer or third-party specialist need not be fluent in the detailed programming and user interface procedures of the particular system being tested. The controls contractor should be present for the verification testing in order to perform the system-specific tasks dictated by the tester, and this requirement should be specified in the design documents.

The start-up/commissioning of the controls system will include the following three steps:

Calibration

All sensors, but especially temperature and relative humidity sensors, should be calibrated to insure that they are reading actual conditions. This process can be time consuming but straightforward with a sling psychrometer in the hands of an experienced user.

Whenever air flows are being controlled against setpoint quantities for pressurization or indoor air quality purposes, it is imperative that the air-flow sensor be calibrated in its installed location. This will require the cooperation of the air balancer to provide the actual air-flow readings against sensor output.

Automatic dampers need to be calibrated to insure that their positions are those required by the control system. If outside air dampers are to be set at a specified minimum during occupied hours to insure proper ventilation, the air balancer will again need to be consulted to determine exactly what damper position corresponds to the desired outside air flow.

Automatic valves for heating, cooling, and humidification processes also need to be calibrated to insure that their positions are those required by the control system. It is also important to coordinate the operation of different valves to insure that simultaneous heating and cooling do not occur unless specifically required by the control system.

Testing

The testing procedure involves "exercising" the control system components. This includes changing setpoints and physically watching valves and dampers modulate. The tests should also override parameters such as time of day and occupancy mode so that testers can observe fans starting, stopping, or changing speed. A test procedure can be developed for each control system strategy specified in the design to insure its proper implementation under most conditions.

By putting a system through its paces during the commissioning process, an institution is less likely to be plagued by unexpected control-system behavior after occupying the building. This is especially true of control systems that are commissioned during the summer and have not been operated during the winter. Summer operation may be acceptable, but without verification testing, there is no way to tell what is going to occur when the weather changes. By that time the controls contractor may be long gone and has no financial motivation for performing additional work on the system. Obviously, the same problems apply to systems commissioned in the winter and never properly tested for summer operation.

An unexpected control system malfunction could be disastrous to collections. Therefore it is imperative to subject the system to all conditions, whether real or artificially simulated, prior to occupancy of the building.

Fine Tuning

The final commissioning task is the fine tuning of the control system. This involves adjusting control-system parameters as required to achieve the desired accuracy and speed of response. Again, because each control system is unique, the actual work should be performed by the controls contractor, but the designer should verify the results.

In simple terms, the control of a single device, such as a hot-water valve, boils down to a mathematical formula with a number of parameters that can be changed to achieve different performance characteristics. The control system receives an input signal from a temperature sensor, for example, and compares that signal against the desired setpoint value for that sensor. If the signal indicates that the actual temperature is lower than the setpoint, the control system sends an output signal to the hot water valve that forces the valve to open a certain amount to provide more heat.

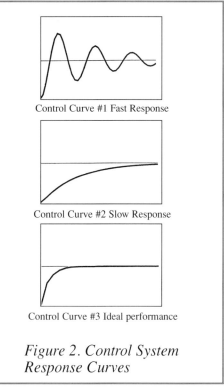

Control Curve #1 Fast Response

Control Curve #2 Slow Response

Control Curve #3 Ideal performance

Figure 2. Control System Response Curves

The graphs in Figure 2 plot an input signal (temperature) on the vertical axis against time on the horizontal axis for different values of the control formula parameters. Control Curve #1 shows a fast response, with undesirable large fluctuations around the setpoint temperature. Control Curve #2 shows a formula that eliminates fluctuation around the setpoint, but produces an extremely slow response. Control Curve #3 shows an "ideal" control formula that provides a fast response with no need for corrections (overshoot). Overshoot describes the creation of a condition that is too extreme, to which the system responds with a correction that is too radical. In this situation conditions bounce back and forth between extremes before gradually reaching the desired value, as in Control Curve #1.

The design documents should specify the acceptable limits of overshoot and undershoot, eg., ±1°F, ±3% RH, etc. It is the control contractor's responsibility to determine the parameters required to achieve the fastest response within those limits. This is often a painstaking, time-consuming, trial-and-error process. Many contractors will fly through using default rule-of-thumb parameters. These may be acceptable for standard commercial buildings where tight environmental control is not critical, but contractors must understand that they will be required to optimize their controls for a museum or archives application.

NORMAL OPERATION

Once there is a newly tested fine-tuned mechanical system functioning as designed, the institution is on its own. The institution may feel particularly poor after the capital-improvements budget has been exhausted, but this is no time to skimp. In order to insure the continued proper operation of the new system and the longest life possible for its components, the institution must pay attention to the continuing performance of the system. The level of attention required will be dependent on the complexity of the system, but even the simplest arrangements of equipment and controls will need periodic preventive maintenance, cleaning, and calibration.

Left to its own devices, a system will appear to operate just fine until a catastrophic failure occurs or until the environment in one or more spaces falls so far away from the desired setpoints that an institution has no choice but to notice. By that time, the required cure is likely to involve a significant effort and expense, because there may be multiple problems in the system. Add to this the fact that the expense is totally unexpected and the money is not available to return the system to its original "as designed" operating state, and one faces the prospect of losing the benefit of the building or renovation project. In order to avoid this outcome, money needs to be budgeted for proper maintenance of the new equipment.

One of the most cost-effective methods of achieving continuous peak performance from a mechanical system is to have at least one knowledgeable and trustworthy person who will take responsibility for the equipment. This person, whom we shall call the Mechanical System Coordinator (MSC), can be on staff, a consultant, a service contractor, or a combination of the three. The job is the same: regular monitoring, maintaining, and servicing of the mechanical systems. Except in the largest installations, this should not require a full-time person.

A good maintenance program will anticipate problems before they reach the critical stage. This can be accomplished by monitoring, at a minimum, the following system characteristics:

Monitor Space Temperature and Relative Humidity

This task must be performed in any facility requiring tightly controlled environmental conditions. The MSC should review these records frequently, looking for trends indicative of degrading system performance. Armed with this information, the MSC can have filters changed, coils cleaned, controls recalibrated, etc. prior to the development of conditions that are unacceptable and perhaps harmful to the contents of a space.

Monitor Utility Bills

The MSC should be provided with all electrical, gas, and oil bills as they are received by the facility. By tracking energy consumption over months and years, the MSC will become familiar with what is "normal" and will quickly identify anomalies that may be evidence of an underlying equipment problem. Anomalies can be investigated and solved before the environment being controlled is affected.

Monitor Filter Status

By keeping a constant awareness of the condition of both particle filters and gaseous pollutant filters, the MSC will know exactly when each type of filter requires replacement. Particle filter monitoring is straightforward and simply requires the installation and regular monitoring of a differential pressure gauge across each bank of filters. As the filter collects dirt, it becomes more and more difficult for air to pass through, causing the pressure to drop across the filters.

Particle Filters. If no more definitive information is available, the differential pressure limit for particle filters can be the manufacturer's recommended maximum, but it is best to learn what pressure drop was assumed by the designer for each bank of filters. The manufacturer's recommended maximums are typically quite high, and the designers probably did not assume all the filters were that dirty when specifying fan size. When the pressure drop across filters rises above the designer's maximum level, the amount of air distributed to the system decreases and, therefore, inhibits the ability of the system to heat, cool, humidify, and dehumidify.

There is another reason it is undesirable to wait until filters are extremely dirty before changing them. Under those circumstances dirt may fall off the filters into the ductwork during filter changeout and be carried into the conditioned spaces. Clearly this should be avoided. Depending on the type of filter, location of the facility, and the ambient air quality, particle filters can be expected to be effective for a duration of three to six months.

Gaseous Pollutant Filters. Monitoring and maintenance of gaseous pollutant filters is more complex and will depend on the type of filter in use.

Standard carbon filter trays require that a sample of the carbon be tested periodically, usually by the manufacturer, to determine its life expectancy. When the carbon is "spent," i.e., has absorbed as much contaminant as possible, the carbon in the trays must be replaced. Other types of filters will require different procedures to determine when they should be replaced or replenished. None of them is as simple as the particle filter procedure. Gaseous pollutant filters typically last for a minimum of one year and often much longer, depending on the ambient air quality and the particular pollutants being absorbed.

Monitor Control System Operation

The automatic control system also requires regular attention to insure that it continues to operate as designed. It is essential that the MSC be familiar with control system basics, but he or she does not have to be an expert in the programming and adjustment of the controllers. The MSC needs to know only enough to identify and intelligently communicate perceived problems to the original controls contractor or other service contractor. Ongoing control system monitoring tasks are similar to those performed during the start-up/commissioning phase, i.e., checking the calibration of sensors and verifying proper operation of all devices. Problems are often identified when the conditioned environment degrades, but this may be too late for some collections. The emphasis needs to be on preventive, not reactive, maintenance.

Renovations

There is one final note for the "Normal Operation" phase of a system, and that applies to subsequent space and/or system modifications. It can be safely assumed that space use and configuration will change many times before a building or mechanical system is replaced or comprehensively upgraded. These alterations must be approached with caution to insure that the original performance of the mechanical system is not sacrificed.

The mechanical system will need to be modified to accommodate most architectural changes, but this fact is often neglected by the people planning a "small" renovation. Mechanical equipment is usually out of sight and, therefore, out of mind. This problem is most likely to be avoided when there is a Mechanical Systems Coordinator looking after the equipment. The MSC should be consulted to determine what affect the proposed changes will have on the system, how the system can serve the new spaces, and whether or not further expertise, e.g., design engineers, will be required for the renovation.

CONCLUSION

In summary, the people who have the greatest interest in the final outcome of any project are those who will use and depend on the new or renovated building and mechanical systems. It is advantageous for them to be involved in the design process, and to become familiar with the construction, start-up/commissioning, and normal operation processes inherent in all building projects. It may not be the institution's responsibility to perform all these tasks, but it is a good idea to be cognizant of how an individual project is progressing and to ask the right questions at the right time as "reminders" to those who do have responsibility.

The tasks discussed here apply to all building projects, not just to major new construction. They should be repeated for each subsequent renovation, no matter how small. In fact, it may be even more important that the institution be actively involved in "minor" renovations, because the smaller jobs are the ones most likely to be taken less seriously by designers and contractors.

While each building project is unique, with its own set of problems and constraints, this paper's suggestions are universal in their application. It is important to understand the construction process and what you have a right to expect as a future occupant of the space. Armed with this information, any institution can intelligently insist that systems be installed and operated as designed.

SOURCES OF EQUIPMENT AND SERVICES

Sources of equipment will depend on the specifications and experience of the designer. It is important to confirm the continued availability of local service and support for equipment components. The length of time a company has been in business, their rating with the Better Business Bureau, and designer and contractor experience with the product should provide some guides. It is always a good idea to ask for references to other institutions where similar equipment or systems have been installed, and to follow up with a call to these institutions.

Another institution with experience in a similar project can be asked to recommend a third party for verification and testing. A regional museum association or an experienced conservator may also have good suggestions.

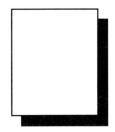

Northeast Document
Conservation Center
100 Brickstone Square
Andover, MA 01810-1494
www.nedcc.org
Tel: (978) 470-1010
Fax: (978) 475-6021

PROTECTION FROM LIGHT DAMAGE

by Beth Lindblom Patkus
Preservation Consultant
Walpole, MA

INTRODUCTION

Light is a common cause of damage to library and archival collections. Paper, bindings, and media (inks, photographic emulsions, dyes, and pigments, and many other materials used to create words and images) are particularly sensitive to light. Light damage manifests itself in many ways. Light can cause paper to bleach, yellow, or darken, and it can weaken and embrittle the cellulose fibers that make up paper. It can cause media and dyes used in documents, photographs, and art works to fade or change color. Most of us recognize fading as a form of light damage, but this is only a superficial indication of deterioration that extends to the physical and chemical structure of collections. Light provides energy to fuel the chemical reactions that produce deterioration. While most people know that ultraviolet (UV) light is destructive, it is important to remember that all light causes damage. Light damage is cumulative and irreversible.

THE NATURE OF LIGHT

Light is a form of electromagnetic energy called radiation. The radiation that we know from medicine and nuclear science is energy at wavelengths far shorter than the light spectrum; radio waves are much longer wavelengths. Visible light, the form of radiation that we can see, falls near the center of the electromagnetic spectrum.

The visible spectrum runs from about 400 nanometers (nm, the measurement applied to radiation) to about 700 nm. Ultraviolet wavelengths lie just below the short end of the visible spectrum (below 400 nm). The wavelengths of infrared light lie just above the long end but our eyes cannot see them. This type of light also damages collections.

HOW DOES LIGHT DO ITS DAMAGE?

Light energy is absorbed by molecules within an object. This absorption of light energy can start many possible sequences of chemical reactions, all of which damage paper. The general term for this process is *photochemical deterioration*. Each molecule in an object requires a minimum amount of energy to begin a chemical reaction with other molecules. This is called its *activation energy*. Different types of molecules have different activation energies.

If the light energy from natural or artificial light equals or exceeds the activation energy of a particular molecule, the molecule is "excited," or made available for chemical reactions. Once this happens, the molecule may behave in a variety of ways. The excess energy may show up as heat or light; the energy may break bonds within the molecule (this will create smaller molecules and weaken the paper); the energy may cause a rearrangement of atoms within the molecule; or the

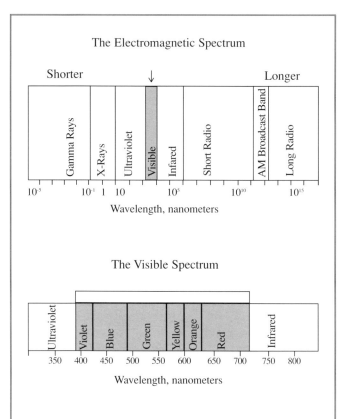

Figure 1. Electromagnetic and Visible Spectrums Taken from: Susan E. Weiss, "Proper Exhibition Lighting: Protecting Collections from Damage," Technology & Conservation (Spring 1977): 20.

energy may be transferred to another molecule. One of the primary photochemical reactions is oxidation, in which the "excited" molecule transfers its energy to an oxygen molecule, which then reacts with other molecules to initiate damaging chemical reactions. While the sequence of events can be extremely complex, the end result is always deterioration.

Shorter wavelengths of light (UV light) have a greater frequency (that is, they occur closer together) as well as more energy than longer wavelengths. This means that they bombard an object with more energy in a shorter time, and that their energy is likely to meet or exceed the required activation energy for many different types of molecules. Thus they cause photochemical deterioration to happen more quickly, and they are extremely damaging. As wavelengths become longer, toward the red end of the spectrum, they have less energy, less frequency, and reduced capacity to "excite" molecules.

It is important to remember, however, that even longer wavelengths of light damage paper and other materials. The energy absorbed from infrared light raises an object's temperature. This in turn increases the speed of damaging chemical reactions already occurring within the paper.

ULTRAVIOLET LIGHT VS. VISIBLE LIGHT

Since UV radiation is the most energetic and destructive form of light, we might assume that if UV light is eliminated, visible light is of minimal concern. This is not true; all wavelengths of light do significant damage.

In practical terms, UV light can be easily eliminated from exhibit, reading, and storage areas, since our eyes do not perceive it and will not miss it. Visible light is far more problematic, but it should be eliminated from storage areas as much as possible and carefully controlled in other areas.

SOURCES OF LIGHT

Light has two sources: natural and artificial. Libraries and archives should avoid natural light. Sunlight has a high percentage of ultraviolet. Daylight is also brighter and more intense, and therefore causes more damage, than most artificial light.

The two primary artificial light sources currently in use in libraries, museums, and archives are **incandescent** and **fluorescent** lamps. (The term "lamp" is used by architects and engineers to refer to the various types of light bulbs, rather than to the fixtures containing the bulbs.) Driven by the need for energy conservation and cost savings, manufacturers continue to refine lamp technologies to produce longer-lived lamps that consume less energy and provide better light. Compact fluorescent, tungsten-halogen, high intensity discharge (HID), and electrodeless lamps have all been developed in response to these concerns.

Conventional incandescent lamps produce light when an electric current is passed through a tungsten filament, heating it to about 2700 degrees Celsius. Incandescent lamps convert only a small percentage of this electricity into light; the rest becomes heat. Conventional incandescent lamps emit very little ultraviolet light and do not require UV filtering. Examples of conventional incandescent lamps include the ordinary household light bulb and a variety of lamps used for exhibition lighting, such as the Reflectorized (R), Ellipsoidal Reflectorized (ER), and Parabolic Aluminized Reflector (PAR) lamps.

Tungsten-halogen lamps (also called quartz lamps) are a variation on the traditional incandescent lamp; they contain halogen gas inside a quartz bulb, which allows the light to burn brighter and longer. These lamps emit significant UV light and do require filtering. Filters can be expensive and special housings designed to accept the UV filters may be necessary. Tungsten-halogen lamps are also used in exhibition lighting; examples include the Halogen PAR and the Mirrored-Reflector (MR) lamp.

Fluorescent lamps contain mercury vapor inside a glass lamp whose inside surface is painted with white fluorescent powder. When electricity is passed through the lamp (via a filament), the mercury vapor emits UV radiation which is absorbed by the fluorescent powder and re-emitted as visible light. Some UV light passes through most fluorescent lamps, however, so they are more damaging than incandescent lamps. The newest type of fluorescent is the compact fluorescent lamp; these are smaller, last longer, and have a more pleasant color than traditional fluorescents, and they can usually be used in incandescent sockets. These lamps must still be filtered, however.

Like fluorescents, **high intensity discharge (HID)** lamps contain a vapor inside a glass lamp coated with a fluorescent powder, but they are much more intense than normal fluorescents. There are two types. Mercury or metal halide HID lamps should not be used, since they have a dangerously strong UV output and filtering can be difficult. High-pressure sodium HID lamps are too intense for direct lighting (and do not provide good color rendering), but they can be used for indirect lighting (i.e., bouncing light off the ceiling) in large storage spaces with high ceilings. Sodium HID lamps have very low UV emissions, which can be further reduced by painting the ceiling with white titanium dioxide paint, a UV-absorber. Sodium HID lamps generate little heat, are efficient, and have low operating costs.[1]

Fiber optic lighting is an energy-efficient means of providing display lighting, particularly in exhibition cases. In a fiber optic system, light is transmitted from a light source through glass or acrylic fibers. The fibers do not conduct infrared or ultraviolet light, and unlike fluourescent lamps, fiber optic lighting does not cause buildup of heat within the case (provided the light source is mounted outside the case).

The **electrodeless lamp** is the newest type of light source. A normal incandescent lamp is subject to the eventual failure ("burn out") of its electrode, which is a piece of metal (usually tungsten) that is heated until it produces light. Electrodeless lamps produce light in other ways, including the use of radio frequencies to excite a coil or microwave energy directed at the element sulfur to produce visible light. Electrodeless lamps produce a lot of illumination, so thus far they have only been used as sources of ambient light (the light produced by one electrodeless sulfur lamp equals more than 250 standard 100 watt incandescent lamps). They are more energy efficient than HID lamps, and they provide excellent color rendition, low infrared and ultraviolet light, and long life. It is expected that this technology will eventually be miniaturized for use in smaller exhibit spaces and in exhibit cases.[2]

HOW MUCH LIGHT IS TOO MUCH?

Do we have to eliminate all UV light? Since all visible light cannot be eliminated, particularly in exhibition areas, how low should the levels be?

Control of ultraviolet light is relatively straightforward. The standard limit for UV for preservation is 75 µW/l (see below). Any light source with a higher UV emission must be filtered. Control of visible light is obviously more problematic. It is essential to understand that light damage is cumulative, and that lower levels of illumination will mean less damage over the long term. Another important concept in controlling visible light is the law of reciprocity. This says that limited exposure to a high-intensity light will produce the same amount of damage as long exposure to a low-intensity light. For example, exposure to 100 lux for 5 hours would cause the same amount of damage as exposure to 50 lux for 10 hours.

For many years, generally accepted recommendations in the preservation community have limited visible light levels for light-sensitive materials (including paper) to 55 lux (5 footcandles) or less and for less sensitive materials to 165 lux (15 footcandles) or less. In recent years, however, there has been some debate about these recommendations. Some have argued the importance of aesthetic concerns: older visitors need more light to see exhibited objects well, and any visitor will find that more fine detail is apparent and colors appear brighter as light levels increase. In addition, the assumption that all paper objects are equally sensitive to light has been challenged.[3] Scientists at the Canadian Conservation Institute (CCI) and others have begun to gather data on rates of light fading for specific media and colors in an effort to begin developing more specific guidelines based on the International Standards Organization (ISO) Blue Wool light fading standards (see "Practical Tips for Estimating Light Damage," below).

In the absence of universal guidelines, it is recommended that each institution establish its own limits on exhibition for its collections. Factors to consider include: the amount of time the lights are turned on in the exhibit space (this may be more than first thought, since lights are often turned on for housekeeping or other purposes when the exhibit is closed to the public); the sensitivity of the items or groups of items being exhibited; the desired lifespan of these items or groups of items; and the importance of aesthetic concerns in exhibition. Ultimately, every institution should decide on an acceptable upper limit of exposure (i.e., a certain number of lux hours per year), which may differ for different parts of an institution's collection. Publications by CCI and the exhibition policy developed by the Montreal Museum of Fine Arts for works of art on paper may be helpful in estimating the sensitivity of various types of paper-based collections.[4]

Using the law of reciprocity, an exhibition limit can be achieved in different ways; for example, a limit of 50,000 lux hours per year could be achieved by keeping the lights on for

10 hours per day, either at 100 lux for 50 days or at 50 lux for 100 days. It is important to remember that even with such guidelines, some fading will occur. The goal is to achieve a workable compromise between exhibition and preservation.

HOW DO YOU MEASURE LIGHT LEVELS?

Visible light levels are measured in lux ("lumens per square meter") or footcandles. One footcandle equals about 11 lux. A light meter measures the level of visible light. The meter should be placed at the spot where you want to take a reading (for example, close to the surface of an object being exhibited). The meter should face the light just as the object does in order for it to get an accurate reading.

If you do not have access to a light meter, you can measure the approximate lux level using a 35 mm single-lens reflex camera with a built-in light meter, using the following procedure.

- Place a sheet of white board measuring 30 cm x 40 cm at the position where the light level is to be measured and at the same angle as the artifacts.
- Set the camera ASA/ISO rating at 800. Set the shutter speed at 1/60 second.
- Aim the camera at the white board and position it just close enough so that the field of view is filled by the board. Be sure not to cast a shadow on the board.
- Adjust the aperture until the light meter indicates a correct exposure, and note the aperture setting. The approximate level of light in lux at the white board relates to the aperture setting as follows:

F4	represents	50 lx
F5.6	represents	100 lx
F8	represents	200 lx
F11	represents	400 lx
F16	represents	800 lx[5]

A light meter measures only the level of illumination; a UV meter must be used to measure the UV component of light. UV light is measured in microwatts per lumen (SYMBOL -µW/l). The most common UV meter is the Crawford monitor, but all UV meters will measure the proportion of ultraviolet in visible light. Again, this should not exceed 75 µW/l.

A word of caution regarding UV meters: some older UV meters (costing from $500 to $1500) may not be adequately sensitive to UV light; they may indicate that levels are safe when in reality they are not. Newer more expensive ($3000 to $5000) meters are designed to measure UV levels more accurately.[6]

PRACTICAL TIPS FOR ESTIMATING LIGHT DAMAGE

It is possible to estimate the damage that might result to an artifact from particular intensities of light and lengths of exposure. This can be done using the ISO's Blue Wool standards cards, available from TALAS, and the light-damage slide rule, available from the Canadian Conservation Institute (CCI).

The Blue Wool standards can clearly demonstrate the destructive powers of light. These cards provide a standard against which subsequent fading can be judged, and therefore can be used to convince skeptics that light really is a problem. Each Blue Wool standard contains eight samples of blue-dyed wool. Sample 1 is extremely light sensitive, while sample 8 is the most stable dye available (although not permanent). Sample 2 takes twice as long to fade as sample 1, sample 3 takes twice as long as sample 2, and so forth.

To demonstrate the degree of fading caused by the intensity of light in a particular location, cover half of the card with a light-blocking material to protect it completely from light damage. Write the date on the card, and set it out in the desired location. Check the card periodically (every couple of weeks) to determine how long it takes for the various samples to fade. Since the sensitivity of the first few samples on the card corresponds to light sensitive materials such as paper and textiles, the results will give you a general idea of the amount of damage you might expect if materials were exhibited for the same period of time at the current light level in that location.

CCI's light-damage slide rule is a sliding plastic scale that aligns projected light types, light levels, and exposure times to predict the fading of a blue wool card under these conditions. For example, it shows that an artifact displayed at 150 lux for 100 years will fade at the same rate as an artifact displayed at 5000 lux for 3 years. The above-mentioned exposure of 150 lux for 100 years would cause significant fading of Blue Wool standard 4 and below. The slide rule also compares damage that would be caused by UV-filtered and unfiltered light. In the above case, standards 4 and below are noticeably more faded when exposed to unfiltered light.

The tools described above can be useful in demonstrating the effect your lighting choices will have on exhibited materials. In most cases a general correlation between the sensitivity of the artifact and the Blue Wool standard's scale will be sufficient to allow informed decision-making. If more detail is needed, the publications from CCI and the Montreal Museum of Fine Arts cited above may be helpful.

CONTROLLING ULTRAVIOLET LIGHT

UV light can be filtered by passing the light through a material that is transparent to visible light but opaque to ultraviolet. The ideal filter would prevent all wavelengths of UV below 400 nm from passing through, but this is difficult to achieve. There are many products available that do the job adequately. In setting priorities, it is usually important to deal with natural light first, and then fluorescent light.

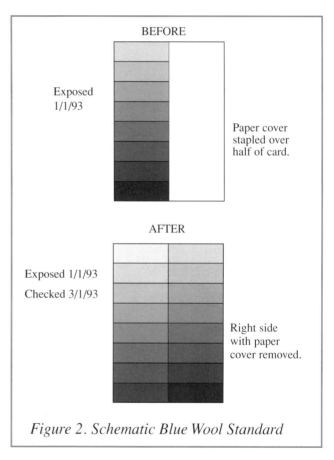

Figure 2. Schematic Blue Wool Standard

Ultraviolet-filtering plastic is available to cover windows and skylights. It must cover the surface completely so that all light passes through it. This plastic is available either in self-supporting sheets of acrylic or in thin film (usually acetate) that is cut to shape with a knife or scissors and adhered to the glass. The acrylic panels can be used in place of window glass (if fire regulations allow), mounted as secondary glazing on existing windows, or hung inside the window from hooks (the panel must be cut larger than the window glass, so that all light passes through it). Tinted panels are also available, to reduce overall light.

Varnishes that absorb ultraviolet light are also available. A supplier applies these coatings on window glass with a special tool. Currently, varnish is not recommended; it is very difficult to apply uniformly, and it deteriorates over time. Plastic is more convenient, lasts longer, and does the job better.

UV filters are normally needed on fluorescent lamps. Filters are available in the form of soft, thin plastic sleeves and hard plastic tubes. The tubes are generally several times more expensive, and do not provide any more protection than thin sleeves. If hard tubes do not fit the lamp exactly, unfiltered light can slip by at uncovered ends. The thin plastic sleeves should also be properly sized for the lamp. If necessary, two sleeves can be overlapped to extend the length of a single sleeve. Whatever type of filter is used, maintenance staff must be trained to transfer the filter when they change lamps.

If the fluorescent lights are housed in recesses that are completely covered by a plastic shield, however, UV light levels should be tested before an institution spends money on UV-filtering sleeves. Experience has shown that these plastic shields often provide UV filtering, reducing UV levels to 10-20 µW/l.

Some fluorescent lamps produce significantly less UV than others. To insure maximum protection, one suggestion is to use lamps that produce relatively low UV in combination with UV filters. This will further reduce UV levels, reduce damage caused by improper installation or failure to replace filters, and extend the lives of the filters themselves.[7] Some manufacturers now make fluorescent lamps with UV-filtering glass, but these can be much more expensive than standard lamps. Replacements must be kept on hand, and care must be taken not to replace a custom UV-filtering lamp with an ordinary one.

Another option available for protecting against UV light is the use of white paint containing titanium dioxide. While this method is not as effective, it will cut down on UV light significantly. Titanium dioxide paint absorbs ultraviolet light, and can be painted directly on windows or skylights, if they do not provide the only source of light.

HOW LONG DO UV FILTERS LAST?

At this time there is no definitive data to indicate how long UV filtering products retain their effectiveness. In a CCI Note published in 1984, the Canadian Conservation Institute reported that both soft plastic filtering sleeves and hard plastic filtering tubes retain their UV-absorbing properties for at least 10 years. UV-filtering window films may also have limited life-spans; some manufacturers quote a life of 5-15 years for these films.[8] In climates with intense sunlight these filters may not last as long.

The only conclusive way to determine the continued effectiveness of UV-filtering products is to measure the UV levels emitted using a UV monitor (see cautions on UV monitor accuracy given above). Since these monitors are expensive, smaller institutions should make arrangements to borrow one every few years from a nearby large museum or other institution.

CONTROLLING VISIBLE LIGHT

It would be ideal to keep collections sheltered from all light, but this is clearly impractical. Even collections stored away from light must sometimes be used. Often, in fact, storage and research areas cannot be separated. Materials must be exhibited, particularly in a museum setting. A difficult balance must be maintained between the desire to protect materials and the need to make them accessible. Any reduction of visible light reduces long-term damage. Storage areas that are not routinely occupied by staff or researchers should be kept dark; they should be windowless, or the windows should be blocked. Lights should be turned off in such areas except when needed. This can be done with timers, but at the very least staff should be trained to turn off the lights when the space is unoccupied. Occupancy sensors can also be installed that turn off lights when no movement is sensed in the area. Lighting should be incandescent (tungsten) rather than fluorescent wherever possible.

Many situations are not ideal and space is often at a premium. If you cannot keep an object out of the light, keep the light from reaching the object. Boxes from archival suppliers made by professional box-makers to fit the exact dimensions of individual objects are useful. While boxes will prevent damage from direct light exposure, it is uncertain whether they will protect objects from the fluctuations in temperature and humidity that may be caused by solar heating.

The specifics of determining guidelines for exhibition lighting of objects have been discussed above. All windows in exhibit areas should be covered with drapes, shades, or blinds, in addition to being filtered for UV. Skylights should be covered to block the sun. Light levels should be low, and materials should never be exposed to direct sunlight. Never display objects permanently unless they are expendable.

Exceptionally fragile and vulnerable objects should not be displayed, and research use should be limited. If materials must be exhibited, great care must be taken to minimize damage. Books that are opened for display should have the pages turned weekly so that one page is not constantly exposed. Photographic and photocopy facsimiles of objects should be used whenever possible for display and research.

Spotlights should never be trained directly on an object. Indirect and low lighting will spare the object, and it will also require less adjustment of the eye from areas of intense light to those of relative darkness, allowing the use of lamps with a lower wattage throughout exhibit spaces. A gradual diminution of light levels through a series of rooms may accustom viewers' eyes to lower exhibition light levels. Strategic placement of labels explaining the reason for low light levels can be used to educate patrons.

SUMMARY

All light contributes to the deterioration of library and archival collections by providing energy to fuel destructive chemical reactions within the paper. Light also damages bindings, photographic emulsions, and other media, including the inks, dyes, and pigments used in many library and archival materials. Institutions should follow the guidelines given above for measurement of light levels and control of light exposure. All sources of ultraviolet light illuminating collections should be filtered, and the exposure of collections to visible light should be strictly controlled.

NOTES

[1] William P. Lull, with the assistance of Paul N. Banks, *Conservation Environment Guidelines for Libraries and Archives* (Ottawa, ON: Canadian Council of Archives, 1995), pp. 44-45.

[2] See Frank Florentine, "The Next Generation of Lights: Electrodeless," in *WAAC Newsletter* 17:3 (September 1995), for more information and details on the use of electrodeless lamps at the Smithsonian Institution's Air and Space Museum.

[3] Stefan Michalski, "Towards Specific Lighting Guidelines," in proceedings of "Museum Exhibit Lighting—Beyond Edison: Lighting for the Next Century," a workshop presented by the National Park Service and the Washington Conservation Guild, March 6-8, 1996.

[4] See Stefan Michalski, "Towards Specific Lighting Guidelines"; "A Light Damage Slide Rule," *CCI Notes* 2/6, Canadian Conservation Institute, Ottawa (1989); and Karen M. Colby, "A Suggested Exhibition/Exposure Policy for Works of Art on Paper" (available at The Lighting Resource website: http://www.webcom.com/~lightsrc/policy1.html).

[5] Taken from "Using a Camera to Measure Light Levels," *CCI Notes* 2/5, (Ottawa: Canadian Conservation Institute, 1992).

[6] Lull, p. 19.

[7] Lull, p. 44.

SUGGESTED FURTHER READING

Anson, Gordon. "The Light Solution." *Museum News* (September/October 1993): 27.

Canadian Conservation Institute. *A Light Damage Slide Rule.* CCI Note No. 2/6. Ottawa: Canadian Conservation Institute, December 1988, 10 pp.

Canadian Conservation Institute. *Ultraviolet Filters for Fluorescent Lamps.* CCI Note No. 2/1. Ottawa: Canadian Conservation Institute, June 1983, 1 p.

Canadian Conservation Institute. *Using a Camera to Measure Light Levels.* CCI Note No. 2/5. Ottawa: Canadian Conservation Institute, 1992, 1 p.

Colby, Karen M. "A Suggested Exhibition/Exposure Policy for Works of Art on Paper." July 1993. Available at The Lighting Resource web site: http://www.webcom.com/~lightsrc/policy1.html.

Feller, Robert L. *The Deteriorating Effect of Light on Museum Objects.* Museum News Technical Supplement No. 3. Washington, DC: American Association of Museums, June 1964, 8 pp.

Florentine, Frank. "The Next Generation of Lights: Electrodeless," in *WAAC Newsletter* 17:3 (September 1995).

Lull, William P, with the assistance of Paul N. Banks. *Conservation Environment Guidelines for Libraries and Archives.* Ottawa, ON: Canadian Council of Archives, 1995. 102 pp.

Museum Exhibit Lighting, An Interdisciplinary Approach: Conservation, Design, and Technology. Proceedings of a workshop presented by the National Park Service and the American Institute for Conservation at the 1997 AIC Annual Meeting. Available from AIC, 1717 K St., NW, Suite 301, Washington, DC 20006; 202-452-9545.

Nicholson, Catherine. "What Exhibits Can Do to Your Collection." *Restaurator* 13 (1992): 95-113.

Thomson, Garry. *The Museum Environment.* 2nd edition. London and Boston: Butterworth in association with The International Institute for Conservation of Historic and Artistic Works, 1986, 308 pp.

SOURCES OF SUPPLIES

This list is not exhaustive, nor does it constitute an endorsement of the suppliers listed. We suggest that you obtain information from a number of vendors so that you can make comparisons of cost and assess the full range of available products.

A more complete list of suppliers is available from NEDCC. Consult the Technical Leaflets section of NEDCC's website at www.nedcc.org or contact NEDCC for the most up-to-date version in print.

3M Product Information Center
3M Center, Building 304-1-01
St. Paul, MN 55144-1000 U.S.A.
Toll Free: (800) 3M HELPS or (800) 364-3577
Telephone: (651) 737-6501
Fax: (800) 713-6329 or (651) 737-7117
E-mail: innovation@mmm.com
http://www.mmm.com
UV-filtering window film (call for local distributor)

Canadian Conservation Institute (CCI)
1030 Innes Road
Ottawa, Ontario K1A OC8 CANADA
Telephone: (613) 998-3721
Fax: (613) 998-4721
http://www.pch.gc.ca
Light-damage slide rule, CCI Notes and Technical Bulletins

Cole-Parmer
7425 North Oak Park Avenue
Niles, IL 60714-9930
Telephone: (800) 323-4340
http://www.cole-parmer.com
Light meters - regular

The Cooke Corporation
600 Main Street
Tonawanda, NY 14150
Telephone: (716) 833-8274
Fax: (716) 836-2927
E-mail: sales@cookecorp.com
http://www.cookecorp.com
Light meters - regular

Gaylord Brothers
P. O. Box 4901
Syracuse, NY 13221-4901
Toll Free: (800) 448-6160
Toll Free: (800) 428-3631 (Help Line) Toll Free Fax: (800) 272-3412
http://www.gaylord.com
UV filters, light meter - regular, light damage, slide rule

Light Impressions
439 Monroe Avenue
P.O. Box 940
Rochester, NY 14603-0940
Toll Free: (800) 828-6216
Telephone: (716) 271-8960
Fax: (800) 828-5539
http://www.lightimpressionsdirect.com
UV filters

Littlemore Scientific Engineering Co. - ELSEC
Railway Lane
Littlemore, Oxford
Oxfordshire, England
OX4 4PZ
Phone: 01865 747437
Fax: 01865 747780
E-mail: bilko@cix.compulink.co.uk
http://www.elsec.co.uk
UV meters

Rohm and Haas
Independence Mall West
Philadelphia, PA 19105
Telephone: (215) 592-3000
Fax: (215) 592-3377
http://www.rohmhaas.com
UV-filtering Plexiglas

Solar-Screen Company
53-11 105th Street
Corona, NY 11368
Telephone: (718) 592-8222
Fax: (718) 271-0891
UV-filtering products

Talas
568 Broadway
New York, NY 10012
Telephone: (212) 736-7744
Fax: (212) 219-0735
Blue Wool standard cards

Thermoplastic Processes, Inc.
1268 Valley Road
Stirling, NJ 07980
(908) 647-1000
Fax: (800) 874-3291
http://www.thermoplasticprocesses.com
Arm-a-Lite UV-filtering tubes (hard plastic)

University Products
517 Main Street
P. O. Box 101
Holyoke, MA 01041
Toll Free: (800) 628-1912
Telephone: (413) 532-3372
Toll Free Fax: (800) 532-9281
Fax: (413) 432-9281
E-mail: info@universityproducts.com
http://www.universityproducts.com
UV filters, light meters - regular and UV

Northeast Document
Conservation Center
100 Brickstone Square
Andover, MA 01810-1494
www.nedcc.org
Tel: (978) 470-1010
Fax: (978) 475-6021

PROTECTING PAPER AND BOOK COLLECTIONS DURING EXHIBITION

by Mary Todd Glaser
Director of Paper Conservation
Northeast Document Conservation Center

Exhibitions are educational and enjoyable. Exhibiting works of art or artifacts, especially the unique, the rare, and the wonderful, is an important part of the educational mission of many institutions. It is also an effective way of attracting the attention and support of the public. Exhibition is the chief activity of most museums. Many libraries and archives exhibit as well, albeit on a smaller scale than museums. Although exhibition can complicate or even compromise preservation efforts, measures can be taken to minimize risk or damage.

There are preservation considerations with all exhibits, even the most modest. Too often preservation issues are overlooked in favor of other priorities. It is essential that the planning of every exhibit include input from a staff member or consultant who is knowledgeable about preservation issues. The involvement of such a person can avoid costly mistakes and limit possible damage to the collection.

For sheet materials one especially effective strategy is to copy the originals and display the copies. This practice has become increasingly common, especially for photographs and documents. Laser color copiers make facsimile documents that are almost indistinguishable from originals, and high quality copying services are available in most areas. Copying can be used to improve photographic images. Digital scanning technology can copy a photograph and remove all blemishes and evidence of physical damage.

There are times, of course, when only the original can be exhibited. It must be protected from light, air, and touching by the public. Sealed frames or cases with preservation-quality components are essential as is control of light, temperature, and relative humidity (RH) in the exhibit area.

LIGHT

Light can be a serious problem for objects on display. Paper is one of the most light sensitive materials, as are certain other writing and drawing media. Light can cause darkening of paper and fading of media and book covers. Damage by light goes beyond visual alteration by attacking the physical structure of paper, causing weakening and embrittlement. Light also damages the emulsions of photographs.

All light is damaging. The higher the light levels, the greater the potential danger. Sources rich in ultraviolet (UV) radiation are especially hazardous. Because light damage is cumulative, even low levels can degrade paper if the exposure is long enough. Conservators therefore recommend that no valuable artifact be permanently displayed.

Natural Light (Daylight) Is Especially Harmful

Exposure to natural light is undesirable because of its intensity and high UV content. If there are windows in the exhibit area, they should be covered with blinds, shades, or curtains for as much of the day as possible. In addition, ultraviolet filters should also be installed to control this damaging component of light.

UV filters are available as plastic sheeting or as rigid panels. The sheeting, usually acetate film, can be cut with scissors and applied directly to windows or cases. Tinted UV films will reduce the intensity of the light as well. Although film is less expensive than rigid panels, it is less attractive and may be difficult to remove later on. At present it is not known how long UV-filtering films remain effective, although informal experiments suggest that they have limited life. The only way to determine if the film is still filtering is to measure the transmitted light with a UV meter (see below).

UV-filtering panels can be used in windows, cases, or frames. They are available in either glass or acrylic sheets. For several decades museums have used an acrylic, UF-3 Plexiglas made by Rohm and Haas. More recently other companies have introduced UV-filtering acrylics or glass. When choosing such glazing, check the product information to make certain the UV-filtering capacity is greater than 90%. Some acrylics and most types of glass filter little or no UV. Ordinary non-glare glass is not UV-filtering, although there are non-glare products with this feature.

Before using acrylic panels as window glazing, check that local fire regulations are not being violated. Filtering panels can also be used as secondary glazing on existing windows. If mounted inside in a manner similar to interior storm windows, filters give thermal control as well as UV filtration. If the budget does not permit this type of installation, hanging the sheets inside the windows from hooks is effective as long as the panels are larger than the window glass so that all light from outside is filtered.

White paint containing titanium dioxide on the walls and ceiling of a room will absorb a certain amount of ambient UV radiation. However, other measures to control UV are still necessary.

Artificial Light

Lighting in areas where paper materials are on exhibit must be maintained at low levels. In addition, lamps that give off little or no UV should be used.

- **Fluorescent Lighting.** Although fluorescent lamps are common in most institutions, they have decided disadvantages in exhibit areas. Fluorescents cannot be dimmed, and most emit UV radiation. There are many brands of fluorescent lamps, however, and they vary greatly in the amount of UV they produce, from 0.5% to 12%. Purchase those with low UV output, not more than 2% UV.[1] For added safety, cover all fluorescent tubes with UV-filtering plastic sleeves. Be sure the sleeves are long enough to cover the ends of the tube, where much of the UV is emitted.

- **Incandescent (Tungsten) Lamps.** Because these can be used with dimmers and because they give off little or no UV, incandescent lamps are suitable for exhibition. The ordinary household light bulb is an example of a tungsten lamp. This type of light does generate heat, however, and must be placed well away from objects, never inside cases. Tungsten sources should be equipped with dimmers.

- **Tungsten-Halogen (Quartz-Iodine) Lamps.** These current favorites in the museum community can be dimmed but give off significant amounts of UV. Tungsten-Halogen sources should be used with the UV filters made for this type of lamp.

It cannot be stressed enough that illumination must always be kept as low as possible. Good lighting designers know how to light exhibits effectively with low to moderate levels of light. If lighting is diffused rather than direct, for example, less light is needed. Visual interest can be created without subjecting a collection to intense spot lights.

Lights should be turned off when visitors are not in the room. Some museums have lights that do this automatically. Other institutions put cloth covers on cases containing especially valuable or light-sensitive objects.

How Much Light is Allowed? The Lux Hour Concept

If all light is potentially damaging and the damage is cumulative, any exposure is harmful, especially to a highly light-sensitive material like paper. Because works of art and cultural artifacts are meant to be seen, however, guidelines for limiting exposure are desirable. A limit of 50,000 lux hours has been suggested for very light-sensitive materials.[2] Lux hours or lx·h are determined by multiplying the level of light, numerically expressed in lux, by the hours the object is exposed to that light (light can also be measured in footcandles or lumens; one footcandle [lumen] equals approximately 11 lux). If an object is lit for 10 hours a day at 50 lux, the limit of 50,000 lx·h is reached in 100 days (50 lux x 10 hours x 100 days). At 100 lux the limit is reached in 50 days. The higher the light level the shorter the exposure time. Some institutions have started to keep exposure histories for their most valuable or light-sensitive materials.

Rooms lit at 50 lux may seem very dim, especially to someone who comes inside on a bright day. The eye does adjust, however, and good lighting design helps a great deal. A sign explaining the reason for the low levels usually mollifies the public. Light is measured with a light meter. Lacking this, the built-in meter of a single-lens reflex camera can be used. UV meters measure the proportion of UV in visible light, expressing it in microwatts per lumen. Paper collections should never be exposed to UV in amounts exceeding 75 microwatts per lumen. If your institution does not have access to a dependable UV meter (they are expensive), you can safely assume that all daylight and most fluorescent or tungsten-halogen sources will contain unacceptable amounts of UV. Such light sources should have UV filters.

CASES

Paper materials must always be displayed in cases or in frames. If made of appropriate materials and properly sealed, cases and picture frames will protect against a variety of airborne hazards as well as physical contact by the public. These enclosures also reduce the effects of temperature and humidity fluctuations on a daily if not on a long-term basis.

Although it is not possible to prevent moisture from entering cases during seasonal periods of high humidity, silica gel will help stabilize the RH in a case if the latter is well sealed. Silica gel is a crystalline material that acts as a desiccant. In exhibit cases, frames, packing crates, and other micro-environments silica gel can be used also as a buffer to maintain a specified RH. Prior to use, the gel must be conditioned to the desired relative humidity (to do this, follow the supplier's instructions). Once conditioned, the gel will absorb moisture when the RH is too high and will release moisture when the micro-environment becomes too dry.

There are two types of silica gel. Regular silica gel is white, and the indicating type is blue. Indicating gel is especially useful because it shows when it has reached the saturation point by turning a dull pink. Indicating gel is much more expensive, but you can save money by purchasing a small amount of indicating gel and mixing it with the regular type. Once saturated, silica gel can be dried and reused by heating it in a 300 degrees F oven for three hours.

The proper quantity of silica gel for the volume of the case must be carefully calculated.[3] Contact the supplier for guidance on this. Art-Sorb and Arten are high performance silica gels that can absorb five times as much as regular silica gel. These come in the form of sheets, beads, fiber cassettes filled with beads, or tiles. These can be inserted into frames and small boxes as well as into cases.

As useful as these products are, controlling the environment in the room as a whole with 24-hour air conditioning and dehumidification is the most effective way of protecting an exhibit from seasonal changes.

Materials used for case construction should be chosen carefully. Woods, wood sealants, paints, adhesives, gasketing materials, and display fabrics can give off harmful gaseous emissions. These volatiles, often acidic in nature, build up in sealed cases. Although they cause obvious damage to materials like silver or lead, these gases can attack paper in subtle ways. Although some conservators recommend ventilation holes in cases, free air exchange would subject the contents to dust and external pollutants. High-tech cases have been developed, including some with filtered air exchange, but at this stage they are beyond the means of most institutions. It is more practical to use cases built with safe materials. If your institution has inappropriate cases and lacks the resources to replace them, the cases should be lined with a barrier material as described below. Sealing the wood as well will give added protection.

Wood and Wood Products

Wood is often used for cases because it is readily available, easy to work with, and attractive. Resulting degradation products, however, pose a great danger for paper. Although there is wide variation, all wood, even old and well seasoned examples, generate volatile acids.

If the budget allows, one can avoid use of wood in new case interiors. Anodized aluminum or properly manufactured coated steel frames are available, but are expensive. Cases can also be designed without a wooden floor, with the frame on the outside of a Plexiglas or glass box.

If wood must be used, choose a type that is comparatively low in harmful emissions. Certain softwoods, notably poplar and basswood, are recommended. One hardwood, mahogany, is also low in volatiles, but true African mahogany must be used. Oak, frequently found in older cases, is the most acidic wood and potentially the most dangerous.

Because they are both strong and economical, plywood and other wood composites are frequently used for case construction. These can be even more problematic than solid wood because they may be fabricated with adhesives or resins containing formaldehyde, which oxidizes to formic acid. Of the composites, exterior plywood bonded with exterior glue, a phenol formaldehyde adhesive, is recommended.[4] Phenol formaldehyde is more stable (off-gasses less) than urea formaldehyde, which is common in wood composite products. A particle board that does not give off formaldehyde, such as Medite II, is also acceptable[5] as are MDO (Medium Density Overlay) and HDO (High Density Overlay), plywood signboards faced with Kraft paper. The American Plywood Association (APA), which creates standards and specifications for the industry, endorses only products bonded with phenol formaldehyde resins,[6] and these bear the APA stamp.

Most important, collection materials should never be placed in direct contact with wood, and all wood surfaces in both new and old cases should be covered with appropriate barrier materials. This protection is especially important with cases made of wood composites or oak.

Barrier Materials

Barrier materials can be active or passive. Passive barriers that are chemically stable and relatively impermeable include polyester film (e.g., Mylar), 4-ply 100% ragboard, and polyethylene foam sheeting (e.g. Ethafoam or Volara). Marvelseal, an adhesive-free laminate of aluminum foil, polyethylene, and polypropylene, is especially recommended because it is the one product that is totally impermeable to gases and moisture. In addition, Marvelseal is a flexible sheet that can bend and wrap.

Active barriers are relatively new. These "scavengers" react chemically with polluting gases, trapping them and removing them from the enclosure. A well known example is MicroChamber, which is available as board or sheets and is being used for storage containers. The active ingredients in MicroChamber products are activated carbon and zeolites. Because these scavenger products are fairly new, little is known about their long-term effectiveness. It is possible they could get used up in time. Such products have great possibilities and bear watching.

Barriers should cover the sides of cases as well as the floor. They can be attached to the sides with Scotch brand #415 double-sided tape (made by 3M). Marvelseal is heat sensitive on one side and can be ironed onto many wood surfaces.

Sealants and Paints

Before the barrier material is installed, sealing the wood will further reduce gaseous emissions. One must choose a sealant that does not give off problematic volatiles of its own. In general, avoid oil-based products. The coatings currently favored by conservators are moisture-borne polyurethanes (not the more common oil-based types) and two-part epoxy sealants. Not all water-based polyurethanes are safe, however, and formulas may change. It is best to check with a preservation professional for the name of the polyurethane currently being recommended. Should you want to test the products yourself, a simple test requiring no special equipment is found in the NEDCC leaflet, "Storage Furniture: A Brief Review of Current Options."

When using a sealant, allow at least three weeks for it to air after application. Proper safety precautions must be taken during application and drying.

If the case is to be painted, use acrylic or latex paint, not oil. Do not use acrylic or latex paints as sealers because they are too porous to seal well. The best paint for that purpose is a two-part epoxy.[7] Two-part epoxy paints and sealants have to be mixed carefully, however, according to the manufacturer's instructions. An incorrect ratio of hardener to adhesive produces an unstable paint.

Cloth, Gaskets, and Adhesives in Cases

Other case components such as fabric linings, adhesives, and the gaskets used to seal the case must also be chosen with care. Fabrics made of silk are acidic and those made of wool emit sulphur compounds and are therefore not recommended. Undyed cotton, linen, polyester, or cotton-polyester blends are acceptable. All fabrics should be washed before use to remove any sizing. Fabrics may also be purchased from a provider that guarantees no additives. If it is necessary to use a dyed fabric, and the wash water shows color, wash it until the dye stops running. As an added precaution, allow no object to come in direct contact with the fabric.

For gaskets, acrylic or Teflon should be used rather than rubber. The best adhesives for use in cases are acrylics or hot-melt glues rather than protein glues or cellulose nitrate. For attaching linings, Scotch #415 tape is preferred over other commercial tapes.

If the exhibition time is limited (as it should be), do all case components have to be absolutely emission free? Can any of the volatiles be tolerated for short periods? In what amounts can they be tolerated and for how long? Until we know the answers to these questions, it is best to be safe and use proven materials, even for such minor case components as gasketing and adhesives.

PLACEMENT WITHIN CASES

Sheet Materials

If the case is well sealed, objects inside need not be glazed or otherwise covered. Unless they are matted or encapsulated, paper materials should be attached to pieces of ragboard or other archival material cut slightly larger than the size of the sheet. This mount not only adds another barrier between object and case but provides support when the object is moved. For appearance, exhibit designers often specify that the edges of the object be flush with the edges of the ragboard mount. A larger mount, however, gives better protection to the sheet. In the design of an exhibit, preservation concerns such as this must be addressed.

Paper sheet materials should be attached securely to the mounts. Sheets may be mounted in window mats (see below) or onto ragboard backings. They can be hinged or attached with corner supports. Edge strips may be used if the edges of the object are covered by a mat. Strips and corner supports are becoming popular because adhesive need not be applied to the object. For non-adhesive mounting, commercially available archival paper or plastic (polyester) photo corners will work on small documents or photographs. Most artifacts, however, require the more substantial support of corner strips. These can be made of polyester film or woven polyester. Finely woven polyester is both transparent and matte and therefore less conspicuous than polyester film.[8] For further information about mounting systems, see the NEDCC leaflets, "Mats and Frames for Art and Artifacts on Paper" and "How To Do Your Own Matting and Hinging."

Objects may also be encapsulated in polyester film, which will protect and support the object during and after the exhibit. Research at the Library of Congress, however, shows that acidic papers deteriorate more rapidly within polyester envelopes and other closed systems. Since almost all old, untreated papers are acidic to some extent, they should be professionally deacidified or at least washed prior to encapsulation. If such treatment is not possible, an alkaline sheet inserted behind the object will slow the acid degradation.

A potential problem with encapsulation is slippage. If positioned vertically, large or heavy objects encapsulated in enclosures with double-sided tape may slip and become embedded in the tape seal. When possible, encapsulation should be done with ultrasonic or heat seals, which are also more attractive.

If unframed artifacts are displayed vertically, a safe and visually acceptable method of securing them must be found. Some institutions use hot-melt adhesives to attach ragboard mounts to vertical surfaces. These can be used in small amounts, and they hold well. Like other materials, however, they must be chosen with care and applied only to the back of the mount. Investigations by the Canadian Conservation Institute indicate that the ethylene vinyl acetate-based type of hot-melt adhesives that are clear or whitish are the least problematic, such as Black and Decker's Thermo Grip Hot Melt Glue GS-14.[9]

Books

Books and pamphlets have their own special exhibition requirements. Volumes should be displayed horizontally or at a gentle angle. It is especially important that books not be propped upright as that can cause the volume to warp or weaken its binding. When ordering or designing exhibition cases for books, specify types that allow horizontal display.

If a volume is shown open, it should be supported so that the binding is not under strain. An open book must never be laid out flat (at a 180° angle). Open it only as much as its binding will comfortably allow. Because books differ in this respect, book cradles custom-made to fit each volume are recommended. Such cradles can be ordered from mount makers or made in-house; instructions are available in the conservation literature. Cradles should always be large enough to support the whole book. If the pages do not remain open naturally, a strip of polyester film can be placed around each side of the open book. The strip can be closed with double-sided tape. Commercially-made molded acrylic cradles or wedges, available in different sizes and angles from conservation suppliers, offer an alternative to custom cradles. At the very least, supports can be made with folded museum board or polyethylene foam wedges.

Turning the pages every few days will protect the text from long-term exposure to light. If a title page must be displayed long term, consider using a copy. Even with page turning, periods of exhibit should be limited. Keeping a book open for long periods can damage its structure.

Although showing a volume closed is less stressful to the book, remember that most book cover materials can be damaged by long-term light exposure. Even closed volumes should be shown for limited periods with low light levels.

FRAMING

Framing plays an important role in exhibition. Use of stable framing and mounting materials is especially important since the objects may remain in the frames after the exhibition is over.

Glazing is a must with artifacts on paper. The glazing should not come in contact with the object. Ultraviolet-filtering glazing is recommended especially if the room has sources of UV radiation. Note, however, that acrylics are not always appropriate for use in frames since these plastics carry a static charge that can dislodge pastel and other friable media. In such cases, ultraviolet-filtering glass can be used.

The mounting materials inside the frame must adhere to conservation standards. Conservators recommend use of pH-neutral or slightly alkaline (buffered) mats or mounts. Hinges or the non-adhesive systems described in the NEDCC leaflets cited above should be used to attach the objects to the mount. If hinges are used, a high-quality, strong paper such as Japanese kozo must be used with an appropriate permanent, non-staining adhesive such as starch-based paste. Further information is given in the leaflets.

Emissions from wooden frames can damage the edges of paper objects. One frequently encounters "burned" edges on old prints or other artifacts that have been framed for many years. Visible damage seems not to occur if the object is an inch or more away from the wood. If for historical reasons it is necessary to keep an artifact in its original frame and the sheet extends to the wood, line the wood with strips of Marvelseal, polyester film, or ragboard. Sometimes Marvelseal can be ironed onto the frame rabbet with a small tacking iron. Unless the artifactual value of the frame prohibits alteration, the rabbet can be enlarged slightly with a router. If this is done, the inside of the frame should still be sealed and lined.

The back of the frame should contain backing layers of archival cardboard that are thick or dense enough to protect the object. Frames should be well sealed and hung securely. Avoid hanging items in damp areas such as on uninsulated outside walls, which can be problematic in winter or during periods of high humidity. If it is necessary to exhibit on an outside wall, a moisture barrier of polyester film or Marvelseal can be inserted between the backing layers or over the back of the frame. The frame should be deep enough so that its back is recessed, allowing a space for air circulation between the frame and the wall. Frames can also be held away from the wall slightly by small rubber bumpers or by push pins attached to the reverse of the frame.

EXHIBITION WITHOUT CASES OR FRAMES

Any object made of paper must be protected from airborne particulates and pollutants and from the fingers of visitors. Some institutions, however, may lack the resources to purchase cases or frames especially for large or complex paper objects that would be costly to frame and are too large for the available cases. If there is no other solution and if the objects are not of great value, they may be encapsulated and mounted on walls temporarily. Note that such display creates a greater risk for damage and theft, and the object is more vulnerable to adverse environmental conditions. Once encapsulated, the objects can be attached to an archival board with double-sided tape (Scotch brand #415) and the board securely fastened to the wall. If the encapsulation is sealed with double-sided tape, the object should be watched and taken down if it appears to be slipping toward the tape at the bottom edge. If the object has not been deacidified or encapsulated with alkaline paper behind, it should be removed from the envelope immediately after exhibition.

LOANS

Lending objects from the collections is a standard practice for many institutions. Although loans promote the collection and the institution, exhibition at remote sites understandably involves additional risk. Potential dangers can be minimized, however, with an appropriate loan policy and procedures.

All lending institutions should establish a formal policy governing loans for exhibition. A written summary of your institution's loan policy would be helpful in negotiations with prospective borrowers.

It is important to establish well in advance that conditions at the borrowing institution are reasonably safe. A visit to the site is recommended if possible. It is the responsibility of the borrower to submit a loan agreement and a facility report. The lender should review these and negotiate amendments as necessary. There is a standard facility report form that was adopted by the Registrars Committee of the American Association of Museums (AAM) in 1988. This 21-page questionnaire, available from the AAM, covers all aspects of an institution's operation that could affect exhibition safety: security (fire and theft), light levels, case materials, environmental controls in the building as a whole, shipping and receiving facilities, and personnel and insurance coverage.

When shipping is necessary, it goes without saying that objects must be well packed and a reliable shipper must be used. Framed materials should be glazed with acrylic rather than glass. If the framing can be done at your institution prior to the loan, an additional measure of control is gained.

STANDARDS FOR EXHIBITION

A committee of the National Information Standards Organization (NISO) has spent several years developing standards for exhibition of library and archival materials. The report of this committee will be available, probably in 1999, and will address criteria such as maximum permissible light exposure, relative humidity, temperature, and pollutants. It will also deal with materials for case construction. For more information, contact NISO Committee MM, Cathy Henderson, Chair, HRHRC, PO Drawer 7219, University of Texas at Austin, Austin, Texas 78713.

FINALLY, INVOLVE THE CONSERVATORS

Do not ignore the risks of exhibiting paper and books. A conservator or other collections-care professional should be involved with the exhibit from the earliest stages of planning. Preservation concerns must not be overlooked in favor of other priorities such as exhibit design.

In collections-holding institutions an ongoing relationship with a preservation professional has become a necessity. If the staff of an institution does not include a specialist on collections care, such a person should be consulted on a regular basis. The field of collections care is changing rapidly as scientific investigation uncovers new information about materials and the mechanisms of deterioration. New products are being introduced and existing products are subject to change. Information in print can become obsolete in a short time. Because a preservation professional is best able to keep up with changes in this increasingly complex field, an ongoing relationship with such a person is essential for responsible collections care.

NOTES

[1] William P. Lull, "Selecting Fluorescent Lamps for UV Output," *Abbey Newsletter* 16.4 (August 1992), pp. 54-55.

[2] Catherine Nicholson, "What Exhibits Can Do To Your Collection," *Restaurator* 13.3 (1993), p. 103.

[3] Barbara Appelbaum, *Guide to Environmental Protection of Collections* (Madison, CT: Sound View Press 1991), pp. 43-47.

[4] Pamela Hatchfield, Museum of Fine Arts, Boston. Personal communication.

[5] Robert Herskovitz, Minnesota Historical Society. Personal communication. P. Hatchfield.

[6] John A. Emery, *Formaldehyde Release from APA Trademarked Structural Panels* (Tacoma, WA: American Plywood Association, 1989).

[7] P. Hatchfield.

[8] Kathy Ludwig, National Archives and Records Administration. Personal communication.

[9] R. Scott Williams, Canadian Conservation Institute. Personal communication. R. Herskovitz.

SUGGESTED FURTHER READING

Blaser, Linda. "Construction of Plexiglas Cradles." *The Book and Paper Group Annual.* Washington, DC: American Institute for Conservation of Historic and Artistic Works, 1996, pp. 3-23.

Craddock, Anne Brooke. "Construction Materials for Storage and Exhibition." In *Conservation Concerns: A Guide for Collectors and Curators.* K. Bachmann, ed. Washington: Smithsonian Institution, 1992, pp. 23-28.

Hatchfield, Pamela. "Choosing Materials for Museum Storage." In *Storage of Natural History Collections: Basic Concepts,* Carolyn L. Rose and Catherine A. Hawks, eds. Pittsburgh, PA: Society for the Preservation of Natural History Collections, 1994.

Hatchfield, Pamela, and Jane Carpenter. *Formaldehyde: How Great is the Danger to Museum Collections?* Cambridge, MA: Center for Conservation and Technical Studies, Harvard University Art Museums, 1987, 44 pp.

Lull, William P., with the assistance of Paul N. Banks. *Conservation Environmental Guidelines for Libraries and Archives.* Albany, NY: New York State Library Division of Library Development, 1990, 87 pp.

Lull, William P., and Linda Merk. "Preservation Aspects of Display Lighting." *Electrical Consultant* (November-December 1980): 8, 9, 12, 14, 20, 39.

Nicholson, Catherine. "What Exhibits Can Do to Your Collection." *Restaurator* 13.3 (1993): 95-113.

Rhodes, Barbara. *Hold Everything!* New York, NY: Metropolitan Reference and Research Library Agency, 1990, 63 pp.

Smith, Merrily. *Matting and Hinging Works of Art on Paper.* Washington, DC: Library of Congress, 1981, 32 pp.

Thomson, Garry. *The Museum Environment.* Boston, MA: Butterworth, 1978, rev. 1986, 293 pp.

SOURCES OF SUPPLIES

This list is not exhaustive, nor does it constitute an endorsement of the suppliers listed. We suggest that you obtain information from a number of vendors so that you can make comparisons of cost and assess the full range of available products.

A more complete list of suppliers is available from NEDCC. Consult the Technical Leaflets section of NEDCC's website at www.nedcc.org or contact NEDCC for the most up-to-date version in print.

Art Preservation Services
315 East 89th Street
New York, NY 10128
Telephone: (212) 722-6300
Fax: (212) 427-6726
Environmental monitoring equipment for cases; silica gel

Archivart
7 Caesar Place
P.O. Box 428
Moonachie, NJ 07074
Telephone: (201) 804-8986
Fax: (201) 935-5964
Archival matting board

Benchmark
P.O. Box 214
Rosemont, NJ 08556
Telephone: (609) 397-1131
Fax: (609) 397-1159
Adjustable book cradles

Cole-Parmer
625 East Bunker Court
Vernon Hills, IL 60061-1844
Toll Free: (800) 323-4340
Telephone: (847) 247-2929
http://www.colepalmer.com
Light meters - regular

Conservation Resources International, Inc.
8000-H Forbes Place
Springfield, VA 22151
Toll Free: (800) 634-6932
Telephone: (703) 321-7730
Fax: (703) 321-0629
MicroChamber Products

J. Freeman Company
65 Tenean Street
Dorchester, MA 02122
Telephone: (617) 282-1150
Fax: (617) 282-7507
UF-3 Plexiglas

Gaylord Brothers
P.O. Box 4901
Syracuse, NY 13221-4901
Toll Free: (800) 448-6160
Toll Free: (800) 428-3631(Help Line)
Toll Free Fax: (800) 272-3412
http://www.gaylord.com
Book cradles, archival board

Light Impressions
439 Monroe Avenue
P.O. Box 940
Rochester, NY 14603-0940
Toll Free: (800) 828-6216
Telephone: (716) 271-8960
Toll Free Fax: (800) 828-5539
http://www.lightimpressionsdirect.com
Polyester film, archival board

Rohm and Haas
100 Independence Mall West
Philadelphia, PA 19106-2399
Telephone: (215) 592-3000
Fax: (215) 592-3377
UF-3 Plexiglas

Solar Screen Company
53-11 105th Street
Corona, NY 11368
Telephone: (718) 592-8222
Fax: (718) 271-0891
UV-filtering products

Testfabrics, Inc.
415 Delaware Avenue
P.O. Box 26
West Pittston, PA 18643
Telephone: (717) 603-0432
Fax: (717) 603-0433
E-mail: testfabrics@aol.com
Archival case fabrics

University Products
517 Main Street
P. O. Box 101
Holyoke, MA 01041
Toll Free: (800) 628-1912
Telephone: (413) 532-3372
Toll Free Fax: (800) 532-9281
Fax: (413) 432-9281
E-mail: info@universityproducts.com
http://www.universityproducts.com
Light meters - regular and UV; archival board; Marvelseal; book cradles

EMERGENCY MANAGEMENT

Northeast Document
Conservation Center

100 Brickstone Square
Andover, MA 01810-1494
www.nedcc.org
Tel: (978) 470-1010
Fax: (978) 475-6021

**TECHNICAL
LEAFLET**

**EMERGENCY
MANAGEMENT**

Section 3, Leaflet 1

PROTECTION FROM LOSS: WATER AND FIRE DAMAGE, BIOLOGICAL AGENTS, THEFT, AND VANDALISM

**by Sherelyn Ogden
Head of Conservation
Minnesota Historical Society**

Providing the best protection for collections from the most common causes of loss is a basic principle of preventive maintenance. The guidelines below will help immeasureably to secure collections. Consult the NEDCC technical leaflets listed at the end of this leaflet for more in-depth information on the topics introduced here.

WATER AND FIRE DAMAGE

The best way to deal with water and fire damage is to be prepared for it. Emergency preparedness is an important component of overall preservation planning. An emergency preparedness plan should cover all hazards, including water and fire, that pose a reasonable threat to collections. A systematically organized, formally written plan enables you to respond efficiently and quickly to an emergency, minimizing danger to staff and damage to collections and the building. Such a plan should cover preventive measures as well as recovery procedures. It should also include a training component. For example, all staff should be shown the location and taught the operation of shut-off valves for water-bearing pipes in buildings where collections are housed. The plan should be reviewed with staff regularly, at least annually. The plan should include lists of steps to follow if a disaster strikes and sources of assistance and supplies that may be needed. The importance of having the plan in written form cannot be overstated. In the excitement and confusion of an emergency, procedures and sources of help are easily forgotten. Information recorded in writing is much less likely to be overlooked. Much valuable time can be lost during emergencies if staff members are unfamiliar with recovery methods. Copies of the plan should be distributed to all personnel responsible for emergency prevention and recovery. Several copies of the plan should be stored off-site as well as in the building(s) where materials are housed.

Protection from water damage is essential to the preservation of library and archival materials. Even a minor water accident such as a leaky pipe can cause extensive and irreparable harm to collections. Several precautions can be taken. Roof coverings and flashings should be inspected regularly and repaired or replaced as needed. Gutters and drains should be cleaned frequently. Materials should never be stored under water pipes, steam pipes, lavatories, mechanical air-conditioning equipment, or other sources of water.

Materials should always be stored at least four inches above the floor, never directly on the floor. Storage in basements or in other areas where the threat of flooding is great should be avoided. If collections must be stored in areas where they are vulnerable to flooding, water-sensing alarms should be installed to insure quick detection of water.

Damage caused by fire can be even more serious than that caused by water. If collections survive at all, they are likely to be charred, covered with soot, brittle from exposure to high heat, wet from water used to extinguish the fire, moldy, and smelling of smoke. Several fire-suppression methods are available. Every institution should have at least one method in operation.

Although water mist systems, which are about to become available commercially, look promising, automatic sprinklers are now considered by most fire safety professionals, librarians, archivists, and conservators to be the best protection from fire for libraries and archives. The preferred type of sprinkler system depends upon the institution's objectives. Before making a choice, staff should consult an experienced fire safety engineer who is familiar with libraries and archives and with current developments in the field. Also, all relevant publications of the National Fire Protection Agency (NFPA), located in Quincy, Massachusetts, should be reviewed. Collections of very special value, which may be irretrievably damaged by water from a sprinkler system, have until recently often been protected by an automatic Halon gas suppression system. Halon contains chloroflurocarbons, however, and its use is now generally prohibited because of its damaging effect on the environment. Other methods of fire suppression for collections of special value are being developed. At the very least, every storage and use area should have several portable fire extinguishers of the ABC dry chemical type, and staff should be trained in their use. All fire-suppression systems should be regularly inspected and properly maintained. The manufacturer's specifications should be followed.

All repositories that house library and archival materials should be equipped throughout with a fire detection and alarm system wired directly to the local fire department or to another 24-hour monitor. Several types of detection and alarm systems are available. The most appropriate type for a particular institution depends upon several factors specific to that institution, such as the building's construction, its use, and its content value. A fire safety engineer who understands fire problems and the various detection and alarm systems available should be consulted. All detectors and alarms should be regularly tested and maintained according to the manufacturers' specifications.

Staff members should work with the local fire department to develop a fire safety program. All existing fire hazards should be eliminated. Regular fire inspections and drills should be held, and staff should be trained in evacuation procedures.

BIOLOGICAL AGENTS

The primary biological agents that cause damage to library and archival collections are mold, rodents, and insects, although dogs, cats, birds, and humans also harm materials. Mold damage can pose a serious threat, especially to institutions located in a hot, humid climate or near a large body of water where humidity is high. Mold spores are ever-present in the environment. Mold damage can be devastating, and measures should be taken to avoid its occurrence. The most important measures are maintaining proper levels of temperature and relative humidity, good circulation of air, and clean, clutter-free storage areas. Ideally temperature should never go above 70°F or relative humidity above 50%. The higher the temperature and humidity, the greater the risk of mold. If a water-related emergency occurs, such as a flood or fire, wet materials should be dealt with immediately before mold develops.

Once mold appears, the affected items should be isolated from the collection. Gloves and a respirator should be worn when handling moldy materials. The items should be dried thoroughly and, once they are dry, the mold should be removed from them. A conservator should be contacted for advice on how best to do this given the particular circumstances.

Library and archival materials are appetizing to rodents and insects, and all possible steps should be taken to control them. They are attracted by clutter and food remains. Clutter, dust, and dirt should not be allowed to accumulate, and storage areas should be kept clean at all times. Eating and drinking should be prohibited in buildings containing collections, especially in storage areas. Staff members should eat only in a staff room that is located as far away from collections as possible. All garbage receptacles containing food should be removed from buildings every day.

High temperature and, in particular, high relative humidity also encourage rodent and insect activity so these should be controlled. Windows, doors, and vents should be kept closed as much as possible because insects enter through these. Buildings should be well maintained because cracks or breaks in the building fabric are another point of entry. Grass and plantings should be trimmed back at least 18 inches from any building that houses collections. If possible all materials entering the building should be checked for rodents and especially insects. This includes new items for the collection, items being returned after a loan, and all equipment, supplies, and packing materials. A program of integrated pest management should be implemented.

Once an infestation is discovered, immediate action is required. Several kinds of traps for catching rodents are available commercially, but hiring a professional exterminator is advisable for reasons of staff safety. If an insect infestation is discovered, the affected items should be isolated from the rest of the collection. Items adjacent to affected ones should also be isolated. The insect should be identified, as this will aid in extermination and may help determine the source of the infestation. Spray-type insecticides should not be sprayed directly onto collections; the chemicals may damage them. Controlled freezing is another method of treating insect-infested library and archival materials, often preferred because it avoids the use of toxic chemicals. Other methods of nonchemical fumigation, such as modified atmospheres, are available. If an infestation is discovered, contact a preservation professional for the most up-to-date information.

THEFT AND VANDALISM

Because of the high value of materials in libraries and archives, adequate protection from theft and vandalism must be provided. This protection can range in complexity from simple locks to elaborate security systems. In general, collections of permanent value should be well secured when the building is closed to the public. Usually the best protection is provided by perimeter intrusion alarms and internal motion detectors connected directly to the local police department or to another outside 24-hour monitoring agency. During working hours it is best to have only one entrance/exit, to be used by researchers and staff alike. All other doors should be alarmed so that unauthorized use can be detected. Windows should be kept closed and locked. Building keys and keys to areas where materials of special value are kept should be strictly limited. A list of keyholders should be kept current, and staff members should be required to return keys when they leave the employ of the institution. Access to storage areas should be strictly limited, and researchers should be accompanied by a staff member if they enter these areas.

Use of materials by researchers should be carefully controlled and strictly monitored. Researchers should never be left unattended. Ideally, they should use materials in a room separate from book storage areas. Coats, bags, and personal belongings of all kinds should be left outside the reading area, and researchers should be allowed to bring only a pencil and paper into the room. Researchers should sign a register, present an identification card, and leave that identification card in the hands of a staff member, who should retrieve the requested object. Requests for the use of materials in special collections should be made in writing. Call slips should be retained to provide a record of use. One object at a time should be given to researchers. If several objects are needed, they should be carefully counted out by the staff member in front of the researcher before and after use. Staff should check the materials visually before and after use for evidence of vandalism. Identification cards should be returned to researchers only when the objects are returned to the staff member and when the staff member is satisfied that no damage has been done.

If you discover that valuable materials have been stolen from your collection, contact the police, the insurance company, and any appropriate organizations as required. You may want to contact the Antiquarian Booksellers Association of America (ABAA). The telephone number is (212) 944-8291, fax is (212) 944-8293, and e-mail is abaa@panix.com. Their online resource provides links to related information sources including reports of stolen books, recovered materials, and forgeries, http://www.abaa-booknet.com. Once a theft occurs, you will need a way to prove ownership of valuable materials. Marking the item itself is a curatorial decision. Written descriptions as well as photographs or high-quality photocopies of identifying details should be kept on file.

TECHNICAL LEAFLET

Northeast Document
Conservation Center

100 Brickstone Square
Andover, MA 01810-1494
www.nedcc.org
Tel: (978) 470-1010
Fax: (978) 475-6021

EMERGENCY MANAGEMENT

Section 3, Leaflet 2

AN INTRODUCTION TO FIRE DETECTION, ALARM, AND AUTOMATIC FIRE SPRINKLERS

by Nick Artim, Director
Fire Safety Network
Middlebury, Vermont

Abstract

Cultural property management is entrusted with the responsibility of protecting and preserving an institution's buildings, collections, operations and occupants. Constant attention is required to minimize adverse impact due to climate, pollution, theft, vandalism, insects, mold and fire. Because of the speed and totality of the destructive forces of fire, it constitutes one of the more serious threats. Vandalized or environmentally damaged structures can be repaired and stolen objects recovered. Items destroyed by fire, however, are gone forever. An uncontrolled fire can obliterate an entire room's contents within a few minutes and completely burn out a building in a couple hours.

The first step toward halting a fire is to properly identify the incident, raise the occupant alarm, and then notify emergency response professionals. This is often the function of the fire detection and alarm system. Several system types and options are available, depending on the specific characteristics of the protected space.

Fire protection experts generally agree that automatic sprinklers represent one of the single, most significant aspects of a fire management program. Properly designed, installed, and maintained, these systems can overcome deficiencies in risk management, building construction, and emergency response. They may also provide enhanced flexibility of building design and increase the overall level of fire safety.

The following text presents an overview of fire detection, alarm and sprinkler systems including system types, components, operations, and answers to common anxieties.

1: Fire Growth and Behavior

Before attempting to understand fire detection systems and automatic sprinklers, it is beneficial to possess a basic knowledge of fire development and behavior. With this information, the role and interaction of these supplemental fire safety systems in the protection process can then be better realized.

Basically, a fire is a chemical reaction in which a carbon based material (fuel), mixes with oxygen (usually as a component of air), and is heated to a point where flammable vapors are produced. These vapors can then come in contact with something that is hot enough to cause vapor ignition, and a resulting fire. In simple terms, something that can burn touches something that is hot, and a fire is produced.

Libraries, archives, museums, and historic structures frequently contain numerous fuels. These include books, manuscripts, records, artifacts, combustible interior finishes, cabinets, furnishings, and laboratory chemicals. It should be recognized that any item containing wood, plastic, paper, fabric, or combustible liquids is a potential fuel. They also contain several common, potential ignition sources including any item, action, or process which produces heat. These encompass electric lighting and power systems, heating and air conditioning equipment, heat producing conservation and maintenance activities, and electric office appliance. Flame generating construction activities such as soldering, brazing, and cutting are frequent sources of ignition. Arson is unfortunately one of the most common cultural property ignition sources, and must always be considered in fire safety planning.

When the ignition source contacts the fuel, a fire can start. Following this contact, the typical accidental fire begins as a slow growth, smoldering process which may last from a few minutes to several hours. The duration of this "incipient" period is dependent on a variety of factors including fuel type, its physical arrangement, and quantity of available oxygen. During this period heat generation increases, producing light to moderate volumes of smoke. The characteristic smell of smoke is usually the first indication that an incipient fire is underway. It is during this stage that early detection (either human or automatic), followed by a timely response by qualified fire emergency professionals, can control the fire before significant losses occur.

As the fire reaches the end of the incipient period, there is usually enough heat generation to permit the onset of open, visible flames. Once flames have appeared, the fire changes from a relatively minor situation to a serious event with rapid flame and heat growth. Ceiling temperatures can exceed 1,000° C (1,800° F) within the first minutes. These flames can ignite adjacent combustible contents within the room, and immediately endanger the lives of the room's occupants. Within 3-5 minutes, the room ceiling acts like a broiler, raising temperatures high enough to "flash", which simultaneously ignites all combustibles in the room. At this point, most contents will be destroyed and human survivability becomes impossible. Smoke generation in excess of several thousand cubic meters (feet) per minute will occur, obscuring visibility and impacting contents remote from the fire.

If the building is structurally sound, heat and flames will likely consume all remaining combustibles and then self extinguish (burn out). However, if wall and/or ceiling fire resistance is inadequate, (i.e. open doors, wall/ceiling breaches, combustible building construction), the fire can spread into adjacent spaces, and start the process over. If the fire remains uncontrolled, complete destruction or "burn out" of the entire building and contents may ultimately result.

Successful fire suppression is dependent on extinguishing flames before, or immediately upon, flaming combustion. Otherwise, the resulting damage may be too severe to recover from. During the incipient period, a trained person with portable fire extinguishers may be an effective first line of defense. However, should an immediate response fail or the fire grow rapidly, extinguisher capabilities can be surpassed within the first minute. More powerful suppression methods, either fire department hoses or automatic systems, then become essential.

A fire can have far reaching impact on the institution's buildings, contents and mission. General consequences may include:

- **Collections damage.** Most heritage institutions house unique and irreplaceable objects. Fire generated heat and smoke can severely damage or totally destroy these items beyond repair.

- **Operations and mission damage.** Heritage occupancies often contain educational facilities, conservation laboratories, catalogue services, administrative/support staff offices, exhibition production, retail, food service, and a host of other activities. A fire can shut these down with adverse impact on the organization's mission and its clientele.

- **Structure damage.** Buildings provide the "shell" that safeguards collections, operations and occupants from weather, pollution, vandalism and numerous other environmental elements. A fire can destroy walls, floors, ceiling/roof assemblies and structural support, as well as systems that illuminate, control temperature and humidity, and supply electrical power. This can in turn lead to content harm, and expensive relocation activities.

- **Knowledge loss.** Books, manuscripts, photographs, films, recordings and other archival collections contain a vast wealth of information that can be destroyed by fire.

- **Injury or loss of life.** The lives of staff and visitors can be endangered.

- **Public relations impact.** Staff and visitors expect safe conditions in heritage buildings. Those who donate or loan collections presume these items will be safeguarded. A severe fire could shake public confidence and cause a devastating public relations impact.

- **Building security.** A fire represents the single greatest security threat! Given the same amount of time, an accidental or intentionally set fire can cause far greater harm to collections than the most accomplished thieves. Immense volumes of smoke and toxic gases can cause confusion and panic, thereby creating the ideal opportunity for unlawful entry and theft. Unrestricted firefighting operations will be necessary, adding to the security risk. Arson fires set to conceal a crime are common.

To minimize fire risk and its impact, heritage institutions should develop and implement comprehensive and objective fire protection programs. Program elements should include fire prevention efforts, building construction improvements, methods to detect a developing fire and alert emergency personnel, and means to effectively extinguish a fire. Each component is important toward overall accomplishment of the institution's fire safety goal. It is important for management to outline desired protection objectives during a fire and establish a program that addresses these goals. Therefore, the basic question to be asked by the property's managers is, "What maximum fire size and loss can the institution accept?" With this information, goal oriented protection can be implemented.

2: Fire Detection and Alarm Systems

2.1: Introduction

A key aspect of fire protection is to identify a developing fire emergency in a timely manner, and to alert the building's occupants and fire emergency organizations. This is the role of fire detection and alarm systems. Depending on the anticipated fire scenario, building and use type, number and type of occupants, and criticality of contents and mission, these systems can provide several main functions. First they provide a means to identify a developing fire through either manual or automatic methods and second, they alert building occupants to a fire condition and the need to evacuate. Another common function is the transmission of an alarm notification signal to the fire department or other emergency response organization.

They may also shut down electrical, air handling equipment or special process operations, and they may be used to initiate automatic suppression systems. This section will describe the basic aspects of fire detection and alarm systems.

2.2: Control Panels

The control panel is the "brain" of the fire detection and alarm system. It is responsible for monitoring the various alarm "input" devices such as manual and automatic detection components, and then activating alarm "output" devices such as horns, bells, warning lights, emergency telephone dialers, and building controls. Control panels may range from simple units with a single input and output zone, to complex computer driven systems that monitor several buildings over an entire campus. There are two main control panel arrangements, conventional and addressable, which will be discussed below.

Conventional or "point wired" fire detection and alarm systems were for many years the standard method for providing emergency signaling. In a conventional system one or more circuits are routed through the protected space or building. Along each circuit, one or more detection devices are placed. Selection and placement of these detectors is dependent upon a variety of factors including the need for automatic or manual initiation, ambient temperature and environmental conditions, the anticipated type of fire, and the desired speed of response. One or more device types are commonly located along a circuit to address a variety of needs and concerns.

Upon fire occurrence, one or more detectors will operate. This action closes the circuit, which the fire control panel recognizes as an emergency condition. The panel will then activate one or more signaling circuits to sound building alarms and summon emergency help. The panel may also send the signal to another alarm panel so that it can be monitored from a remote point.

In order to help insure that the system is functioning properly, these systems monitor the condition of each circuit by sending a small current through the wires. Should a fault occur, such as due to a wiring break, this current cannot proceed and is registered as a "trouble" condition. The indication is a need for service somewhere along the respective circuit.

In a conventional alarm system, all alarm initiating and signaling is accomplished by the system's hardware which includes multiple sets of wire, various closing and opening relays, and assorted diodes. Because of this arrangement, these systems are actually monitoring and controlling circuits, and not individual devices.

To further explain this, assume that a building's fire alarm system has 5 circuits, zones A through E, and that each circuit has 10 smoke detectors and 2 manual stations located in various rooms of each zone. A fire ignition in one of the rooms monitored by zone "A" causes a smoke detector to go into alarm. This will be reported by the fire alarm control panel as a fire in circuit or zone "A". It will not indicate the specific detector type nor location within this zone. Emergency responding personnel may need to search the entire zone to determine where the device is reporting a fire. Where zones have several rooms, or concealed spaces, this response can be time consuming and wasteful of valuable response opportunity.

The advantage of conventional systems is that they are relatively simple for small to intermediate size buildings. Servicing does not require a large amount of specialized training.

A disadvantage is that for large buildings, they can be expensive to install because of the extensive amounts of wire that are necessary to accurately monitor initiating devices.

Conventional systems may also be inherently labor intensive and expensive to maintain. Each detection device may require some form of operational test to verify it is in working condition. Smoke detectors must be periodically removed, cleaned, and recalibrated to prevent improper operation. With a conventional system, there is no accurate way of determining which detectors are in need of servicing. Consequently, each detector must be removed and serviced, which can be a time consuming, labor intensive, and costly endeavor. If a fault occurs, the "trouble" indication only states that the circuit has failed, but does not specifically state where the problem is occurring. Subsequently, technicians must survey the entire circuit to identify the problem.

Addressable or "intelligent" systems represent the current state-of-the-art in fire detection and alarm technology. Unlike conventional alarm methods, these systems monitor and control the capabilities of each alarm initiating and signaling device through microprocessors and system software. In effect, each intelligent fire alarm system is a small computer overseeing and operating a series of input and output devices.

Like a conventional system, the address system consists of one or more circuits that radiate throughout the space or building. Also, like standard systems, one or more alarm initiating devices may be located along these circuits. The major difference between system types involves the way in which each device is monitored. In an addressable system, each initiating device (automatic detector, manual station, sprinkler waterflow switch, etc.) is given a specific identification or "address". This address is correspondingly programmed into the control panel's memory with information such as the type of device, its location, and specific response details such as which alarm devices are to be activated.

The control panel's microprocessor sends a constant interrogation signal over each circuit, in which each initiating device is contacted to inquire its status (normal or emergency). This active monitoring process occurs in rapid succession, providing system updates every 5 to 10 seconds.

The addressable system also monitors the condition of each circuit, identifying any faults which may occur. One of the advancements offered by these systems is their ability to specifically identify where a fault has developed. Therefore, instead of merely showing a fault along a wire, they will indicate the location of the problem. This permits faster diagnosis of the trouble, and allows a quicker repair and return to normal.

Advantages provided by addressable alarm systems include stability, enhanced maintenance, and ease of modification. Stability is achieved by the system software. If a detector recognizes a condition which could be indicative of a fire, the control panel will first attempt a quick reset. For most spurious situations such as insects, dust, or breezes, the incident will often remedy itself during this reset procedure, thereby reducing the probability of false alarm. If a genuine smoke or fire condition exists, the detector will reenter the alarm mode immediately after the reset attempt. The control panel will now regard this as a fire condition, and will enter its alarm mode.

With respect to maintenance, these systems offer several key advantages over conventional ones. First of all, they are able to monitor the status of each detector. As a detector becomes dirty, the microprocessor recognizes a decreased capability, and provides a maintenance alert. This feature, known as Listed Integral Sensitivity Testing, allows facilities personnel to service only those detectors that need attention, rather than requiring a labor and time consuming cleaning of all units.

Advanced systems, such as the FCI 7200 incorporate another maintenance feature known as drift compensation. This software procedure adjusts the detector's sensitivity to compensate for minor dust conditions. This avoids the ultra sensitive or "hot" detector condition which often results as debris obscures the detector's optics. When the detector has been compensated to its limit, the control panel alerts maintenance personnel so that servicing can be performed.

Modifying these systems, such as to add or delete a detector, involves connecting or removing the respective device from the addressable circuit, and changing the appropriate memory section. This memory change is accomplished either at the panel or on a personal computer, with the information downloaded into the panel's microprocessor.

The main disadvantage of addressable systems is that each system has its own unique operating characteristics. Therefore, service technicians must be trained for the respective system. The training program is usually a 3-4 day course at the respective manufacturer's facility. Periodic update training may be necessary as new service methods are developed.

2.3: Fire Detectors

When present, humans can be excellent fire detectors. The healthy person is able to sense multiple aspects of a fire including the heat, flames, smoke, and odors. For this reason, most fire alarm systems are designed with one or more manual alarm activation devices to be used by the person who discovers a fire. Unfortunately, a person can also be an unreliable detection method since they may not be present when a fire starts, may not raise an alarm in an effective manner, or may not be in perfect heath to recognize fire signatures. It is for this reason that a variety of automatic fire detectors have been developed. Automatic detectors are meant to imitate one or more of the human senses of touch, smell or sight. Thermal detectors are similar to our ability to identify high temperatures, smoke detectors replicate the sense of smell, and flame detectors are electronic eyes. The properly selected and installed automatic detector can be a highly reliable fire sensor.

Manual fire detection is the oldest method of detection. In the simplest form, a person yelling can provide fire warning. In buildings, however, a person's voice may not always transmit throughout the structure. For this reason, manual alarm stations are installed. The general design philosophy is to place stations within reach along paths of escape. It is for this reason that they can usually be found near exit doors in corridors and large rooms.

The advantage of manual alarm stations is that, upon discovering the fire, they provide occupants with a readily identifiable means to activate the building fire alarm system. The alarm system can then serve in lieu of the shouting person's voice. They are simple devices, and can be highly reliable when the building is occupied. The key disadvantage of manual stations is that they will not work when the building is unoccupied. They may also be used for malicious alarm activations. Nonetheless, they are an important component in any fire alarm system.

Thermal detectors are the oldest type of automatic detection device, having origin in the mid 1800's, with several styles still in production today. The most common units are fixed temperature devices that operate when the room reaches a predetermined temperature (usually in the 135°-165°F/57°-74°C). The second most common type of thermal sensor is the rate-of-rise detector, which identifies an abnormally fast temperature climb over a short time period. Both of these units are "spot type" detectors, which means that they are periodically spaced along a ceiling or high on a wall. The third detector type is the fixed temperature line type detector, which consists of two cables and an insulated sheathing that is designed to breakdown when exposed to heat. The advantage of line type over spot detection is that thermal sensing density can be increased at lower cost.

Thermal detectors are highly reliable and have good resistance to operation from nonhostile sources. They are also very easy and inexpensive to maintain. On the down side, they do not function until room temperatures have reached a substantial temperature, at which point the fire is well underway and damage is growing exponentially. Subsequently, thermal detectors are usually not permitted in life safety applications. They are also not recommended in locations where there is a desire to identify a fire before substantial flames occur, such as spaces where high value thermal sensitive contents are housed.

Smoke detectors are a much newer technology, having gained wide usage during the 1970's and 1980's in residential and life safety applications. As the name implies, these devices are designed to identify a fire while in its smoldering or early flame stages, replicating the human sense of smell. The most common smoke detectors are spot type units, that are placed along ceilings or high on walls in a manner similar to spot thermal units. They operate on either an ionization or photoelectric principle, with each type having advantages in different applications. For large open spaces such as galleries and atria, a frequently used smoke detector is a projected beam unit. This detector consists of two components, a light transmitter and a receiver, that are mounted at some distance (up to 300 ft/100m) apart. As smoke migrates between the two components, the transmitted light beam becomes obstructed and the receiver is no longer able to see the full beam intensity. This is interpreted as a smoke condition, and the alarm activation signal is transmitted to the fire alarm panel.

A third type of smoke detector, which has become widely used in extremely sensitive applications, is the air aspirating system. This device consists of two main components: a control unit that houses the detection chamber, an aspiration fan and operation circuitry; and a network of sampling tubes or pipes. Along the pipes are a series of ports that are designed to permit air to enter the tubes and be transported to the detector. Under normal conditions, the detector constantly draws an air sample into the detection chamber, via the pipe network. The sample is analyzed for the existence of smoke, and then returned to atmosphere. If smoke becomes present in the sample, it is detected and an alarm signal is transmitted to the main fire alarm control panel. Air aspirating detectors are extremely sensitive and are typically the fastest responding automatic detection method. Many high technology organizations, such as telephone companies, have standardized on aspiration systems. In cultural properties they are used for areas such as collections storage vaults and highly valuable rooms. These are also frequently used in aesthetically sensitive applications since components are often easier to conceal, when compared to other detection methods.

The key advantage of smoke detectors is their ability to identify a fire while it is still in its incipient. As such, they provide added opportunity for emergency personnel to respond and control the developing fire before severe damage occurs. They are usually the preferred detection method in life safety and high content value applications. The disadvantage of smoke detectors is that they are usually more expensive to install, when compared to thermal sensors, and are more resistant to inadvertent alarms. However, when properly selected and designed, they can be highly reliable with a very low probability of false alarm.

Flame detectors represent the third major type of automatic detection method, and imitate the human sense of sight. They are line of sight devices that operate on either an infrared, ultraviolet or combination principle. As radiant energy in the approximate 4,000 to 7,700 angstroms range occurs, as indicative of a flaming condition, their sensing equipment recognizes the fire signature and sends a signal to the fire alarm panel.

The advantage of flame detection is that it is extremely reliable in a hostile environment. They are usually used in high value energy and transportation applications where other detectors would be subject to spurious activation. Common uses include locomotive and aircraft maintenance facilities, refineries and fuel loading platforms, and mines. A disadvantage is that they can be very expensive and labor intensive to maintain. Flame detectors must be looking directly at the fire source, unlike thermal and smoke detectors which can identify migrating fire signatures. Their use in cultural properties is extremely limited.

2.4: Alarm Output Devices

Upon receiving an alarm notification, the fire alarm control panel must now tell someone that an emergency is underway. This is the primary function of the alarm output aspect of a system. Occupant signaling components include various audible and visual alerting components, and are the primary alarm output devices. Bells are the most common and familiar alarm sounding device, and are appropriate for most building applications. Horns are another option, and are especially well suited to areas where a loud signal is needed such as library stacks, and architecturally sensitive buildings where devices need partial concealment. Chimes may be used where a soft alarm tone is preferred, such as health care facilities and theaters. Speakers are the fourth alarm sounding option, which sound a reproducible signal such as a recorded voice message. They are often ideally suited for large, multistory or other similar buildings where phased evacuation is preferred. Speakers also offer the added flexibility of emergency public address announcements. With respect to visual alert, there are a number of strobe and flashing light devices. Visual alerting is required in spaces where ambient noise levels are high enough to preclude hearing sounding equipment, and where hearing impaired occupants may be found. Standards such as the Americans with Disabilities Act (ADA) mandate visual devices in numerous museum, library, and historic building applications.

Another key function of the output function is emergency response notification. The most common arrangement is an automatic telephone or radio signal that is communicated to a constantly staffed monitoring center. Upon receiving the alert, the center will then contact the appropriate fire department, providing information about the location of alarm. In some instances, the monitoring station may be the police or fire departments, or a 911 center. In other instances it will be a private monitoring company that is under contract to the organization. In many cultural properties, the building's inhouse security service may serve as the monitoring center.

Other output functions include shutting down electrical equipment such as computers, shutting off air handling fans to prevent smoke migration, and shutting down operations such as chemical movement through piping in the alarmed area. They may also activate fans to extract smoke, which is a common function in large atria spaces. These systems can also activate discharge of gaseous fire extinguishing systems, or preaction sprinkler systems.

2.5: Summary

In summary, there are several options for a building's fire detection and alarm system. The ultimate system type, and selected components, will be dependent upon the building construction and value, its use or uses, the type of occupants, mandated standards, content value, and mission sensitivity. Contacting a fire engineer or other appropriate professional who understands fire problems and the different alarm and detection options is usually a preferred first step to find the best system.

3: Fire Sprinklers

3.1: Introduction

For most fires, water represents the ideal extinguishing agent. Fire sprinklers utilize water by direct application onto flames and heat, which causes cooling of the combustion process and prevents ignition of adjacent combustibles. They are most effective during the fire's initial flame growth stage, while the fire is relatively easy to control. A properly selected sprinkler will detect the fire's heat, initiate alarm, and begin suppression within moments after flames appear. In most instances sprinklers will control fire advancement within a few minutes of their activation, which will in turn result in significantly less damage than otherwise would happen without sprinklers.

Among the potential benefits of sprinklers are the following:

- **Immediate identification and control of a developing fire.** Sprinkler systems respond at all times, including periods of low occupancy. Control is generally instantaneous.
- **Immediate alert.** In conjunction with the building fire alarm system, automatic sprinkler systems will notify occupants and emergency response personnel of the developing fire.
- **Reduced heat and smoke damage.** Significantly less heat and smoke will be generated when the fire is extinguished at an early stage.
- **Enhanced life safety.** Staff, visitors and fire fighters will be subject to less danger when fire growth is checked.
- **Design flexibility.** Egress route and fire/smoke barrier placement becomes less restrictive since early fire control minimizes demand on these systems. Many fire and building codes will permit design and operations flexibility based on the presence of a fire sprinkler system.
- **Enhanced security.** A sprinkler controlled fire can reduce demand on security forces by minimizing intrusion and theft opportunities.
- **Decreased insurance expenditure.** Sprinkler controlled fires are less damaging than fires in nonsprinklered buildings. Insurance underwriters may offer reduced premiums in sprinkler protected properties.

These benefits should be considered when deciding on the selection of automatic fire sprinkler protection.

3.2: Sprinkler System Components and Operation

Sprinkler systems are essentially a series of water pipes that are supplied by a reliable water supply. At selected intervals along these pipes are independent, heat activated valves known as sprinkler heads. It is the sprinkler that is responsible for water distribution onto the fire. Most sprinkler systems also include an alarm to alert occupants and emergency forces when sprinkler activation (fire) occurs.

During the incipient fire stage, the heat output is relatively low and is unable to cause sprinkler operation. However, as the fire intensity increases, the sprinkler's sensing elements become exposed to elevated temperatures (typically in excess of 57-107°C (135-225°F), and begin to deform. Assuming temperatures remain high, as they would during an increasing fire, the element will fatigue after an approximate 30 to 120 second period. This releases the sprinkler's seals allowing water to discharge onto the fire and begin the suppression action. In most situations less than 2 sprinklers are needed to control the fire. In fast growing fire scenarios, however, such as a flammable liquid spill, up to 12 sprinklers may be required.

In addition to normal fire control efforts, sprinkler operation may be interconnected to initiate building and fire department alarms, shutdown electrical and mechanical equipment, close fire doors and dampers, and suspend some processes.

As fire fighters arrive their efforts will focus on ensuring that the system has contained the fire, and, when satisfied, shut off the water flow to minimize water damage. It is at this point that staff will normally be permitted to enter the damaged space and perform salvage duties.

3.3: System Components and Types

The basic components of a sprinkler system are the sprinklers, system piping, and a dependable water source. Most systems also require an alarm, system control valves, and means to test the equipment.

The sprinkler itself is the spray nozzle, which distributes water over a defined fire hazard area (typically 14-21 m2/150-225 ft2) with each sprinkler operating by actuation of its own temperature linkage. The typical sprinkler consists of a frame, thermal operated linkage, cap, orifice, and deflector. Styles of each component may vary but the basic principles of each remain the same.

- **Frame.** The frame provides the main structural component which holds the sprinkler together. Water supply piping is connected to the sprinkler at the base of the frame. The frame holds the thermal linkage and cap in place, and supports the deflector during discharge. Frame styles include standard and low profile, flush, and concealed mount. Some are designed for extended spray coverage, beyond the range of normal sprinklers. Standard finishes include brass, chrome, black, and white, while custom finishes are available for aesthetically sensitive spaces. Special coatings are available for areas subject to high corrosive effect. Selection of a specific frame style is dependent on the size and type of area to be covered, anticipated hazard, visual impact features, and atmospheric conditions.

- **Thermal linkage**. The thermal linkage is the component that controls water release. Under normal conditions the linkage holds the cap in place and prevents water flow. As the link is exposed to heat, however, it weakens and releases the cap. Common linkage styles include soldered metal levers, frangible glass bulbs, and solder pellets. Each link style is equally dependable.

Upon reaching the desired operating temperature, an approximate 30 second to 4 minute time lag will follow. This lag is the time required for linkage fatigue and is largely controlled by the link materials and mass. Standard responding sprinklers operate closer to the 3-4 minute mark while quick response (QR) sprinklers operate in significantly shorter periods. Selection of a sprinkler response characteristic is dependent upon the existing risk, acceptable loss level, and desired response action.

In heritage applications the advantage of quick response sprinklers often becomes apparent. The faster a sprinkler reacts to a fire, the sooner the suppression activity is initiated, and the lower the potential damage level. This is particularly beneficial in high value or life safety applications where the earliest possible extinguishment is a fire protection goal. It is important to understand that response time is independent of response temperature. A quicker responding sprinkler will not activate at a lower temperature than a comparable standard head.

- **Cap**. The cap provides the water tight seal which is located over the sprinkler orifice. It is held in place by the thermal linkage, and falls from position after linkage heating to permit water flow. Caps are constructed solely of metal or a metal with a teflon disk.

- **Orifice**. The machined opening at the base of the sprinkler frame is the orifice from which extinguishing water flows. Most orifice openings are 15 mm (1/2 inch) diameter with smaller bores available for residential applications and larger openings for higher hazards.

- **Deflector**. The deflector is mounted on the frame opposite the orifice. Its purpose is to break up the water stream discharging from the orifice into a more efficient extinguishing pattern. Deflector styles determine how the sprinkler is mounted, with common sprinkler mounting styles known as upright (mounted above the pipe), pendent (mounted below the pipe, i.e. under ceilings), and sidewall sprinklers which discharge water in a lateral position from a wall. The sprinkler must be mounted as designed to ensure proper action. Selection of a particular style is often dependent upon physical building constraints.

A sprinkler that has received wide spread interest for museum applications is the on/off sprinkler. The principle behind these products is that as a fire occurs, water discharge and extinguishing action will happen similar to standard sprinklers. As the room temperature is cooled to a safer level, a bimetallic snap disk on the sprinkler closes and water flow ceases. Should the fire reignite, operation will once again occur. The advantage of on/off sprinklers is their ability to shut off, which theoretically can reduce the quantity of water distributed and resultant damage levels. The problem, however, is the long time period that may pass before room temperatures are sufficiently cooled to the sprinkler's shut off point. In most heritage applications, the building's construction will retain heat and prevent the desired sprinkler shut down. Frequently, fire emergency response forces will have arrived and will be able to close sprinkler zone control valves before the automatic shut down feature has functioned.

On-off sprinklers typically cost 8-10 times more than the average sprinkler, which is only justifiable when assurance can be made that these products will perform as intended. Therefore, on/off sprinkler use in heritage facilities should remain limited.

Selection of specific sprinklers is based on: risk characteristics, ambient room temperature, desired response time, hazard criticality and aesthetic factors. Several sprinkler types may be used in a heritage facility.

All sprinkler systems require a reliable water source. In urban areas, a piped public service is the most common supply, while rural areas generally utilize private tanks, reservoirs, lakes, or rivers. Where a high degree of reliability is desired, or a single source is undependable, multiple supplies may be utilized.

Basic water source criteria include:

- **The source must be available at all times.** Fires can happen at any time and therefore, the water supply must be in a constant state of readiness. Supplies must be evaluated for resistance to pipe failure, pressure loss, droughts, and other issues that may impact availability.

- **The system must provide adequate sprinkler supply and pressure.** A sprinkler system will create a hydraulic demand, in terms of flow and pressure, on the water supply. The supply must be capable of meeting this demand. Otherwise, supplemental components such as a fire pump or standby tank must be added to the system.

- **The supply must provide water for the anticipated fire duration.** Depending of the fire hazard, suppression may take several minutes to over an hour. The selected source must be capable of providing sprinklers with water until suppression has been achieved.

- **The system must provide water for fire department hoses operating in tandem with the sprinkler system**. Most fire department procedures involve the use of fire attack hoses to supplement sprinklers. The water supply must be capable of handling this additional demand without adverse impact on sprinkler performance.

Sprinkler water is transported to fire via a system of fixed pipes and fittings. Piping material options include various steel alloys, copper, and fire resistant plastics. Steel is the traditional material with copper and plastics utilized in many sensitive applications.

Primary considerations for selection of pipe materials include:

- **Ease of installation**. The easier the material is installed, the less disruption is imposed on the institution's operations and mission. The ability to install a system with the least amount of disturbance is an important consideration, especially in sprinkler retrofit applications where building use will continue during construction.

- **Cost of material versus cost of protected area.** Piping typically represents the greatest single cost item in a sprinkler system. Often there is a temptation to reduce costs by utilizing less expensive piping materials that may be perfectly acceptable in certain instances, i.e. office or commercial environs. However, in heritage applications where the value of contents may be far beyond sprinkler costs, appropriateness of the piping rather than cost should be the deciding factor.

- **Contractor familiarity with materials.** A mistake to be avoided is one in which the contractor and pipe materials have been selected, only to find out that the contractor is inexperienced with the pipe. This can lead to installation difficulties, added expense, and increased failure potential. A contractor must demonstrate familiarity with the desired material before selection.

- **Prefabrication requirements or other installation constraints.** In some instances, such as in fine art vaults, requirements may be imposed to limit the amount of work time in the space. This will often require extensive prefabrication work outside of the work area. Some materials are easily adapted to prefabrication.

- **Material cleanliness.** Some pipe materials are cleaner to install than others. This will reduce the potential for soiling collections, displays, or building finishes during installation. Various materials are also resistant to accumulation in the system water, which could discharge onto collections. Cleanliness of installation and discharge should be a consideration.

- **Labor requirements.** Some pipe materials are heavier or more cumbersome to work with than others. Consequently additional workers are needed to install pipes, which can add to installation costs. If the number of construction workers allowed into the building is a factor, lighter materials may be beneficial.

The benefits and disadvantages of each material should be evaluated prior to selection of pipe materials.

Other major sprinkler system components include:

- **Control valves.** A sprinkler system must be capable of shut down after the fire has been controlled, and for periodic maintenance and modification. In the simplest system a single shutoff valve may be located at the point where the water supply enters the building. In larger buildings the sprinkler system may consist of multiple zones with a control valve for each. Control valves should be located in readily identified locations to assist responded emergency personnel.

- **Alarms**. Alarms alert building occupants and emergency forces when a sprinkler water flow occurs. The simplest alarms are water driven gongs supplied by the sprinkler system. Electrical flow and pressure switches, connected to a building fire alarm system, are more common in large buildings. Alarms are also provided to alert building management when a sprinkler valve is closed.

- **Drain and test connections**. Most sprinkler systems have provisions to drain pipes during system maintenance. Drains should be properly installed to remove all water from the sprinkler system, and prevent water from leakage onto protected spaces, when piping service is necessary. It is advisable to install drains at a remote location from the supply, thereby permitting effective system flushing to remove debris. Test connections are usually provided to simulate the flow of a sprinkler, thereby verifying the working condition of alarms. Test connections should be operated every 6 months.

- **Specialty valves.** Drypipe and preaction sprinkler systems require complex, special control valves that are designed to hold water from the system piping until needed. These control valves also include air pressure maintenance equipment and emergency operation/release systems.

- **Fire Hose Connections.** Fire fighters will often supplement sprinkler systems with hoses. Firefighting tasks are enhanced by installing hose connections to sprinkler system piping. The additional water demand imposed by these hoses must be factored into the overall sprinkler design in order to prevent adverse system performance.

3.4: System Types

There are three basic types of sprinkler systems: wet pipe, dry pipe and preaction, with each having applicability, depending on a variety of conditions such as potential fire severity, anticipated fire growth rates, content water sensitivity, ambient conditions, and desired response. In large multifunction facilities, such as a major museum or library, two or more system types may be employed.

Wet pipe systems are the most common sprinkler system. As the name implies, a wet pipe system is one in which water is constantly maintained within the sprinkler piping. When a sprinkler activates this water is immediately discharged onto the fire.

Wet pipe system advantages include:

- **System simplicity and reliability.** Wet pipe sprinkler systems have the least number of components and therefore, the lowest number of items to malfunction. This produces unexcelled reliability, which is important since sprinklers may be asked to sit in waiting for many years before they are needed. This simplicity aspect also becomes important in facilities where system maintenance may not be performed with the desired frequency.

- **Relative low installation and maintenance expense.** Due to their overall simplicity, wet pipe sprinklers require the least amount of installation time and capital. Maintenance cost savings are also realized since less service time is generally required, compared to other system types. These savings become important when maintenance budgets are shrinking.

- **Ease of modification.** Heritage institutions are often dynamic with respect to exhibition and operation spaces. Wet pipe systems are advantageous since modifications involve shutting down the water supply, draining pipes, and making alterations. Following the work, the system is pressure tested and restored. Additional work for detection and special control equipment is avoided, which again saves time and expense.

- **Short term down time following a fire.** Wet pipe sprinkler systems require the least amount of effort to restore. In most instances, sprinkler protection is reinstated by replacing the fused sprinklers and turning the water supply back on. Preaction and drypipe systems may require additional effort to reset control equipment.

141

The main disadvantage of these systems is that they are not suited for subfreezing environments. There also may be concern where piping is subject to severe impact damage, such as some warehouses.

The advantages of wet systems make them highly desirable for use in most heritage applications, and with limited exception, they represent the system of choice for museum, library and historic building protection.

The next system type, a dry pipe sprinkler system, is one in which pipes are filled with pressurized air or nitrogen, rather than water. This air holds a remote valve, known as a dry pipe valve, in a closed position. The drypipe valve is located in a heated area and prevents water from entering the pipe until a fire causes one or more sprinklers to operate. Once this happens, the air escapes and the dry pipe valve releases. Water then enters the pipe, flowing through open sprinklers onto the fire.

The main advantage of dry pipe sprinkler systems is their ability to provide automatic protection in spaces where freezing is possible. Typical dry pipe installations include unheated warehouses and attics, outside exposed loading docks and within commercial freezers.

Many heritage managers view dry pipe sprinklers as advantageous for protection of collections and other water sensitive areas, with a perceived benefit that a physically damaged wet pipe system will leak while dry pipe systems will not. In these situations, however, dry pipe systems will generally not offer any advantage over wet pipe systems. Should impact damage happen, there will only be a mild discharge delay, i.e. 1 minute, while air in the piping is released before water flow.

Dry pipe systems have some disadvantages that must be evaluated before selecting this equipment. These include:

- **Increased complexity.** Dry pipe systems require additional control equipment and air pressure supply components, which increases system complexity. Without proper maintenance this equipment may be less reliable than a comparable wet pipe system.

- **Higher installation and maintenance costs.** The added complexity impacts the overall drypipe installation cost. This complexity also increases maintenance expenditure, primarily due to added service labor costs.

- **Lower design flexibility.** There are strict requirements regarding the maximum permitted size (typically 750 gallons) of individual drypipe systems. These limitations may impact the ability of an owner to make system additions.

- **Increased fire response time.** Up to 60 seconds may pass from the time a sprinkler opens until water is discharged onto the fire. This will delay fire extinguishing actions, which may produce increased content damage.

- **Increased corrosion potential.** Following operation, drypipe sprinkler systems must be completely drained and dried. Otherwise, remaining water may cause pipe corrosion and premature failure. This is not a problem with wet pipe systems where water is constantly maintained in piping.

With the exception of unheated building spaces and freezer rooms, dry pipe systems do not offer any significant advantages over wet pipe systems and their use in heritage buildings is generally not recommended.

The third sprinkler system type, preaction, employs the basic concept of a dry pipe system in that water is not normally contained within the pipes. The difference, however, is that water is held from piping by an electrically operated valve, known as a preaction valve. The operation of this valve is controlled by independent flame, heat, or smoke detection. Two separate events must happen to initiate sprinkler discharge. First, the detection system must identify a developing fire and then open the preaction valve. This allows water to flow into system piping, which effectively creates a wet pipe sprinkler system. Second, individual sprinkler heads must release to permit water flow onto the fire.

In some instances, the preaction system may be set up with an interlock feature in which pressurized air or nitrogen is added to system piping. The purpose of this feature is twofold: first to monitor piping for leaks and second to hold water from system piping in the event of inadvertent detector operation. The most common application for this system type is in freezer warehouses.

The primary advantage of a preaction system is the dual action required for water release: the preaction valve must operate and sprinkler heads must fuse. This provides an added level of protection against inadvertent discharge, and for this reason, these systems are frequently employed in water sensitive environments such as archival vaults, fine art storage rooms, rare book libraries and computer centers.

There are some disadvantages to preaction systems. These include:

- **Higher installation and maintenance costs.** Preaction systems are more complex with several additional components, notably a fire detection system. This adds to the overall system cost.

- **Modification difficulties.** As with drypipe systems, preaction sprinkler systems have specific size limitations which may impact future system modifications. In addition, system modifications must incorporate changes to the fire detection and control system to ensure proper operation.

- **Potential decreased reliability.** The higher level of complexity associated with preaction systems creates an increased chance that something may not work when needed. Regular maintenance is essential to ensure reliability. Therefore, if the facility's management decides to install preaction sprinkler protection, they must remain committed to installing the highest quality equipment, and to maintaining these systems as required by manufacturer's recommendations.

Provided the application is appropriate, preaction systems have a place in heritage buildings, especially in water sensitive spaces.

A slight variation of preaction sprinklers is the deluge system, which is basically a preaction system using open sprinklers. Operation of the fire detection system releases a deluge valve, which in turn produces immediate water flow through all sprinklers in a given area. Typical deluge systems applications are found in specialized industrial situations, i.e. aircraft hangers and chemical plants, where high velocity suppression is necessary to prevent fire spread. Use of deluge systems in heritage facilities is rare and typically not recommended.

Another preaction system variation is the on/off system which utilizes the basic arrangement of a preaction system, with the addition of a thermal detector and nonlatching alarm panel. The system functions similar to any other preaction sprinkler system, except that as the fire is extinguished, a thermal device cools to allow the control panel to shut off water flow. If the fire should reignite, the system will turn back on. In certain applications on/off systems can be effective. Care, however, must be exercised when selecting this equipment to ensure that it functions as desired. In most urban areas, it is likely that the fire department will arrive before the system has shut itself down, thereby defeating any actual benefits.

3.5: Sprinkler Concerns

Several common misconceptions about sprinkler systems exist. Consequently, heritage building owners and operators are often reluctant to provide this protection, especially for collections storage and other water sensitive spaces. Typical misunderstandings include:

- **When one sprinkler operates, all will activate.** With the exception of deluge systems (discussed later in this leaflet), only those sprinklers in direct contact with the fire's heat will react. Statistically, approximately 61% of all sprinkler controlled fires are stopped by two or less sprinklers.

- **Sprinklers operate when exposed to smoke.** Sprinklers function by thermal impact against their sensing elements. The presence of smoke alone will not cause activation without high heat.

- **Sprinkler systems are prone to leakage or inadvertent operation.** Insurance statistics indicate a failure rate of approximately 1 head failure per 16,000,000 sprinklers installed per year. Sprinkler components and systems are among the most tested systems in an average building. Failure of a proper system is very remote.

Where failures do occur, they are usually the result of improper design, installation, or maintenance. Therefore, to avoid problems, the institution should carefully select those who will be responsible for the installation and be committed to proper system maintenance.

- **Sprinkler activation will cause excessive water damage to contents and structure.** Water damage will occur when a sprinkler activates. This issue becomes relative, however, when compared to alternative suppression methods. The typical sprinklerwill discharge approximately 25 gallons per minute (GPM) while the typical fire department hose delivers 100-250 GPM. Sprinklers are significantly less damaging than hoses. Since sprinklers usually operate before the fire becomes large, the overall water quantity required for control is lower than situations where the fire continues to increase until firefighters arrive.

The table below shows approximate comparative water application rates for various manual and automatic suppression methods.

Fire Suppression Water Application Rates.

Delivery Method	Liters/min.	Gallons/min.
Portable Fire Extinguisher/Appliance	10	2.5
Occupant Use Fire Hose	380	100
Sprinkler (1)	95	25
Sprinkler (2)	180	47
Sprinkler (3)	260	72
Fire Department, Single 1.5" Hose	380	100
Fire Department, Double 1.5" Hose	760	200
Fire Department, Single 2.5" Hose	950	250
Fire Department, Double 2.5" Hose	1900	500

One final point to consider is that the water damage is usually capable of repair and restoration. Burned out contents, however, are often beyond mend.

- Sprinkler systems look bad and will harm the buildings appearance . This concern has usually resulted from someone who has observed a less than ideal appearing system, and admittedly there are some poorly designed systems out there. Sprinkler systems can be designed and installed with almost no aesthetic impact.

To ensure proper design, the institution and design team should take an active role in the selection of visible components. Sprinkler piping should be placed, either concealed or in a decorative arrangement, to minimize visual impact. Only sprinklers with high quality finishes should be used. Often sprinkler manufacturers will use customer provided paints to match finish colors, while maintaining the sprinkler's listing. The selected sprinkler contractor must understand the role of aesthetics.

To help ensure overall success, the sprinkler system designer should understand the institution's protection objectives, operations, and fire risks. This individual should be knowledgeable about system requirements and flexible to implement unique, thought-out solutions for those areas where special aesthetic or operations concerns exist. The designer should be experienced in the design of systems in architecturally sensitive applications.

Ideally, the sprinkler contractor should be experienced working in heritage applications. However, an option is to select a contractor experienced in water sensitive applications such as telecommunications, pharmaceuticals, clean rooms, or high tech manufacturing. Companies including AT&T, Bristol Meyers Squibb, and IBM have very stringent sprinkler installation requirements. If a sprinkler contractor has demonstrated success with these type of organizations, then they will be capable of performing satisfactorily in a heritage site.

The selected sprinkler components should be provided by a reputable manufacturer, experienced in special, water sensitive hazards. The cost differential between average and the highest quality components is minimal. The long term benefit, however, is substantial. When considering the value of a facility and its contents, the extra investment is worth while.

With proper attention to selection, design, and maintenance, sprinkler systems will serve the institution without adverse impact. If the institution or design team does not possess the experience to ensure the system is proper, a fire protection engineer experienced in heritage applications can be a great advantage.

3.6: Water Mist

One of the most promising automatic extinguishing technologies is the recently available fine water droplet, or mist systems. This technology represents another tool that can provide automatic fire suppression in some cultural property applications. Potential uses include locations where reliable water supplies do not exist, where even sprinkler water discharges are too high, or where building construction and aesthetics impact the use of standard sprinkler pipe dimensions. Mist systems may also be an appropriate solution to the protection void left by the environmental concerns, and subsequent demise, of Halon 1301 gas.

Mist technology was originally developed for offshore uses such as on board ships and oil drilling platforms. For both of these applications, there is a need to control severe fires while limiting the amount of extinguishing water, which could impact vessel stability. These systems have been extensively approved by a number of domestic and international marine organizations, and have been a protection standard for the past 8-10 years. They have a solid track record dealing with maritime fires. These systems have also been used in several land based applications, and have a number of listings, primarily in Europe, where their effectiveness has been recognized. Some systems have recently received approvals for North American land based uses.

Mist systems discharge limited water quantities at higher pressures than sprinkler systems. These pressures range from approximately 100 to 1,000 psi, with the higher pressure systems generally producing larger volumes of fine sprays. The produced droplets are usually in the 50 to 200 micron diameter range (compared to 600-1,000 microns for standard sprinklers), resulting in exceptionally high efficiency cooling and fire control, with significantly little water. In most situations, fires are controlled with approximately 10-25% of the water normally associated with sprinklers. Water saturation that is often associated with standard firefighting procedures is decreased. Other benefits include lower aesthetic impact and known environmental safety.

Typical water mist systems consist of the following components:

- **Water supply:** Water for a system may be provided by either the piped building system or a dedicated tank arrangement. In some instances, lower pressure systems may use existing sprinkler piping. For most, however, supplemental pumps will be required. Other options include dedicated water/nitrogen storage cylinders, which can deliver a limited duration supply.

- **Piping and nozzles:** Piping can be greatly reduced when compared to sprinklers. For low pressure systems, pipes are generally 25-50% smaller than comparable sprinkler piping. For high pressure systems, piping is even smaller with the 0.50-0.75 inch diameters as the norm. Like sprinklers, nozzles are individually activated by the fire's heat, and are selected to cover a certain size hazard. Their sizes are comparable to a low profile sprinkler.

- **Detection and control equipment.** In some instances, mist discharge can be controlled by selected, high reliability intelligent detectors or by an advanced technology VESDA smoke detection system. These systems represent the premier, stateoftheart, fire detection technology that can provide very early warning of a developing fire, as well as reduce the probability of inadvertent discharge.

At this point, one of the main drawbacks to mist systems is their higher cost, which can be 50-100% greater than standard sprinklers. This cost, however, may be reduced due to possible installation labor savings. In rural applications, where reliable sprinkler water supplies can be expensive, mist systems may be comparable or less than standard sprinklers. Another problem is that these systems do not have the variety of approvals and listings commonly associated with sprinklers. As such, they may not be as recognized by fire and building authorities. In addition, the number of contractors who are familiar with the technology is limited. These concerns are diminishing, however, as use of these systems becomes more widespread.

3.7: Summary:

In summary, automatic sprinklers often represent one of the most important fire protection options for most heritage applications. The successful application of sprinklers is dependent upon careful design and installation of high quality components by capable engineers and contractors. A properly selected, designed and installed system will offer unexcelled reliability. Sprinkler system components should be selected for compliance with the institution's objectives. Wet pipe systems offer the greatest degree of reliability and are the most appropriate system type for most heritage fire risks. With the exception of spaces subject to freezing conditions, dry pipe systems do not offer advantages over wet pipe systems in heritage buildings. Preaction sprinkler systems are beneficial in areas of highest water sensitivity. Their success is dependent upon selection of proper suppression and detection components and management's commitment to properly maintain systems. Water mist represents a very promising alternative to gaseous agent systems.

4.0: Additional Information.

The following information sources are available to assist with selection of fire sprinkler systems:

- **Fire Safety Network**; Post Office Box 895; Middlebury, Vermont 05753; USA. Telephone: (802) 388-1064. firesafe@together.net

- **National Fire Protection Association**; Batterymarch Park; Quincy, Massachusetts 02269; USA. Telephone: (617) 770-3000. www.nfpa.org

- **Reliable Automatic Sprinkler, Inc.**; 525 North MacQuesten Parkway, Mount Vernon, New York 10552 USA. Telephone: (800) 668-3470. Attention: Ms Kathy Slack, Marketing Manager. www.reliablesprinkler.com

- **Fire Control Instruments**; 301 Second Street, Waltham, Massachusetts 02154. Telephone: (781) 487-0088. Attention: Mr. Randy Edwards.

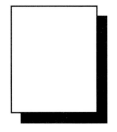

Northeast Document
Conservation Center
100 Brickstone Square
Andover, MA 01810-1494
www.nedcc.org
Tel: (978) 470-1010
Fax: (978) 475-6021

DISASTER PLANNING

by Beth Lindblom Patkus
Preservation Consultant
Walpole, MA and
Karen Motylewski
formerly Director of Field Service
Northeast Document Conservation Center

Natural disasters, such as hurricane Andrew's August 1992 assault on southern Florida and Louisiana, make all of us acutely aware of our vulnerabilities to disaster. Fortunately, catastrophes of this magnitude are rare, but disaster can strike in many ways. For example, a broken water main inundated the Chicago Historical Society in 1986; fire severely damaged the Cabildo in New Orleans in 1988; the Loma Prieta earthquake damaged several San Francisco area museums and libraries in 1989; smoke from an electrical fire covered collections throughout the Huntington Gallery in 1985; mold damage threatened Mount Vernon's archival collections. Large or small, natural or man-made, emergencies put an institution's staff and collections in danger.

It is unfortunate that institutional staff often learn about the advantages of emergency preparedness through hard experience, but an emergency does not have to become a full-fledged disaster. In fact, hazards can often be mitigated or avoided altogether by a comprehensive, systematic, emergency-preparedness program. Such programs provide a means for recognizing and preventing risks, and for responding effectively to emergencies.

An increasing number of professionals know that small-scale emergencies can be contained if staff members are prepared to react quickly. Damage can be limited even in the face of a large-scale disaster. For example, cultural institutions in Charleston, South Carolina, formed a consortium that focused on disaster preparedness several years before they were hit by hurricane Hugo in 1989. Many of those institutions sustained only minor damage because they were able to put their early warning procedures into operation.

Disaster planning is complex; the written plan is the result of a wide range of preliminary activities. The entire process is most efficient if it is formally assigned to one person who acts as the disaster planner for the institution and is perhaps assisted by a planning team or committee. The institution's director may play this primary role or may delegate the responsibility, but it is important to remember that the process must be supported at the highest level of the organization if it is to be effective. The planner should establish a timetable for the project and should define the scope and goals of the plan, which will depend largely on the risks faced by the institution.

For any collection, the risk of disaster is a combination of environmental hazards plus the vulnerabilities of buildings, mechanical systems, and collections. An institution-wide risk survey is the best way to assess these factors. Research into past events and previous problems will also help identify dangers. An article of this length cannot cover all of the possibilities, but there are many helpful guides in interactive computer programs, published books and articles, and technical leaflets from regional conservation programs.

IDENTIFYING RISKS

A prudent first step is to list geographic and climatic hazards and other risks that could jeopardize the building and collections. These might include the institution's susceptibility to hurricanes, tornadoes, flash flooding, earthquakes, or forest fires, and even the possibility of unusual hazards such as volcanic eruptions. Consider man-made disasters such as power outages, sprinkler discharges, fuel or water supply failures, chemical spills, arson, bomb threats, or other such problems. Take note of the environmental risks that surround your institution. Chemical industries, shipping routes for hazardous materials, and adjacent construction projects all expose your institution to damage. While all institutions are not vulnerable to all disasters, any event that is a real possibility should be covered under your emergency plan.

Look carefully at your building and site. Check the surrounding terrain. Is the building located on a slope? Is the basement above flood level? Are there large trees near the building? Are such things as utility poles and flagpoles secure? Is the roof flat? Does water accumulate? Do gutters and drains work properly? Are they cleaned regularly? Are windows and skylights well sealed? Is there a history of leaks or other building and structural problems?

Within the building, fire protection systems, electrical systems, plumbing, and environmental systems are of primary concern. Are there enough fire extinguishers, and are they regularly inspected? Does the building have fire alarms and a fire-suppression system? Are they well maintained? Are they monitored twenty-four hours a day? Are fire exits blocked? How old is the wiring? Is it overloaded? Are electrical appliances unplugged at night? Is auxiliary power available if needed? Are water pipes in good shape? Are there water detectors, and do they work? Are there any problems with the climate-control system? You may have already thought of many other questions, and you should create a risk-assessment checklist of your own.

It is also important to determine the vulnerability of the objects within the collections. What types of materials are included? Are they easily damaged? Are they particularly susceptible to certain types of damage such as moisture, fire, breakage, and the like? How and where are collections stored? Are they protected by boxes or other enclosures? Is shelving anchored to structural elements of the building? Is it stable? Are any artifacts stored directly on the floor where they could be damaged by leaks or flooding? All items should be raised at least four inches from the floor on waterproof shelves or pallets. Are materials stored under or near water sources? Analyze your security and housekeeping procedures. Do they expose collections to the dangers of theft, vandalism, or insect infestation?

Consider administrative vulnerabilities. Are your institution's collections insured? Is there a complete and accurate inventory? Is a duplicate of the inventory located at another site? Have collection priorities been set? In other words, do you know which collections should be salvaged first in the event of fire, water, or other emergency? Do you have a back-up priority list if you cannot reach the highest-priority objects due to building damage or the nature of the disaster?

While these questions may seem overwhelming, by the time you complete your survey, you will have a good idea of the significant risks your institution faces. Although there may be a wide range of disaster scenarios, the most common are water, fire, physical or chemical damage, or some combination of these. The specific procedures of a disaster plan focus on the prevention and mitigation of these types of damage.

DECREASING RISKS

Once your institution's hazards are specified, the disaster planner should devise a program with concrete goals, identifiable resources, and a schedule of activities for eliminating as many risks as possible. Geography and climate cannot be changed, but other vulnerabilities can be reduced. If building and collection conditions are regularly monitored, repaired and improved, many emergency situations will be eliminated.

A regular program of building inspection and maintenance should be a very high priority if one is not already in place. It can prevent or reduce common emergencies resulting from burst pipes, defective climate-control equipment, worn electrical wiring, clogged drains, or other problems. If all improvements cannot be undertaken at once, make a schedule and follow it. If some items on your schedule prove impossible or are delayed, move on to the next goal and return to the earlier problem when it becomes more practical.

Once building systems are in proper working order, devise a maintenance schedule. Patchwork repairs and deferred maintenance only result in accelerated deterioration, leading to an increased risk of emergencies. Keep a log of building events like clogged drains, furnace cleaning, and equipment failures. The more you know about your building and its operation, the faster (and more economically) repairs can be made.

While water damage is the most common form of disaster for museums, every institution with collections of enduring value needs a good fire-protection system. Since most emergencies seem to happen outside normal working hours, reliable fire detection systems on professional, twenty-four-hour monitors are a wise investment. Wherever possible, collections should also be protected by a fire-suppression system. The use of halon is no longer recommended. Preservation professionals now recommend wet-pipe sprinklers for most libraries and archives. In addition, water misting suppression systems have become available within the last several years; these can provide fire suppression using much less water than conventional sprinkler systems. Before choosing a fire-protection system, be sure to contact a preservation professional or a fire-protection consultant for information about the latest developments in fire protection and for advice appropriate to your collections and situation.

All fire-protection systems should be designed and installed by professionals with experience in servicing museums, archives, and libraries, because the needs of these institutions differ from the needs for home protection. Talk to colleagues at other local institutions or a preservation professional in your region for recommendations, and always check references.

Other actions that reduce building and collection vulnerability include maintaining a collection inventory, improving collection storage, and following good security and housekeeping procedures. An inventory will provide a basic list of holdings to assist in assigning priorities for salvage, and will be essential for insurance purposes. Improved collection storage, such as boxing and raising materials above the floor level, will reduce or eliminate damage when emergencies occur. Comprehensive security and housekeeping procedures will ward off emergencies such as theft, vandalism, and insect infestation. They will also ensure that fire exits are kept clear and fire hazards eliminated.

A COOPERATIVE PLAN

Disaster planning should not take place in a vacuum. To work effectively, it must be integrated into the routine operating procedures of the institution. In fact, you will probably find that in planning for disasters you will also be working toward the accomplishment of other goals. For example, a properly functioning climate-control system will prevent fluctuations in temperature and relative humidity, resulting in a better preservation environment and a longer life for all collections. At the same time, this prevents disasters such as water leaks from air-handling units. Similarly, if an institution surveys its collections and creates an inventory for disaster planning, a corollary benefit is better access to the collections for researchers and staff.

Remember three important characteristics of an effective disaster plan: comprehensiveness, simplicity, and flexibility. The plan needs to address all types of emergencies and disasters that your institution is likely to face. It should include plans for both immediate response and long-term salvage and recovery efforts. The plan should also acknowledge that normal services may be disrupted. How will you proceed if there is no electrical power, no water, and no telephone?

The plan must be easy to follow. People faced with a disaster often have trouble thinking clearly, so concise instructions and training are critical to the success of the plan. The key is to write in a clear, simple style without sacrificing comprehensiveness. Above all, remember that you cannot anticipate every detail, so be sure that while your plan provides basic instructions, it also allows for some on-the-spot creativity.

Decide who will be responsible for various activities when responding to an emergency. Who will be the senior decision-maker? Who will interact with fire officials, police, or civil defence authorities? Who will talk to the press? Who will serve as back-up if any of your team members are unable to get to the site? Identify a location for a central command post (if necessary), and space for drying collections. Set up a system for relaying information to members of the salvage team. Because written information is less susceptible to misunderstanding, your communications strategy might include notes to be delivered by "runners." Good communication is essential to avoid confusion and duplication of effort in an emergency.

Finally, if the planning process seems overwhelming, approach it in stages. Decide what type of disaster is most likely to occur in your institution, and begin to plan for it. The plan can always be expanded to include other scenarios.

IDENTIFYING RESOURCES

Some important steps should be taken before you write your plan. First, identify sources of assistance in a disaster. Determine the supplies you will need for disaster response and salvage efforts for your specific collections. Basic supplies like polyethylene dropcloths, sponges, flashlights, and rubber gloves should be purchased and kept on hand. They should be kept in a clearly marked location, inventoried periodically, and, if necessary, replaced. If you choose to lock the cabinet containing the supplies, make sure the keys will be available in an emergency. A sample list of basic supplies is included with this article. Keep a list of additional supplies that might be needed. This list should include suppliers' names, addresses, and phone numbers, and should provide backup sources for supplies. Arrangements should also be made for emergency cash or credit, because it is sometimes difficult to get money quickly in a disaster situation.

In recent years, many disaster-planning guides have published lists of supplies and companies that provide disaster services as well as sources of technical assistance. Research these services thoroughly—it is an essential part of the planning process. If possible, invite local service providers to visit your institution to become familiar with your site plan and collections in advance of an emergency. It is also a good idea to plan for back-up companies to provide critical supplies and services in case there is a community-wide or regional disaster. Consider coordinating with other local institutions.

The disaster planner should identify all appropriate disaster-response and recovery services. These can range from police, fire, and ambulance services to maintenance workers, insurance adjustors, and utility companies. Several national companies provide disaster-recovery services such as dehumidification and vacuum freeze drying. Liaisons should be maintained with local emergency services so that they can respond appropriately in case of disaster. For example, you may want to provide the fire department with a list of high-priority areas to be protected from water if fire-fighting efforts permit. You may be able to arrange with the fire department to allow specific staff members from your institution to enter the building for evaluation or salvage if safety allows. It may be possible to rope off areas for arson investigation while allowing accessibility to other areas. All such arrangements must be prepared for in advance for efficient response.

Other valuable sources of assistance are local, state, or federal government agencies. While it is widely known that the Federal Emergency Management Agency (FEMA) provides disaster assistance programs, institutions may not be aware that this can include support for recovery of art objects and cultural resources. An October 1991 policy change allows federal assistance to pay for conservation of objects that are damaged in a disaster. Conservation is defined by FEMA as "the minimum steps which are both necessary and feasible to place the items back on display without restoring them to their pre-disaster condition." FEMA does not cover the replacement of destroyed items.

SETTING PRIORITIES

The first priority in any disaster is human safety. Saving collections is never worth endangering the lives of staff or patrons. In a major event, the fire department, civil defense authorities, or other professionals may restrict access to the building until it can be fully evaluated. Once safety concerns are met, the next consideration will be records and equipment crucial to the operation of the institution, such as registrar's records, inventories, and administrative files. Collections salvage and building rehabilitation will be the next priority.

Objects or collections of great importance to the institution must be identified ahead of time. If this is not done, valuable time may be wasted salvaging materials of little value or spent arguing about what should be saved first. Ideally, this step includes a floor plan that clearly states the priority of collections for salvage. This should be attached to the disaster plan, but the security of this type of information should be considered. It may be wise to allow only upper-level staff access to this part of the plan prior to an actual emergency.

Salvage priorities should be based not only on the value of objects, but on their vulnerability to the particular damage caused by the emergency. If you are not knowledgeable about the hazards for various materials, contact a conservator to help you incorporate these considerations into your salvage plan. Paper and textiles, for instance, are susceptible to mold when they are warm and damp. Many metals will corrode rapidly under the same conditions. Salt water may accelerate this damage. Ivory, small wooden objects, and lacquer may swell and crack with rapid changes in moisture and temperature. Veneers and furniture may be constructed with water-soluble adhesives. Objects may become brittle after exposure to the temperatures of a fire. All categories of collections have special handling and salvage procedures developed by experienced professionals. Because the instructions for salvage of the wide variety of objects found in collections is beyond the scope of this article, a brief reading list has been included for further information.

WRITING THE PLAN

Once the necessary preliminary steps have been taken, writing the plan should be relatively straightforward. Although each plan will be different, a sample outline is given below:

1. Introduction—stating the lines of authority and the possible events covered by the plan.

2. Actions to be taken if advance warning is available.

3. First response procedures, including who should be contacted first in each type of emergency, what immediate steps should be taken, and how staff or teams will be notified.

4. Emergency procedures with sections devoted to each emergency event covered by the plan. This will include what is to be done during the event, and the appropriate salvage procedures to be followed once the first excitement is over. Include floor plans.

5. Rehabilitation plans for getting the institution back to normal.

6. Appendices, which may include evacuation/floor plans; listing of emergency services; listing of emergency response team members and responsibilities; telephone tree; location of keys; fire/intrusion alarm procedures; listing of collection priorities; arrangements for relocation of the collections; listing of in-house supplies; listing of outside suppliers and services; insurance information; listing of volunteers; prevention checklist; record-keeping forms for objects moved in salvage efforts; detailed salvage procedures.

MAINTAINING THE PLAN

No matter how much effort you have put into creating the perfect disaster plan, it will be largely ineffective if your staff is not aware of it, if it is outdated, or if you cannot find it during a disaster. A concentrated effort must be made to educate and train staff in emergency procedures. Each staff member should be made aware of his or her responsibilities, and regular drills should be conducted if possible. Keep several copies of the plan in various locations, including off-site (ideally in waterproof containers). Each copy of the plan should indicate where other copies may be found.

Most important, the disaster plan must be updated periodically. Names, addresses, phone numbers, and personnel change constantly. New collections are acquired, building changes are made, and new equipment is installed. If a plan is not kept completely up to date, it may not be able to assist you effectively in dealing with disasters.

Disaster planning is essential for any institution to provide the best possible protection for its collections. Disaster can strike at any time—on a small or a large scale—but if an institution is prepared, the damage may be decreased or avoided. A disaster plan must be considered a living document. Its risk-assessment checklist must be periodically reviewed, its lists must be updated, and its collection priorities revised as needed. An effective disaster plan will do its best to insure that historical collections in our cultural institutions are safeguarded for the future.

SUGGESTED READING

The following sources provide further basic reading on disaster planning for libraries and archives. Please consult NEDCC's leaflet "Emergency Management Bibliography" for additional references.

Artim, Nick. "An Introduction to Automatic Fire Sprinklers." *WAAC Newsletter* 15.3 (September 1994): 20-27, and 17.2 (May1995): 23-28. Available at http://palimpsest.stanford.edu/waac/.
Describes the various types of sprinkler systems and their advantages and disadvantages in a clear, readable style.

Artim, Nick. "An Update on Micromist Fire Extinguishment Systems." *WAAC Newsletter* 17.3 (September 1995): 14. Available at http://palimpsest.stanford.edu/waac/.
Provides information on development and testing of water misting fire-suppression systems.

Artim, Nick. "Cultural Heritage Fire Suppression Systems: Alternatives to Halon 1301." *WAAC Newsletter* 15.2 (May 1993): 34-36. Available at http://palimpsest.stanford.edu/waac/.
Useful for institutions deciding whether to retain or replace a Halon fire-suppression system.

Canadian Conservation Institute. "Emergency Preparedness for Cultural Institutions." *CCI Note* 14/1, and "Emergency Preparedness for Cultural Institutions: Identifying and Reducing Hazards." *CCI Note* 14/2. (Ottawa: CCI, 1995).
A good starting point; has an excellent checklist for reducing hazards.

Fortson, Judith. *Disaster Planning and Recovery: A How-To-Do-It Manual for Librarians and Archivists.* (New York: Neal-Schuman Publishers, 1992).
Excellent, comprehensive guidance for emergency preparedness: risk prevention, response, and recovery. Includes resource lists, bibliography, decision tree. If you can buy only one emergency planning guide, this should be it.

Fox, Lisa L. "Management Strategies for Disaster Preparedness." *The ALA Yearbook of Library and Information Services* 14 (1989): 1-6.
An excellent summary of management and implementation strategies for putting theory into practice.

Lyall, Jan. "Disaster Planning For Libraries and Archives: Understanding the Essential Issue." *Provenance: The Electronic Magazine* 1.2 (March 1996). Available at http://www.nla.gov.au/nla/staffpaper/lyall1.html.

O'Connell, Mildred. "Disaster Planning: Writing and Implementing Plans for Collections-Holding Institutions." *Technology and Conservation* (Summer 1983): 18-24.
A succinct and practical approach to disaster planning. Every planning committee should read it before undertaking the task.

Walsh, Betty. "Salvage Operations for Water Damaged Archival Collections: A Second Glance" and "Salvage at a Glance." *WAAC Newsletter* 19.2 (May 1997). Available at http://palimpsest.stanford.edu/waac/.
Excellent recovery guidelines for minor, moderate, and major disasters.

BASIC EMERGENCY SUPPLIES AND EQUIPMENT:

Dehumidifier
Metal cart
Plastic (milk) crates
Flashlights
50-ft. extension cord (grounded)
Portable electric fan
Wet vacuum
Blank newsprint
Freezer or waxed paper
Plastic trash bags
Plastic buckets and trash can
Paper towels

Sponges
Mop
Monofilament nylon (fishing) line
Broom
Gloves (rubber/leather)
Rubber boots and aprons
Safety glasses
Plastic sheeting (stored with scissors and tape)
First aid kit
Clipboards, paper, pens, markers
Emergency funds (cash and purchase orders)

Acknowlegements

Reprinted with permission from *Disaster Planning for Cultural Institutions*, by Beth Lindblom and Karen Motylewski, published originally as *Technical Leaflet #183* by the American Association for State and Local History, Nashville, TN, 1993. All rights reserved.

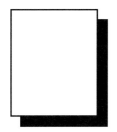

Northeast Document
Conservation Center
100 Brickstone Square
Andover, MA 01810-1494
www.nedcc.org
Tel: (978) 470-1010
Fax: (978) 475-6021

WORKSHEET FOR OUTLINING A DISASTER PLAN

by Karen E. Brown
Field Service Representative
Northeast Document Conservation Center

A. Institutional Information

Name of institution _____

Date of completion _____

Date of next update of this form/plan _____

List all locations where this plan is on file (on and off premises)

_____   _____

_____   _____

_____   _____

_____   _____

_____   _____

_____   _____

Staff members to be called in case of disaster:

Position	Name	Home Phone	Specific Responsibility in Case of Disaster
Chief Administrator	_____	_____	_____
Disaster Recovery Team Leader	_____	_____	_____
Person in charge of building maintenance	_____	_____	_____
Cataloger/ Registrar	_____	_____	_____
Preservation Administrator/ Conservator	_____	_____	_____

In-house disaster-recovery team members:

NAME	HOME PHONE
_____	_____
_____	_____
_____	_____
_____	_____

Who on the staff has a copy of this plan and is familiar with its contents?

_____	_____
_____	_____
_____	_____
_____	_____

B. Services Needed in an Emergency

Service	Company and/or Name of Contact	Phone #
In-house Security	_____	_____
Fire Department	_____	_____
Police or Sheriff	_____	_____
Ambulance	_____	_____
Civil Defense	_____	_____
Professional Advice/ Conservator	_____	_____
Insurance Company	_____	_____
Freezer	_____	_____
Freeze-dry Service	_____	_____
Document Recovery/Salvage	_____	_____
Computer Records Recovery/Salvage	_____	_____
Microfilm Recovery/Salvage	_____	_____
Videotape Recovery/Salvage	_____	_____
Computer Emergency	_____	_____
Legal Advisor	_____	_____
Electrician	_____	_____
Plumber	_____	_____
Carpenter	_____	_____
Exterminator	_____	_____
Fumigation Service	_____	_____
Locksmith	_____	_____
Utility Companies		
Electric	_____	_____
Gas	_____	_____
Telephone	_____	_____
Water	_____	_____
Architect or Builder	_____	_____
Janitorial Service	_____	_____
Glass Company	_____	_____
Photographer	_____	_____
Other	_____	_____

C. In-house Emergency Equipment (List locations and attach floor plans with locations labeled)

1. Keys _____
2. Main Utilities
   a) Main electrical cut-off switch _____
   b) Main water shut-off valve _____
   c) Main gas shut-off _____
3. Sprinkler system _____
4. Heating/cooling system _____
5. Fire extinguishers
   a) Wood, paper, combustible (Type A) _____
   b) Gasoline and flammable liquid (Type B) _____
   c) Electrical (Type C) _____
   d) All routine types of fire (Type ABC) _____
6. Master fire alarm (pull box) _____
7. Smoke and heat detectors _____
8. Cellular telephone _____
9. Portable pump _____
10. Extension cords (50 ft., grounded) _____
11. Flashlights _____
12. Camera with film _____
13. Battery-operated radio _____
14. Tool kit (crowbar, hammer, pliers, screwdriver) _____
15. Brooms and dustpans _____
16. Mop, bucket, sponges _____
17. Wet-vacuum _____
18. Metal book trucks _____
19. Portable folding tables _____
20. Portable fans _____
21. Protective masks/glasses _____
22. Hard hats _____
23. Rubber boots _____
24. Rubber or plastic aprons _____
25. Gloves (leather, rubber) _____
26. Drying space _____

D. In-house Emergency Supplies (List locations and attach floor plans with locations labeled)

27. First aid kit _____

28. Heavy plastic sheeting
    (with scissors and tape) _____

29. Paper towel supply _____

30. Plastic garbage bags _____

31. Polyethylene bags (various sizes) _____

32. Waxed or freezer paper _____

33. Absorbent paper
    (blank newsprint, blotter, etc.) _____

34. Dry chemical sponges (for removing soot) _____

35. Clipboards (also paper pads, pencils,
    waterproof pens, large self-adhesive labels) _____

36. Emergency funds _____

   a) cash _____

   b) purchase orders _____

   c) institutional credit cards _____

Are all staff familiar (by tour, not map) with location of a copy of this plan, the location and use of numbers 1-36 above, thermostats, regular exits, fire exits, fire extinguishers, flashlights, radio, and civil defense shelter?

E. Additional Sources of Emergency Equipment and Supplies

Item	Supplier	Phone
Wet vacuum	_____	_____
Sand bags	_____	_____
Portable dehumidifiers	_____	_____
Portable electric fans	_____	_____
Portable generator	_____	_____
Portable pump	_____	_____
Refrigerator trucks	_____	_____
Nearest off-site phone	_____	_____
Nearest CB radio	_____	_____
Portable lighting	_____	_____
Extension cords (50 ft., grounded)	_____	_____
Metal book trucks	_____	_____
Plastic (milk) crates	_____	_____
Sturdy boxes	_____	_____
Heavy plastic sheeting	_____	_____
Plastic garbage bags	_____	_____
Polyethylene bags (various sizes)	_____	_____

Freezer or waxed paper   _____   _____

Dry ice   _____   _____

Drying space   _____   _____

Portable tables   _____   _____

Absorbent paper
(blank newsprint, blotter, etc.)   _____   _____

Paper towels   _____   _____

Plastic buckets and trash cans   _____   _____

Water hoses with spray nozzles   _____   _____

Brooms and dustpans   _____   _____

Mops, buckets, sponges   _____   _____

Monofilament nylon (fishing) line   _____   _____

Hard hats   _____   _____

Rubber boots   _____   _____

Rubber and/or plastic aprons   _____   _____

Gloves (rubber/leather)   _____   _____

Protective masks/glasses   _____   _____

Photographic equipment/supplies   _____   _____

Portable toilets   _____   _____

Construction materials
(wood, screws, nails)   _____   _____

Ladders   _____   _____

Extra security personnel   _____   _____

Other   _____   _____

F. Daily Upkeep Checklist

The following should be checked during opening and closing procedures, and included in overnight security patrols.

	Y	N
Keys are secure and accounted for	_____	_____
Vaults and safes are secured	_____	_____
Doors that are supposed to be locked are locked	_____	_____
Evidence of tampering with locks or access points	_____	_____
Evidence of tampering with major utilities	_____	_____
Anyone hiding in the building	_____	_____
Central panels or local monitors for trouble indicators	_____	_____
Doorbells, buzzers, intercom are working	_____	_____
Lights are working (including emergency lighting)	_____	_____
Surveillance equipment is operating	_____	_____
Alarms are armed or disarmed as required	_____	_____
Equipment is operating properly		
HVAC	_____	_____
Water tanks	_____	_____
Pumps	_____	_____
Special equipment	_____	_____
Unusual or off-hours activity	_____	_____
Construction / renovation areas	_____	_____
Unusual smells or sounds	_____	_____
Evidence of water leakage (walls, ceilings, floors)	_____	_____
Known problem areas	_____	_____
Refrigerators and freezers are plugged in and operating	_____	_____
Small appliances are unplugged	_____	_____
Sinks and toilets are in working order	_____	_____

G. Weekly Upkeep Checklist

	Y	N
Emergency numbers are posted near every telephone	____	____
Fire extinguishers are updated and operable	____	____
Smoke and/or heat detectors are operable	____	____
Sprinkler system is operable	____	____
Water detectors are operable	____	____
Halon or other fire suppression system is operable	____	____
Fire alarms are operable	____	____
Internal detection devices are in working order	____	____
Internal alarms are in working order	____	____
External detection devices are in working order	____	____
External alarms are in working order	____	____
Back-up systems have been tested		
Emergency lights	____	____
Power	____	____
Alarm panels	____	____
Incident reports have been reviewed	____	____
All keys are accounted for	____	____
Flashlights are operable (one in each dept., public desk, and civil defense shelter)	____	____
Transistor radio is operable	____	____

H. Other Emergency Issues

Date of last fire drill: _____

Frequency: _____   Required? (Y/N)   Next scheduled date: _____

Date of last inspection by local fire department:

Frequency _____   Required? (Y/N)   Next scheduled date: _____

Date of last civil defense drill:

Frequency: _____   Required? (Y/N)   Next scheduled date: _____

Date of last analysis/update of insurance coverage

Frequency: _____   Required? (Y/N)   Next scheduled date: _____

Photographs of interior and exterior stored off-site? (Y/N)

Frequency: _____   Required? (Y/N)   Next scheduled date: _____

Is there an off-site record (microform, computer tape) of the collection?   (Y/N)

Frequency of update:

_____

Location:

_____

(Insert copies of last inventory report and insurance policies here)

I. Salvage Priorities

Compile a list of items that should be salvaged first following a disaster for each department, area, and/or office. Keep these considerations in mind when setting priorities.

- Is the item critical for ongoing operations of the institution?

- Can the item be replaced?

- Would the cost of replacement be more or less than the cost of restoring the object? (Replacement cost figures should include ordering, cataloging, shipping, etc., in addition to the purchase price.)

- Is the item available in another format, or in another collection?

- Does the item have a high or low collection priority?

- Does the item require immediate attention because of its composition (coated paper, vellum, water-soluble inks)?

J. Procedures

Compile and attach a detailed list of procedures to be followed in case of disaster. These should accommodate your institution's particular needs and collections. Consult the NEDCC Technical Leaflet "Disaster Management Bibliography" for sources of information.

Acknowledgements

This material is based on statewide disaster plans developed by the State Libraries of Wyoming and Iowa, and "Guidelines for Protecting Your Organization's Memory From Disaster," by H. Holland, Provincial Archives New Brunswick, and is used with their kind permission.

EMERGENCY INSTRUCTION SHEET

This sheet should contain in brief and easy-to-read steps all the instructions that any staff member, volunteer, or student needs to follow in case of an emergency affecting the collections. Copies of this one-page sheet should be posted near all staff telephones and at public service desks. All staff should receive instruction in its use. Examples of what it might contain are listed below.

FIRE

1. **Call Fire Department**   Phone _____

2. **Assist in evacuation of building**

3. **Notify**
    Disaster response leader   Phone _____

    Immediate supervisor   Phone _____

    Library Director   Phone _____

WATER

1. **Call**

    Disaster response leader   Phone _____

    Plumber/facilities staff   Phone _____

    Immediate supervisor   Phone _____

2. **Cover stacks with plastic located** _____ **OR**

    Move books higher on shelves OR
    Move books off shelves using a booktruck OR
    Carry books to another location.

Continue to list brief instructions relevant to the building, collections, and location. Make them clear, so that even excited staff will understand and know what to do.

Acknowledgements

Modified from a document kindly provided by Sally Buchanan, 1992.

Copyright 1999, Northeast Document Conservation Center. All rights reserved.

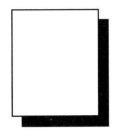

Northeast Document
Conservation Center
100 Brickstone Square
Andover, MA 01810-1494
www.nedcc.org
Tel: (978) 470-1010
Fax: (978) 475-6021

EMERGENCY MANAGEMENT BIBLIOGRAPHY

Karen E. Brown
Field Service Representative
Northeast Document Conservation Center

There are many good publications dealing with the subject of emergency planning, preparedness, and recovery for museum, library, and archival materials. Many have been designed for use as templates, simplifying the process. In addition, as attachments to your formal plan, portions of many articles and manuals can provide a fast reference for detailed information about materials, technologies, experts, ideas, and suggestions during an emergency.

EMERGENCY PLANNING

Brooks, Constance. *Preservation Planning Program Guides: Disaster Preparedness.* Washington, DC: Association of Research Libraries, Spring1993. 184 pp.
This volume is one of a set of 7 guides. Cost is $15 each, or $70 for the set. To order, contact ARL at ARL Publications-WEB, Department #0692, Washington, DC 20073-0692 or order through their Web site, http://arl.cni.org/pubscat.html.

Buchanan, Sally A. *Disaster Planning: Preparedness and Recovery for Libraries and Archives.* RAMP Publication PGI-88/WS/6. Paris: United Nations Education, Scientific, and Cultural Organization, 1988. 187 pp.
An efficient review of Buchanan's conceptual structure for disaster preparedness, which remains a model for the library field. Available from UNESCO, Division of the General Information Programme, 7 Place de Fontenoy, 75700 Paris, France. Single copies are free.

Canadian Conservation Institute. "Emergency Preparedness for Cultural Institutions," *CCI Notes* 14/1, and "Emergency Preparedness for Cultural Institutions: Identifying and Reducing Hazards," *CCI Notes* 14/2. Ottawa: CCI, 1995.
A good starting point. Available from CCI, 1030 Innes Road, Ottawa, ON K1A 0M5 Canada, or tel. (613) 998-3721.

Coleman, Christopher. "Practical Large-Scale Disaster Planning." *Westwords 2* (May 1992): 1-20.
Covers the problems of large institutions with many independent units (e.g.,multi-library university systems or branch libraries).

Fortson, Judith. *Disaster Planning and Recovery: A How-To-Do-It-Manual for Librarians and Archivists. How-To-Do-It Manuals for Libraries, No. 21. New York: Neal Schuman Publishers, 1992. 181 pp. $45.00.*
Excellent, comprehensive guidance for emergency preparedness, risk prevention, response, and recovery. Includes resource lists, bibliography, decision tree. If you can buy only one emergency planning guide, this should be it.

Fox, Lisa L. *Disaster Preparedness Workbook for U.S. Navy Libraries and Archives.* Newport, RI: U.S. Naval War College Library, 1998. Forthcoming.
A comprehensive guide to emergency planning, including topics such as response to wildfire. Extensive bibliography.

George, Susan, comp. *Emergency Planning and Management in College Libraries.* CLIP Note No. 17. Chicago: Association of College and Research Libraries, and ALA, 1994. 146 pp.
Compiled from a survey of small college and university library policies. Includes sample plans. To order, call ALA at (800) 545-2433 and press 7 to reach ALA's Customer Service Representatives (Open 8:00 am-5:00 pm, CST, Monday-Friday). For 24-hour service, FAX your order: (312) 836-9958. Or, mail your order to American Library Association, Order Fulfillment, 155 N. Wacker Drive, Chicago, IL 60606.

Haskins, Scott M. *How to Save Your Stuff From a Disaster.* Santa Barbara, CA: Preservation Help Publications, 1996.
A basic response guide for the general public touching on most aspects of disaster preparedness, with emphasis on recovering collections (e.g., paper and books, fine art, furniture, etc.). The advice and information are sound, and the presentation is user-friendly. Available from Preservation Help Publications, PO Box 1206, Santa Barbara, CA, 93102, tel. (800) 833-9226, or tel. (805) 899-9226. Cost: $19.95.

Kahn, Miriam. *Disaster Prevention and Response for Special Libraries: An Information Kit.* Washington, D.C.: Special Libraries Association, 1995.
This has a very useable checklist format designed to aid in preventing disasters, with an extensive bibliography for further information. Good coverage on machine-readable strategies. Available from Special Libraries Association, 1700 18th Street, N.W., Washington, DC. 20009-2508, tel. (202) 234-4700, ext. 643.

Lord, Allyn, Carolyn Reno, and Marie Demeroukas. *Steal This Handbook! A Template for Creating a Museum's Emergency Preparedness Plan.* Columbia, SC: Southeastern Registrars Association, 1994.
Covers everything from mechanical failure to volcanic eruption and is an excellent reference resource. Out of print, but well worth trying to obtain a used copy, or through interlibrary loan.

Merrill-Oldham, Jan, and Jutta Reed-Scott, eds. *Preservation Planning Program: An Assisted Self-Study Manual for Libraries.* Rev. ed. Washington, D.C.: ARL Office of Management Studies, 1993.
"Developed to help libraries plan and implement preservation programs in a process that educates and involves a large number of staff members. Outlines a comprehensive self-study process, and augmented by a guide to disaster planning." Lisa Fox. Available from ARL/OMS Dept. #0692, Washington, D.C. 20073-0692 (202) 296-2296.

O'Connell, Mildred. "Disaster Planning: Writing and Implementing Plans for Collections-Holding Institutions." *Technology and Conservation* (Summer 1983): 18-24.
A succinct and practical approach to disaster planning. Every planning committee should read it before undertaking the task.

Ogden, Sherelyn, ed. *Preservation of Library and Archival Materials: A Manual.* Third edition, revised and expanded. Andover, MA: Northeast Document Conservation Center, 1999. *A compilation of technical leaflets or brief guides to significant preservation concepts and procedures. Topics include salvage procedures for books, documents, and photographs; mold control; sources of services; short-form emergency-preparedness plan. Contact NEDCC at (978) 470-1010, or access these leaflets at http://www.nedcc.org.*

Reilly, Julie A. *Are You Prepared?* Omaha, Nebraska: The Nebraska State Historical Society, 1997. *Useful to institutions creating their first disaster plan. Designed to be used as a template. Available from the Nebraska State Historical Society, c/o The Gerald R. Ford Conservation Center, 1326 South 32nd Street, Omaha, Nebraska 68105. Cost is $10.00 including shipping.*

Roberts, Barbara O. "Emergency Preparedness." *In Storage of Natural History Collections: A Preventive Conservation Approach,* Vol. I, eds. Carolyn L. Rose, Catharine A. Hawks, and Hugh H. Genoways, 81-99. Iowa City, Iowa: Society for the Preservation of Natural History Collections, 1995. *Discusses the issues associated with creating a disaster plan and practical tips for ensuring effective implementation. Useful detailed appendices contain information resources and emergency checklists.*

Schur, Susan E. "Disaster Prevention, Response, and Recovery: A Selected Bibliography." *Technology & Conservation* (Summer 1994): 21-23, and (Fall 1995): 23-34. *A must for anyone doing in-depth research into any disaster topic; retrospective to 1962.*

MANAGEMENT

Association of Research Libraries, Office of Management Services. *Insuring Library Collections and Buildings.* SPEC Kit 178. ARL, Oct. 1991. Cost $46.00.

Brawner, L.B. "Insurance and Risk Management for Libraries." *Public Library Quarterly* *13*.1 (1993): 5-16, and 13.2 (1993): 29-34. *Part I covers the function of insurance and defines risk and insurance categories. Part II discusses supplemental coverages. Good starter articles.*

Flitner, Arthur. "An Insurance Primer for the Local Historical Organization." *American Association for State and Local History (AASLH) Technical Leaflet 147.* Nashville, TN: AASLH, 1983. *Brief, helpful description of levels and types of insurance coverage for any collecting institution. This and other excellent publications can be ordered through their Web site, http://www.aaslh.org, by writing to 530 Church Street, Suite 600, Nashville, TN 37219-2325, or by tel. (615) 255-2971.*

Fox, Lisa L. "Management Strategies for Disaster Preparedness." *The ALA Yearbook of Library and Information Services* 14 (1989): 1-6. *An excellent summary of management and implementation strategies for putting theory into practice. To order, call ALA at 1-800-545-2433 and press 7 to reach ALA's Customer Service Representatives (Open 8:00 am-5:00 pm, CST, Monday-Friday). For 24-hour service, FAX your order: (312) 836-9958. Or, mail your order to American Library Association, Order Fulfillment, 155 N. Wacker Drive, Chicago, IL 60606.*

Higginbotham, Barbra Buckner, and Miriam B. Kahn. "Disasters for Directors: The Role of the Library or Archives Director in Disaster Preparedness and Recovery." *In Advances in Preservation and Access*, Vol. 2, ed. Barbra Buckner Higginbotham, pp. 400-12. Medford, NJ: Learned Information, Inc., 1995.
Describes the critical role of the director during an emergency. A must read if you are in charge.

Inland Marine Underwriters Association. *Libraries & Archives: An Overview of Risk and Loss Prevention.* IMUA: 1994.
A 35-page report that includes information on the libraries and archives industry, coverage and policy issues, valuation, exposures and loss prevention, and disaster planning. Available free to members, $50.00 for non-members. This and other publications can be ordered through the IMUA Web site, http://www.imua.org.

Lunde, Diane B. "Aftermath of a Disaster: Establishing a Rebinding Program." *The New Library Scene* 17.2 (June 1998): 10-13, 19, 22-23.
Describes a large-scale book-recovery and repair program at Colorado State University Libraries following the 1997 flood in Fort Collins.

McGiffin, Gail E. "Sharing the Risk." *History News* 48.1 (January/February 1993): 16-19.
Uses case studies to describe the advantages of insurance coverage to minimize the impact of disaster.

Smith, Scott. "Insurance Planning." *History News* 48.1 (January/February 1993): 18-19, 37.
Common sense advice for working with an insurance provider.

Sylves, Richard T., and William L. Waugh. *Disaster Management in the U.S. and Canada. Second Endition.* Springfield, IL: Charles C. Thomas,1996.
Discussion papers and analysis of disaster preparedness and response based on actual incidents. Extensive bibliography.

FIRE

Artim, Nick. "An Introduction to Automatic Fire Sprinklers." *WAAC Newsletter* 15.3 (September 1994): 20-27, and 17.2 (May1995): 23-28.
Explains the various types of sprinkler systems and their advantages and disadvantages.

Frens, Dale H. "Specifying Temporary Protection of Historic Interiors During Construction and Repair." *Preservation Tech Note.* Washington, D.C.: National Park Service. 1993.
A must for anyone considering renovations, a time when buildings and collections are at high risk of fire damage. Copies can be obtained from Heritage Preservation Services Information Desk (2255), National Center for Cultural Resource Stewardship and Partnerships, PO Box 37127, Washington, D.C., 20013-7127, tel. (202) 343-9538, or email hps_info@nps.gov.

National Fire Protection Association. *NFPA 909: Protection of Cultural Resources; NFPA 913: Protection of Historic Structures and Sites; NFPA 914: Fire Protection in Historic Structures.* Quincy, MA: National Fire Protection Association. Contact them at 1 Batterymarch Park, Quincy, MA 02269-9101, tel. (617) 770-3000, or order through their Web site, http://www.nfpa.org.
These standards discuss the causes, prevention, detection, and suppression of fire in libraries, museums, archives, and historic structures. They contain descriptions and standards for fire detection/suppression equipment, synopsis of the role of the institution's staff in fire protection, and a bibliography of resources. Each includes useful self-inspection checklists.

Stoppacher, Linda Swenson. "Culture Shock: Fire Protection for Historic and Cultural Property." Videorecording. Boston University, American Studies Program 1996, 23 minutes.
An excellent introduction to fire safety equipment for those responsible for disaster prevention in historic house museums, or anyone interested in fire protection for cultural collections. Write to the National Center for Preservation Technology and Training, c/o Training and Education, MSU Box 5682, Natchitoches, LA 71497. Free.

Trinkley, Michael. "Protecting Your Institution From Wild Fires: Planning Not to Burn and Learning to Recover." http://palimpsest.stanford.edu /byauth/trinkley/wildfire.html (14 August 1998).
Good advice for site preparation to help prevent wildfire damage to buildings.

Wilson, J. Andrew. "Fire Protection." In *Storage of Natural History Collections: A Preventive Conservation Approach,* Vol. I, eds. Carolyn L. Rose, Catharine A. Hawks, and Hugh H. Genoways, 57-79. Iowa City, Iowa: Society for the Preservation of Natural History Collections, 1995.
Comprehensive discussion of all aspects of fire protection for cultural institutions, including disaster planning, prevention and reaction to fire, and building design.

FLOOD

Berry, Michael A., Jeff Bishop, Claude Blackburn, Eugene C. Cole, William G. Ewald, Terry Smith, Nathan Suazo, and Steve Swan. "Suggested Guidelines for Remediation of Damage from Sewage Backflow into Buildings." *Journal of Environmental Health* 57.3 (October 1994): 9-15.
Overview of the risks associated with sewage, including guidelines for safe recovery.

Canada Mortgage and Housing Corporation. *Cleaning Up Your House After a Flood.* Ottawa, ON: CMHC, 1993. Order number 6789E, $3.95.
Outlines the health risks associated with flood, with clear instructions for drying out and cleaning flood- or water-damaged buildings and contents. A standard reference guide for everyone, especially homeowners. Call CMHC at (800) 668-2642, or order through their Web site at http://www.cmhc-schl.gc.ca/Boutique/Info-products/nfrm/index.html.

Department of the Interior. National Park Service. Preservation Assistance Division. *After the Flood: Emergency Stabilization and Conservation Measures.* Washington, D.C.: NPS, 1995. Provides first response procedures for historic structures affected by flood. With good bibliography. For a free copy, contact Division of Publications, National Park Service, Harpers Ferry, WV 25425-0050, tel. (304) 535-6018.

Federal Emergency Management Agency/Federal Insurance Administration. "Flood-Resistant Materials Requirements for Buildings Located in Special Flood Hazard Areas." *Technical Bulletin* 2-93. Washington, D.C.: FEMA/FIA, 1993.
A good guide for anyone building or renovating in areas at risk of flooding. Prepared in accordance with the National Flood Insurance Program. Available from FEMA/FIA Office of Reduction, Technical Standards Division, 500 C St., SW, Room 417, Washington, D.C., 20472.

National Trust for Historic Preservation. "Treatment of Flood-Damaged Older and Historic Buildings." *Technical Booklet No. 82* (1993), 16 pages. NTHP Order No. 2182.
Illustrated explanations of the risks associated with floodwaters, and practical suggestions for stabilizing buildings after the water recedes. Available from the National Trust for Historic Preservation through their online catalog, http://www.infoseries.com, under "Natural Disasters and Historic Resources." Free. Other publications are also available on earthquake hazard reduction and hurricane readiness.

United States Environmental Protection Agency. *"Flood Cleanup: Avoiding Indoor Air Quality Problems." Fact Sheet 402-F-93-005. Washington, D.C.: EPA, 1993. 2 pp. Discusses the serious problems caused by microbial growth and steps for cleaning. Copies are available from IAQ INFO, U.S. Environmental Protection Agency, tel. (800) 438-4318.*

ELECTRONIC AND BUSINESS RECORDS

Disaster Recovery Journal. *A quarterly journal covering all aspects of disaster recovery, but especially strong from a business perspective, including electronic data and impact analysis. Available free in the US and Canada for those involved in contingency planning. Contact the Circulation Department, P.O. Box 510110, St. Louis, MO 63151, or order through their Web site, http://www.drj.com.*

Drewes, Jeanne. "Computers: Planning for Disaster." *Law Library Journal* 81.103 (1989): 103-16.
A guide to main concerns and strategies.

Ianna, Frank. "Disaster Recovery for Businesses." *Disaster Recovery Journal* (Summer 1997): 39, 40, 42.
Brief but informative discussion on the risk of permanent loss of business due to disaster. A few good statistics with a synopsis of a simulated drama by AT&T.

Jones, Virginia A., and Kris E. Keyes. *Emergency Management for Records and Information Programs.* Prairie Village, Kansas: ARMA, 1997.
An in-depth detailed sourcebook covering risk management, preparedness, recovery, and resumption of business.

Kahn, Miriam. *Disaster Response and Prevention for Computers and Data.* Columbus, OH: MBK Consulting, 1994.
An excellent desk reference manual for first response. Includes checklists to assist with planning. Available by contacting MBK at 60 N. Harding Rd., Columbus, OH 43209-1524, tel. (614) 239-8977, or email mbkcons@netexp.net.

PESTS

Butcher-Younghans, Sherry, and Gretchen E. Anderson. *A Holistic Approach to Museum Pest Management.* American Association for State and Local History (AASLH) Technical Leaflet 191. Nashville, TN: AASLH, 1990.
Detailed, practical advice for controlling a range of common museum pests. This and other publications can be ordered through their Web site, http://www.aaslh.org, by writing to 530 Church Street, Suite 600, Nashville, TN 37219-2325, or tel. (615) 255-2971.

Harmon, James. *Integrated Pest Management in Museum, Library, and Archival Facilities: A Step by Step Approach for the Design, Development, Implementation, and Maintenance of an Integrated Pest Management Program.* Indianapolis: Harmon Preservation Pest Management (P.O. Box 40262, Indianapolis, IN 46240), 1993. 140 pp.
A thorough, useful guide to IPM for collections-holding institutions; in a 3-ring binder. Covers monitoring, identification, and non-chemical and chemical strategies for pest control for insects and other pests like pigeons.

Parker, Thomas A. *Study on Integrated Pest Management for Libraries and Archives.* Paris: UNESCO, General Information Program and UNISIST, 1988. Publication number PGI-88/W3/20. 119 pp.
The basics of pest management for cultural institutions.

Story, Keith O. *Approaches to Pest Management in Museums.* Suitland, MD: Conservation Analytical Laboratory, Smithsonian Institution, 1985. Out-of-print.
Some of the chemical treatment information is outdated, but identification and IPM strategies are good.

Wellheiser, Johanna G. *Nonchemical Treatment Processes for Disinfection of Insects and Fungi in Library Collections.* NY: K.G. Saur, 1992.
Excellent discussions on the various options for controlling pests in libraries.

RESPONSE AND RECOVERY

Environmental Hazards Management Institute. *Emergency Action Wheel.* Durham, NH: EHMI, 1995.
Like its counterpart, the Emergency Response and Salvage Wheel (below), this is a practical, portable tool to assist in preparing for disaster, and protecting oneself from personal hazard. Especially useful ideas for community-wide disaster preparedness. Available for $3.95 each from EHMI, PO Box 932, Durham, NH 03824, or through their Web site, http://www.ehmi.org.

National Task Force on Emergency Response. *Emergency Response and Salvage Wheel.* Washington, D.C.: The Task Force, 1997.
A compact reference tool to assist in immediate response procedures for cultural collections in the event of a disaster. Available from the National Task Force on Emergency Response, c/o National Institute for Conservation of Cultural Property, 3299 K Street, Washington, D.C., 20007 or tel. (888) 979-2233. $9.95 each.

Trinkley, Michael. *Hurricane! Surviving the Big One: A Primer for Libraries, Museums, and Archives.* Atlanta: Southeastern Library Network, Inc. (SOLINET), 1993. 76 pp.
A thorough planning aid for institutions in hurricane areas. Portions will be useful in planning for recovery from any region-wide natural disaster. Available for $10 from SOLINET, 1438 Peachtree Street, Station 200, Atlanta, GA 30309-2955, or tel. (800) 999-8558.

Walsh, Betty. "Salvage Operations for Water Damaged Archival Collections: A Second Glance." *WAAC Newsletter* 19.2 (March 1997): 12-23.
Excellent recovery guidelines for minor, moderate, and major disasters. A summary chart is available with the Newsletter when sold as a standard back issue. The cost is $10; volume discounts given on larger orders. For copies of the Newsletter see the WAAC Web site at http://palimpsest.stanford.edu/ waac. Printed back issues with the chart can be ordered through the WAAC Membership Secretary, Chris Stavroudis, 1272 N. Flores St., Los Angeles, CA 90060, tel. (323) 654-8748 or email at cstavrou@ix7.ix.netcom.com.

INTERNET RESOURCES

The internet has a seemingly limitless number of excellent disaster preparedness and recovery information resources. Other internet listings are available in the Regional Alliance for Preservation newsbrief (September 1997), in Linda Musser and Lisa Recupero's "Internet Resources on Disasters," *College & Research Libraries News* (June 1997): 403-407, and at the Natural Hazards Observer Web site (Natural Hazards Center at the University of Colorado, Boulder), http://www.colorado.edu/hazards. The following is a selection of sites to get you started:

The Boulder Creek Flood Notebook	http://www.colorado.edu/hazards/bcfn/
The Chubb Corporation Library	http://www.chubb.com
Disaster Mitigation Planning Assistance	http://disaster.lib.msu.edu/disaster/
Disaster Preparedness and Response	http://palimpsest.stanford.edu/bytopic/disasters
Emergency Information Infrastructure Partnership	http://www.emforum.org
The EnviroCenter	http://envirocenter.com
Federal Emergency Management Agency	http://www.fema.gov
Halon Alternatives Research Corporation	http://www.harc.org
Harvard University Libraries Preservation	http://preserve.harvard.edu
Library of Congress Preservation Directorate	http://www.lcweb.loc.gov/preserv
National Fire Protection Association (NFPA)	http://www.nfpa.org
National Institute of Disaster Restoration	http://www.ascr.org/nidr.htm
Water Mist Information Index	http://members.aol.com/fpekek/mist_I.htm

Acknowledgements

The author and NEDCC gratefully acknowledge the previous work of Karen Motylewski in the preparation of this technical leaflet.

Northeast Document
Conservation Center
100 Brickstone Square
Andover, MA 01810-1494
www.nedcc.org
Tel: (978) 470-1010
Fax: (978) 475-6021

EMERGENCY MANAGEMENT SUPPLIERS AND SERVICES

This list is not exhaustive, nor does it constitute an endorsement of the suppliers listed. We suggest that you obtain information from a number of vendors so that you can make comparisons of cost and assess the full range of available products.

A more complete list of suppliers is available from NEDCC. Consult the Technical Leaflets section of NEDCC's website at www.nedcc.org or contact NEDCC for the most up-to-date version in print.

- SUPPLIES
- EQUIPMENT AND TRANSPORTATION RENTAL
- COLD STORAGE FACILITIES
- DRYING FACILITIES
- CLEANING SERVICES, FUMIGATION, FIRE AND SMOKE RECLAMATION
- ENVIRONMENTAL STABILIZATION
- CONSULTING SERVICES
- PEST MANAGEMENT
- SALVAGE - ELECTRONIC DATA AND EQUIPMENT
- SALVAGE - MAGNETIC MEDIA
- SALVAGE - MICROFILM
- SALVAGE - PAPER OBJECTS
- SALVAGE - PHOTOGRAPHIC MATERIALS

SUPPLIES

Abbott Box Co., Inc.
10 Campanelli Circle
Canton, MA 02021
Telephone: (781) 821-8200
Fax: (781) 821-1919
Hours: 8 am - 2 pm. Although there is usually someone available after 2 pm, they do have voice mail.

Can supply corrugated boxes in various sizes. Cubic-foot boxes (file #104) are $0.75 for 250 to 499 boxes, and $0.69 for 500 to 999 boxes.

Gentle Giant
29 Harding Street
Cambridge, MA 02143
Toll Free: (800) 287-3030
Hours: 8:00 am -5:00 pm M-F

Moving company that has 1.5-cubic-foot boxes available @ $1.25 a piece.

Gold Star Trucking
2449 Massachusetts Avenue
Cambridge, MA 02140
Telephone: (617) 354-5543
Fax: (617) 497-4551 Hours: 7:00 am - 5:00 pm M-F

Moving company that has small moving boxes available @ $2.50 per box (20 or more).

Protext
3315 Leland Street
Bethesda, MD 20815
Telephone: (301) 718-1659
Fax: (301) 654-6153
Contact: Linda Nainis

Source of innovative emergency supplies, including the Rescube, a collapsible corrugated plastic container that is sturdy and durable.

The Quality Rubber Company
P.O. Box 71
Sedalia, MO 65302-0071
Toll Free: (800) 597-9947
Telephone: (660) 826-4641
Toll Free Fax: (800)676-5807
Fax: (660) 827-0713
Hours: 8:30 am - 5:00 pm M-F

Sponges for soot removal

Rentacrate
39 Rumford Avenue
Waltham, MA 02154-3844
Telephone: (781) 899-4477
Fax: (781) 899-4695
Contact: Michael Shanley

Stocks a variety of stackable plastic crates, dollies, and carts. Rental of a 1.6-cubic-foot crate costs $2.00 per month. (Arrangements can be made for longer periods.)

EQUIPMENT AND TRANSPORTATION RENTAL

AMI Leasing
South Union Street
Lawrence, MA 02155
Telephone: (978) 975-2550
Hours: M-F 7:00 am - 5:00 pm, Saturdays 8 am - noon

Can supply 18-ft. refrigerator trucks. Weekly rental is $500. Must have commercial driver's license (Class B).

Budget
Rolling Green
Andover, MA 02139
Telephone: (978) 497-1801
Hours: 7:00 am - 6:00 pm M-F

Budget rents trucks of various sizes and types. No refrigerated trucks are available.

C.J. & J. Leasing
5 Claflin Street
South Boston, MA 02210
Telephone: (617) 423-5695
Fax: (617) 426-8912
Contact: Rocky Hicks

Hours: 7:00 am - 6:00 pm. M-F. There is no guaranteed evening or weekend availability. However, a 24-hr. road service can try to expedite rental arrangements; call (617) 423-6720 to page Rocky Hicks. An affiliate of ThermoKing, this company can provide electric or diesel refrigerated trailers and trucks which can operate below 32 degrees Fahrenheit. Drivers are also available on a limited basis.

Century Leasing Corporation
366 Second Street
Everett, MA 02149
Telephone: (618) 387-1000 or (617) 844-5780
Fax: (617) 389-7105
Contact: Joe Panniello
Hours: 8:00 am - 4:30 pm. M-F. No evening or weekend availability

Century Leasing can provide electric or diesel 40-ft. refrigerator trailers that can operate below freezing.

Cummings Northeast, Inc.
100 Allied Drive
Dedham, MA 02026
Telephone: (781) 329-1750
Contact: Vince
Hours: 8:00 am - 5:00 pm M-F

For the rental of both diesel and electric generators, as well as other types of equipment.

Dorlen Products
6615 West Layton Avenue
Milwaukee, WI 53220
Telephone: (414) 282-4840
Toll Free: (800) 533-6392
Fax: (414) 282-5670
http://www.wateraltert.com
Hours: 8:00 am - 4:30 pm M-F

Surface water detectors.

Fire Equipment
88 Hicks Avenue
Medford, MA 02155
Telephone: (781) 391-8050
Fax: (781) 391-8835
Hours: 8:00 am - 4:30 pm M-F

Fire extinguishers/detectors.

Raychem Corporation
TraceTek Products Group
300 Constitution Drive
Menlo Park, CA 94025
Telephone: (650) 361-4602 or (650) 361-5579
Hours: 7:00 am - 5:00 pm M-F

Water-sensing cable.

Rent-a-tool
777 Shore Road
Revere, MA 02151
Telephone: (617) 289-3800 (24 hours)
Hours: 7:30 am - 5:30 pm M-F, Saturdays 8 am - 5:30 pm

Rent HEPA & Euroclean U2-930 vacuum cleaners.

COLD STORAGE FACILITIES

Americold
555 Pleasant Street
Watertown, MA 02172
Telephone: (617) 269-6330 or (617) 923-2100
Contact: Paul Martell, General Manager ext. 210
or Betty Frongillo, Sales Representative ext. 244
Hours: 8:00 am - 3:30 pm

A large company with freezer storage space available throughout the country. They have 8 local MA warehouses, one of which is in Watertown. Freezers operate at sub-zero temperatures. Americold in Watertown is a seasonal business, making it difficult to estimate space availability.

Millbrook Cold Storage
9 Medford Street
Somerville, MA 02143
Telephone: (617) 354-3800
Fax: (617) 661-4134
Contact: Charlie Petrie (home phone [617] 729-9348)
Hours: 7:30 am - 4:30 pm M-F

Located near East Cambridge, the building's capacity is 840,000 cubic feet. Operating temperature is between -4 degrees & +4 degrees. As with many cold-storage facilities, business is seasonal and space is not always available.

DRYING FACILITIES

American Freeze-Dry, Inc.
411 White Horse Pike
Audubon, NJ 08106
Telephone: (609) 546-0777
Contact: John Magill
Hours: 9:00 am -5:00 pm M-F

Able to vacuum freeze-dry 50 cubic feet of wet library materials (approximately 625 volumes) at a cost of $55-60 per cubic foot. Can also make arrangements for larger quantities with McDonnell Douglas (thermal vacuum drying) or a Canadian company with a 500-cubic-foot vacuum freeze-dry chamber.

Blackman-Mooring Steamatic Catastrophe, Inc.
International Headquarters
303 Arthur Street
Fort Worth, TX 76107
Toll Free: (800) 433-2940
Telephone: (817) 332-2770; 24-hour hotline
Fax: (817) 332-6728
Hours: 8:00 am -5:30 pm M-F

Disaster recovery services, odor removal, vacuum freeze-drying; provides extensive recovery and restoration services and is able to handle almost any size emergency. Recovery services include paper-based materials as well as electronic equipment and magnetic media. Book and document collections are vacuum freeze-dried for approximately $40 per cubic ft. based on a 500-cubic-foot (approx. 6,250 volumes) load. Offers a free standby service agreement that creates a customer profile, capturing information that is vital in an emergency prior to an event. Portable blast freezer available.

Disaster Recovery Services
2425 Blue Smoke Court South
Ft. Worth, TX 76105
Toll Free: (800) 856-3333 (24-hr. hotline)
Telephone: (817) 535-6793
Fax: (817) 536-1167
Hours: 8:00 am - 5:00 pm M-F; 24-hr hotline

Disaster recovery and recovery planning services, vacuum freeze-drying.

Document Reprocessors
5611 Water Street
Middlesex (Rochester), NY 14507
Telephone: (716) 554-4500
(888) 437-9464; 24-hr. hotline
Fax: (716) 554-4114
Hours: 8:00 am - 5:00 pm M-F

Vacuum freeze-drying, disaster recovery of computer media, microfiche and microfilm, books, business records.

Uses vacuum freeze-drying to recover water-damaged materials. The vacuum freeze-dry chamber has an 800-cubic-ft. capacity which translates to approximately 10,000 volumes. The rate for freeze-drying varies but is generally about $60 per cubic foot. Also has a thermal freeze-drying process that employs heat and a cold trap. During the drying operation materials cycle from -40 to 60 degrees.

Midwest Freeze-Dry, Ltd.
Midwest Center for Stabilization and Conservation
7326 North Central Park
Skokie, IL 60076
Telephone: (847) 679-4756
Fax: (847) 679-4191
Hours: Open by Appointment M-F; 24-hr. call monitoring

Freeze-drying of historical volumes, manuscripts, microfilm, blueprints. Uses vacuum freeze-drying to salvage wet books and documents. Their chamber will hold 150 milk crates (approximately 2500 cubic feet, or 31,250 volumes). Call for price.

Munters Corporation—Moisture Control Services
79 Monroe Street
Amesbury, MA 01913
Contact: Barry Kray
Toll Free: (800) 797-5020; 24-hr. hotline
Telephone: (978) 241-1100
Fax: (978) 241-1218
Hours: 7:30 am - 8:00 pm M-F

Disaster recovery services, building dehumidification, drying services, microfilm drying services. Will dry to customer's specifications or will recommend an appropriate method. Choices include: vacuum freeze-drying, in situ drying through dehumidification, or stabilization by freezing materials to be dried at a later time. The vacuum freeze-dryer has a 100-cubic-foot, or 1,250 volume, capacity. Cost is approximately $50 per cubic foot with a reduction for quantities greater than 500-cubic-ft.

Solex Environmental Systems
P.O. Box 460242
Houston, TX 77056
Contact: Don Hartsell
Toll Free: (800) 848-0484; 24-hr. hotline
Telephone: (713) 963-8600
Fax: (713) 461-5877
Hours: 8:00 am - 6:00 pm M-F

Disaster recovery, dehumidification, building drying services. Specialty is drying wet materials. Solex's cryogenic dehydration chamber can accommodate a 40 ft. trailer of materials. Solex also offers vacuum freeze-drying and additional services, such as dehumidification of large spaces. The vacuum freezer has a capacity of 1000 cubic feet (12,500 volumes) at $40 per cubic foot. The minimum job is 250 cubic feet.

CLEANING SERVICES, FUMIGATION, FIRE, AND SMOKE

ECS Companies, Inc.
19 Wheeling Avenue
Woburn, MA
Telephone: (800) 696-4054; 24-hours or (617) 935-4455
Contact: Andy Eromine

Clean-up after fire and water damage.

Pro-Care
3 North Maple Street
Woburn, MA 01801
Toll Free: (800) 660-1973
Telephone: (617) 933-7400
Contact: Otto Marenholz
Hours: 8:30 am -5:00 pm M-F (24 hour answering service)

Can help with the clean-up after a fire or water emergency, including mold removal. Also offers air-duct cleaning services. Uses compressed air and HEPA filtration to clean both supply and return duct work.

UNICCO Service Company
89 South Street
Boston, MA 02116
Telephone: (617) 330-7878 or (617) 782-3300
Fax: (617) 864-5829
Contact: Paul B. McAleer
Hours: 8:30 am -5:00 pm M-F

Offers a variety of maintenance, operations, and engineering services and can provided highly specialized cleaning services to libraries.

ENVIRONMENTAL STABILIZATION

Munters Corporation - Moisture Control Services
79 Monroe Street
Amesbury, MA 01913-4404
Toll-Free: (800) 797-5020 (24-hr.)
Telephone: (978) 241-1100
Fax: (978) 241-1218
Hours: 7:30 am - 8:00 pm M-F
Contact: Barry Kray

Known for drying out buildings after water emergencies. Structural drying is one of their specialties. Charges for drying vary widely based on the type of structures to be dried and the type of equipment used.

World Wide Drying
Silver City Restoration
24 Weir Avenue
P.O. Box 750
Taunton, MA 02780
Toll Free: (800) 442-1911
Telephone: (508) 823-0189
Fax: (508) 823-9374
Contact: Kathy Zoll

Specialize in dehumidification and restoration services. Use portable refrigerating dehumidifiers in a wide range of sizes in conjunction with forced air movement. Focus and experience is with the structural and interior drying of buildings, although the companies also offer salvage of books, documents, and magnetic tape. Fees vary based on the type of equipment used and the type of job.

CONSULTING SERVICES

Conservation Center for Art and Historic Artifacts
264 South 23rd Street
Philadelphia, PA 19103
Telephone: (215) 545-0613
Contact: Ingrid Bogel, Executive Director

CCAHA Field Services can provide advice about recovery of various types of collections, specializing in conservation of paper-based materials. Conservators are able to advise on special collections. Photographic conservator on staff. Consultation services over the phone are free; the rate for on-site work is $70/hr.

Federal Emergency Management Agency (FEMA) Headquarters
500 C Street, SW
Washington, DC 20472
Telephone: (202) 646-4600
http://www.fema.gov

Free publications relating to emergency preparedness.

Fogg Art Museum
28 Quincy Street
Cambridge, MA 02138
Telephone: (617) 495-2392
Contact: Craigen Bowen

Offers consultation for paper artifacts, objects, and paintings. Treatment for damaged items can also be arranged. No assistance for textiles is provided.

National Fire Protection Association
1 Batterymarch Park
Quincy, MA 02269-9101
Toll Free: (617) 770-3000
Fax: (617) 770-0700
E-mail: library@nfpa.org
http://www.nfpa.org

Fire prevention information and standards.

Northeast Document Conservation Center
100 Brickstone Square
Andover, MA 01810-1494
Telephone: (978) 470-1010 (24-hr.)
Fax: (978) 475-6021
Contact: Steve Dalton or Karen Brown
http://www.nedcc.org

Able to provide basic advice and references in the event of an emergency. Staff conservators are also available for expert consultation. The field rate for conservation is $530/day. There is no charge in case of dire emergency.

Peabody Museum
Conservation Department
11 Divinity Avenue
Cambridge, MA 02138
Telephone: (617) 495-2487
Contact: T. Rose Holdcraft

Conservators at the Peabody Museum will consult or advise on the recovery and treatment of archaeological, ethnographic, and historic objects and textiles. Strauss Center for Conservation.

Williamstown Art Conservation Laboratory, Inc.
Clark Art Institute
225 South Street
Williamstown, MA 01267
Telephone: (413) 458-5741
Contact: Lori van Handel
Hours: 9:00 am - 5:00 pm M-F. Nights and weekends call the Clark Art Institute and specify nature of emergency: (413) 458-9545.

Field service provides basic recovery information. Specializes in the conservation of paper, paintings, furniture, and wooden objects, as well as sculpture and the decorative arts. Not a source for textile information. Fees are charged on a case-by-case basis. Generally there is no charge for emergency consultation services.

PEST MANAGEMENT

Archos
126 Prospect Street
Cambridge, MA 02139
Telephone: (617) 492-8621
Chicora Foundation, Inc.
P.O. Box 8664
861 Arbutus Drive
Columbia, SC 29202-8664
Telephone: (803) 787-6910
http://palimpest.stanford.edu/byorg/chicora

While telephone consultations are free, more in-depth consulting is offered on a for-fee basis. Call for more information on services and associated costs.

Insects Limited, Inc.
Fumigation Service & Supply, Inc.
16950 Westfield Park Road
Westfield, IN 46074
Telephone: (317) 896-9300
Fax: (317) 867-5757
http://www.insectslimited.com/insects.htm

Speciliazing in bio-rational means of pest control, pheromones, and other least toxic measures as well as advanced fumigation techniques.

Keepsake Systems Inc.
59 Glenmount Park Road
Toronto, ON M4E 2N1
Canada
Telephone: (416) 703-4696
Fax: (416) 703-5991
E-mail: keepsafe@interlog.com
http://www.interlog.com/~keepsafe/
Contact: Jerry Shiner, President

Supplier of anoxic packaging materials and services, barrier films, bags, "Ageless," etc.

Pest Control Services
14 East Stratford Avenue
Lansdowne, PA 19050
Telephone: (610) 284-6249
Fax: (610) 622-3037

IPM inspections and development of IPM programs for museums, historical societies, libraries, and archives. Services also include mold remediation.

Society for the Preservation of New England Antiquities
Haverhill, MA
Telephone: (978) 521-4788
Contact: Gary Rattigan

Fumigates using a carbon-dioxide bubble. The 2-week process has a 95% kill rate. The remaining 5% are usually eggs or adult carpet beetles. The bubble is 11' x 11' x 8'.

SALVAGE - ELECTRONIC DATA & EQUIPMENT

ACS Data Recovery Service
42-220 Green Way, Suite B
Palm Desert, CA 92211
Telephone: (760) 568-4351
Fax: (760) 341-8694
http://www.averdrivetronics.com/acs-data-recovery.html

In business since 1979. Specializes in repairing damaged data caused by hardware failure, virus contamination, and user error.

Data Mechanix Services
Irvine, CA
Toll Free: (800) 886-2231
Fax:
E-mail:
http://www.datamechanix.com

Specializing in the rescue of lost data from hard disk drives and other storage media.

Data Recovery Labs
85 Scarsdale Road, Suite 100
Toronto, ON M3B 2R2
Canada
Toll Free: (800) 563-1167
Toll Free: (877) datarec
Telephone: (416) 510-6990
Toll Free Fax: (800) 563-6979
Fax: (416) 510-6992
Telephone Support: 8 am - 8 pm EST
E-mail: helpme@datarec.com
http://www.datarec.com

Provides custom-engineered data-recovery solutions and data-evidence investigations. Free pre-recovery analysis.

Data Recovery and Reconstruction (Data R&R)
P.O. Box 35993
Tucson, AZ 85740
Telephone: (520) 742-5724
E-mail: datarr@datarr.com
http://www.datarr.com

A charge of $75.00/per drive is required for decontamination of fire- or water-damaged drives. Offers a $150.00 discount for non-profit organizations. No charge for preliminary diagnostics.

ECO Data Recovery

4115 Burns Road
Palm Beach Gardens, FL 33410
Toll Free: (800) 339-3412
Telephone: (561) 691-0019
Fax: (561) 691-0014
http://www.eco-datarecov.com

Specializing in electronic data retrieval and restoration of failed hard drives.

ESS (Electronic System Services)

118 Parkwood Road
Carbondale, IL 62901
Telephone: (888) 759-8758 or (618) 529-4138
Fax: (618) 529-5152
E-mail: info@datarecovery.org
http://www.datarecovery.org

Charges no evaluation fee, and can provide 24-hour turnaround. Disks may be sent to the address above with or without prior approval. Please enclose your contact information with your hard drive.

Excalibur

101 Billerica Avenue
5 Billerica Park
North Billerica, MA 01862-1256
Toll Free: (800) 726-3669
Telephone: (978) 663-1700
Fax: (978) 670-5901
Contact: http://www.excaliburdr.com

A computer-recovery service that can recover data from loss caused by many types of disaster. They have experience working with many types of media and more than twenty operating systems.

Micro-Surgeon

6 Sullivan Street
Westwood, NJ 07675
Telephone: (201) 666-7880
After 5:00 PM EST: (201) 619-1796 (please enter " #" after leaving your number)
E-mail: datarr@datarr.com
http://msurgeon.com/

Offers evaluations based upon a flat rate of $75 per drive and includes all diagnostic services related to determination of recovery feasibility. Special discounts for the educational market are offered.

Ontrack
6321 Bury Drive
Eden Prairie, MN 55346
Toll Free: (800) 872-2599
Phone: (612) 937-5161
Fax: (612) 937-5750
http://www.ontrack.com

Offers emergency and on-site data-recovery services as well as Remote Data Recovery (RDR).

Restoration Technologies, Inc.
3695 Prairie Lake Court
Aurora, IL 60504
Toll Free: (800) 421-9290
Fax: (708) 851-1774

Offers a broad range of cleaning services, from cleaning and disinfecting heating, ventilation, and air conditioning systems (HVAC) to computer media. However their specialty is electronic equipment, including computers, printers, video tape recorders, cameras, etc.

TexStar Technologies
3526 FM 528, Suite 200
Friendswood, Texas 77546
Telephone: (281) 282-9902
Fax : (281) 282-9904
http://www.texstartech.com/index.html

Specializes in data recovery, computer security, software design, systems integration, and Internet services.

SALVAGE - MAGNETIC MEDIA

Film Technology Company, Inc.
726 North Cole Avenue
Hollywood, CA 90038
Telephone: (323) 464-3456
Fax: (323) 464-7439
E-mail: filmtech@primenet.com

Nitrate movie film duplication.

John E. Allen, Inc.
116 North Avenue
Park Ridge, NJ 07656
Telephone: (201) 391-3299
Fax: (201) 391-6335

Nitrate movie film duplication.

Karl Malkames
1 Sherwood Place
Scarsdale, NY 10583
Telephone: (914) 723-8853

Nitrate movie film duplication.

Restoration House
Film Group, Inc.
PO Box 298
Belleville, ON K8N 5A2
Canada
Telephone: (613) 966-4076
Fax: (613) 966-8431

Nitrate movie film duplication.

Smolian Sound Studios
1 Wormans Mill Court
Frederick, MD 21701
Telephone: (301) 694-5134
Contact: Steve Smolian

Well known for offering all types of audio tape restoration. Also works with acetate and shellac discs.

Sound Studios, Inc.
1296 East 48th Street
Brooklyn, NY 11234-2102
Telephone: (718) 338-8284 or (212) 870-1694
Contact: Seth B. Winner

Consulting and treatment of audio tape collections. Able to work with a variety of formats.

SPECS Brothers
PO Box 5
Ridgefield Park, NJ 07660
Toll Free: (800) 852-7732
Telephone: (201) 440-6589
Fax: (201) 440-6588
URL: www.specsbros.com
Contact: Peter Brothers

Specializies in the recovery of videotapes after any type of disaster. Offers recovery advice, assistance, and cleaning and copying services for affected tapes. Also cleans and copies archival video and audio tapes.

SALVAGE - MICROFILM

Eastman Kodak Company
Disaster Recovery Laboratory
1700 Dewey Avenue
B-65, Door G, Room 340
Attention: Howard Schartz
Rochester, NY 14650-1819
Toll Free: 800-EKC-TEST (352-8378)
Telephone: (716) 253-3907

Reprocesses original camera films (only Kodak brand) free of charge. There is no limit on the number of rolls. Films should be packaged according to Kodak's instructions which are given when Kodak is notified.

New England Micrographics
750 E. Industrial Park Drive
Manchester, NH 03109
Telephone: (603) 625-1171
Fax: (603) 625-2515

Reprocesses any amount of water-damaged microfilm, and also provides off-site storage for microfilm and computer media. Cost is based on the size and nature of the request. Works with Fuji film and Ilford color film.

SALVAGE - PHOTOGRAPHIC MATERIALS

Conservation Center for Art and Historic Artifacts
264 South 23rd Street
Philadelphia, PA 19103
Telephone: (215) 545-0613
Contact: Virgilia Rawnsley

Provides advice about recovery of various types of collections. A photograph conservator is on staff to advise on recovery and treatment options for photographic collections.

Northeast Document Conservation Center
100 Brickstone Square
Andover, MA 01810-1494
Telephone: (978) 470-1010 (24 hrs.)
Fax: (978) 475-6021
http://www.nedcc.org
Contact: Steve Dalton or Karen Brown

Has 3 photograph conservators with a wide range of knowledge of the various photographic formats. Conservators are available for expert consultation, advice, and treatment of collections involved in natural or other disasters.

Northeast Document
Conservation Center
100 Brickstone Square
Andover, MA 01810-1494
www.nedcc.org
Tel: (978) 470-1010
Fax: (978) 475-6021

EMERGENCY SALVAGE OF
WET BOOKS AND RECORDS

**by Sally Buchanan, Associate Professor
School of Information Science
University of Pittsburgh**

The recovery of books and records after exposure to a water-based emergency can be successful and cost-effective if staff and management are prepared ahead of time and react in a timely way. Many libraries and archives have recovered in splendid form because staff knew precisely what to do in an emergency. However, if decisions and actions are delayed more than a few hours, collections may be lost or so seriously damaged that recovery becomes a major undertaking. Funds must be diverted from other projects. Service for the public and scholars is interrupted, and public relations suffer. The key steps for a satisfactory emergency recovery include:

- Timely initial response
- A detailed disaster plan
- Educated staff
- Committed management
- Effective communication
- Quick, informed decisions

Rapid response is essential for an effective recovery effort. Paper-based collections begin to distort physically immediately after becoming wet. Books swell and distort; paper cockles; inks and pigments run; coated papers begin to adhere to one another. Materials that could be dried easily and relatively inexpensively if attended to quickly become candidates for rebinding, expert conservation, or discard. Unfortunately, many librarians believe that replacement of water-damaged materials is the best solution, only to find that many items are not replaceable. Or they are replaceable in formats that are not acceptable to users or compatible with service goals. Collections of some breadth and depth may never recover their former distinction.

If environmental conditions are poor after a water problem, mold will begin to bloom in as little as 2-3 days, developing first in the gutters and spines of bound materials, and spreading rapidly thereafter. Once established, mold is extremely difficult to control and eradicate, frequently causing problems in the facility for many months after the recovery effort is concluded.

Recovery from exposure to water is more successful if collections and facilities are stabilized as soon as possible. This means that the immediate environment must receive attention. Water must be removed; temperature and humidity controlled; and dry collections protected. At the same time, wet books and records should, in most instances, be removed from the site following accepted procedures, and stabilized by freezing.

After a serious water emergency, questions often arise that deserve attention. Are any of these materials expendable because they no longer are used, have no relationship to the current collection development plan, or have no value? Can they be purchased in another format that will be acceptable to users? Would the purchase in another format create hidden expenses in the future? For example, will there be a need to upgrade equipment, hardware, or software to access the information? Does the institution have obligations to the region or even the world's library?

For books and records that have been water damaged, there are several drying techniques which have been tested and perfected over the past decade. The selection of one or more of these depends upon the extent and severity of water damage, the composition of the materials affected, the expected use and retention of the collections, and the documented facts related to the overt and hidden costs of recovery using various drying methods. These will be described briefly with comments about the kinds of damage and the specific collection materials for which they were developed as well as the short- and long-term costs of employing them.

Advice from a preservation manager or a conservator experienced in disaster recovery can be helpful before making final decisions. If rare books or unique materials are involved, a conservator should always be consulted so mistakes can be avoided. Successful recovery operations over the past decade have demonstrated repeatedly that if sound recovery methods are followed, it is less expensive to dry original collections than to replace them.

It is important to understand that no drying method restores collections. If time must be taken to make critical decisions and materials have distorted badly, that is the way they will look when dry. However, if collections are stabilized quickly, they can often be dried and returned to the shelves with little discernible damage.

Air Drying

Air drying is the oldest and most common method of dealing with wet books and records. It can be employed for one item or many, but it is most suitable for small numbers of damp or slightly wet books and documents. Because it requires no special equipment, it is often believed to be an inexpensive method of drying. But it is extremely labor intensive, it can occupy a great deal of space, and it usually results in badly distorted bindings and textblocks. It is seldom successful for drying bound volumes with coated paper. The rehabilitation costs after air drying tend to be extensive because most bound material requires rebinding. Single sheets are often distorted requiring flattening and rehousing. It is not unusual for mold to develop during extensive air-drying operations. Another hidden cost of air drying is the extra amount of shelf space required for collections. Depending upon how quickly wet materials are stabilized, the minimum amount of additional space required after drying will be 20%-30%.

Dehumidification

Drying by dehumidification has been employed for many years by business and industry to dry out buildings, the holds of ships, and mammoth storage containers. Large, commercial dehumidifiers are placed in a facility with all the collections, equipment, and furnishings left in place. Temperature and humidity are carefully controlled to specifications. This drying method is especially effective for library or archives buildings that have suffered extensive water damage to the structure itself. It can be used for collections that have suffered only slight to moderate water damage, but is not safe for water-soluble inks or pigments. Slightly damp coated paper may be dried this way if swelling and adhesion have not taken place before the process is initiated. The number of items that can be treated with dehumidification is limited only by the expertise or the equipment of the company. This drying method has the advantage of leaving the collections in place on the shelves and in storage containers, eliminating the costly step of removal to a freezer or vacuum chamber. Dehumidification is especially effective in conjunction with other drying methods and for stabilizing the building and environment.

Freezer Drying

A modest number of books and records that are only damp or moderately wet may be dried quite successfully in a self-defrosting blast freezer if left there long enough. The temperature in the freezer must be maintained no warmer than -10 degrees F. Materials should be placed in the freezer as soon as possible after becoming wet. Books will dry best if their bindings are supported firmly to inhibit initial swelling. One method is to support books between clear acrylic "boards" with holes drilled in them to facilitate drying. The book and boards can be wrapped with a strong elastic cord which will keep them firmly supported as the books dry and shrink slightly. Documents may be placed in the freezer in stacks or spread out for faster drying. Small numbers of leather and vellum bindings can be dried successfully this way. Expect this method to take from several weeks to many months, depending upon the temperature of the freezer and the extent of water damage, because it is a passive technology. Caution is advised with coated paper as leaves may adhere to one another while drying. If items are placed in the freezer very soon after becoming wet, additional shelf or storage space will be held to a minimum.

Thermaline or Cryogenic Drying

This is the copyrighted name for a new drying technique currently being tested and revised to meet special needs. Intended primarily for rare book and manuscript collections, the process was developed to address the difficulty of drying large numbers of rare books bound in leather or vellum. It employs blast freezers at very low temperatures and is an advanced variation of the Freezer Drying method described above, using sophisticated technology to hasten the drying in a more active approach. Because books receive a great deal of individual handling to ensure the most effective drying with the least amount of damage, this process is the most expensive of the drying methods. It is safe for water-soluble media and for coated papers. As with vacuum freeze drying, if carried out properly, Thermaline Drying never distorts materials as a result of the process.

Vacuum Freeze Drying

This process calls for sophisticated equipment and is especially suitable for large numbers of wet books and records as well as for water-soluble inks and for coated paper. Frozen books and records are placed in a vacuum chamber. The vacuum is pulled, a source of heat introduced, and the collections, dried at temperatures below 32 degrees F, remain frozen. The physical process known as sublimation takes place—i.e., ice crystals vaporize without melting. This means that there is no additional wetting, swelling, or distortion beyond that incurred before the frozen materials were placed in the chamber. If materials have been stabilized quickly after becoming wet, very little extra shelf or storage space will be required when they are dry. 10% additional shelf space is a sound estimate to use for planning.

Many coated papers can be difficult to dry without adhering once they are wet. Because it is nearly impossible to determine which paper will block, all coated papers should be treated the same way for the purpose of vacuum freeze drying: before any drying takes place, and ideally within six hours of exposure, materials should be frozen at -10 degrees F or lower. They may then be vacuum freeze dried with a high potential for success. Rare and unique materials can be dried successfully by vacuum freeze drying, but leathers and vellums may not survive. Although this method may initially appear to be more expensive because of the equipment required, the results are often so satisfactory that additional funds for rebinding are not necessary, and mud, dirt and/or soot are lifted to the surface, making cleaning less time-consuming. If only a few books are dried, vacuum freeze drying can be expensive. However, companies that offer this service are often willing to dry one client's small group of books with another client's larger group, reducing the per-book cost and making the process affordable.

Vacuum Thermal Drying

Books and records that are slightly to extensively wet may be dried in a vacuum thermal drying chamber into which they are placed either wet or frozen. The vacuum is drawn, heat is introduced, and the materials are dried just above 32 degrees F. This means that the materials stay wet while they dry. This method is used extensively in the food industry for freeze drying certain foods. It is an acceptable method of drying wet records that have no long-term value. The method often produces extreme distortion in books, and almost always causes blocking of coated paper. For large numbers of collections, vacuum thermal drying is easier than air drying and almost always more cost-effective. However, extensive rebinding or recasing of books should be expected as should the need for expanded shelf or storage space.

How to Air Dry Wet Records

Wet records may be air dried if care is taken to follow guidelines suggested by preservation experts. The technique is most suitable for small numbers of records that are damp or water damaged only around the edges. If there are hundreds of single pages, or if the water damage is severe, other methods of drying will be more satisfactory and cost-effective. Stacks of documents on coated, or shiny, paper must be separated immediately to prevent adhesion, or they must be frozen to await a later drying decision. Care must be taken with water-soluble inks as well. Records with running or blurred inks should be frozen immediately to preserve the written record. After the items are frozen, conservators can be contacted for advice and assistance.

If records must be air dried, the following steps will help achieve satisfactory results. Wet paper is extremely fragile and easily torn or damaged, so care must be exercised. Once wet, records will never look the same, and at least some cockling should be expected.

1. Secure a clean, dry environment where the temperature and humidity are as low as possible. The temperature must be below 70 degrees F. and the humidity below 50%, or mold will probably develop and distortion will be extreme.

2. Keep the air moving at all times using fans in the drying area. This will accelerate the drying process and discourage the growth of mold. If materials are dried outside, remember that prolonged exposure to direct sunlight may fade inks and accelerate the aging of paper. Be aware that breezes can blow away single records. Train fans into the air and away from the drying records.

3. Single leaves can be laid out on tables, floors, and other flat surfaces, protected if necessary by paper towels or clean, unprinted newsprint, or clotheslines may be strung close together and records laid across them for drying.

4. If records are printed on coated paper, they must be separated from one another to prevent them from sticking. This is a tedious process that requires skill and patience. Practice ahead of time will prove useful. Place a piece of polyester film on the stack of records. Rub it gently down on the top sheet. Then slowly lift the film while peeling off the top sheet. Hang the polyester film up to dry on a clothesline using closepins. As the document dries, it will separate from the surface of the film, so it must be monitored carefully. Before it falls, remove it and allow it to finish drying on a flat surface.

5. Once dry, records may be rehoused in clean folders and boxes, or they may be photocopied or reformatted in other ways. Dried records will always occupy more space than ones that have never been water damaged.

How to Air Dry Wet Books

Air drying is most appropriate for books that are only damp or wet in limited places such as along the edges. Books that are soaking wet should be frozen and vacuum freeze dried to minimize cockling of pages and distortion of the text block and binding. Books containing coated paper should be frozen while still wet and vacuum freeze dried for best results. Books with running or blurred inks must be frozen immediately to preserve the contents.

1. Refer to steps 1 and 2 in the section How to Air Dry Wet Records.

2. Interleave every few pages, starting from the back of the book, turning pages carefully. For interleaving, use paper towels or clean, unprinted newsprint. Be careful to avoid interleaving too much or the spine will become concave and the volume distorted. Complete the interleaving by placing clean blotter paper inside the front and back covers. Close the book gently and place it on several sheets of absorbent paper. Change the interleaving frequently. Turn the book from head to tail each time it is interleaved.

3. When books are dry but still cool to the touch, they should be closed, laid flat on a table or other horizontal surface, gently formed into the normal shape, with convex spine and concave front edge (if that was their original shape), and held in place with a light weight. Do not stack drying books on top of each other. In no case should books be returned to the shelves until thoroughly dry; otherwise mold may develop, particularly along the gutter margin.

4. Dampness will persist for some time in the gutter, along the spine, and between boards and flyleaves. This is particularly true of volumes sewn on an oversewing machine. Check often for mold growth while books are dying.

5. If the edges of the book are only slightly wet, the book may be stood on end and fanned open slightly in the path of a flow of air (as from a fan). To minimize distortion of the edges, lay volumes flat under light pressure just before drying is complete. Paper or cloth-covered bricks work well for weights.

6. If you can establish an air-conditioned room capable of maintaining a constant relative humidity of 25 to 35% and temperature between 50 and 65 degrees F, books with only wet edges can be dried successfully in approximately two weeks without interleaving. Do not try to dry books printed on coated paper by this method. In most cases, the only chance of saving such books is to freeze them while they are wet and dry them by vacuum freeze dying.

Acknowledgements

The author acknowledges expertise from many people who have contributed to the understanding of emergency recovery methods. These include Willman Spawn, Peter Waters, Olivia Primanis, and the staff at NEDCC.

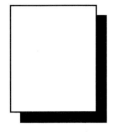

Northeast Document
Conservation Center
100 Brickstone Square
Andover, MA 01810-1494
www.nedcc.org
Tel: (978) 470-1010
Fax: (978) 475-6021

**TECHNICAL
LEAFLET**

**EMERGENCY
MANAGEMENT**

Section 3, Leaflet 8

EMERGENCY SALVAGE OF WET PHOTOGRAPHS

by Gary Albright
Senior Paper/Photograph Conservator
Northeast Document Conservation Center

Because of the number of photographic processes and their wide variety, responsible advice for the emergency salvage all kinds of wet photographs is difficult to provide. Some processes can withstand immersion in water for a day or more, whereas others would be permanently disfigured or even destroyed by a couple of minutes of exposure. In general, wet photographs should be air dried or frozen as quickly as possible. Once they are stabilized by either of these methods, there is time to decide what course of action to take.

Ideally, salvage should occur under the supervision of a conservator who can minimize damage to a collection if he or she can direct the salvage and treat the collection immediately after the damage has occurred. Time is of the essence: the longer the period of time between the emergency and salvage, the greater the amount of permanent damage that will occur.

MINIMIZE IMMERSION TIME

Photographs in water will quickly deteriorate: images can separate from mounts, emulsions can dissolve or stick together, and staining can occur. Mold can grow within 48 hours at 60% relative humidity and 70°F, and it often causes permanent staining and other damage to photographs. For these reasons photographs need to be dried as quickly as possible. If photographs cannot be dried they should be frozen.

SALVAGE PRIORITIES FOR WET PHOTOGRAPHS

- In general, films (plastic-based materials) appear to be more stable than prints (paper-based materials); therefore, prints should be salvaged first. Important exceptions include deteriorated nitrate and safety films, which are extremely susceptible to water damage.

- Photographs made by the following processes should be salvaged first: ambrotypes, tintypes, collodion wet plate negatives, gelatin dry plate negatives, lantern slides, deteriorated nitrate or safety film, autochromes, carbon prints, woodburytypes, deteriorated or unhardened gelatin prints, and color materials. Photographs made by many of these processes will not survive immersion.

- Photographs that are more stable in water include: daguerreotypes, salted paper prints, albumen prints, collodion prints, platinum prints, and cyanotypes.

AIR DRYING PHOTOGRAPHS

- If personnel, space, and time are available, photographs can be air dried.

- Separate photographs from their enclosures, frames, and from each other. If they are stuck together or adhered to glass, set them aside for freezing and consultation with a conservator.

- Allow excess water to drain off the photographs.

- Spread the photographs out to dry, face up, laying them flat on an absorbent material such as blotters, unprinted newsprint, paper towels, or a clean cloth.

- Keep the air around the drying materials moving at all times. Fans will speed up the drying process and minimize the risk of mold growth.

- Negatives should be dried vertically. They can be hung on a line with plastic clips placed at the edges.

- Photographs may curl during drying. They can be flattened later.

FREEZING PHOTOGRAPHS

- If immediate air drying of photographs is not possible or if photographs are stuck together, freeze them.

- Wrap or interleave photographs with waxed paper before freezing.

- Interleave or wrap individual photographs or groups of photographs before freezing with a non-woven polyester material or waxed paper. This will make them easier to separate when they are eventually treated.

DRYING FROZEN PHOTOGRAPHS

- Frozen photographs are best dried by thawing, followed by air drying. As a stack of photographs thaws, individual photographs can be carefully peeled from the group and placed face up on a clean, absorbent surface to air dry.

- Vacuum thermal drying, where the frozen material is thawed and dried in a vacuum, is not recommended for photographs. Gelatin photographs undergoing this procedure have a tendency to mottle severely and stick together.

- Photographs can be vacuum freeze dried; in this process no thawing occurs. Gelatin photographs may mottle during the procedure, but they will not stick together.

- Wet collodion glass plates must never be freeze dried; they will not survive. This is also true for all similar collodion processes such as ambrotypes, collodion lantern slides, and tintypes.

SALVAGING SLIDES

- Slides can be rinsed and dipped in a water/Photo-flo mixture, slide cleaner, or a similar commercial product and air dried; preferably they should be hung on a line or propped on edge.

- Ideally, slides should be removed from their frames for drying and then remounted.

- Slides mounted between glass must be removed from the glass or they will not dry.

CALL A QUALIFIED CONSERVATOR

Dried or frozen photographs are reasonably stable. Store them until you can talk to a conservator who has experience with photographs and can advise you of treatment needs.

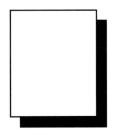

Northeast Document
Conservation Center

100 Brickstone Square
Andover, MA 01810-1494
www.nedcc.org
Tel: (978) 470-1010
Fax: (978) 475-6021

EMERGENCY SALVAGE OF MOLDY BOOKS AND PAPER

by Beth Lindblom Patkus
Preservation Consultant
Walpole, MA

INTRODUCTION

Most librarians and archivists have seen the effects of mold on paper materials, but many have never experienced an active mold outbreak. Dealing with such an outbreak (large or small) can be overwhelming. This leaflet provides some basic information about mold and outlines the steps that need to be taken to stop mold growth and begin to salvage collections.

Please note that the actions recommended here are basic stabilization techniques to be undertaken in-house for small to moderate outbreaks. The complexities of dealing with a large number of wet and moldy materials will usually require outside assistance, and some suggestions for dealing with a major mold outbreak, appear at the end of this leaflet. In all cases, a conservator or preservation professional should be consulted if any questions arise or if further treatment is necessary.

WHAT IS MOLD?

Mold and *mildew* are generic terms that refer to various types of fungi, microorganisms that depend on other organisms for sustenance. There are over 100,000 known species of fungi. The great variety of species means that patterns of mold growth and the activity of mold in a particular situation can be unpredictable, but it is possible to make some broad generalizations about the behavior of mold.

Mold propagates by disseminating large numbers of spores, which become airborne, travel to new locations, and (under the right conditions) germinate. When spores germinate, they sprout hair-like webs known as mycelium (visible mold); these in turn produce more spore sacs, which ripen and burst, starting the cycle again. Molds excrete enzymes that allow them to digest organic materials such as paper and book bindings, altering and weakening those materials. In addition, many molds contain colored substances that can stain paper, cloth, or leather. It is also important to realize that mold can be dangerous to people and in some cases can pose a major health hazard. Mold outbreaks should never be ignored or left to "go away on their own."

WHY DOES MOLD GROW?

To germinate (become *active*), spores require a favorable environment. If favorable conditions are not present, the spores remain inactive (*dormant*); in this state they can do little damage.

The most important factor in mold growth is the presence of moisture, most commonly in the air, but also in the object on which the mold is growing. Moisture in the air is measured as relative humidity (RH). In general, the higher the RH the more readily mold will grow. If the RH is over 70% for an extended period of time, mold growth is almost inevitable. It is important to remember, however, that it is possible for some species of mold to grow at lower RH as well. If collections have become wet as the result of a water disaster, this increases their susceptibility to mold growth. Other factors that will contribute to mold growth in the presence of moisture are high temperature, stagnant air, and darkness.

Mold spores, active or dormant, are everywhere. It is not possible to create an atmosphere free of spores. They exist in every room, on every object in the collection, and on every person entering the collection area. The only wholly dependable control strategy is to keep the humidity and temperature moderate so the spores remain dormant, keep collections as clean as possible, and prevent the introduction of new active mold colonies.

BASIC PRINCIPLES OF SALVAGE

REDUCE THE HUMIDITY: As noted above, moisture initiates mold growth. Reducing the humidity is essential to stopping the mold growth.

DO NOT TURN UP THE HEAT: This will not help to dry out collections and storage areas. Additional heat in the presence of moisture will cause the mold to grow faster.

IF COLLECTIONS ARE WET, DRY OR FREEZE THEM: Mold will normally grow on wet materials in about 48 hours (sometimes sooner). If you know you cannot get the affected material dry within 48 hours, it is best to freeze it. This will not kill the mold, but it will stop further growth until you have a chance to dry and clean the material.

CONSIDER THE HEALTH RISKS: A few mold species are toxic to people, and many molds are powerful sensitizers. Exposure to mold can lead to debilitating allergy even among people not prone to allergies. Everyone who works with moldy objects must be properly protected.

AVOID "QUICK AND EASY" CURES: "Quick cures" that you may have heard about (such as spraying Lysol on objects or cleaning them with bleach) may cause additional damage to items or be toxic to people; they are also often ineffective. In the past, mold-infested collections were often treated with fumigants. Ethylene oxide (ETO) will kill active mold and mold spores; other chemicals that have been used are less effective. **All** of these chemicals can have adverse effects on both collections and people, and none of them will keep the mold from recurring.

STEP-BY-STEP SALVAGE

This section provides specific steps for responding to a small or moderate mold outbreak. While the steps are numbered for convenience, they may not be carried out in exactly this order, and some of these activities will occur simultaneously.

1. **Find out what is causing the mold growth.** You need to know what is causing the problem so that additional mold on collections not yet affected can be avoided.

- Look first for an obvious source of moisture, such as a water leak.

- If there is no obvious source of moisture, use a monitoring instrument to measure the relative humidity in the affected area. If the humidity is elevated, there might be a problem with the HVAC (heating, ventilating, and air conditioning) system, or the area might be subject to higher humidity for another reason, such as having shelves placed against an outside wall. Mold might also develop in areas with poor air circulation or in areas where there is a lot of dust and dirt that might provide a food source for mold.

- Initiate repairs or resolve the problem as soon as possible. If the problem cannot be resolved quickly, salvage the collections as directed below and develop a strategy for frequent monitoring of the area for additional mold growth.

2. **Take steps to modify the environment so that it is no longer conducive to mold growth.**

- Mop up and/or use a wet-dry vacuum to remove any standing water. Bring in dehumidifiers, but be sure that a mechanism is in place to drain them periodically so they do not overflow. Bring in fans to circulate the air, and open the windows (unless the humidity is higher outside).

- Your goal should be to reduce the relative humidity to 55% or lower. Temperature should be moderate, below 70°F. Get a monitoring instrument that can measure the relative humidity and temperature accurately, and record the measurements in a log several times a day. Do not rely on your own impression of climate conditions.

3. **Implement safety precautions for staff and others working with moldy items.**

- A mycologist should be consulted to insure that no toxic mold species are present (a local hospital or university should be able to provide a reference). If toxic molds are present, DO NOT attempt to salvage materials yourself.

- If there are no toxic molds present, collections can be salvaged in-house, but everyone working with the affected materials must wear disposable plastic gloves and clothing, and use a protective mask when working with moldy objects.

- Use a respirator with a **HEPA** (high efficiency particulate) filter; pollen dust masks available in drug and hardware stores are not adequate. If you cannot use disposable clothing, be sure to leave dirty clothes in a designated area and wash them in hot water and bleach. Respirators should be wiped periodically with rubbing or denatured alcohol.

- Be aware that some people cannot wear respirators. The respirator must fit well with good contact around the nose and mouth area. In addition, they make breathing somewhat difficult and can be problematic for people with asthma or heart conditions, or people who are pregnant. It is a good idea to consult your doctor before wearing a respirator to work with moldy materials. [1]

4. **Isolate the affected items.**

- Quarantine items by removing them to a clean area with relative humidity below 45%, separate from the rest of the collection. Items should be transferred in sealed plastic bags to avoid transfer of mold to other items during the move, but they should not remain in the bags once in the clean area, since this will create a micro-environment that can foster further mold growth.

- In the case of a large mold outbreak it may be impractical to move the items; in that case the area in which they are housed should be quarantined and sealed off from the rest of the building to the extent possible (remember that this includes shutting off air circulation from the affected area).

5. **Begin to dry the materials.** Your goal is to make the mold go dormant, so that it will appear dry and powdery rather than soft and fuzzy. This will allow you to remove the mold residue more easily.

- Wet material should be dried in a cool, dry space with good air circulation. An air-conditioned space is the best for this purpose, but if that is impossible, use fans to circulate air (do not aim fans directly at objects, however, as this can damage materials and further scatter mold spores). Place paper toweling or unprinted newsprint (regular newspapers may transfer print to the wet objects) under the drying items to absorb moisture, and change this blotting material often. Air drying takes time and attention, since you must check drying materials often, and you must maintain cool, dry conditions and air circulation in the space.

- Collections may also be dried outside in the sun (sunlight or ultraviolet light can cause some molds to become dormant). The outside humidity must be low. Be aware that the sun causes fading and other damage to paper-based collections, however. Materials should be monitored closely and left outside no more than an hour or so.

- Special attention should be paid to framed objects (such as prints and drawings) and to the interior of the spines of books. A frame provides an ideal environment for mold; the back is dark, air does not circulate, and humidity can be trapped inside. Similarly, the interior of the spine of a book is particularly vulnerable to mold growth. Spines should be checked regularly during the drying process. Framed materials should be unframed immediately, and dried as above. If the item appears to be stuck to the glass in the frame, remove the backing materials from the frame and leave the item in the frame and attached to the glass. Place the framed item in a cool, dry space as described above, and consult a professional conservator.

6. **If immediate drying is not possible, freeze the affected items.**

- If the item is small enough, it can be placed in the freezer compartment of a home refrigerator, with freezer paper loosely wrapped around it to prevent it from sticking to other items.

- For items that are too big for a freezer compartment or for larger numbers of items, a commercial freezer may be necessary (grocery store, university food service, commercial cold storage facility, etc.). It is a good idea to make arrangements for commercial freezer storage before an emergency arises, since there may be restrictions on storing moldy items in a freezer that normally holds foodstuffs.

- Once time and resources are available, frozen materials can be thawed and dried in small batches, or they can be freeze-dried or vacuum freeze-dried (with the exception of photographs, which should not be freeze-dried or vacuum freeze-dried).

7. **Clean the affected items. DO NOT** try to clean active mold (soft and fuzzy) yourself. This should be done only by a conservator, who will use a vacuum aspirator to avoid further embedding the mold into the paper. The following instructions apply only to inactive (dry and powdery) mold and materials that do NOT have artifactual value: [2]

- Remove mold residue outdoors rather than in an enclosed space whenever possible. Be sure to wear protective gear (see above). If you must work indoors, use a fume hood with a filter that traps mold or in front of a fan, with the fan blowing contaminated air out a window. Close off the room from other areas of the building (including blocking the air circulation vents).

- Vacuum the mold. Use a vacuum with a HEPA filter; this will contain the mold spores. A normal vacuum will simply exhaust the spores out into the air. You can also use a wet-dry commercial-strength vacuum if the tank is filled with a solution of a fungicide such as Lysol diluted according to the label instructions. A tube from the hose inlet should extend into the solution so that incoming spores are directed there.

- Do not vacuum fragile items directly, since the suction can easily cause damage. Papers can be vacuumed through a plastic screen held down with weights. A brush attachment covered with cheesecloth or screening should be used for books to guard against loss of detached pieces. Boxes can be vacuumed directly. When disposing of vacuum bags or filters, seal them in plastic trash bags and remove them from the building.

- It is also acceptable to clean off mold with a soft brush, but this must be done carefully. Once moldy material is dry and the residue appears powdery, take a soft, wide brush (such as a watercolor wash brush) and lightly brush the powdery mold off the surface of the item. This should be done outside or the mold should be brushed into a vacuum nozzle. Be careful not to rub the mold into the surface, since that will attach it permanently to paper fibers or the cover of a book.

8. **Dry and thoroughly clean the room(s) where the mold outbreak occurred.** You may do this yourself or hire a company to provide dehumidification and/or cleaning.

- Vacuum shelves and floors with a wet-dry vacuum filled with a fungicide solution such as Lysol, then wipe them down with Lysol or a similar solution. Allow them to dry fully before returning any materials. If a musty odor lingers in the room, open containers of baking soda may help.

- It is also a good idea to have the HVAC system components (heat-exchange coils, ductwork, etc.) cleaned and disinfected, particularly if you suspect they have caused the problem.

9. **Return materials to the affected area.** Do this ONLY after the area has been thoroughly cleaned AND the cause of the mold outbreak has been identified and dealt with.

10. **Continue to monitor conditions and take steps to avoid additional mold growth.**

- Take daily readings of temperature and relative humidity, and be sure that the climate is moderate. It is particularly important to keep humidity below 55% to insure that mold will not reappear. Temperature should not exceed 70°F.

- Check problem areas frequently to insure that there is no new mold growth. Be sure to examine the gutters of books near the endbands and inside the spines.

- Keep areas where collections are stored and used as clean as possible, since dust and dirt are a source of spores, both active and dormant. Clean floors with a HEPA filter vacuum rather than sweeping, since sweeping scatters dust. House collections in protective enclosures whenever possible to keep them free of dust. Vacuum shelves and the tops of unboxed, shelved books, or clean them with a magnetic wiping cloth.

- If funds permit, install a multi-stage particulate filtration system in the building or storage area.

- Keep windows closed to prevent active spores from entering, and prohibit live plants in collection storage or use areas, since these are also a source of spores.

- Quarantine new acquisitions for a few days, and check them carefully for signs of mold.

- Avoid storing collections in potentially damp areas or in locations where water accidents are possible. Insure that regular maintenance is carried out on the building to reduce the chance of water emergencies.

- Regularly inspect the HVAC system, which is a good breeding ground for mold. Regularly clean the heat exchange coils, drip pan, and ductwork. Change air filters frequently.

- Prepare a disaster plan. This will prevent some accidents and provide strategies for dealing quickly and effectively with problems. Be sure that all employees are familiar with the plan.

DEALING WITH A MAJOR MOLD OUTBREAK

If a large portion of the collection is affected by the mold outbreak, if dangerous species of mold are present, or if the HVAC system and the building itself are also infected with mold, outside assistance will be needed. Particularly in the latter cases, it is essential to make sure that the building is safe for occupancy by staff. There are a variety of companies experienced in working with cultural collections that can assist institutions with recovery.

Most of the disaster recovery companies that provide drying services will also clean surface mold off collections. Conservators or regional conservation centers provide treatment services for individual items with artifactual value.

There are also several disaster recovery companies that specialize in dehumidifying and cleaning of buildings. In the case of a severe infestation of mold and/or an infestation that poses serious health risks to staff, companies specializing in indoor air quality can help to insure that the building is safe for occupancy. In severe cases, fumigation of the affected area may be necessary. Due to the potential for damage, fumigants should not be used directly on or in the presence of collections unless there is no other choice. Fumigation should always be done by a licensed professional.

A list of service providers is given at the end of this leaflet. Be sure that the company you choose is familiar with the requirements of cultural collections. If you are not sure how to choose a service provider, always contact a conservator or preservation professional for advice.

SUMMARY

Spores, active or dormant, are ubiquitous. Although it is impossible to get rid of all the spores, mold growth can be controlled. Most important for mold control is maintaining RH conditions below 55%, or, better, below 45%. Use of protective enclosures, meticulous housekeeping, monitoring of RH and temperature, and a watchful eye are also important. If resources allow, high-level filtration of storage areas, if not of the whole building, is recommended. Protecting library and archival collections from water accidents should be among the highest priorities for any institution. Wet collections must be immediately dried or stabilized by freezing. Moldy materials must be isolated, dried if wet, then cleaned using the strictest precautions.

NOTES

[1] Hilary Kaplan. "Mold: A Follow-up." Available on-line at http://palimpsest.stanford.edu/bytopic/mold.

[2] For these and other cleaning suggestions, see Lois Olcott Price, *Managing a Mold Invasion: Guidelines for Disaster Response*. (Philadelphia, PA: Conservation Center for Art and Historic Artifacts, 1996). CCAHA Technical Series No. 1.

FURTHER READING

Chamberlain, William R. "A New Approach to Treating Fungus in Small Libraries." *Abbey Newsletter* 15.7 (November 1991): 109.
A practical article describing the response to a mold outbreak and the preventive measures that were subsequently undertaken at the Virginia State Library. Available online at http://palimpsest.stanford.edu/byorg/abbey/.

"Mold As a Threat to Human Health." *Abbey Newsletter* 18.6, (Oct 1994).
A short article on mold as a workplace hazard for library and archival workers. Summarizes articles relevant to the subject and anecdotes from the field. Available online at http://palimpsest.stanford.edu/byorg/abbey/.

Nyberg, Sandra. *Invasion of the Giant Spore*. SOLINET Preservation Program Leaflet Number 5 (Atlanta, GA: Southeastern Library Network, 1987), 19 pp.
An updated version of this leaflet (emphasizing preventive activities and non-chemical treatments) is available from SOLINET on its web page at http://www.solinet.net/presvtn/preshome.htm or from Alicia Riley-Walden, Preservation Administrative Assistant, SOLINET Preservation Services, 1438 West Peachtree Street, NW, Suite 200, Atlanta, GA 30309-2955 (email: alicia_riley-walden@solinet.net or ariley@solinet.net). The older version of the leaflet gives a good summary of mold prevention and treatment, and also presents detailed information on various chemical treatment methods that in most cases would no longer be recommended.

Price, Lois Olcott. *Managing a Mold Invasion: Guidelines for Disaster Response.* Philadelphia, PA: Conservation Center for Art and Historic Artifacts, 1996. CCAHA Technical Series No. 1.
An excellent summary of response and recovery techniques. Includes a good bibliography that cites articles on the effects of fumigation on collections. Available from CCAHA, 264 South 23rd Street, Philadelphia, PA, 19103; (215) 545-0613, FAX (215) 735-9313, or email CCAHA@shrsys.hslc.org.

SOURCES OF SUPPLIES AND SERVICES

This list is not exhaustive, nor does it constitute an endorsement of the suppliers and services listed. We suggest that you obtain information from a number of vendors so that you can make comparisons of cost and asses the full range of available products and services.

A more complete list of suppliers is available from NEDCC. Consult the Technical Leaflets section of NEDCC's website at www.nedcc.org or contact NEDCC for the most up-to-date version in print.

Aldrich Corporation
1001 West St. Paul Avenue
Milwaukee, WI 53233
Toll Free: (800) 558-9160 (within USA)
Telephone: (414) 273-3850
Toll Free Fax: (800) 962-9591 (within USA)Fax: (414) 273-4979
http://www.sigma/aldrich.com
Respirators

American Freeze Dry
411 White Horse Pike
Audubon, NJ 08106
Telephone: (609) 546-0777
Fax: (609) 547-4158
Vacuum freeze drying, cleaning of collections

BMS Catastrophe
303 Arthur Street
Fort Worth, TX 76107
Toll Free: (800) 433-2940
Telephone: (817) 332-2770
Fax: (817) 332-6728
http://www.bmscat.com
Vacuum freeze drying, cleaning of collections, cleaning of interiors

Disaster Recovery Services, Inc.
2425 Blue Smoke Court South
Fort Worth, TX 76105
Toll Free: (800) 856-3333
Telephone: (817) 535-6793
Fax: (817) 536-1167
Vacuum freeze drying, cleaning of collections, dehumidification

Document Reprocessors
5611 Water Street
Middlesex, NY 14507
Telephone: (888) 437-9464
Telephone: (716) 554-4500
Fax: (716) 554-4114
http://www.documentreprocessors.com
Vacuum freeze drying, cleaning of collections

EnviroCenter
http://envirocenter.com
A web resource specializing in the indoor environment and indoor air quality. Provides a list of companies that specialize in indoor air quality products and services.

Ethylene Oxide Sterilization Association
1815 H Street NW, Suite 500
Washington, DC 20006
Telephone: (202) 296-6300
Fax: (202) 775-5929
E-mail: info@eosa.org
http://www.eosa.org
An industry trade group established by parties with an interest in ethylene oxide sterilization. A place to start if a company specializing in ETO fumigation is needed.

Lab Safety Supply
P.O. Box 1368
Janesville, WI 53547-1368
Toll Free: (800) 356-0783
Fax: (800) 543-9910
http://www.labsafety.com
Respirators, HEPA filter vacuums

Munters Moisture Control Services
79 Monroe Street
Amesbury, MA 01913
Telephone: (800) I CAN DRY
Telephone: (978) 241-1229
Fax: (978) 241-1218
http://www.muntersmcs.com
Dehumidification, cleaning of interiors

Nilfisk-Advance of America
300 Technology Drive
Malvern, PA 19355
Toll Free: (800) NILFISK or
Toll Free: (800) 645-3475
http://www.pa.nilfisk-advance.com
HEPA filter vacuums

Northeast Document
Conservation Center
100 Brickstone Square
Andover, MA 01810-1494
www.nedcc.org
Tel: (978) 470-1010
Fax: (978) 475-6021

PROTECTING COLLECTIONS DURING RENOVATION

by Karen Motylewski
former Director of Field Service
Northeast Document Conservation Center

INTRODUCTION

Renovation of a building is frequently a key element in developing an institutional preservation program. Renovations can correct such physical plant problems as inadequate fire protection, poor environmental control, roof leaks, and inefficient use of functional space.

Unfortunately, there are hazards associated with all construction projects. Book and paper collections are highly susceptible to damage from fire, smoke, water, dirt, chemical pollutants, and mishandling—all commonly associated with renovation. Libraries, archives, and museums need more than the protections routinely provided for standard building construction. An accident on any scale will require staff time for response and salvage and may require replacement, reformatting, or conservation treatment of the damaged materials.

In the worst case, a building itself may be lost to construction-related fire. It is highly desirable to relocate collections away from work spaces or to seal them off completely during construction, but this is often impractical. In many cases personnel are insufficient and no suitable space is available for relocation. Thorough seals require labor-intensive efforts and make collections largely inaccessible, and an institution's mission may require continued access to its holdings. An acceptable compromise must be designed to fit each situation. This leaflet is intended to alert institutions to common sources of construction-related damage and to provide some solutions for foreseeable problems.

In all cases it is critical to provide enough detail in contract specifications to insure that contractors: (1) understand the client's requirement of strict contract compliance on safety issues; (2) allow for increased costs to cover strict safety precautions; and (3) employ effective risk management strategies. Do not assume a contractor will supply even contractually specified protections without active monitoring by the client. It is difficult to project costs accurately for large-scale projects, and competitive bids often underestimate. Contractors may try to balance deficits by cutting corners. Many feel it is cheaper to clean up after a (presumably unlikely) disaster than to prevent it. Documenting conservation or replacement costs for representative collections as an attachment to requests for bids may help persuade bidders to take accident prevention seriously.

ADMINISTRATIVE AND SUPERVISORY CONCERNS

Adequate protection requires systematic staging of construction activities and good communication between the architect, the contractor, client administration, and the project liaison. An institution's staff must be able to plan for continued access to heavily used and critical collections. They must be notified of construction plans and schedules for special collection areas as soon as these are known, since these areas require unusual attention to protection and security. They must also get advanced notice of the inevitable changes in schedule as a project progresses. Details of responsibility for notification and dissemination of information should be included in the contract specifications and the institution's internal plan for project management.

It is ideal to appoint a project liaison, either from the staff or as a hired consultant. The project liaison should make sure that evacuation procedures are in place and that the staff is appropriately trained to use them. This person should coordinate a fire-fighting plan with the local fire-fighting unit, and should work in conjunction with local officials and the contractor to insure that applicable regulations are being met. The liaison should also coordinate security arrangements with staff and contractors.

The project liaison should review all contracts and specifications to insure adequate protection for collections as well as recovery in the event of damage. This should be done with the advice of the institution's legal counsel. Responsibility and contract specifications should be established for such necessary practices as on-going clean-up or sealing of areas to prevent pollutant migration and water damage. It is equally important that the contract specify the contractor's responsibility for salvage (personnel, freezing and drying collections, dehumidification of spaces, clean-up) and for restoration activities (microfilming, binding, photocopying, and conservation).

Specifications for safety practices for crew members during construction or renovations should be detailed in the contract. All smoking, eating, and drinking should be forbidden in work areas. Although library staff will most likely have primary responsibility for the handling of collections, workmen should be made aware of the vulnerability of collections and should be trained to handle books, boxes, and other materials with care if handling becomes necessary.

The contract should specify fire-protection management responsibility; normally such a function is filled by the contractor's or construction manager's staff. In addition, a client staff member should, daily, inspect collection areas affected by construction, to insure that protective wraps or seals are in place before construction starts, that clean-up is being provided, that fire and water protections are satisfactory, and that suitable ventilation is available for the use of solvents and coatings or other sources of gaseous pollutants. This person should also be responsible for advising administration of the status of the collections on a regular basis. Ideally, this would be someone other than the project liaison, but monetary and staff resources may be such that no one else can fill this role.

The staff should review the provisions of their disaster plan to make sure critical services can be rapidly obtained, and that personnel understand their role in an emergency. Phone numbers and the staff-notification system should be reviewed internally, and with the police or fire department as necessary. Immediate response procedures in the event of fire or flood should be reviewed with the contractor, staff, and local services.

A backup for catalog and inventory records for the current collection should be available in duplicate and should be stored off site. While off-site storage of backup records is recommended at all times, it is essential during renovation. For computerized records, a secondary storage site needs to be chosen and a duplication schedule established. Depending on the volume of data entry, records should be duplicated daily or weekly, and the duplicate transferred to the off-site storage location. If data entry volume is small, daily or weekly backups could be stored on site, with monthly backups at the off-site location. Hard-copy catalog and inventory records require at a minimum a duplicate shelf/storage location list, which should be stored off site. Any original (master) microfilms stored on site should be relocated. The location of master films should be documented.

The disaster plan should also include (for confidential staff and possibly fire-fighter use) the locations of collections or objects that have a high priority for salvage. These should receive preferential attention in an emergency.

FIRE HAZARDS

The second most common cause of library fires (arson is the first) is construction or renovation. Workmen often use heaters, mechanical equipment, and torches. Potentially dangerous situations include the installation of heating, ventilating, and air conditioning (HVAC) equipment, roof replacement, plumbing, and paint removal. Masonry removal, duct work, sprinklers, and electrical wiring also pose fire hazards.

Books and paper burn readily. Smoke and soot produce odors and can chemically damage paper and bindings. It is often impossible to remove all residual soot; anyone handling smoke-damaged collections will pick up the soot on his or her hands and transfer it to interior pages or to other books and papers in the collection. The intrinsic value of materials in special collections can be destroyed or severely diminished in the event of a fire.

NFPA's *Standard for the Protection of Cultural Resources* (NFPA 909) provides a brief summary of precautions necessary during renovations. Other pertinent NFPA publications are suggested at the end of this leaflet.

Fire Safety Precautions

Enhanced fire protection and emergency procedures must be in place before any construction employing electrical, mechanical, or heat-producing equipment begins.

Existing alarm systems should be inspected before any construction activities take place. Inspection should consider sensors and the integrity of their connection to the police and/or fire department or other monitor. The detection system should be tested weekly for the duration of the project. *It is critical to specify that electrical work and replacement or augmentation of fire-sensing equipment will not result in discontinuity of fire protection during non-working hours.*

The fire-safety practice of the construction crew should be evaluated by the project liaison. State or local regulations may require construction crew supervisors and journeyman workers to be trained in the use of extinguishers; most laborers are not. Ask the contractor to specify what procedures crew members will follow in the event of fire. Appropriate portable extinguishers (usually ABC-type) must be available and visible in the vicinity of any construction activities. Extinguishers can be moved with work crews as work progresses. Staff members should also know where extinguishers are located and how to use them. If there is an institutional safety officer, he or she should be able to provide or arrange for this training. The local fire marshal or fire department is often a good source of training.

Smoldering fires caused by welding or cutting may be slow to be detectable. The contract should specify protections such as halting heat-generating operations early in the construction day and posting a 30-minute (or longer) fire watch immediately afterward. See Dale Frens, *Temporary Protection,* and NFPA publications for additional detailed recommendations for fire safety during construction activities.

WATER HAZARDS

Water is a major hazard to the survival of paper-based materials. It can cause glues to dissolve, books, paper, and parchment to swell and deform, bindings to fall off, inks to run, and coated papers (glossy paper) to stick together permanently. Some photographs dissolve, while others stick together. Wet collections are highly susceptible to mold damage, which may be irreversible.

Roof and skylight replacement, the installation of pipes, fan coils, or sprinklers, and the excavation and removal of existing plumbing all pose flooding hazards during renovations. In addition, water draining into light fixtures can create a fire hazard. Areas vulnerable to broken pipes, leaks, or flooding should be identified. Roofs are highly vulnerable to damage from the weight of human traffic. A frequent cause of leaks in an already faulty system is roof evaluation or pilot work by the contractor.

Water Protection

Potential water damage will be decreased by the fire protections above, since water from fire-fighting efforts can cause extensive damage. The contractor needs to be made aware of the special vulnerability of collection materials to damage from water and mold. The client institution should specify that any area of a roof under construction will be completely secured against water infiltration before work stops each day. The project liaison should review the contract to see what provisions it contains for covering areas of the roof while work is in progress and should regularly check for compliance. A routine check of construction locations should be made at closing. These cautions pertain to skylights and patches as well as to full-scale roofing projects.

No area of roof over collection spaces should be left open unless workmen are present. Sheeting or tarps are insufficient protection over night or over weekends unless they are completely secured at joints and edges, and drainage is provided. This can be achieved by slanting coverings toward functional drainage routes. Heavy rain can pool in a flat covering; when buildup is sufficient, the covering could collapse, deluging spaces below.

Staff should always be notified about areas of skylight and roof work at least 48 hours in advance. The staff also needs to be notified 48 hours in advance when work requiring the removal or trial of water-bearing systems is scheduled, so that waterproof protections can be provided for collections, or collections can be temporarily relocated. Collections can be draped with polyethylene, but if drapes leave gaps or cover only the upper levels of stacks, they may shed water on anything in dripping range below them.

All protections should be treated and rated for fire resistance by Underwriters Laboratory (UL). Drapes should cover an entire storage unit, and should be long enough to reach slightly farther than the floor. Shelf units should be completely covered. All collections must be shelved or placed on water-resistant pallets at least 4" off the floor. Water alarms should be installed in any area containing irreplaceable research materials or artifacts. These alarms can be wired into automatic monitoring systems.

The police, the contractor, the project liaison, or other authorized personnel should know the location and operating procedures for all water mains governing pipes to building areas. Phone numbers for authorized personnel should be immediately available at all times. If a pipe is accidently ruptured, or a sprinkler system fails at any point during installation or testing, the water must be shut off at its source without delay. These provisions must be made in advance, and qualified/authorized personnel must be available on a 24-hour basis (ideally on site, from building maintenance or security departments if the institution is large enough to have such staff).

Freezer facilities, and dehumidification and water clean-up services listed in the disaster plan should be contacted by the staff or project liaison to make sure telephone numbers are current, and that services remain available in an emergency.

Procedures for the salvage of wet materials should be reviewed by the staff, so that fast, appropriate action can be taken in the event of an emergency.

ABRASION AND CHEMICAL DAMAGE

Plaster dust, sawdust, and other particulates filter onto, then into collections. They abrade paper and act as a catalyst for chemical damage. They are spread by air-handling systems, normal air currents, and traffic from one area to another.

Gases or fumes from plumbing and electrical work, paint and coatings, and epoxy-based construction materials (including much plywood, particle board, and insulating material) are similarly distributed. Many of these will react with moisture in books and paper to produce acids or other detrimental chemical reactions. It is critical to provide adequate ventilation to prevent fumes from solvents and other restoration or cleaning agents from creating a fire hazard, damaging collections, or exposing staff and users to health hazards.

Protection from Construction Materials

It is extremely important to control dust, grit, and other abrasives as much as possible by constructing temporary barriers (e.g., framing and sheeting), by hanging tarpaulins or drapes over book shelves, and by providing between-room or area seals in stack and storage spaces. All such protections must be of fire-retardant materials. *Air-handling systems must not be tested unless physical protection for collections is in place, and until obvious particulate residues have been removed.* If this recommendation is ignored, dust, grit, and other particulates will be distributed throughout a building.

Here again, the project liaison or other appropriate person should review the contract to see what routine clean-up, protection of building contents, and pollutant controls have been specified. The contractor is committed to provide reasonable protections for building occupants and contents where those are not specified by contract. The definition of "reasonable" or other defining terminology with respect to the collection's materials should be articulated.

If the contractor is not responsible for constructing barriers or temporary compartmentalization during construction, the staff will require at least 48-hour (or more) notice of work in collection areas so the collections can be relocated or protected, and so users can be warned which collections will be inaccessible. If regular staff must prepare the collections, expect routine services to be severely interrupted.

To the extent that sections of the building (e.g., floors, rooms) can be compartmentalized, they will be protected from dust and fumes generated in other areas. Effective protections may include fire-retardant framed barriers along the route of HVAC installation (floor excavations, masonry openings, duct and pipe installations). To prevent the migration of dust, such barriers need to include a ceiling and a mechanism for exhausting plaster, sawdust, fumes, etc. out of the building.

Openings between rooms or levels may pose particular problems. Such openings need to be sealed before construction begins. Sheeting fastened with tape or staples could be used, if it meets fire safety requirements, if plaster/paint layers will permit, and if fire exit routes are not obstructed. If fastenings would unacceptably damage the walls, it may be necessary to create framed barriers.

If compartmentalization is not possible, tarps or drapes may be sufficient to protect collections, which would remain accessible. Given the potential fire and health hazards (for workmen) of poorly ventilated compartments in construction areas, however, it may be better to seal and package collections themselves, e.g., shrink wrap or box books. Sealed wraps should extend from the top of each shelf unit to the floor, and from wall to wall. Emergency access to volumes would be possible by slitting the wraps and sealing the slits with duct tape after a book or box has been replaced. This should be kept to a minimum, since dust will penetrate with each opening, and the drapes themselves will deteriorate.

While wraps, drapes, and compartmentalization will provide some protection, construction-related grime is so pervasive that damage needs to be controlled by regular cleaning. Dust *cannot* be allowed to accumulate for the several years a project may require. *There should be a clean-up (vacuuming, dusting of books and furniture) as each phase of construction is completed in each area.* Back-pack or hand-held vacuums are extremely useful for this kind of cleaning. Disposable-bag vacuums are preferred. If the contractor is not responsible for this cleaning it will be necessary to assign the task to regular or temporary maintenance staff. Remember that routine services will be interrupted or compromised if regular staff must also provide this maintenance.

A complete shelf-by-shelf and item-by-item cleaning of all areas needs to be scheduled at the end of any renovation.

SECURITY

A construction project often requires that workmen have unsupervised access to areas of a building that are normally closed to the public. To protect the collection from vandalism and theft, the staff must be notified of work schedules so that they can routinely (e.g., daily, before closing) inspect areas where work is taking place. This should help identify losses or other problems rapidly, so corrective actions can be taken.

Areas containing special or rare collections should be closed to workmen (by locked doors) unless staff assigned to these collections can be present. Special collections staff should provide unobtrusive, but visible, supervision while construction-related activities are taking place. Daily inspections of special collections areas following construction activities are essential.

If unusual routes (security doors, temporary openings, or windows) are opened to expedite traffic, they must be closed when workmen leave the area. An entire facility is more vulnerable to vandalism during construction activities.

SUMMARY

Collections are exposed to predictable, increased hazards and potential loss during renovation. While it is impossible to foresee every danger or prevent all damage, it is imperative to protect collections from destructive factors that can be anticipated. A checklist of major recommendations follows.

General

_____ a. Staff of the institution have read pertinent literature and become familiar with risks and precautions common to construction projects.

_____ b. Responsibility for protecting collections from dirt, fire, and water is specified by contract. Specifications include the form protections will take and identify the party responsible for installation and maintenance.

_____ c. A project liaison is assigned (or hired) to work in close cooperation with administration, the contractor, and collections' staff liaison to insure protections are implemented and maintained.

_____ d. The disaster plan has been reviewed and updated in the light of recommendations throughout this leaflet and additional readings. It includes a means of identifying losses (e.g., catalog or shelf-list duplication) in the event of a major disaster. Salvage priorities have been identified by the staff.

_____ e. Emergency response supplies (e.g., sponges, paper towels, polyethylene sheeting) are on hand. Additional sources of supply and funds for purchase are identified.

Fire Safety

_____ a. Current safety practices, detection system, and suppression equipment have been evaluated and improved as necessary before commencement of construction activities.

_____ b. Expert opinions have been sought from the institution's safety officer or the local fire marshal regarding necessary precautions, specifications for fire-retardant materials for the construction of dust barriers, and fire-fighting plans.

_____ c. An emergency evacuation procedure has been designed and rehearsed. Staff are familiar with procedures (which are provided in writing) and are trained in their use.

_____ d. Routine monitoring of safety precautions is provided by the institution's staff.

Water Hazards

_____ a. The contractor and his representatives have been told in writing of the irreversible damage water can produce in paper-based collections. The contract specifies the increased precautions that the contractor's representatives will exercise in collection areas.

_____ b. Contractual specifications include securing the roof against water infiltration during work that opens areas of the roof. Routine monitoring is provided by the institution's staff.

_____ c. Temporary barriers (e.g., fire-retardant waterproof sheeting) are constructed to prevent water from draining onto collections and through floors during pauses in construction activities.

_____ d. If water-related construction will impact special collection areas, water alarms have been installed. Response procedures in the event of alarm have been designed and rehearsed. The contractor, security team, and other professionals are informed of the provisions of this plan.

_____ e. Salvage procedures for water-damaged materials have been reviewed.

Abrasion and Chemical Damage

_____ a. Responsibility and procedures for controlling particulate and gaseous pollutants generated by construction activities are specified.

_____ b. Where possible, collections have been temporarily relocated away from construction areas.

_____ c. Arrangements have been made to compartmentalize spaces, erect barriers, and/or wrap collections on the shelves as necessary to protect them from the spread of particulate and gaseous materials.

_____ d. Interim and post-construction cleanup programs have been designed. Responsibility has been specified and the institution's staff have been assigned to monitor compliance and performance.

_____ e. Adequate ventilation has been specified for construction activities that will generate significant chemical fumes (e.g., paint removal). Compliance is monitored by the institution's staff.

Security

_____ a. The contractor will notify the client in advance of work schedules and changes so that security can be maintained.

_____ b. Workmen cannot enter limited-access collection storage without staff knowledge. Workmen do not have access to high-security areas without direct staff supervision.

SUGGESTED FURTHER READING

Frens, Dale H. *Temporary Protection: Specifying Temporary Protection of Historic Interiors During Construction and Repair.* Washington, D.C.: National Park Service, 1993, 8 pp. Preservation Tech Notes No. 2. Available from Tech Notes, Preservation Assistance Division, National Park Service, P.O. Box 37127, Washington, DC 20013.
An excellent introduction to protecting a building from accidental damage and losses during renovation activities. Greatest detail is provided for fire safety.

National Fire Protection Association. *Standard for the Protection of Cultural Resources* (NFPA 909); *Fire Protection for Archives and Records Centers* (NFPA 232A); and *Safeguarding Building Construction and Demolition Operations* (NFPA 241). Quincy, MA: National Fire Protection Association, avg. 25 pp.
Causes, prevention, detection, and suppression of fire in each type of repository or operations are discussed. Contain descriptions and standards for fire-detection/suppression equipment, synopsis of the role of the institution's staff in fire protection, and a bibliography of resources. Each includes a useful self-inspection checklist. Many other codes and standards are available. Contact NFPA at 1 Batterymarch Park, P.O. Box 9101, Quincy, MA 02269-9101, Telephone: (800) 344-3555.

Northeast Document
Conservation Center

100 Brickstone Square
Andover, MA 01810-1494
www.nedcc.org
Tel: (978) 470-1010
Fax: (978) 475-6021

INTEGRATED PEST MANAGEMENT

by Beth Lindblom Patkus
Preservation Consultant
Walpole, MA

INTRODUCTION

A variety of insects and other pests attack binding materials, adhesives, and other substances in library and archival collections. Since some insects are attracted to the tight, dark places that abound in storage areas, and since many materials are handled infrequently, insects and other pests may do significant damage before they are discovered.

Libraries and archives have traditionally relied on pesticides for routine pest prevention and response to observed infestation. Pesticides often do not prevent infestation, however, and application of pesticides after the fact cannot correct the damage already done. Pesticides have also become less attractive because of a growing awareness that the chemicals in pesticides can pose health hazards to staff and damage paper-based collections. Newer extermination methods such as controlled freezing and oxygen deprivation have shown promise as alternatives for treatment of existing infestations, but like pesticides, they do not prevent infestation. Prevention can be achieved only through strict housekeeping and monitoring procedures.

Preservation professionals increasingly recommend a strategy called *integrated pest management* (IPM). This approach relies primarily on non-chemical means (such as controlling climate, food sources, and building entry points) to prevent and manage pest infestation. Chemical treatments are used only in a crisis situation threatening rapid losses or when pests fail to succumb to more conservative methods.

LIBRARY AND ARCHIVES PESTS

Most of the insect species likely to infest paper collections are attracted not by the paper itself but by sizes, adhesives, and starches, all of which are more easily digested than the cellulose that makes up paper. Some insects will also attack cellulose (i.e., paper and cardboard) and proteins (i.e., parchment and leather). Insect damage does not come solely from dining habits; collections are also damaged by tunnelling and nesting activities, and by bodily secretions.

Silverfish, firebrats, psocids (also called *booklice*), and cockroaches are among the most common library pests. Silverfish and firebrats can reach up to 12.5 mm in length; they feed on paper sizing, chew holes in paper (especially glossy paper), and damage book bindings and wallpaper to get to the adhesives underneath. They also feed on textiles, primarily rayon, cotton, and linen. They prefer dark, humid areas that are undisturbed for long periods of time.

Psocids feed on microscopic mold growing on paper, and thus their presence usually indicates a humidity problem in the storage area. They are much smaller than silverfish and firebrats (about 1-2 mm), and may also feed on pastes and glues, but they do not produce holes in paper.

Cockroaches are omnivorous, but are especially fond of starchy materials and protein; they will eat book pages, bindings, adhesives, leather, and wallpaper. Cockroaches will chew holes in paper and bindings, but also can badly stain materials with their secretions. Cockroaches are thigmotactic, meaning that they like to contact a surface on all sides of the body; they seek very small crevices, between framed objects and the wall, etc.

The above discussion of library pests is far from exhaustive. Additional information on library and museum pests can be found in Harmon, Zycherman & Schrock, and Story, referenced at the end of this leaflet. Although other pests such as rodents may be encountered in libraries and archives, this leaflet will concentrate primarily on the prevention of insect infestations.

WHAT DO PESTS EAT?

All insects go through a metamorphosis during their life cycle; their growth proceeds in a series of steps until they reach adult stage. Other stages include egg, larva, pupa, and nymph; not all insects go through all stages. For many insects, the larva stage is the most damaging since that is when the most feeding takes place, but others (such as booklice) also inflict damage in the adult stage.

It is important to remember that collections themselves are not the only source of food for insects. There is a huge spectrum of foodstuffs for insects and other pests in library and archives buildings. The most obvious attractant is human food waste and stored food in offices and kitchens, but there are many other less obvious food sources.

Dermestid beetles may attack leather and wool, including rugs. They may also be attracted by dead birds and/or abandoned birds nests. Some species of beetles feed on the pollen and nectar from flowering plants, while others eat shed hair and skin cells from humans and other animals. Dust mites, which are numerous and almost invisible, feed on this human dander.

Although some insects may not be a direct threat to collections, their presence may attract insects that do pose a threat. Some insects feed on the bodies of other insects. Most pests (insect and otherwise) are attracted by debris from human or other animal activities.

Since most buildings and collections offer a seemingly endless supply of food for insects and other pests, it is clear that the first priority for effective pest prevention must be to eliminate sources of food and strongly emphasize strict housekeeping.

HABITATS AND BREEDING HABITS

Insect species require specific ranges of temperature, relative humidity, and other conditions in order to flourish. The first condition for their presence is the existence of openings in the building envelope through which they can enter. Once insects have entered a building, they seek out moisture, food sources, and undisturbed spaces for breeding.

Routes of entry

Inadequately sealed windows and doors, or windows and doors that are left open routinely, can provide an entry point for insects. Cracks and crevices in walls or foundations or openings around pipes can also be an entry route. Insects can squeeze through extremely small openings. Vents and air ducts can provide an entry point for birds, rodents, and insects. Plantings close to a building provide an excellent habitat for insects, which may then migrate into the building through various openings. Insects also can be brought into the building in books and papers themselves.

Climate

Optimum temperature for many insects is between 68-86°F. Most insects will die if exposed to temperatures below 28°F or above 113°F for a period of time. Optimum humidity levels for their proliferation are generally between 60%-80%.[1] Insects need moisture to survive, and some (such as psocids and silverfish) thrive on high humidity.

Water sources

Many insects are attracted to damp areas. Sources of water and potential insect habitats include water pipes running through collections, restrooms, kitchens, water fountains, custodial closets, and climate-control equipment. Standing water on a roof or in other locations can raise humidity levels and provide an excellent environment for insects.

Food sources

Food waste in kitchens and offices provides sustenance for insects, particularly if it remains in a building and uncovered for long periods of time. Potted plants and cut flowers, water in vases and over-watered plants, dead and dying plants, and the nectar and pollen of flowering plants all encourage the presence of insects.

Storage conditions

Some insect species that threaten collections thrive in small, dark, undisturbed spaces, in other words, in conditions that are common to storage areas. Insects will set up housekeeping inside dark, tight spaces (such as corrugated boxes), and are attracted to piles of boxes or other materials that are left undisturbed for long periods. Insects also live in quiet spaces like corners, the undersides of bookcases, and behind furniture. Dust and dirt help to provide a hospitable atmosphere for pests. Dead insects or insect debris can attract other insects. Dirt and clutter also make it difficult to see pests, so a problem may go unnoticed for some time.

Control of insect infestation requires elimination insofar as possible of potential insect habitats and food sources.

IPM STRATEGIES

Integrated pest management strategies encourage ongoing maintenance and housekeeping to insure that pests will not find a hospitable environment in a library or archives building. Activities include building inspection and maintenance; climate control; restriction of food and plants; regular cleaning; proper storage; control over incoming collections to avoid infestation of existing collections; and routine monitoring for pests.

It is best to begin a formal pest management program with an initial survey of the building and all collection storage areas. Have there been any pest problems in the past? If so, what type of pest was involved and what materials were affected? What was done to solve the problem? Any potential insect habitats should be eliminated. There are several steps that can be taken to reduce the number of insects in a library or archive.

Routes of entry

Windows and doors should be tightly sealed; weatherstripping may be necessary. Doors should not be propped open regularly. Openings around pipes should be sealed, as should cracks in the walls or foundation. Vents should be screened to keep out birds and rodents. A planting-free zone of about 12 inches should be maintained around buildings to discourage insects from entering. Plantings should be properly cared for and not over watered. The area around foundations should be graveled and graded away from a building to avoid basement flooding.

Climate

Climate should be moderate; conditions should be cool and dry; specifics depend on the needs of different materials. Temperature should be 68°F or lower, and relative humidity should be kept below a maximum of 50%. Maintaining climate conditions recommended for the preservation of books and paper will help to control insect populations.

Water sources

Pipes in collections areas and other sources of water such as restrooms, kitchens, or climate-control equipment should be inspected routinely to guard against water leakage. Wrap sweating pipes with insulating tape. Close off unused drains or drainpipe openings. Roofs and basements should be inspected periodically to insure that there is no standing water or flooding. Where problems recur, frequent inspections are necessary.

Food sources

Plants and cut flowers should be removed from the building. If this is impossible, plants should be well cared for and kept to a minimum; flowering plants should certainly be avoided. Avoid over watering and watch plants carefully for signs of infestation or disease. Food consumption should be confined to a staff lounge; staff should not eat at their desks. If functions that include refreshments are held in other spaces, all leftovers should be tightly sealed or removed by the caterers. Vacuuming and kitchen cleanup should be done immediately. All food should be stored in tightly sealed glass or metal containers or refrigerated, and a plastic garbage can with a tight-fitting lid should be provided for food waste. Trash should be removed from the building daily.

Housekeeping

Collection storage areas (and other areas) should be cleaned routinely and thoroughly, at least every 6 months. All areas should be checked for signs of pests at least once a month. Look at collections for stains and signs of insect grazing (small holes in paper, or areas of loss on the surface of paper or bindings). Check window sills; under bookcases and radiators; on and behind shelves; and inside boxes and drawers for signs of insect activity. Look for small piles of dust, insect bodies, frass (insect droppings), egg cases, and live insects; clean up any insect debris immediately.

Incoming collections

It is particularly important to develop strict procedures for dealing with newly acquired collections, since such collections have often been stored in attics or basements that are hospitable to pests.

Examine incoming material immediately to see if there is evidence of infestation. Work over a clean surface covered with blotter or other light paper. Remove all objects from storage or shipping enclosures and look at the binding, pages, and hollow (if any) in books. Examine frame backings and mats, wrappings, and other accompanying materials. Look for live creatures, insect droppings, larvae, or bodies.

Transfer materials to clean archival boxes until you can process them. If possible, isolate rehoused, incoming materials in a space away from other collections until processing. Space that will provide preservation conditions is cool, dry, clean, outfitted with shelving, etc., to discourage mold and insects. Throw the old boxes away unless they are archival quality and you are absolutely certain they are clean.

The clean archival boxes can be used over and over for this temporary holding use as long as the contents and boxes continue free of evidence of insects. Ideally, of course, incoming material should be processed and rehoused in its permanent enclosures promptly. Realistically, processing may be delayed, and the interior of boxes should be inspected routinely at least every few weeks. A tent or motel-type sticky trap can be placed on a side wall inside each box to improve monitoring.

If there is evidence of insects, talk to a preservation professional for detailed advice before proceeding further. Materials can be vacuumed thoroughly (assuming the objects are not deteriorated or fragile) through a nylon or other soft screen, using a high-filtration vacuum. Discard both filter and disposable bag outside the building or in a sealed container which is provided for food wastes and is emptied daily.

Pest monitoring

Effective implementation of a pest management program requires routine monitoring of pest activity. Routine monitoring using traps provides information about the type of insect(s), their entry points, the number of insects, where they are taking up residence, and why they are surviving. This information allows for identification of problem areas and development of a species-specific treatment program.

The most commonly used insect traps are sticky traps, available from most hardware and grocery stores. Several types are available: flat traps, rectangular box-shaped traps (motels), and tent-shaped traps. Many conservators recommend the tent traps as the easiest to handle. Whatever type and brand is chosen, consistency should be maintained so that data can be interpreted accurately.

The basic procedure for monitoring is as follows: 1) identify all doors, windows, water and heat sources, and furniture on a building floor plan; 2) identify likely insect routes, and mark trap locations on a floor plan; 3) number and date the traps; 4) place the traps in the area to be monitored, as indicated on the floor plan; 5) inspect and collect the traps regularly; and 6) refine trap placement and inspection as necessary, according to the evidence collected. Relocate traps (if initial results are negative) and try again.

If infestation is suspected in a particular area, place traps every 10 feet. Care should be taken to insure that traps do not come into contact with collection materials, since the adhesive can cause damage. Checking the traps 48 hours after placement will identify the area most seriously infested. Traps should be inspected weekly for at least three months and should be replaced every two months, when they are full, or when they lose their stickiness.

Documentation is essential; monitoring will be useless without it. The number of insects, the types of insects, and their stage of growth should all be recorded for each trap. Dates and locations of trap replacements should be noted. Detailed records should also be kept of any other evidence of activity, such as live or dead insects or their droppings.

Once insects have been trapped, they must be identified to determine what threat they pose to collections. There are several good books with drawings and descriptions of common library and archives pests; these are listed in the bibliography. An excellent resource for identification is the local or state Agricultural Extension agency, which will usually identify insects free of charge (the insect must be sent to them, and the entire body must be intact). Other potential resources include the biology department of a local university or a local history museum with an entomologist on staff.

TREATMENT METHODS

It is important to remember that sighting one or two insects is an occasion for monitoring to determine the extent of the problem; it is not necessarily a crisis situation. In the past, insect sightings often occasioned an indiscriminate use of pesticides.

If a serious insect infestation occurs, or if insect problems do not respond to the preventive techniques discussed above, direct treatment for insect infestation may be necessary. This strategy should be used as a last resort. Both chemical and non-chemical treatments are available; non-chemical means should be used wherever possible.

Chemical treatments

Pesticides are divided into categories, depending on the way they are used and their physical state.

Common chemical treatments used to control insects include *aerosol sprays; attractants* (which lure insects into traps, sometimes killing them); *baits and pellets* (which are eaten by the insects); *contact and residual sprays* (normally sprayed into cracks and crevices; these kill on contact and/or by absorption of the pesticide when the insect walks through the residue); *dusts* (e.g., boric acid or silica dust, which dehydrate insects or interfere with internal water regulation); *fogging concentrates* (these use equipment that suspends a pesticide and oil formulation in the air); *fumigants* (these expose infected material to a lethal gas); and *residual and vapor pest strips* (the insect absorbs pesticide by walking across residual pest strips, while pesticide evaporates from vapor pest strips to become a fumigant). *Repellents* (such as mothballs) are also sometimes used; these are meant to discourage rather than kill insects.

Fumigants are among the most toxic of pesticides; other pesticides are usually suspended in a liquid and sprayed, so that they tend to settle out of the air. Fumigant gases remain in the air and can easily spread over a wide area. *Ethylene oxide (ETO)*, a gaseous fumigant, was commonly used in libraries and archives until the 1980s; many libraries had their own ETO chambers. ETO is effective against insect adults, larvae, and eggs. It poses serious health hazards to workers, and there is evidence that ETO can change the physical and chemical properties of paper, parchment, and leather. Acceptable limits on ETO exposure have been steadily lowered by the government, and most existing ETO chambers in libraries cannot meet these restrictions. Some residual ETO remains in treated materials, and little is known about the long-term risks to collections and staff from off-gassing toxins. ETO should be used only as a last resort; materials should be sent to a commercial facility and allowed to off-gas for at least several weeks before being returned to the library or archives.

In general, fumigants and other pesticides can cause long- and short-term health problems, ranging from nausea and headaches to respiratory problems to cancer. Many chemical treatments may cause no ill effects at the time of exposure, but may be absorbed into the body to cause health problems years later. Many of the chemicals also damage the treated materials and no chemical treatments provide a residual effect that will prevent reinfestation. Growing awareness of the risks has brought about increased emphasis on non-chemical pest-control methods.

Non-chemical treatments

A variety of non-chemical processes for exterminating insects have been explored. The most promising are controlled freezing and the use of modified atmospheres. Methods that have not proved as successful include the use of heat, gamma radiation, and microwaves.

Controlled freezing has been undertaken in various institutions over the past 15 years, and reports on its effectiveness have been largely favorable. Freezing is attractive because it involves no chemicals and thus poses no hazard to library staff. It can be used on most library materials and does not appear to damage collections (according to existing literature on experimental efforts), but research into this question is not yet complete. Very fragile objects, those made from a combination of materials, and artifacts with friable media should probably not be frozen; a conservator should always be consulted before any method is chosen.

Materials can be treated in household or commercial freezers, blast freezers, or controlled-temperature and humidity freezers. It is necessary to bag and seal items unless a freezer with specially controlled temperature and humidity is used. Bags must be sealed immediately to prevent insects from escaping. Some institutions box materials and then bag them. Bagging protects objects from changes in moisture content during defrost cycles and from condensation on cold books when they are removed from the freezer.

It is essential to guard against freeze resistance; some insects can acclimate to cold temperatures if they are kept in a cool area before freezing or if freezing happens too slowly. Research is incomplete in this area; it is not known if common library pests are able to develop freeze resistance.

In the absence of definitive data, material must be kept at room temperature until freezing begins. Items should not be packed too tightly within a freezer, since this can slow the freezing process. Most important, material should be frozen quickly. Freezer temperature should reach 0°C within 4 hours and -20°C within 8 hours. The most commonly reported successful treatments have been carried out at -29°C for a period of 72 hours.[2] It is unknown whether higher temperatures for a shorter time would be equally effective; there are reports that 20°C for 48 hours has also been used with success.[3]

Collections should be slowly thawed (brought up to 0°C over 8 hours) and brought up to room temperature. The entire process should then be repeated to insure effectiveness. Objects should remain bagged (some institutions leave them bagged for 6-8 months) until monitoring in the space indicates that the insect problem has been solved. Detailed documentation of each phase of treatment should be maintained.

Like chemical treatments, freezing provides no residual benefits. If collections are not returned to a well maintained storage area, reinfestation will almost certainly occur.

Modified atmospheres have been used widely in the agricultural and food industries to control insect infestation. The term refers to several processes: decreased oxygen, increased carbon dioxide, and the use of inert gases, primarily nitrogen. Various experiments with modified atmospheres have been undertaken by cultural institutions over the past 10 years, with generally successful results. Modified atmospheres show great promise, but additional research is needed to determine optimum exposure times and methods for particular types of insects. There appears to be no obvious damage to collections, but little research has been done on long-term effects. There is potential danger to staff from exposure to high levels of carbon dioxide, if that is used, but there are no residual effects on collections.

Modified atmospheres can be applied 1) in a traditional fumigation chamber or a portable fumigation bubble or 2) in low-permeability plastic bags. With a chamber or a bubble, materials are prepared for treatment (quarantined, documented, and loaded into the treatment chamber), air is evacuated from the chamber, and carbon dioxide (generally about 60% concentration) or nitrogen (to achieve an atmosphere of less than 1% oxygen) is introduced. Once the desired atmospheric concentration is reached, conditions are maintained at a specific temperature and relative humidity for the required amount of time.

Once treatment is finished, the vacuum is released, the carbon dioxide or nitrogen is removed, the chamber is aerated, and materials are removed to a quarantine area so that the effectiveness of treatment can be assessed. The process for treating materials in low-permeability plastic bags is similar, except that materials are sealed in bags with an oxygen scavenger that will reduce the oxygen level in the enclosure to less than what is needed for insect respiration. In some cases, the bags are purged with nitrogen before sealing.

In the tests conducted thus far, a variety of exposure times, temperatures, and relative humidities have been used. Since requirements for achieving an acceptable kill rate seem to vary according to the type of insect being exterminated and the type of process being used, there are not yet any generally-accepted guidelines for the application of modified atmospheres. Always contact a preservation professional for advice before proceeding with modified atmosphere treatment.

Heat can effectively exterminate insects; it has been used widely in food processing and medicine. A temperature of 140°F for at least one hour will kill most insects. Heat should not be used to eliminate insects from paper collections, however, because heat at the levels needed to kill insects greatly accelerates oxidation and paper aging; materials can become brittle and otherwise damaged.

Gamma radiation is used to sterilize cosmetics, food and agricultural products, medical supplies, and hospital and lab equipment. It poses some danger to personnel during treatment, but there is no residual radiation in the treated material. Gamma radiation can be effective against insects, but the minimum lethal dose for various species is still unknown and is affected by variables such as climate conditions and the nature of the infested material. Most important, research has shown that gamma radiation may initiate oxidation and cause scission of cellulose molecules; it has the potential to seriously damage paper-based materials. There is also a cumulative effect from repeated exposures. As a result, gamma radiation is *not* recommended.

Rumors about the effectiveness of *microwaves* for killing insects have circulated in the library community over the past several years. Microwaves are used successfully in the food, agricultural, and textile industries to control insects, but *this strategy is not recommended for library collections.* Microwaves have a limited penetration, and may not penetrate thick books. Their effectiveness also depends on the type of insect and the intensity and frequency of the radiation. Microwave ovens vary in intensity, so it is extremely difficult to determine standard times and temperatures for treatment. The primary argument against microwaves is the danger of damage to treated materials. Evidence from a variety of experiments indicates that pages and covers can scorch; metal attachments like staples can cause arcing; and adhesives can soften, causing pages to detach from their bindings in certain books.

Freezing and modified atmospheres currently show the most promise as alternatives to traditional pesticides. They remain experimental until more research has been done, however, so a preservation professional should be consulted before undertaking either treatment.

SUMMARY

Library and archival collections can be threatened by a variety of pests that damage paper-based and other materials. The method of pest control least damaging to collections and staff involves preventive measures and regular monitoring. If infestation does occur, treatment should be tailored to the specific insect species and the type of material that is infested. Chemical treatments should be avoided except as a last resort. Emerging technologies such as blast freezing and modified atmospheres have significant potential as alternatives to chemical control.

NOTES

[1] Johanna G. Wellheiser, *Nonchemical Treatment Processes for Disinfestation of Insects and Fungi in Library Collections.* (Munich: K.G. Saur, 1992), p. 5.

[2] Wellheiser, p. 27.

[3] Wellheiser, p. 27

SOURCES FOR FURTHER INFORMATION

"A Virtual Exhibition of the Ravages of Dust, Water, Moulds, Fungi, Bookworms and other Pests." Available at http://www.knaw.nl/ecpa/expo.htm.
A general introduction to the topic, prepared by the European Commission on Preservation and Access (ECPA).

"Integrated Pest Management." Audiovisual Department, Universite du Quebec a Montreal and Canadian Conservation Institute and Centre de Conservation du Quebec. 1995. Videotape, 22 minutes.
A professionally produced video that provides good basic information for museums and archives. Comes with a short, informative booklet that gives the key points and suggests further reading.

Butcher-Younghans, Sherry, and Gretchen E. Anderson. *A Holistic Approach to Museum Pest Management.* American Association for State and Local History (AASLH) Technical Leaflet 191 (1990). Nashville, TN: AASLH.
Detailed, practical advice for controlling a range of pests commonly found in museums. This and other excellent publications can be ordered through their Web site, http://www.aaslh.org, by writing to 530 Church Street, Suite 600, Nashville, TN 37219-2325, or by tel. 615/255-2971.

Canadian Conservation Institute. "Preventing Infestations: Control Strategies and Detection Methods," and "Detecting Infestations: Facility Inspection Procedure and Checklist." *CCI Notes* 3/1 and 3/2. Ottawa: CCI, 1996. 4 pp. and 3 pp.
Short leaflets written primarily for museums providing general information about monitoring with traps and inspecting a building for infestation.

Daniel, Vinod, Gordon Hanlon, and Shin Maekawa. "Eradication of Insect Pests in Museums Using Nitrogen." *WAAC Newsletter* 15.3 (September 1993): 15-19.
Describes Getty Conservation Institute tests of low-oxygen atmospheres for treatment of pest-infested museum objects. Air was replaced with nitrogen in a bag encapsulating the infested object so that the oxygen concentration was reduced to less than 0.1%. Available online at: http://palimpsest.stanford.edu/waac/.

Elert, Kerstin, and Shin Maekawa. "Rentokil Bubble in Nitrogen Anoxia Treatment of Museum Pests." *Studies in Conservation* 42 (1997): 247-52.
Describes tests conducted on a commercially available portable fumigation enclosure to determine its suitability for nitrogen fumigation. Addresses set-up, safety considerations, and limitations of the technology.

Goldberg, Lisa. "A History of Pest Control Measures in the Anthropology Collections, National Museum of Natural History, Smithsonian Institution." *Journal of the American Institute for Conservation* 35.1 (Spring 1996): 23-43.
An interesting review of pest eradication techiques (particularly pesticides and fumigants) used at the National Museum of Natural History during the 19th and 20th centuries. Discusses the effects of such techniques on the collections.

Harmon, James D. *Integrated Pest Management in Museum, Library, and Archival Facilities: A Step by Step Approach for the Design, Development, Implementation, and Maintenance of an Integrated Pest Management Program.* Indianapolis: Harmon Preservation Pest Management (P.O. Box 40262, Indianapolis, IN 46240), 1993. 140 pp.
A thorough, useful guide (in a three-ring binder) to IPM for collections-holding institutions. Covers monitoring, identification, and non-chemical and chemical strategies for pest control for insects and other pests like pigeons.

Hengemihle, Frank H., Norman Weberg, and Chandru J. Shahani. "Desorption of Residual Ethylene Oxide from Fumigated Library Materials." Washington, DC: Preservation Research and Testing Office, Preservation Directorate, The Library of Congress, November 1995. Preservation Research and Testing Series No. 9502.
Describes studies undertaken to compare the relative capacity of selected library materials for offgassing of ethylene oxide. Useful for those concerned about exposure to collections that were fumigated with ethylene oxide in the past. Available at: http://lcweb.loc.gov/preserv/rt/fumigate/fume.html.

Jacobs, Jeremy F. "Pest Monitoring Case Study," in *Storage of Natural History Collections: A Preventive Conservation Approach,* Volume 1. Carolyn Rose, Catharine A. Hawks, and Hugh H. Genoways, eds. Society for the Preservation of Natural History Collections, 1995.
A detailed description of the pest-monitoring activities undertaken by the Division of Mammals in the National Museum of Natural History.

Jessup, Wendy Claire. "Integrated Pest Management: A Selected Bibliography for Collections Care." February 1997.
An excellent annotated bibliography that covers museum, library, and archival pests; integrated pest management methods; the effects of pesticides on collections; and occupational safety and health. Available at http: palimpsest.stanford.edu.

Odegaard, Nancy. "Insect Monitoring in Museums"; and Dale Paul Kronkright. "Insect Traps in Conservation Surveys." Both in *WAAC Newsletter* 13.1 (January 1991): 19-23.
Both articles offer practical tips for monitoring insect populations using various types of traps. Available online at: http://palimpsest.stanford.edu/waac/.

Parker, Thomas A. *Study on Integrated Pest Management for Libraries and Archives.* Paris: UNESCO, General Information Program and UNISIST, 1988. Publication number PGI-88/W3/20. 119 pp.
Excellent publication covering the basics of pest management for cultural institutions.

Story, Keith O. *Approaches to Pest Management in Museums.* Washington, DC: Smithsonian Institution, 1985, 165 pp.
Out of print. Some of the chemical-treatment information is outdated, but identification and IPM strategies are good.

Wellheiser, Johanna G. *Nonchemical Treatment Processes for Disinfestation of Insects and Fungi in Library Collections.* Munich: K.G. Saur, 1992, 118 pp.

An excellent review of the various options for controlling pests in libraries; covers fumigants, freezing, gamma radiation, microwaves, and modified atmospheres. Includes information about treatment procedures; costs; results reported by various institutions; and benefits and risks of each treatment.

Zycherman, Linda A., and J. Richard Schrock, eds. *A Guide to Museum Pest Control.* Washington, DC: American Institute for Conservation and Association of Systematics Collections, 1988. 205 pp.
Some information is outdated, but still a good basic text.

SOURCES OF SUPPLIES AND SERVICES

This list is not exhaustive, nor does it constitute an endorsement of the suppliers and services listed. We suggest that you obtain information from a number of vendors so that you can make comparisons of cost and asses the full range of available products.

A more complete list of suppliers is available from NEDCC. Consult the Technical Leaflets section of NEDCC's website at www.nedcc.org or contact NEDCC for the most up-to-date version in print.

BMS Catastrophe, Inc.
303 Arthur Street
Fort Worth, TX 76107
Toll Free: (800) 433-2940
Telephone: (817) 332-2770
Fax: (817) 332-6728
http://www.bmscat.com/contents.html
Blast freezing (client must request blast freezing)

Cooper Mill Ltd.
RR3
Madoc, ON K0K 2K0
CANADA
Telephone: (613) 473-4847
Fax: (613) 473-5080
E-mail: ipm@coopermill.com
http://www.coopermill.com/
Pheromones and insect monitoring traps

Dallas Ft. Worth Pest Control
11312 LBJ Freeway #500
Dallas, TX 75238
Telephone: (214) 349-2847
Telephone: (972) 240-2847
Telephone: (817) 595-2847
Fax: (214) 349-6866
http://www.dfwpest.com/company.htm
Insect monitoring traps

Keepsafe Systems Inc.
570 King Street W.
Toronto, ON M5V 1M3
CANADA
Telephone: (416) 703-4696
Fax: (416) 703-5991
E-mail: keepsafe@interlog.com
http://www.interlog.com/~keepsafe
Supplies and kits for anoxic treatment and storage

Midwest Freeze-Dry, Ltd.
Midwest Center for Stabilization and Conservation
7326 North Central Park
Skokie, IL 60076
Telephone: (847) 679-4756
Fax: (847) 679-4191
E-mail: mfd7326@aol.com
http://members.aol.com/mfd7326/midwest.html
Blast freezing

Munters Moisture Control Services
79 Monroe Street
Amesbury, MA
Toll Free: (800) I CAN DRY
Telephone: (978) 388-4900
Fax: (978) 388-4939
http://www.muntersmcs.com/
Blast freezing

National Pest Control Association
http://
National organization that provides general information about pest control and pest control firms

Tom Parker
Pest Control Services
14 East Stratford Avenue
Lansdowne, PA 19050
Telephone: (610) 284-6249
Fax: (610) 622-3037
Pest management consulting

Pest Control Supplies
1700 Liberty
Kansas City, MO 64102
Toll Free: (800) 821-5689
Telephone: (816) 421-4696
Fax: (816) 472-0966
http://www.pcspest.com/
Insect monitoring traps

Rentokil Ltd.
Felcourt
East Grinstead
West Sussex RH19 2JY
UNITED KINGDOM
http://www.rentokil-initial.com
Supplier of bubble for anoxic fumigation

Society for the Preservation of New England Antiquities Haverhill, MA
Telephone: (978) 521-4788
Contact: Gary Rattigan
Fumigation using a carbon dioxide bubble

Northeast Document
Conservation Center
100 Brickstone Square
Andover, MA 01810-1494
www.nedcc.org
Tel: (978) 470-1010
Fax: (978) 475-6021

COLLECTIONS SECURITY: PLANNING AND PREVENTION FOR LIBRARIES AND ARCHIVES

by Karen E. Brown
Field Service Representative
Northeast Document Conservation Center and
Beth Lindblom Patkus
Preservation Consultant
Walpole, MA

INTRODUCTION

Many archives and libraries fail to recognize the vulnerability of their collections to loss. Collections can be threatened not just by theft and vandalism, but by disasters (e.g., fire or flood) and damage from careless handling or poor environmental conditions. Any repository seeking to provide the best possible security for its collections must put in place coordinated policies that address all of these threats. Since other leaflets in this series can be consulted for information on disaster planning, environmental control, and proper storage and handling, this leaflet will focus on the problems traditionally associated with collections security: theft and vandalism.

Most library and archives staff members have heard stories describing trusted patrons, other outsiders, or even valued staff who have pilfered collections (for personal gain, to add to private collections, or perhaps for moral or ethical reasons), but many do not believe such things could happen in their repository. While most libraries and archives have basic security policies, universal enforcement can be difficult. Some patrons (and indeed some staff) see security measures as unnecessary inconveniences.

If a security program is to be effective, there must be widespread understanding of the importance of security to the mission of the repository. It seems obvious that missing or damaged collections cannot be made available for use, but too often staff and management do not recognize the occurrence or the effects of theft and vandalism. It is important to understand that while some damage or loss can be alleviated (for example, a stolen journal might be replaced through purchase, books missing in one library may be loaned from another, or missing pages may be photocopied), other materials may be irreplaceable (if the material is unique, rare, or difficult and expensive to replace).

This leaflet will discuss strategies for preventing theft and vandalism of collections, responding to any breach of security that might occur, and creating an effective, universally enforced security plan.

SECURITY PLANNING

If collections are to be protected against loss, libraries and archives must consider security as a management issue deserving a serious investment of resources. Security planning must be supported at the highest level of the institution. A collections security plan will be most effective if it is coordinated among the various departments and/or areas of activity involved in maintaining security. Such coordination can be a challenge, to say the least, so long-term institutional commitment is essential. Activities that may have a security component include proper collection storage, cataloging or processing, circulation, reference services, special events, building maintenance, staff training, insurance, and conservation services.

Basic Components of Security Planning

1. Prepare a written security policy. If appropriate, form a security planning group to help develop policies and procedures. Always insure that the policy is endorsed at the highest managerial level.

2. Appoint a security manager to develop and implement your security plan.

3. Perform a security survey to assess your needs.

4. Initiate preventive measures:

   - Eliminate weaknesses to insure the security of the building.
   - Install appropriate security systems.
   - Insure that collection storage is secure and that good records are kept.
   - Establish patron regulations.
   - Establish staff regulations.

5. Identify likely emergencies and plan your response to any breach of security. Tell staff what to do, practice response plans, and coordinate plans with outside officials.

6. Maintain and update your security plan.

These planning elements are discussed in more detail below. While specific security measures may differ from repository to repository, depending on the institution's size and available resources, this planning process is appropriate for any repository.

THE SECURITY POLICY

Every cultural institution should develop a written security policy that underlines a commitment to security management. The policy should include a statement supporting security planning, prevention of incidents, and the implementation of response procedures. Staff in all areas of the organization should be involved in drafting both policy and procedures. An important part of the security program will be regular policy review and updating.

THE SECURITY MANAGER

A security manager should be appointed to coordinate security planning. In smaller institutions, a staff member may be assigned this responsibility along with many others; in a large repository this might be a full-time position. Particularly in the case of a part-time security manager, security responsibilities should be clearly stated and incorporated into the staff member's job description. A certain amount of time should be set aside for that person to work on the security program. The security manager should prepare regular assessments of the program and work to improve systems and procedures as needed.

The security manager will need to work with all staff members that have contact with the collection. The appointee must have direct access to the institution's director, and sufficient authority both to coordinate preventive efforts among the staff and to act during a security emergency.

THE SECURITY SURVEY

Before initiating or upgrading a security program, an assessment of current and projected needs is recommended. The security manager should make a systematic study of the facility and its operations. This survey should evaluate current security policies and procedures, identify potential areas of risk, and rank security threats according to the probability of occurrence. This will allow the institution to concentrate on the most serious problems first, and it will assist in long-term planning and budgeting.

A survey looks at the following: 1) external perimeter and interior areas for inadequacies, such as proximity to other facilities which pose a risk, inappropriate intrusion detection and signaling, poor lighting, poor sight lines, and inadequate locks; 2) current polices and procedures for use of the collection by staff and patrons, including patron registration, reading room procedures, staff access to the collection, and key control; 3) collection protection in storage, in transit, and on exhibition; and 4) any past problems and concerns identified by staff or others.

PREVENTIVE MEASURES

Once a survey has been completed, it is likely that improvements in preventive security measures will be needed. Activities designed to prevent loss or damage fall into several categories: external and internal building security, patron regulations, and staff regulations. Each will be addressed below.

BUILDING SECURITY

The building and collection must be secured both during and after normal working hours. Unauthorized entrance to the building and unauthorized removal of collection material from the building must be prevented.

The perimeter of a building can be protected in various ways, ranging from the use of door and window locks to more expensive strategies like the posting of security guards and/or installation of an automated security system.

Internal building security is important both during and after working hours. Most institutions should have a security room to protect valuable items when they are not being used; this room should be secured even when the repository is open, and the number of personnel having access should be strictly limited. Valuable materials should always be stored in this room when the repository is closed.

Automated security systems are discussed separately in the following section. Other strategies for upgrading building security include:

- Installing high-quality, heavy-duty locks, dead bolts, and hinges on all exterior doors
- Installing grills or screens on ground-floor windows
- Requiring patrons and staff to enter and exit the building by one door, which is monitored at all times.
- If appropriate, installing a book security system (this is NOT appropriate for rare or unique materials such as those found in archival and historical collections, but it is normally used for general circulating collections)
- If the collection is located in a library or building with easy access, storing the collection in a locked room and limiting access to the key. Ideally, the room should have no windows, a solid door that opens out, a minimum one-inch dead bolt, and pinned hinges. Door buzzers and alarms are recommended.
- Employing one or more security guards to patrol the repository after closing
- Insuring that alarms (fire, etc.) are always secured, tamper proof, and located away from the main stream of traffic, to prevent accidental false alarms or deliberate use of an alarm to distract from a theft in process
- Taking steps to prevent removal, or duplication of keys, insuring that keys are returned when employees leave, and changing all locks periodically
- Installing after-hours security lighting

SECURITY SYSTEMS

An automated security system serves three main purposes. First, the mere presence of a system can act as a deterrent to crime. Second, if an intrusion occurs, it will be detected. Finally, the system will notify appropriate personnel, making apprehension of the intruder possible.

There are additional advantages: modern alarm installations are relatively inexpensive; other alarms (water alert, fire, power outage, temperature) may be connected to the security control panel; an alarm system can provide two-way communication (opening and closing of gates, arming devices, etc.); recorded data can be used to produce management logs (status summaries, alarm summaries, entry and exit reports, etc.), and most systems are expandable, so it is easy to start with the basics.

Despite these advantages, an automated system should never be an institution's only protection. Since most thefts occur during working hours and occur because of human errors, it is essential to have a broad-based security plan that includes strategies for protecting collections during use.

How Security Systems Work

A basic security system will secure vulnerable perimeter access points such as doors and windows, and it will protect interior spaces via interior motion detectors that monitor movement inside the premises. An electronic security system includes sensors, a control panel (which interprets the report from the sensors and decides whether or not to activate the reporting devices), and reporting devices (which might be a traditional alarm or a signal to a security company monitoring the system).

In order to insure response to an alarm, you must have the security system monitored 24 hours a day by the monitoring station. If you use a local signal only, you must rely on a neighbor to call authorities when the alarm sounds. Costs for a monitoring system normally include a monthly fee plus telephone charges and can be arranged through your alarm installation company. While there are a number of companies that install and monitor their own accounts, there are many more that install systems and contract with a third-party monitoring facility.

How to Contract for a Security System

A qualified company should perform a site inspection and discuss your individual security needs. Each repository is unique and the system should be tailored to fit your needs and price range. The company should provide you with an evaluation of your premises, highlighting the measures you can take to improve the security of your institution over and above the addition of an electronic alarm system.

A great deal can be learned about a company through its sales representative. A sales representative should be knowledgeable about all areas of the alarm industry. It is this person's job to "tailor" a system that will provide the level of protection needed with as little disruption as possible to the facility. This can generally be accomplished through an effective system design.

When comparing companies, be sure to make a true comparison by thoroughly reviewing the number and types of products being installed.

Remember that alarm companies tend to concentrate on night-time protection, without any thought to a public institution's vulnerability during daytime visiting hours. If your security survey has been complete, and the findings incorporated into your plans, you will be better prepared to discuss specific needs and design options with the alarm company.

Always carry out periodic tests of the system to insure that it is in proper working order at all times.

SECURITY GUARDS

The use of security guards may be appropriate in some situations. All staff members (including general staff, management, custodial workers, grounds keepers, and volunteers) will still need to participate in maintaining security, but guards can be a valuable supplement to staff efforts and their presence alone may deter theft and/or vandalism.

It is important for an institution to specify its needs, communicate them clearly to the security guards, and supervise those personnel. This is true especially if services are contracted from a private company. It may also be advisable to incorporate incentives and penalties into the contract to insure that services are performed satisfactorily. The security manager must determine what equipment, instruction, and supervision the security personnel will receive. It is important to work with them to develop a daily schedule for monitoring institution activities and a mechanism for making regular reports.

COLLECTION MANAGEMENT AND SECURITY

Collection management is an important aspect of security. It is difficult to verify that something is missing if collections are not properly cataloged. In the worst-case scenario, cataloging records and identification marks can help prove an object is the item in question and provide proof of rightful ownership. Detailed collection records can also help the archivist or librarian separate intrinsically valuable items for special storage or other special treatment. In addition, regular inventory of collections can identify missing items that might otherwise have been overlooked.

Specific collection management activities that will be helpful in maintaining security include:

- Inventory your collection on a regular basis.
- Ensure that storage areas are arranged for quick and easy inspection. As materials arrive in the repository, identify and segregate valuable and/or marketable materials (monetary or intrinsic value). It is best to store these items separately in a secure area and consider

substituting photocopies or photographic reproductions for the originals for access purposes.

- If valuable and/or marketable items will not be stored separately, place them in separate folders within the collection so they can be easily checked by a staff member. Create procedures to insure the collection is inspected for completeness before and after use.

- Record a physical description of valuable materials to aid recovery and ensure positive identification should a theft occur. Provide insurance coverage for valuable materials.

- Consider using some form of identification mark for the collection. **This may not be an appropriate choice for materials with artifactual value,** but may be useful in some situations.

- Use call slips, sign-out sheets, computer systems, etc. to record and track the use of the collection during research, loan, exhibition, conservation, microfilming, etc.

- Do not allow patrons access to unprocessed collections.

- Remember that in-house finding aids provide important information for collection access. These are also at risk of theft and loss, so up-to-date copies should be stored safely in a remote location.

PATRON MANAGEMENT

Archivists and librarians must maintain healthy patron relations while enforcing reasonable rules and procedures. It is unfortunate that there are many documented cases of "regulars" and trusted professionals gaining privileged access to the collection. Such researchers are often allowed to work without supervision and regular checking of personal effects or the materials being used. It is only later that the repository discovers a pattern of loss, often of the most valuable items. It is essential to remember that the safety of the collection must come first. The great majority of patrons will understand and abide by rules and procedures once the reasons for them are explained.

The cornerstones of managing the use of archival and special collections are supervision of patrons; inspection of patron belongings and of collection materials (before and after use); and the maintenance of records documenting the use of materials. Supervision and inspection will help to prevent theft and vandalism, and records that document use may be invaluable in a theft investigation. The U.S. National Archives currently retains these records for 25 years. If all of these activities are carried out routinely, patron use of collections can be well managed in even the smallest repository.

The following procedures apply to use of collections in an archives or a library special collection with a separate reading room, rather than for a general circulating collection:

Patron Access: Step-by-Step

1. All patrons must be required to register:

    - Each patron should complete a Registration Form that asks for identifying information and information about research interests, and each patron should sign a logbook.

    - All patrons should be required to present photographic identification when they register. A staff member should monitor the registration procedure to ensure that the name appearing on the identification matches the one given on the registration materials.

- If desired, a photographic ID may be retained from each patron until the research materials are returned. The ID should be attached to the completed registration form and stored in a secure place. At a large repository in-house ID might be issued for regular users.

2. Perform a reference interview:

   - Record each patron's interests.
   - Discuss their research topic and evaluate their request.
   - Limit the amount of accessed material by assessing the patron's needs.
   - Scrutinize the patron's intentions.
   - Explain finding aids, catalogs, and services.

3. Explain the rules for use of materials:

   - Allow only necessary research materials into the reading room. The repository should provide lockers or other secure storage for the personal effects of patrons (coats, briefcases, purses and oversize handbags, portfolios, etc.).
   - Separate from the tables all containers and personal effects that are allowed in the reading room.
   - Provide written guidelines for proper handling of materials (e.g., do not damage bindings, use pencil instead of pen when working, etc.).
   - Remind patrons to keep materials in the order in which they are found. Limit the number of boxes they can use at one time. Instruct patrons to put papers away each time they leave the reading room.
   - Explain how to use reference slips. All collection materials that are retrieved must have a slip, and patrons should be required to sign the slip(s).
   - Require patrons to sign a form stating that they understand and agree to comply with the rules for handling and use.

4. Insure that the reading room is adequately staffed at all times. Ideally there should be two staff members so that one can retrieve materials while another supervises the patrons.

5. Check each archival box for collation and completeness before and after it is used by patrons.

6. Each time the patron leaves the reading room, inspect any personal materials that were allowed into the room.

7. Inspect collections for sequencing and completeness before re-shelving. A retention schedule should be established to ensure that registration forms and reference slips are available if they are needed later for investigating a theft. Determine how long these records will be retained.

Patron Access in Small Repositories

The recommendations given above may seem difficult if not impossible to implement for small repositories with few staff members, such as historical societies (which are often staffed by volunteers) and public libraries (which are often responsible for managing both circulating and historical collections). With some effort (and institutional commitment), however, reasonable security can be provided even in a situation where staffing limitations make constant supervision of researchers difficult.

No matter how small or understaffed the archives or library is, patrons should be required to sign in and a record should be kept of the materials they use. It is often a good idea in situations like this to retain identification from the patron until they are finished working. This makes it less likely that they will leave the building with items from the collection. A secure locked drawer must be provided for storage of identification.

Regarding supervision, it is most important to provide an area where readers can be watched while they are working and where it is difficult for them to leave the building unobserved. In a historical society, patron visits should be scheduled when a volunteer is available. In a library where supervision cannot be provided in the special collections reading room, patrons should be required to work at a table in view of the general reference desk or other library personnel.

In a situation where constant supervision cannot be provided, it is crucial to check patrons' belongings when they exit the building and to inspect archival materials before and after use. This can be awkward, but it will be easier if the procedures and the reasons for them are clearly explained to patrons at the outset. Institutions are advised to get counsel to ensure full compliance with laws regarding privacy, search, and seizure. For historical book collections that do not contain unique or rare material, the use of a book security system may also be helpful.

Remember that the purpose of these procedures is not to inconvenience patrons, but rather to safeguard your collection and demonstrate to your patrons that these materials are important to your institution.

STAFF MANAGEMENT

Involving all staff in planning efforts will increase the likelihood of a smoothly run, effective security program. Staff members who work with the public are an excellent source for input on how to improve security procedures, and they should be encouraged to contribute their ideas.

Training staff members to implement the security plan is essential, since the primary reason existing security procedures are not implemented is that staff members find it awkward or inconvenient to do so.

All staff must be instructed to enforce all rules, regulations, and procedures without exception. If exceptions are made routinely, a lax atmosphere conducive to theft and/or vandalism can develop. Staff should be trained in the techniques of observation. The room supervisor should not remain seated. It is essential to move around the reading room on a regular basis to observe as well as to provide assistance to the researchers. All chairs in the reading room should be facing the reading room supervisor and with clear sight lines. Chairs on both sides of the table make observation difficult.

While the importance of universal enforcement of security procedures must be communicated to staff, it is also essential that the staff is trained to deal with difficult situations that can make security procedures difficult to enforce. What should a staff member do if a patron refuses to provide registration information? if a patron refuses to have his/her belongings inspected? if a patron mishandles collections while working with them? If the repository does not have a professional security staff, it is a good idea to bring in a security professional to address these issues in a training session.

Unfortunately, another aspect of staff management is the protection of collections from theft by staff members themselves. There are some basic precautions that can be undertaken. Staff backgrounds can be checked before hiring; staff access to restricted areas can be limited; key control can be strictly enforced; staff belongings can be inspected when staff members exit the building; and staff can be required to sign in and out of the building, both during and after hours.

RESPONDING TO A SECURITY PROBLEM

Since it is impossible to prevent all theft and vandalism, it is important for a security plan to include procedures for responding to a security breach. This might be a loss that is discovered after the fact or it might be a theft in progress, and it might involve a researcher or even a staff member who is behaving suspiciously. In all cases, the goal should be to recover the missing materials and to apprehend the person responsible. The success of this effort will depend on quick action.

Some general guidelines for responding to specific situations are given below.[1] Remember that it is essential to insure that you are familiar with the federal, state, and local laws governing theft and mutilation of library and archival materials before drafting your own procedures.

If a staff member suspects a patron of theft, be sure no action is taken unless the staff member actually sees the theft or discovers that materials are missing in the process of checking them before and after use. The staff member should then request the patron to step into an office or other area away from the reading room. If possible, a second staff member should accompany them so that there is a witness. It is important not to touch or to coerce the patron. If the patron agrees to be detained, notify and await the arrival of security personnel or the police. If the patron insists on leaving, one staff person should notify the authorities and the other should carefully follow the patron to get a description of the patron's car. In either case, staff should write down all pertinent information about the encounter as soon as possible, in case it is needed for future court action.

Some of the warning signs that might indicate theft by a staff member include: one person consistently reports items missing or frequently finds missing materials; attempts have been made to alter collections records; a staff member frequently requests exceptions to the repository's rules and regulations; and a staff member appears to have a lifestyle that does not match his or her known resources. If a staff member is suspected of theft, determine the procedures to be followed before approaching the person. The person should be confronted by at least two supervisors and given a chance to explain his or her actions. It may be necessary to remove the person from the department temporarily and/or to contact police or security personnel.

It is somewhat more likely that a theft will be discovered after the fact, making it more difficult to identify the perpetrator. In such a case the security manager should first determine exactly what is missing (this might require an inventory of the collection if multiple items are involved), then contact the police, insurance company, and any appropriate organizations, as required.[2] All actions taken to locate missing materials and identify the thief should be carefully documented.

It is essential to provide staff with training so they are prepared to respond to a security emergency. Be sure that all staff members have a copy of the security plan, practice response procedures, and coordinate plans with outside officials such as institutional security personnel and/or police.

PREPARING AND MAINTAINING A SECURITY PLAN

Many of the principles for writing and maintaining a disaster plan will also apply to preparing a security plan; in fact, in most institutions these two plans will be closely related. Other leaflets in this series provide in-depth advice on preparing a disaster plan.

When preparing a security plan, the first step should be to put together a committee (in a small institution this may be a committee of one) that will perform a security survey, identify the most serious security risks, determine what should be done about them, and write a security plan. This committee must have the institution director's authority to act.

The security plan should include: information about any security systems in the building, information about distribution and control of keys to the building and to any special storage areas, copies of all policies and procedures relating to security (patron and staff use of the collection, collection management policies, etc.), a checklist of preventive measures to be undertaken, and a list of procedures for responding to a security breach (e.g., a theft, either in progress or one that has already occurred). Remember that in some cases it may not be appropriate to include some of the above information (e.g., security system information and key control information) in all copies of the plan; this information may be limited to upper-level staff members. All copies of the plan must be stored in a secure area where they cannot be accessed by the general public. When you write the plan, it is easy to feel overwhelmed by the amount to be accomplished, particularly if your institution has not had a systematic security plan. It is best to break the writing process into small projects (e.g., start by writing polices for collection use or procedures for responding to a theft in progress). This will make the process less intimidating and there will be a sense of accomplishment once each piece of the project is finished.

Once the plan is finished, do not allow it to gather dust on a shelf. Be sure to review it with all staff periodically, update it when information changes, and revise and improve it as necessary in response to any security emergency that might occur.

CONCLUSION

It is an unfortunate reality that libraries and archives must be concerned about the security of their collections. It is recommended that all repositories conduct a security survey and draw up a security plan. While there is a place for automated security systems of various types, a repository must not depend solely on these systems to protect its collection. Its security plan must also include policies and procedures regulating access to the collection by staff and users; mechanisms for identifying missing items; and procedures for responding to a security breach. Most important, the repository must recognize the difficulties staff members can face in enforcing security policies and provide training that will reinforce the importance of security activities and give staff members the skills they need to carry out these important duties effectively.

NOTES

[1] The guidelines given here in summary are discussed in more detail in Chapter 8, "Crisis Management," in Gregor Trinkaus-Randall, *Protecting Your Collections: A Manual of Archival Security* (Chicago: Society of American Archivists, 1995).

[2] For example, one may wish to report missing, recovered, or forged material to the Antiquarian Booksellers Association of America. For contact information, see Sources for Further Information at the end of this leaflet.

SOURCES FOR FURTHER INFORMATION

The American Society for Industrial Security. ASIS Standing Committee on Museum Security. *Suggested Guidelines in Museum Security.* Arlington, VA: ASIS, 1989; 21 pp. This can be purchased by contacting ASIS Customer Services at (703) 519-6200 for a catalog and/or order form and ordering information. The catalog item is #1036. Cost to members is $16; non-members $25.

_____. ASIS Online. ASIS, a membership organization for security professionals, offers a range of educational and information resources through their web site, including daily summaries of events and articles chosen from over 1000 monitored publications. http://www.asisonline.org

American Risk and Insurance Association. ARIA is the premier professional association of insurance and risk management scholars and professionals. They can be contacted at PO Box 9001, Mount Vernon, NY 10552, tel (914) 699-2020, fax: (914) 699-2025. ARIAWeb, their online resource, is worth consulting for a range of insurance information and links. Members can access ARIA's *The Journal of Risk and Insurance*, http://aria.org.

Antiquarian Booksellers' Association of America (ABAA). Headquarters are located at 20 W. 44th Street, New York, NY 10035-6604, tel. (212) 944-8291, fax (212) 944-8293, email abaa@panix.com. Their online resource was created in part to assist in locating booksellers and advertising upcoming book fairs. Links are provided to related information sources, including report of stolen books, recovered materials, and forgeries. http://www.abaa-booknet.com.

Association of College and Research Libraries, Rare Books and Manuscript Section Security Committee. "Guidelines Regarding Thefts in Libraries." *College & Research Libraries News* 55 (1994): 289-94.
Also available online at http://www.ala.org/acrl/guides/raresecu.html. Anyone entrusted with the care of valued library materials should review this document thoroughly.

Chaney, Michael, and Alan F. MacDougall. *Security and Crime Prevention in Libraries.* Aldershot, Hants.; Brookfield, VT: Ashgate Publishing Company, 1992.

Fennelly, Lawrence J., ed. *Effective Physical Security.* 2nd ed. Boston: Butterworth-Heinemann, 1997. An invaluable resource detailing the essential components of a secure facility, including security hardware and systems.

Interloc Missing and Stolen Books Database. An easily searchable database, including an easy means to contribute new items. Offered as a free service, both direct dial and internet access are provided. For information contact Interloc, Inc., PO Box 5, Southworth, WA, 98386, tel. (206) 871-3617, fax (206) 871-5626, email interloc@shaysnet.com.

INTERPOL (International Criminal Policy Organization). INTERPOL has disseminated information on stolen art since 1947. The recently established Cultural Property Program web site, www.usdoj.gov/usncb/culturehome.htm, will assist in accessing photographs and descriptive information to improve the chances of successful recovery.

Keller, Steven R., and Darrell R. Willson. "Security Systems." In *Storage of Natural History Collections: A Preventive Conservation Approach,* Vol. I, eds. Carolyn L. Rose, Catharine A. Hawks, and Hugh H. Genoways, 51-56. Iowa City, Iowa: Society for the Preservation of Natural History Collections, 1995.

Keller, Steven R. "Conducting the Physical Security Survey." Deltona, Florida: Steven R. Keller and Associates, Inc., 1988. This and many other excellent documents on security of cultural resources by Steven Keller are available online at http://www.horizon-usa.com. See especially the following:

_____. "The Most Common Security Mistakes That Most Museums Make." Deltona, Florida: Steven R. Keller and Associates, Inc., 1994. http://www.horizon-usa.com/horizon/common.txt

_____. "Securing Historic Houses and Buildings." Deltona, Florida: Steven R. Keller and Associates, Inc., 1994. http://www.horizon-usa.com/horizon/histhous.txt

_____. "A Dozen Things You Can Do to Improve Your Security Program." Deltona, Florida: Steven R. Keller and Associates, Inc., 1993. http://www.horizon-usa.com/horizon/dozen.txt

_____. "A Plan for Achieving Internal Security." Deltona, Florida: Steven R. Keller and Associates, Inc., 1990. http://www.horizon-usa.com/horizon/internal.txt

Liston, David, ed. *Museum Security and Protection.* ICOM (International Committee on Museum Security). New York: Routledge Inc., 1993. This volume covers all aspects of building and collection protection, including an excellent section on guard services.

McCabe, Gerard B., ed. *Academic Libraries in Urban and Metropolitan Areas: A Management Handbook.* Westport, CT: Greenwood Press, 1992. The Greenwood Library Management Collection.

movlibs-L. movlibs, created by the LAMA () Moving Libraries Discussion Group, is a forum for librarians interested in issues regarding relocating collections, furniture, equipment, and personnel. To subscribe, send an email message to listproc@ala.org, with the subject line blank, the message "subscribe movlibs-L (first name, last name)."

Museum Security Network. MSN is devoted to the safety and security of cultural property. Their services include a mailing list as well as an extensively linked Web site for excellent sources of information. Contents include access to articles, lists of consultants, security organizations, disaster management resources, and contact information for reporting loss. http://museum-security.org

O'Neill, Robert Keating, ed. *Management of Library and Archival Security: From the Outside Looking In.* Binghamton, NY: The Haworth Press, Inc., 1998. Menzi L. Behrnd-Klodt, JD, Attorney/Archivist, Klodt and Associates, Madison, WI: "Provides useful advice and on-target insights for professionals caring for valuable documents and artifacts. Focusing not just on the aftermath of a catastrophe, but disaster prevention and integration of security with preservation programs, this book is an excellent guide. This useful work should be owned by professionals and administrators at large and small institutions alike."

Patkus, Beth Lindblom. "Collections Security: A Preservation Perspective." *Journal of Library Administration* 25.1 (1998): 67-89. Good overall review of security and disaster concerns for collection preservation.

Robertson, Guy. "The Elvis Biography Has Just Left the Building, and Nobody Checked It Out: A Primer on Library Theft." *Feliciter* 44.10 (October 1998): 20-24. Written with humor, the author describes various techniques for stealing from libraries and archives, then lists basic (and mandatory) preventive measures.

Safety-L. An electronic discussion list, created by the LAMA () Buildings and Equipment Safety/Security Discussion Group, to identify common concerns and examine alternative solutions. To subscribe, send an email message to listproc@ala.org, with the subject line blank, the message "subscribe safety-L (first name, last name)."

Shuman, Bruce A. *Library Security and Safety Handbook: Prevention, Policies and Procedures.* Chicago: American Library Association, forthcoming.

_____. "Designing Personal Safety into Library Buildings." *American Libraries* 27.7 (August 1996): 37-39. Practical guidelines for improving public library spaces and procedures to help ensure patron and staff safety.

Totka, Vincent A., Jr. "Preventing Patron Theft in the Archives: Legal Perspectives and Problems." *American Archivist* 56 (1993): 664-72. For further information on legal matters, see the Museum Security Network Web site listed above.

Trinkaus-Randall, Gregor. *Protecting Your Collections: A Manual of Archival Security.* Chicago: The Society of American Archivists, 1995. An invaluable primer to assist in developing an effective security program, including enough detail to implement the basics.

Wyly, Mary. "Special Collections Security: Problems, Trends, and Consciousness." *Library Trends 36* (1987): 241-56. An older but good basic article reviewing security concerns particular to the use of special collections material.

SAMPLE PATRON REGISTRATION FORM

NAME OF INSTITUTION
Location
Mailing Address
Telephone Number
Fax Number

Researcher Registration and Procedures

1. Please sign the registration book each day you use the reading room.

2. Please complete the following, read the procedures, and sign the agreement below.

Name (print clearly): _____

Identification: _____

Mailing Address:

_____

_____

_____

Current Local Residence:

_____

_____

_____

Professional Affiliation:

_____

Subject of Research:

_____

_____

The following procedures must be observed while conducting research in the Archives. You must sign the statement agreeing to abide by these procedures. They are intended to allow access to the collections while preserving them for future generations.

Sample Procedures Information Sheet

- Coats, parcels, purses, backpacks, briefcases, and other similar belongings must be left at the coat rack in the lobby, or in the lockers provided.
- No documents are to be removed from the research area under any circumstances. Archival materials are never loaned but must be consulted in the archives.
- All food and beverages must be consumed only in designated areas. No smoking anywhere in the building.
- Up to three boxes of materials can be requested at any time, but only one box at a time can be used by the researcher to ensure that materials are not placed into the wrong box.
- Original documents are not made available to the researcher if a copy (microform, photocopy, etc.) is available.
- Original order must be maintained within each box and within each file folder. If you have a problem returning items to original order, or if you find something out of order, please consult a staff member.
- Misconduct or disrespect of the rules may result in the researcher's being refused further access the Archives.

By affixing my signature below, I certify that I have read the list of procedures, and that I agree to abide by said procedures in any use I make of the collections at the (Name of Institution).

Signature _____Date _____

Collections used: _____

Staff member on duty: _____

STORAGE AND HANDLING

Northeast Document
Conservation Center
100 Brickstone Square
Andover, MA 01810-1494
www.nedcc.org
Tel: (978) 470-1010
Fax: (978) 475-6021

STORAGE METHODS AND HANDLING PRACTICES

**by Sherelyn Ogden
Head of Conservation
Minnesota Historical Society**

Unacceptable storage methods have a direct effect on the useful life of materials. Slovenly, haphazard, overcrowded conditions soon result in avoidable damage to collections, and poor-quality storage enclosures accelerate the deterioration of the materials they are intended to protect. Poor handling also takes its toll. Normal handling is inevitably somewhat damaging; rough handling, however, quickly leads to serious, irreparable harm. The longevity of collections will be significantly extended by observing the following basic guidelines.

BOOKS

In general, good air circulation should be maintained in storage areas. Books should never be stored directly against walls but should be at least three inches away from them to facilitate movement of air around the books and to avoid the occurrence of pockets of damp air. This is especially important when bookshelves are positioned against the outside walls of a building. Books stored in a closed cabinet should also be shelved a distance from the back wall of the cabinet, and the cabinet itself should be approximately three inches away from the wall. Care should be taken to ensure that humidity and stagnant air do not build up in closed cabinets, especially those against outside walls.

Books should be held upright on shelves. They should not be allowed to lean to one side or the other, because this causes strain on the binding. Books should be arranged so that shelves are full, preventing books from leaning; however, books should not be shelved so tightly that damage is incurred when they are removed from the shelf. If shelves are not full, bookends should be used to hold books upright. Bookends should be non-damaging, with smooth surfaces and broad edges to prevent bindings from being abraded or leaves from being torn or creased.

Books should not extend beyond the edges of shelves into aisles because they may be bumped or otherwise damaged. Instead, adequate oversized shelving should be provided so that large books can be stored on shelves without extending beyond the edge. Books should not be stored on the fore-edge. If books are too tall to stand upright, either the books should be moved or shelves should be rearranged so that the books fit on the shelves standing upright. Books should be stored spine down until the shelving is rearranged; storing a book spine down rather than spine up will prevent the text from pulling out of the binding due to its weight. Large books should not be stored next to small ones because they are not adequately supported by them. When possible, books should be shelved by size to prevent this. Some books are so large that they should be shelved lying down, especially if upright storage could allow heavy textbooks to sag away from their bindings.

Paper and cloth bindings should not be stored in direct contact with leather bindings. Acidity and oils in the leather migrate into paper and cloth and hasten their deterioration. Furthermore, degraded powdery leather will soil paper and cloth. When possible, books should be boxed to avoid these problems. When this is not possible, paper and cloth bindings should be shelved together, separate from leather bindings. Other alternatives to consider when the binding must remain on view, such as in a period room in a historic house, are the use of book shoes (supports that cover the sides but leave the spines of books visible) or placement of a piece of polyester film between the books.

As a rule, books should not be stacked in piles on shelves. Small, structurally sound books should be shelved upright. Oversized, heavy, structurally weak, or damaged books should be stored flat rather than upright, to give them the overall support they require. If books are stored on their sides, additional shelves may need to be inserted at narrow intervals to avoid having to stack these books. Shelves should be wide enough to support oversized books completely so that books do not protrude into the aisles. Volumes should be stacked only when absolutely necessary, and the stacks should contain only two to three books. Ideally all books that are stacked should be individually boxed. Books with bindings of special value should be stacked only if they are boxed to prevent abrasion to the bindings. Special care should be taken to insure that call number flags or titles of books that are stored flat are visible so the books can be identified without being moved.

Boxing is crucial to the preservation of certain books. Those with fragile bindings of special value that should be retained in their present condition should be boxed for protection. Damaged books that have low value or are rarely used and do not warrant treatment or repair of the binding should also be boxed. Books bound in vellum should be boxed. Vellum responds readily to changes in temperature and relative humidity by expanding and contracting. This can result in warped covers. Boxing helps restrain vellum bindings and thereby minimizes warping. Boxes should be constructed of archival-quality materials and should be custom made to fit a book's dimensions exactly.

Both drop-spine and phase boxes are acceptable. Drop-spine boxes are preferable because they provide better support and keep books cleaner. For volumes that require structural support while being displayed, the book shoe is appropriate. The use of slipcases should be avoided because they often abrade the surface of the binding when the book is slid in and out of the slipcase. Envelopes are sometimes used for the storage of books. These generally do not provide the support books need and should be replaced with boxes. If boxes are too expensive or take up too much space on shelves, books that are infrequently used can be placed in card stock enclosures (best for small books) or wrapped in a permanent durable paper. Damaged books should never be held together with rubber bands or string. They should be boxed, wrapped in paper, or tied with a flat undyed cotton, linen, or polyester tape. Tape should be tied with knots at the top or fore-edge of the text block.

Poor handling procedures can cause irreparable damage to books. They should not be pulled off the shelves by the headcap, a practice that causes the headcap to fail, tearing the spine of the binding. Instead, books on either side of the desired book should be pushed in, and the desired book pulled out gently by grasping it on both sides with the thumb and fingers. The book should be removed, and the remaining books on the shelf and the bookends readjusted. When the book is replaced, the bookend should be loosened, the books moved on the shelf to make a space, and the book reinserted in the space. The bookend should then be readjusted. When oversized books that are stored flat are removed, the upper volumes should be transferred to an empty shelf or book truck. The desired volume should be removed by lifting it with both hands, and then the removed volumes transferred back to the shelf. Replacing the book on the shelf is done in the same way.

To minimize chances of dropping books, one should not stack them too high when they are moved or carried. Books of special value should not be stacked at all. If book trucks are used, they should be easy to maneuver and have wide shelves, protective rails, and bumpers on the corners. Books should not be stacked high on the truck, nor should they protrude beyond the edges; the center of gravity of the loaded truck should be low to help stabilize it.

Books are often unnecessarily damaged during photocopying. Photocopy machines with flat copy platens necessitate jamming the binding flat in order to get a good image. Better machines are those with edge platens or other features that allow a book page to be copied with the book open only to $90°$ instead of $180°$. Photocopying of books of special value should be done only by staff members rather than by researchers, and then only if it can be done without causing damage to the books themselves. The spine of a book should never be pressed down with the hand or the cover of the copier to insure a good quality image. If a book is too brittle or tightly bound to photocopy safely, it should be microfilmed instead and a photocopy made from the film copy.

Call numbers should not be painted on books that are of special value, nor should they be typed onto labels taped to books with pressure-sensitive tape or attached with adhesive. Paint is unattractive and disfiguring; tape and adhesive may discolor and stain the binding. Ideally volumes should be boxed and the call number placed on the box. For volumes that are not boxed, call numbers should be typed onto heavy, acid-free paper flags placed inside the volume. These flags should be about two inches wide, and two to three inches longer than the book is high. An alternative is to construct polyester film jackets and place call number labels on them. Bar code labels should never be applied to books of special value because the books will almost always be damaged. If computerized codes must be used for special books, the label should be attached to a flag of alkaline paper placed in the book or onto a polyester film jacket.

For books that do not have special value, care should be taken to ensure that the label adhesive will remain effective over time. It is especially important that the adhesive does not desiccate, causing labels to come loose or fall off, and does not ooze, causing stickiness on the book, which will attract dirt and may damage other materials that touch it.

If bookplates must be used in books of special value, they should be made of low-lignin, alkaline paper, and should be attached with a stable, reversible adhesive, preferably rice- or wheat-starch paste, or methyl cellulose; or polyester film jackets should be made and the bookplates attached to them. Circulation card pockets should be treated the same way, although books of special value usually should not circulate.

All acidic inserts, such as bookmarks, scraps of paper, and pressed flowers, should be removed from books. This is to prevent acidity in the inserts from migrating into book pages and damaging them. Paper clips on book pages or on inserts into books should be removed.

UNBOUND FLAT PAPER

For paper collections, it should be kept in mind that only objects of the same size and category should be stored together. Differences in bulk and weight create a potential for physical damage, so it is not advisable to store single sheets in the same box with books or pamphlets. Generally speaking, heavy objects should be stored separately from lighter ones, as should bulky objects (which cause uneven pressure inside boxes). It should also be kept in mind that because acid migrates from paper of inferior quality to any other paper with which it comes into direct contact, it is important to separate poor-quality papers from those that are better. Newsclippings and other obviously inferior-quality papers must be removed from direct contact with historical documents and manuscripts on better-quality paper.

Documents and manuscripts should be unfolded for storage if this can be done without splitting, breaking, or otherwise damaging them. If unfolding may result in damage, a conservator should be consulted before proceeding. All damaging fasteners such as staples, paper clips, and pins should be carefully removed and replaced, only if absolutely needed, with nonrusting ones. Documents should be housed in acid-free, buffered file folders. Ideally no more than ten to fifteen sheets should be placed into each folder; the more valuable or fragile the item, the fewer the sheets that should be stored in one folder.

Folders should be kept in archival-quality document-storage boxes. All folders inside a box should be the same size and should conform to the size of the box. The boxes can be stored flat or upright. If boxes are stored flat, they should be stacked only two high to facilitate handling. Flat storage will give the documents overall support and will prevent crumbling edges, slumping, and other mechanical damage to which upright storage might subject them. Flat storage, however, causes documents on the bottom of the box to suffer from the weight of those above. Upright storage is preferable when documents and folders are well supported to prevent slumping and edge damage. Spacer boards made out of stable materials can be used to fill out boxes that are not quite full. Care should be taken not to overfill boxes because this can cause damage when items are removed, replaced, or reviewed. An alternative to boxing is storage in a file cabinet equipped with hanging racks and hanging folders. If hanging folders made of archival-quality materials cannot be found, general office hanging folders may be used, as long as the folders within them are made of acceptable materials.

Vellum documents, like vellum books, are highly susceptible to fluctuations in temperature and relative humidity and should be placed in an enclosure. Suitable enclosures include encapsulation, folders, mats, and boxes, or a combination of these.

OVERSIZED MATERIALS

Oversized materials—like architectural drawings, blueprints, maps, large prints, and wallpaper samples—are best stored flat in the drawers of map cases or in large covered boxes of acceptable quality. The materials should be placed in acid-free buffered folders. Until recently it was recommended that blueprints, which are alkali-sensitive, should not be stored in alkaline-buffered folders. Recent research indicates, however, that if the storage environment is maintained at an acceptable relative humidity (30% to 55%), unbuffered folders may not be necessary and buffered folders may be used. All folders should be cut to fit the size of the drawer or box; drawer- or box-sized folders are preferable to smaller ones, which tend to get jammed at the back of drawers or shift position as the drawers open and close or the boxes are moved. Ideally only one item should be placed in a folder, although several may be stored in a folder if necessary. If several items are placed in one folder, interleaving with acid-free tissue paper is desirable, especially if the items have colors or are of special value. There should be adequate room where oversized materials are stored so that they can be safely removed from drawers or shelves, and there should be a place to put them down once they are removed or prior to replacement in drawers or on shelves.

If they are not brittle or fragile, oversized materials can be rolled when flat storage is not possible. It is important to make sure the materials are not too brittle or fragile to sustain rolling and unrolling. Some items need to be rolled individually; others can be rolled in groups of four to six similar-sized items, the exact number depending on the size and weight of the paper. A tube several inches longer than the largest item being rolled and at least four inches in diameter (larger diameters are preferable) should be used. If the tube is not made of low-lignin, pH-neutral materials, it should be wrapped in neutral or buffered paper or polyester film. Alternatively, the items can be placed in a folder of five-mil polyester film cut several inches larger in both dimensions than the largest item being rolled. The item or items are then rolled face out onto the tube. If a polyester film folder is used, it should be rolled so that the fold is parallel with the length of the tube. The assembly should then be wrapped with neutral or buffered paper or polyester film to protect it from abrasions. The wrapped roll should be loosely tied with flat linen, cotton, or polyester tape. This assembly may be stored inside a larger tube for added protection if desired. Tubes should be stored horizontally.

NEWSPRINT

Much of the newsprint produced after the mid-nineteenth century is made of paper pulp that contains lignin and other impurities, and its long-term preservation is difficult at best. While it is possible to alkalize (deacidify) newsprint to retard its deterioration, this is often not practical because it will still continue to deteriorate at a relatively rapid rate. Also, alkalization after newsprint has become yellow and brittle will not make it white and flexible again. Most newsclippings are important because of the information they contain and not because of the value of the clippings themselves. For this reason, photocopying and microfilming are the most practical preservation options for collections of newsclippings. All photocopying should be done on low-lignin, buffered paper using an electrostatic copier with heat-fused images. Newsclippings that must be retained should be treated and then physically separated from better quality papers in a folder or in an enclosure made of polyester film.

PAMPHLETS

Pamphlets can be stored in boxes or in folders. Several pamphlets of the same cover size can be stored together in a drop-spine or phase box. Pamphlets that differ in size should be stored either individually in drop-spine or phase boxes, or in file folders that are kept in document-storage boxes or in hanging files in file cabinets. If stored in folders, pamphlets should be stored spine down. If single pamphlets must be shelved between books, they should be individually boxed. Groups of pamphlets shelved between books can be boxed together according to the guidelines just given. If pamphlet binders are used, they must be of acceptable quality throughout and should be attached to pamphlets in such a way as to be non-damaging to them. Consult an experienced professional about the advantages and disadvantages of various commercially available binders. They should not be adhered directly to pamphlets. Where stitching is used to join pamphlet and binder, it should be done through the fold and through original sewing holes where possible.

SCRAPBOOKS AND EPHEMERA

Many historical collections include scrapbooks and ephemera (e.g., trade cards, valentines, patterns, paper dolls, etc.). These items pose challenging preservation problems because they often contain a variety of components and media. They may have raised surfaces, three-dimensional decoration, or moving parts. They are frequently unique, fragile, damaged, and of significant associational value. They should never be interfiled with other categories of library and archival materials because damage may result from the different sizes, shapes, weights, and materials represented.

Most scrapbooks and ephemera can be stored according to the general guidelines given above. Scrapbooks that are of special historic value in their original form should be individually boxed in custom-fitted boxes. Unbound ephemera should be grouped by size and type (e.g., photographs, printed material, manuscripts, etc.), individually enclosed to protect items from acid migration and mechanical damage if needed, and stored in a way that will support them structurally. Some vendors of archival supplies offer standard-sized storage boxes and sleeves for common ephemera such as postcards and stereo views. Others can produce custom-sized enclosures in quantity to meet special needs.

PHOTOGRAPHS

For photographs, it is best for each item to have its own enclosure. This reduces damage to the photograph by giving it protection and physical support. Acceptable storage materials can be made of either paper or plastic. Because paper enclosures are opaque, the photograph must be removed from the enclosure when it is viewed; clear plastic enclosures have the advantage of allowing researchers to view the image without handling it, thus reducing the possibility of scratching or abrasion. Paper enclosures should be acid and lignin free. Plastics suitable for photographic storage are polyester, polypropylene, and polyethylene. Polyvinyl-chloride should be avoided at all times. Both paper and plastic enclosures should meet the specifications provided in the American National Standards Institute (ANSI) Standard IT 9.2-1998 and should pass the Photographic activity test (PAT) as specified in ANSI NAPM IT 9.16-1993.

Once materials have been properly housed in folders, sleeves, or envelopes, they should usually be stored flat in drop-front boxes of archival quality. Glass plate negatives are an exception and should be stored vertically in order to prevent breakage of plates stored on the bottom of a pile. The boxes should be housed on metal shelves or in metal cabinets. Where possible, items of similar size should be stored together; the mixing of different sizes can cause abrasion and breakage, and can increase the risk of misplacing smaller items. Regardless of the size of the photograph, all enclosures within a box should be the same size and should be the size of the box. Boxes should not be overfilled.

Horizontal storage of photographs is usually preferable to vertical storage, since it provides overall support and avoids mechanical damage such as bending. Vertical storage, however, may make access to the collection easier and decrease handling. With vertical storage, photographs should be placed in acid-free file folders or envelopes that are themselves housed in hanging file folders or document storage boxes. Overcrowding should be avoided. The use of hanging file folders will prevent photographs from sliding down under each other and will facilitate their handling.

Special care must be given to the storage of oversized photographic prints mounted on cardboard. This board is often acidic and extremely brittle. Embrittlement of the support can endanger the image itself because the cardboard may break in storage or during handling, damaging the photograph. Such prints must be carefully stored, sometimes in specially made enclosures. They should be handled with great care.

FINALLY . . .

Proper storage and handling of library and archival materials can be relatively inexpensive, with several of the measures described above costing little or nothing. In addition, it can lead to future savings by minimizing the need for repair of materials. Following these guidelines is a practical, cost-effective way to extend the useful life of collections.

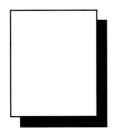

Northeast Document
Conservation Center
100 Brickstone Square
Andover, MA 01810-1494
www.nedcc.org
Tel: (978) 470-1010
Fax: (978) 475-6021

STORAGE FURNITURE: A BRIEF
REVIEW OF CURRENT OPTIONS

**by Sherelyn Ogden
Head of Conservation
Minnesota Historical Society**

The selection of storage furniture for library and archival materials requires careful investigation. Many of the currently available furniture choices contain materials that produce by-products that contribute to the deterioration of the collections they house. In addition, some construction features are damaging and also contribute to deterioration of collections. The information that follows is intended to serve as an introduction to the subject and as a guide to what to look for in selecting storage furniture.

BAKED ENAMEL

Until recently only baked enamel furniture was recommended. Constructed of steel with a baked enamel coating, this furniture was thought to be made of chemically stable materials. Because it is readily available, competitively priced, strong, and durable, it has been a particularly attractive choice. Questions, however, have been raised about the possibility that the baked enamel coating may give off formaldehyde and other volatiles harmful to collections if it has not been properly baked (not long enough at high enough temperatures). This concern is especially serious when collections are stored on book shelves in an area that is enclosed or has poor air circulation, or are stored in closed furniture such as map cases, file cabinet drawers, and book cases with solid doors.

Because of this concern about off-gassing, baked enamel furniture is no longer widely recommended unless it has been properly baked. For us to be certain that it has, the furniture must be tested. Testing should comply with ASTM (American Society of Testing Materials) E-595.[1] This testing requires the use of sophisticated analytical equipment. Furniture can be less conclusively tested in-house with the organic solvent methyl ethyl ketone (MEK).[2] If this crude test, known as the MEK rub test, indicates that the coating may not be properly baked, the furniture should perhaps be tested by a professional testing service to determine for certain if it is off-gassing.

POWDER COATINGS

Steel storage furniture with various powder coatings appears to avoid the off-gassing problems associated with baked enamel. Powder coatings of finely divided, synthetic polymer materials are fused onto the steel. Testing done thus far indicates that the coatings are chemically stable, present minimal threat of volatile evocation, and so are safe for the storage of valuable materials. Nevertheless, conducting the MEK rub test in an inconspicuous area where the steel is the heaviest gauge will confirm that the coating is properly cured and that off-gassing is not a concern. [3]

ANODIZED ALUMINUM

Anodized aluminum storage furniture is another option. This uncoated metal is extremely strong yet light in weight. The metal itself is reported to be non-reactive and, since it has no coating, off-gassing problems are eliminated. Many people consider anodized aluminum to be the best choice, especially for highly sensitive materials, but it tends to be the most expensive.

CHROME-PLATED STEEL SHELVING

Open chrome-plated steel shelving, made of heavy-gauge, chrome-plated steel wire, is a storage choice suitable for boxed materials. The shelving is durable, and the open-wire framework is light in weight and provides good air circulation. The wires, however, can leave permanent marks on items that are not protected, so materials should be boxed or the shelves should be lined.

WOOD

Storage furniture, especially shelving, made of wood has traditionally been popular for reasons of aesthetics, economy, and ease of construction. Harmful acids and other substances, however, are emitted by wood, wood composites, and some sealants and adhesives. Although the levels of emissions are highest initially, in most cases volatiles are present for the life of the materials. To avoid potential damage to collections, storage furniture made of wood or wood products should be avoided. If this is not possible and wood must be used, precautions are necessary. Certain woods and wood composites are more potentially damaging than others. For example, oak, which has been used extensively for the storage of library and archival materials, is considered the wood with the most volatile acidity and should not be used. Also, many wood composites that are advertised as formaldehyde-free may contain potentially damaging acids or other aldehydes. Current information should be obtained prior to selecting new furniture made of wood or a wood product so that the least damaging wood can be chosen. All wood and wood composites should be tested to determine their safety for use. [4]

COATINGS FOR WOOD

For wooden storage furniture that is already in use, safeguards should be taken. All wood should be sealed. It should be noted, though, that no coating or sealant will completely block the emission of acids and harmful volatiles for prolonged periods of time, but it can be useful for short-term exposure. Also, some sealants are better than others at blocking damaging substances. Great care must be taken in selecting a sealant to make sure that the one chosen forms the most effective barrier and does not itself emit harmful substances.

The most readily available sealant that is recommended at this time is a moisture-borne polyurethane. Many kinds of polyurethane are available. Oil-modified polyurethanes are the most common. However, oil-modified polyurethanes, oil-based paints, and other products that contain oil or alkyd resins should be avoided. Only moisture-borne polyurethanes are recommended. Unfortunately not all moisture-borne polyurethanes on the market are safe for use. Also, formulations often change without notice. For these reasons, the polyurethane selected should be tested prior to use to guarantee its acceptability. [5] Contact a preservation professional for brand names of moisture-borne polyurethanes that are currently being recommended and begin testing with these. Because these urethanes do not completely prevent the escape of volatiles, choosing low-emission wood products is of critical importance.

Paints can also be used to seal wood if the natural appearance of the wood does not have to be retained. Oil-based paints and stains should not be used because of the potentially damaging effects of the acids in the drying oils. Two-part epoxy paints form an excellent barrier, but they are difficult to use. Latex and acrylic paints form a less effective barrier but are easier to use.[6] All coatings should be tested prior to use. Contact a preservation professional for current information before making a decision. After furniture is sealed it should be allowed to air for three to four weeks. Because of the toxicity of various components of most sealants, the sealants should be used with caution and appropriate safety measures observed.

ADDITIONAL BARRIERS

In addition to sealing wood, bookshelves and drawers should be lined with an effective barrier material. Barriers that are recommended at present include an inert metallic laminate (e.g., Marvelseal 360 and 470), PCTFE (polychlorotrifluoroethylene) high-barrier films (e.g., Alclar), sheet aluminum, glass, polymethyl methacrylate sheeting (e.g., Plexiglas), or a combination of these.[7] Polymethyl methacrylate sheeting can absorb pollutants and reemit them, so this material should not be reused once it has served as a barrier. Note that printing inks found on some of these barrier materials may be corrosive.[8] Contact the manufacturer to request information on the printing inks, or request products without printing. If these barriers do not provide an appropriate surface for the storage of materials, 100% ragboard can be used in addition. Ragboard, however, should not be used by itself, because it does not provide a sufficient barrier.

CONSTRUCTION FEATURES

Regardless of the construction material chosen, storage furniture should have a smooth, non-abrasive finish. If steel furniture is painted or coated, the finish should be resistant to chipping since chips will leave steel exposed and susceptible to rust. The furniture should be free of sharp edges and protrusions. Exposed nuts and bolts are particularly hazardous. The furniture should be strong enough that it will not bend or warp when filled. Shelving should be bolted together as well as to the floor and perhaps ceiling so it will not wobble when collections are housed on it. Shelves should be adjustable to accommodate items of various sizes, particularly oversized ones. The lowest storage area in the furniture should be at least four to six inches off the floor to protect collections from water damage in the event of a flood. Cabinets with doors are often preferred when security and protection from dust are special concerns. These are available with shelves or drawers. The use of piano hinges for the attachment of the doors is advisable if opening the doors flat will facilitate safe removal of items from the cabinet. Condensation can be a problem in closed steel cabinets when the relative humidity where the cabinets are stored fluctuates.[9] Condensation can result in rusting or mold growth in cabinets. For this reason, conditions in closed cabinets should be monitored. This is most easily accomplished by the use of dial hygrometers or paper-based humidity indicator cards. These devices do not have a high degree of accuracy, but they are sufficient to indicate problematic conditions. If possible, the use of closed steel cabinets should be avoided unless the cabinets are well ventilated or the relative humidity is closely controlled and monitored.[10]

Drawers in flat files should be no more than two inches deep (less if possible). The deeper the drawer the greater the weight on the items in it and the greater the stress on items when they are removed. Drawers should have dust covers or rear hoods to prevent items from being damaged at the back of the drawer. Drawers should have stops to prevent them from coming out of cabinets. Also, they should have ball bearings rather than slide in grooves because they will open and close more smoothly, causing less vibration to items, and the risk that they will fall out of the grooves and become stuck is eliminated. Drawers can be lined with foam core for cushioning as added protection from jarring and vibration.

HIGH-DENSITY STORAGE SYSTEMS

High-density storage systems, often referred to as compact or movable shelving, are used by many institutions with space limitations. These systems minimize the amount of space needed by compacting ranges of shelves or cabinets of drawers tightly together. The ranges slide along tracks so they can be moved apart for retrieval of items on a particular range and then moved back together again. Moving systems such as these can be damaging to items because of the vibrations to which they subject items. Also, items can be jostled off shelves causing further damage. If a high-density storage system must be used, a design should be chosen that minimizes these hazards. It is crucial with high-density storage systems that items do not extend beyond the edge of the shelves to avoid having the items on opposite shelves collide with them when the ranges are closed. When installing high-density systems, enough overall space should be allowed to insure that sufficiently wide aisles can be opened between the ranges for the safe removal of items, particularly oversized ones, from shelves and drawers. Floor loading is a serious concern and should be taken into account if many heavy items are stored in a confined space. This is quite important with compact shelving for books. Weight estimates need to include floor treatment, furniture tracks and fittings, and shelf and drawer loads as well as the furniture. A structural engineer should be consulted. Fire detection and suppression are additional concerns. A space of a few inches always should be left between the ranges so that a fire between them can be detected and suppressed. Leaving a small space will also enhance air circulation, avoiding the build-up of pockets of damp or stagnant air. Another concern is the behavior of compact shelving during floods, fires, or earthquakes, and how to gain access to materials if the shelving fails to open because of increased weight, distortion of the tracks, or failure of electricity. Consult the manufacturer about this.

REMEMBER . . .

The selection of suitable storage furniture and the specification or modification of wooden storage furniture are complicated tasks. Poor-quality storage greatly accelerates the deterioration of collections. Opinion on what constitutes acceptable storage furniture is changing rapidly. A preservation professional should be consulted for the most up-to-date information before decisions with far-reaching impact are made. Making the right choice will add immeasurably to the useful life of collections.

NOTES

[1] Pamela Hatchfield, Conservator, Objects Conservation and Scientific Research, Museum of Fine Arts, Boston, Massachusetts. Personal communication.

[2] Saturate a small-tip cotton swab on a stick with methyl ethyl ketone (MEK) and rub it vigorously over a small inconspicuous area of the furniture to be tested. Rub the swab over the furniture backward and forward thirty times in each direction. The finish on the furniture may soften, take on a moist look, or discolor slightly. This is not a concern. Look at the swab to see how much, if any, paint has been removed. Minimal or slight discoloration on a swab is a reasonable assurance that the coating is properly cured. Medium to heavy discoloration indicates that the coating may not be properly cured and may need to be tested further. **Please note that MEK is toxic and flammable. It must be used in a well ventilated area, and appropriate protective measures must be taken**. B.W. Golden, Vice President, Engineering, Interior Steel Equipment Co., Cleveland, Ohio, and Bruce Danielson, President, Delta Designs, Topeka, Kansas. Personal communication.

[3] Golden.

[4] This procedure is used for testing wood products, sealants, and a variety of other materials. If you are testing a wood or other material, place a sample of the material in a glass jar. If you are testing a sealant, coat a clean glass slide with the sealant you want to test, and place the coated slide in a glass jar. Also place in the jar a piece of cleaned and degreased lead, silver, and iron: rub the metal pieces with 600-grit sandpaper or steel wool and then wipe them with acetone or alcohol. Next dampen a piece of cotton with deionized water and place it in the jar with the metal pieces and wood sample or glass slide. Place the dampened cotton in a small glass beaker or glass vial in the jar so that it is not in direct contact with the metal pieces and glass slide and to slow the evaporation rate. Cover the jar with two thicknesses of aluminum foil and secure the foil tightly with brass or other wire. Prepare a second jar exactly the same way as the first but without the sample or coated glass slide. This jar will serve as a control. Place both jars in an oven at 60°C for three weeks or on a window sill for as long as possible. Watch for changes in the appearance of the metals. Looking under magnification will be helpful. Changes will probably occur in both the test samples and the control samples. If the changes in the test samples differ from those in the

control samples, unacceptable substances are probably present. In the testing of wood composites, it is impossible to determine if the reaction is caused by the wood or by the adhesives in the composite. If a positive reaction is observed, the material is probably unsuitable for use. Hatchfield. Personal communication.

[5] Hatchfield.

[6] Hatchfield.

[7] Hatchfield, "Choosing Materials for Museum Storage," in *Storage of Natural History Collections: Basic Concepts*, Carolyn L. Rose and Catharine A. Hawks, eds. (Pittsburgh, PA: Society for the Preservation of Natural History Collections, 1994), p. 7.

[8] Hatchfifeld, pp. 5-6.

[9] Margaret Holben Ellis, *The Care of Prints and Drawings* (Walnut Creek, CA: Altamira Press, 1995), 148.

[10] Ellis., 148-9.

SUGGESTED FURTHER READINGS

Hatchfield, Pamela. "Choosing Materials for Museum Storage." In *Storage of Natural History Collections: Basic Concepts*. Carolyn L. Rose and Catharine A. Hawks, eds. Pittsburgh, PA: Society for the Preservation of Natural History Collections, 1994.

Hatchfield, Pamela, and Jane Carpenter. *Formaldehyde: How Great Is the Danger to Museum Collections?* Cambridge, MA: Harvard University, 1987.

Miles, Catherine E. "Wood Coatings for Display and Storage Cases." *Studies in Conservation* 31.3 (August 1986): 114-24.

Raphael, T. *Conservation Guidelines: Design and Fabrication of Exhibits.* Harpers Ferry, WV: Division of Conservation, National Park Service, Harpers Ferry Center, 1991.

SOURCES OF SUPPLIES

This list was provided by Pamela Hatchfield, Conservator, Objects Conservation and Scientific Research, Museum of Fine Arts, Boston, Massachusetts. The list is not exhaustive, nor does it constitute an endorsement of the suppliers listed. Obtain information from a number of vendors so that you can make comparisons of cost and assess the full range of available products.

A more complete list of suppliers is available from NEDCC. Consult the Technical Leaflets section of NEDCC's website at www.nedcc.org or contact NEDCC for the most up-to-date version in print.

Alfa Products
30 Bond Street
Ward Hill, MA 01835
Telephone: (978) 521-6300
Fax: (978) 521-6350
Metal foils for materials testing

Allied Signal
PO Box 1039
Morristown, NJ 07962
Toll Free: (800) 934-5679
Alclar transparent vapor barrier

B.F. Goodrich
300 Whitney Street Leominster, MA 01453
Telephone: (978) 537-4748
Fax: (978) 537-8245
available from:
Dexter Brothers
44 Rugg Road
Alston, MA 02134
Telephone: (617) 789-5665
Sancure 878 moisture-borne polyurethane

Conservation Resources
8000-H Forbes Place
Springfield, VA 22151
Telephone: (703) 321-7730
Fax: (703) 321-0629
Carbon based paint in acrylic binder

Fisher Scientific
52 Fadem Road
Springfield, NJ 07081
Toll Free: (800) 766-7000
Fax: (201) 379-7638
Glass beakers and vials and other testing supplies

International Paint Co.
2270 Morris Avenue
Union, NJ 07083
Toll Free: 800-INTRLUX
Interprotect 1000 2-part epoxy paint (clear)

Ludlow Packing Corp.
Laminating & Coating Division
1 Minden Road
Homer, LA
Telephone: (318) 927-9641
Nylon or polyethylene aluminum laminates (e.g., Marvelseal) for lining shelves and drawers

NuSil Technology
1040 Cindy Lane
Carpinteria, CA 93013
Telephone: (805) 684-8780
Fax: (805) 566-0270
Low out-gassing materials testing service; testing in compliance with ASTM E-595

Sure Pure Chemetals
23 Woodbine Road
Florham Park, NJ 07930
Telephone: (201) 377-4081
Fax: (201) 377-4081
Metal foils for materials testing

SOURCES OF STORAGE FURNITURE

Only a few sources of storage furniture are listed below. Numerous sources are listed in *Hold Everything! A Storage and Housing Information Source-Book for Libraries and Archives*, by Barbara Rhodes, General Editor, New York Metropolitan Reference and Research Library Agency (METRO), March 1990. The list below does not constitute an endorsement of the suppliers listed. We suggest that you obtain information from a number of vendors so that you can make comparisons of cost and assess the full range of available products.

A more complete list of suppliers is available from NEDCC. Consult the Technical Leaflets section of NEDCC's website at www.nedcc.org or contact NEDCC for the most up-to-date version in print.

Crystallizations Systems, Inc.
1595A Ocean Avenue
Bohemia, NY 11716
Telephone: (516) 567-0888
Fax: (516) 567-4007
Anodized Aluminum

Delta Designs Ltd.
P.O. Box 1733
Topeka, KS 66601
Telephone: (785) 234-2244
Fax: (785) 233-1021
Powder Coatings

Light Impressions
439 Monroe Avenue
P.O. Box 940
Rochester, NY 14603-0940
Toll Free: (800) 828-6216
Telephone: (716) 271-8960
Toll Free Fax: (800) 828-5539
Open Chrome Shelving

Plan Hold Corp.
17421 Von Karman Avenue
Irvine, CA 92714
Toll Free: (800) 854-6868
Telephone: (714) 660-0400
Toll Free Fax: (800) 735-6869
Powder Coatings

Spacesaver Corporation
1450 Janesville Avenue
Fort Atkinson, WI 53538-2798
Toll Free: (800) 492-3434
Telephone: (920) 563-6362
Fax: (920) 563-2702
Powder Coatings

Acknowledgements

The author gratefully acknowledges the assistance of Pamela Hatchfield in the preparation of this technical leaflet.

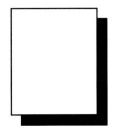

Northeast Document
Conservation Center
100 Brickstone Square
Andover, MA 01810-1494
www.nedcc.org
Tel: (978) 470-1010
Fax: (978) 475-6021

TECHNICAL LEAFLET

STORAGE AND HANDLING

Section 4, Leaflet 3

CLEANING BOOKS AND SHELVES

by Sherelyn Ogden
Head of Conservation
Minnesota Historical Society

Books should be kept clean. This will significantly extend their useful life. Cleaning should be done on a regular basis, with the frequency of cleaning determined by how rapidly dust and dirt accumulate in book storage areas. It is important to note that cleaning itself may damage fragile bindings, which may not be able to withstand the handling required to clean them. Judgment needs to be used in deciding when to clean books.

The organization of a cleaning project and the procedures used to clean books and shelves will vary depending upon several factors. These factors include the physical condition of the books, the amount and type of soil to be removed (light layer of dust versus heavy accumulation of gritty dirt), the nature of the value of the books (if they are valuable solely for the information they contain or if they have historic, artistic, or associational value as well), and the scope of the cleaning to be undertaken (if cleaning is an on-going program intended to maintain every book in the library, or if it is a limited project designed to clean only books in a particular area or collection). These and other factors are discussed in detail by Ann Swartzell in "Preservation," RTSD *Newsletter* 10 (November 7, 1985). What follows here is a general discussion of basic cleaning procedures.

To reduce the amount of dust and dirt that accumulates on books and shelving, floors in book storage areas should be kept as clean as possible. Floors should be vacuumed regularly. Sweeping is discouraged because it tends to stir up and scatter dirt. Floors should be washed and carpets cleaned when needed. It is essential that precautions be taken to prevent books on lower shelves from being splashed by cleaning agents.

Shelves are best cleaned with a magnetic wiping cloth, which attracts and holds dust with an electrostatic charge. This type of cloth is sold commercially under brand names such as the Dust Bunny, the Dust Magnet, and Preserve-It. Two alternatives are dust cloths that are chemically treated to hold dust, such as the One-Wipe, and chemical-based products, such as Endust, that are sprayed onto a cloth. Feather dusters should never be used because they only redistribute the dust. Heavy dust should be removed with a vacuum designed to prevent recirculation of dust through the exhaust, such as one with a HEPA (high efficiency particulate) filter. Thick accumulations of dust and dirt may require that shelves be washed with a mild detergent. Careful consideration, however, should be given to bringing water into book storage areas because of the risk of spillage and of raising the relative humidity in a confined area if many shelves are cleaned at one time. Shelves must be completely dry prior to reshelving books, especially if shelves have been cleaned with water. Fast-drying spray cleaning agents that do not require mixing with water may be preferable.

Books should be cleaned by being held firmly closed and wiped with one of the cloths mentioned above. The magnetic wiping cloth is preferable because it does not contain chemicals or other substances that could be left behind on books. If books are covered with a heavy layer of dust, vacuuming may be advisable. A soft brush attachment is recommended. A piece of cheesecloth or screen should be added between the end of the hose and the brush attachment to prevent loose fragments of deteriorated bindings from being sucked into the vacuum. The suction of the vacuum may need to be decreased for this reason. The vacuum should not be used directly on books of artifactual or associational value. Instead, a soft-bristled brush should be used to sweep dust from the book into the vacuum nozzle. When cleaning books it is important to hold them firmly closed to prevent dirt from slipping down between the leaves. Books should be wiped or brushed away from the spine to avoid pushing dirt into the endcap or down into the spine of the binding. The top of the book, which is usually the dirtiest area, should be cleaned first and then the rest of the book wiped or vacuumed. Dust cloths should be changed frequently, and the cloths used to clean shelves should never be used to clean books.

Several book-cleaning products are available on the market; some are specified for particular types of bindings such as leather, cloth, or paper. There are advantages and disadvantages to the use of these products. Since the magnetic wiping cloth is sufficient for most cleaning tasks, rely on it and avoid the use of the book-cleaning products. When books in your collection present special cleaning problems, however, these products may prove useful. In general these products should be avoided for books of value because components in the cleaners may cause long-term damage to some book materials. Seek the advice of an experienced professional.

Cleaning is usually most efficiently carried out by two-person teams using a book cart, cloths, and a vacuum. The team should work one shelf at a time from top to bottom; books should be removed in shelf-order and placed on the cart, using a bookend to support them. The shelf should then be cleaned. Acidic inserts, such as bookmarks, scraps of paper, and pressed flowers, should be removed from books so that acidity in the inserts does not migrate into pages and damage them. Paper clips and other damaging fasteners should be removed so that they do not stain or crease pages. Each book should be cleaned and then returned to the shelf in order.

Since cleaning has the potential to damage books, personnel should be taught careful handling techniques. Personnel should also be made aware of the importance of cleaning. Because it is such a basic and time-consuming task, cleaning is often overlooked or postponed. However, it is of critical importance in extending the useful life of collections. By eliminating dust and dirt which abrade pages and binding surfaces, attract insects, and contribute to an environment that supports mold growth, personnel are contributing greatly to the preservation of their collections. This basic task is one of the most important in preserving collections.

SOURCES OF SUPPLIES

This list is not exhaustive, nor does it constitute an endorsement of the suppliers listed. We suggest that you obtain information from a number of vendors so that you can make comparisons of cost and assess the full range of available products.

A more complete list of suppliers is available from NEDCC. Consult the Technical Leaflets section of NEDCC's website at www.nedcc.org or contact NEDCC for the most up-to-date version in print.

Magnetic wiping cloths:

Light Impressions
439 Monroe Avenue
P.O. Box 940
Rochester, NY 14603-0940
Toll Free: (800) 828-6216
Telephone: (716) 271-8960
Toll Free Fax: (800) 828-5539
http://www.lightimpressionsdirect.com

Modern Solutions
6370 Copps Avenue
Madison, WI 53716
Telephone: (800) 288-2023
Fax: (608) 222-2704

TestFabrics, Inc.
415 Delaware Avenue
P.O. Box 26
West Pittston, PA 18643
Telephone: (717) 603-0432
Fax: (717) 603-0433
E-mail: testfabrics@aol.com

University Products
517 Main Street
P. O. Box 101
Holyoke, MA 01041
Toll Free: (800) 628-1912
Telephone: (413) 532-3372
Toll Free Fax: (800) 532-9281
Fax: (413) 432-9281
E-mail: info@universityproducts.com
http://www.universityproducts.com

Chemically treated cloths;
Chemical-based spray products:

Available from hardware or grocery stores

HEPA filter vacuums:

Gaylord Brothers
P. O. Box 4901
Syracuse, NY 13221-4901
Toll Free: (800) 448-0160
Fax: (800) 532-9281
Toll Free: (800) 428-3631 help line
http://www.gaylord.com

Light Impressions
439 Monroe Avenue
P.O. Box 940
Rochester, NY 14603
Telephone: (716) 271-8960
Toll Free: (800) 828-6216
Fax: (800) 828-5539
http://www.lightimpressionsdirect.com

University Products
517 Main Street
Holyoke, MA 01041
Toll Free: (800) 762-1165
Toll Free: (800) 628-1919
Fax: (800) 532-9281
http://www.universityproducts.com

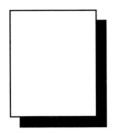

Northeast Document
Conservation Center
100 Brickstone Square
Andover, MA 01810-1494
www.nedcc.org
Tel: (978) 470-1010
Fax: (978) 475-6021

SELECTION OF SUITABLE-QUALITY STORAGE ENCLOSURES FOR BOOKS AND ARTIFACTS ON PAPER

by Sherelyn Ogden
Head of Conservation
Minnesota Historical Society

All materials from which enclosures for books and artifacts on paper are made should meet preservation requirements. The use of poor-quality materials causes irreparable damage. Acidity in poor-quality folders may be transferred into documents that are housed in the folders, discoloring the documents and hastening their deterioration. The same is true for envelopes and portfolios. Storage boxes made from poor-quality materials can become so deteriorated that they may fall apart, threatening the safety of the items they are intended to protect. Poor-quality interleaving papers discolor the items they touch, hastening their deterioration. Discoloration from acidic window mats, often referred to as *mat burn*, disfigures works of art and hastens their deterioration in the area where it occurs. Similar damage results when items are framed with such poor-quality materials as wood or corrugated ground wood backings, and slat burns or striations form in the work of art.[1] Additionally, when mats become acidic, they become brittle. In advanced stages of deterioration they may be unable to support their own weight and may break, causing the work of art to be torn or creased.

Chemical Stability

Acids in paper are responsible for much of the deterioration suffered by books and artifacts on paper. This deterioration is most noticeable as discoloration and embrittlement. Since acids can migrate from storage enclosures into items in direct contact with them, it is essential that storage enclosures be made of acid-free materials. In addition, storage materials should be chemically stable so that they do not form acids over time that can be transferred to the items they contain. Lignin, ground wood, and alum-rosin sizing are common components of paper that lead to the formation of acid.[2] All storage materials should be free of these components. The board for boxes should be lignin-free and chemically purified. The board used for matting works of art on paper should be a 100 per cent cotton ragboard or a lignin-free, chemically purified conservation mounting board. All papers for interleaving sheets, folders, and envelopes should also meet these specifications. Adhesives and tapes for making mats, folders, and boxes should be chemically stable, non-staining, and free of damaging components.

It is important to know *all* the components in storage materials. For example, 100 per cent ragboard can be or become acidic if sized with an unstable sizing agent.[3] Reagent stains can be used to determine the presence of damaging substances such as ground wood or alum. The reagents are available in testing kits from suppliers of storage materials, although these kits are becoming difficult to obtain. The individual reagents are available separately from chemical supply houses. A preservation specialist should be consulted regarding which reagents to obtain. This information is also available in *Analysis of Paper*, Second Edition, Revised and Expanded, by B. L. Browning, Marcel Delcher Inc., New York and Basel, 1977.

Alkaline Buffer

As added protection from the formation of acid, paper-based storage materials may have a buffer, such as calcium carbonate, added during manufacture. The purpose of the buffer is to neutralize acids as they form in the storage materials. Suppliers of storage materials should be able to provide information regarding the type and amount of alkaline buffer used. Many papers and conservation mounting boards contain three per cent calcium carbonate. Buffered materials are appropriate for the storage of most books and artifacts on paper. Common exceptions include works of art that contain dyes or pigments sensitive to high alkalinity, collages with wool or silk components, cyanotypes, diazo reproductions, and some types of photographs.[4]

Molecular Traps

A recently developed type of storage material, based on the combination of one or more alkaline buffers with a molecular trap, either activated carbon or zeolites, is intended to protect items better than storage materials that contain only an alkaline buffer. These new storage materials provide protection against environmental pollutants and by-products of deterioration that do not react with the alkaline buffer in the storage material. Research indicates that acidic pollutant gases in the environment are not neutralized by an alkaline buffer in storage materials, and that these gases pass through the storage materials unaltered. It is assumed that other pollutant gases also pass through buffered storage materials unchanged. The molecular traps capture and remove the harmful molecules that pass by the alkaline buffering.[5]

pH

The acidity and alkalinity of paper-based materials, including various types of board for storage boxes and mats, is expressed by pH, based on a logarithmic scale of zero through fourteen. Seven is the neutral point, with measurements under that being acidic and over being alkaline. Although the recommendation varies for what an ideal pH for storage enclosures should be, a pH of 7.0 through 8.5 is a good general guide for books and artifacts on paper. Photographic materials, however, require special consideration, with different types of photographs having different needs. A photographic materials conservator should be consulted.

Several methods for measuring pH exist. The simplest is the use of a pH detector pencil or pen, which indicates the surface pH of the material being tested. When using these pencils, one should test the core of papers and borads as well as the surface, because a surface reading alone may not be accurate. These pencils leave a disfiguring stain and should never be used to test an object. A more specific pH reading can be obtained by using pH indicator strips. pH meters provide the most accurate readings. When selecting storage materials, one should not rely solely on pH measurements. A pH reading above 7.0 does not necessarily mean that a material is of preservation quality. It has been noted that some newly manufactured wood pulp board can be alkaline, but it will soon become acidic.[6] All the components of storage materials should be identified, and the processing of the components determined. This information should be considered along with the pH when selecting materials for storage enclosures.

Durability

Books and artifacts on paper should be stored only in enclosures that are of an appropriate durability. Storage enclosures should be sufficiently durable to protect items. If enclosures are not sturdy enough to adequately support artifacts, these items may become distorted, creased, or torn, or the storage enclosure itself may become damaged or even fall apart. Overly strong storage enclosures may also be problematic, adding unnecessary weight and bulk, which can lead to handling and spatial difficulties.

ANSI Standards

The term *permanent* or *permanent durable* is sometimes used to describe materials that are chemically stable and durable. The *American National Standard for Permanence of Paper for Publications and Documents in Libraries and Archives*, ANSI/NISO Z39.48-1992, approved by the American National Standards Institute and developed by the National Information Standards Organization, uses these terms. This standard establishes criteria for paper that will last for several hundred years under normal use and storage conditions. It is intended to be used as a guide in the selection of papers for use in publications. It can also be used as a guide in selecting papers for use as storage materials. Different standards exist for storage enclosures for photographic materials. *The American National Standard for Imaging Media – Photographic Processed Films, Plates and Papers – Filing Enclosures and Storage Containers*, ANSI IT9.2-1998, provides specifications for enclosures. Another standard that further specifies criteria for enclosures for photographs is the *American National Standard for Imaging Media – Photographic Activity Test*, ANSI IT9.16-1993. Storage enclosures for photographs should meet both standards.[7]

Plastics

Plastics vary greatly in chemical stability and should be used with caution. Some plastics are unstable chemically and produce by-products as they deteriorate that accelerate the breakdown of paper. Others contain volatile plasticizers that can cause items in contact with them to stick to their surface and media to bleed.[8] Three types of plastic meet preservation standards: polypropylene, polyester, and polyethylene.[9]

Polypropylene is frequently used for boxes and trays. Polyester film is used as an interleaving material to protect the surface of items, for folders, and to encapsulate single items. Only polyesters that are free of plasticizers, ultraviolet inhibitors, dyes, and surface coatings should be used. Polyester film has an electrostatic charge that can lift loosely bound media from the surface of paper. For this reason it should not be used for items with media that are not firmly bound to paper, such as pastel, chalk, charcoal, and soft graphite pencil. Flaking inks and photographic images may also be adversely affected by the static electricity. Polyester film should be used judiciously for items with these problems. For folders and encapsulation, polyester film can be sealed using equipment that forms either an ultrasonic or heat-activated weld. If the equipment required for this welding is not available, the polyester can be sealed using double-sided tape. Only tapes that meet preservation standards should be used. These minimize problems of damaging by-products being emitted as the tapes deteriorate, and of creeping or movement of the adhesive that can cause items to become adhered to it.

Finally . . .

Several suppliers of preservation-quality storage enclosures are available. Obtain catalogs from a number of suppliers so that you can make comparisons of cost and assess the full range of available products. If you have questions about the composition of a product, ask the supplier for details. This information should be readily available. If you require further assistance, contact the Field Services Department at the Northeast Document Conservation Center.

NOTES

[1] Dianne van der Reyden, "Paper Documents," in *Storage of Natural History Collections: A Preventive Conservation Approach.* Carolyn Rose, Catherine A. Hawks, Hugh H. Genoways, eds. (Iowa City: Society for the Preservation of Natural History Collections, 1995), 333.

[2] "Choosing Archival-Quality Storage Enclosures for Books and Paper," in P*reservation of Library and Archival Materials: A Manual,* 2nd ed. Sherelyn Ogden, ed. (Washington, DC: American Association of Museums; 1994), 136.

[3] Margaret Holben Ellis, *The Care of Prints and Drawings* (Walnut Creek, CA: Altamira Press, 1995), 110.

[4] Nancy Carlson Schrock and Gisela Noak, *Archival Storage of Paper* (Syracuse, NY: Gaylord Bros., 1997), 2.

[5] Conservation Resources, *Conservation Resources General Catalog 1997/98* (Cowley, Oxfordshire: Conservation Resources, 1997), vi; Siegfried Rempel, "Zeolite Molecular Traps and their Use in Preventive Conservation," WAAC *Newsletter* 18.1 (1996): 13.

[6] Ellis, *Care of Prints and Drawings*, 112.

[7] "Storage Enclosures for Photographic Materials," in *Preservation of Library and Archival Materials: A Manual,* 2nd ed. Sherelyn Ogden, ed. (Washington, DC: American Association of Museums; 1994), 163.

[8] van der Reyden, "Paper Documents," 333.

[9] Schrock and Noak, "Archival Storage of Paper," 3.

Acknowledgements

This technical leaflet is part of "Storage Of Art On Paper" by Sherelyn Ogden, from the forthcoming book *Conservation Of Works Of Art On Paper*, edited by Margaret Holben Ellis, published by Butterworth Heinemann.

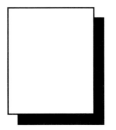

Northeast Document
Conservation Center
100 Brickstone Square
Andover, MA 01810-1494
www.nedcc.org
Tel: (978) 470-1010
Fax: (978) 475-6021

PROTECTING BOOKS WITH CUSTOM-FITTED BOXES

by Richard Horton
Conservator
Bridgeport National Bindery, Inc.

Boxes provide books with structural support and protection from dust, dirt, light, and mechanical damage. Books of great importance merit boxes to prevent damage whatever their condition. Artifactually important volumes with damaged bindings that need to be retained should be boxed rather than treated when treatment would alter their value or character. Damaged books that have low value or are rarely used and do not warrant treatment or repair of the binding should also be boxed. Very thin, small, fragile, limp or oddly shaped books need boxes to hold them in shape, to protect them during handling, and to protect them from adjacent volumes on the shelf.

The two types of boxes appropriate for most books are the drop-spine box (Figure 1), also known as the clamshell or double-tray box, and the phase box (Figure 2).

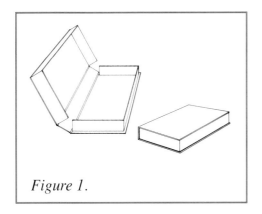

Figure 1.

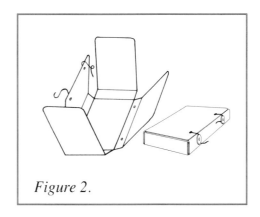

Figure 2.

Drop-spine boxes provide better support and protection from dirt and light than do phase boxes. Phase boxes were originally intended as a temporary preservation measure; books were housed in phase boxes while they awaited conservation treatment. Although they are less rigid and impervious to light and dust than drop-spine boxes, phase boxes have nevertheless become an acceptable, cost-effective storage medium. They are now available in various styles with different types of closures. The slip case (Figure 3) should not be used to hold books. Bindings are abraded as books slide in and out of slip cases. In addition, the spine is left unprotected from light.

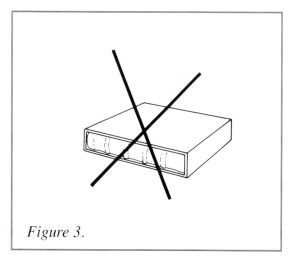

Figure 3.

It is important that a box be accurately fitted to the book. A loose fit does not provide the necessary support and allows the book to shift inside the box, exposing it to the abrasion which the box was constructed to avoid. A tight fit can cause damage to the edges and joints of the cover.

The materials used to construct a box should be permanent, durable, and acid-free. For phase boxes, materials should also be lignin-free and buffered if possible.

SOURCES OF CUSTOM BOOK BOXES

This list is not exhaustive, nor does it constitute an endorsement of the suppliers listed. We suggest that you obtain information from a number of vendors so that you can make comparisons of cost and assess the full range of available products. Check your local telephone directory for individual binders in private practice who make drop-spine boxes.

A more complete list of suppliers is available from NEDCC. Consult the Technical Leaflets section of NEDCC's website at www.nedcc.org or contact NEDCC for the most up-to-date version in print.

Acme Bookbinding Company
100 Cambridge Street
Charlestown, MA 02129-1228
Telephone: (617) 242-1100
Fax: (617) 242-3764
Drop-spine boxes
Phase boxes

Bridgeport National Bindery
662 Silver Street
P.O. Box 289
Agawam, MA 01001-0289
Toll Free: (800) 223-5083
Telephone: (413) 789-4007
E-mail: info@BNBindery.com
E-mail: JNoyes@BNBindery.com
Drop-spine boxes
Phase boxes

Campbell-Logan Bindery
212 Second St., North
Minneapolis, MN 55401
Toll Free: (800) 942-6224
Telephone: (612) 332-1313
Fax: (612) 332-1316
E-mail: 71514.3705@compuserve.com
Drop-spine boxes

Custom Manufacturing, Inc. (CMI)
831 Boyle Road
Fairfield, PA 17320
Telephone: (717) 642-6304
Fax: (717) 642-6596
E-mail: cmiboxes@cvn.net
http://www.cvn.net/~microclimates
Phase boxes

Conservation Resources International
8000-H Forbes Place
Springfield, VA 22151
Toll Free: (800) 634-6932
Telephone: (703) 321-7730
Fax: (703) 321-0629
Drop-spine boxes
Phase boxes

Kater-Craft Bookbinders
4860 Gregg Road
Pico Rivera, CA 90660
Telephone: (562) 692-0665
Fax: (562) 692-7920
Drop-spine boxes
Phase boxes

Ocker & Trapp Library Bindery
17 A Palisade Avenue
P.O. Box 314
Emerson, NJ 07630
Telephone: (201) 265-0262
Fax: (201) 265-0588
Drop-spine boxes

MEASURING FOR CUSTOM BOOK BOXES

Whether you construct your own custom-fitted book boxes or order them from suppliers, you are faced with the task of measuring the height (H), width (W), and thickness (T) of the books to be boxed (Figure 4). The easiest way to do this is by using a measuring device such as the Measurephase, available from Bridgeport National Bindery, Inc. and University Products.

A similar device can be made at home or by a carpenter, with plywood, cardboard, and a ruler (Figure 5). If, however, you must measure books by hand, the following tips may be helpful.

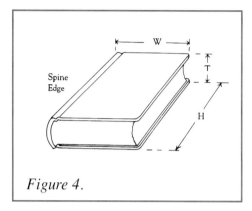

Figure 4.

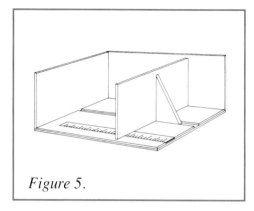

Figure 5.

1. Find a perfectly flat work surface with a smooth vertical wall or surface on one side of it: a table against a wall is one example; a covered brick on a tabletop is another. In the following instructions, this vertical surface will be called a backstop (Figure 6).

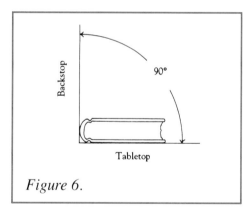

Figure 6.

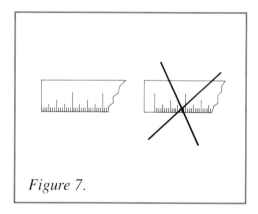

Figure 7.

2. Use the following tools: (a) a ruler at least as long as the longest book to be measured, and (b) a triangle with one side at least as long as the width of the widest book to be measured. Markings on the ruler should begin at the end of the ruler, not slightly in from the end (Figure 7).

3. Measure width (W) by laying the book on the tabletop with its spine touching the backstop. Do not compress the book against the backstop, but allow it to assume its normal size and shape. Pushing the book against the backstop will change its shape, causing the measurement to be too small. Stand the triangle on the tabletop with its vertical side touching the fore edge of the book at the book's widest point. Place the ruler on top of the book with its end touching the backstop. The point on the ruler where it meets the triangle is the book's width (Figure 8). If the location of the book's widest point is in doubt, make measurements at several points, and use the widest of these measurements. Remember to count the protrusions of raised bands or clasps as part of the width of the book (Figure 9)

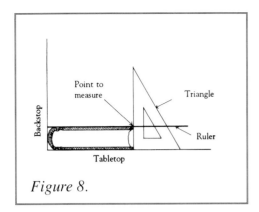

Figure 8.

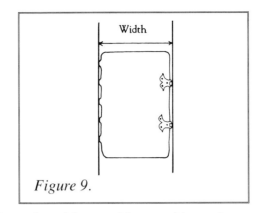

Figure 9.

4. Measure the height (H) by laying the book on the tabletop with one of its ends touching the backstop. Repeat step 3.

5. Thickness (T) must be measured somewhat differently. Lay the book on the tabletop. Stand a ruler on end vertically beside it, and hold a triangle against the backstop so that its vertical edge is flat against the backstop, and its horizontal edge is parallel to the tabletop. Lower the triangle, maintaining its contact with the backstop, until the horizontal edge of the triangle encounters the thickest part of the book. Note the measurement where the horizontal edge of the triangle crosses the ruler (Figure 10).

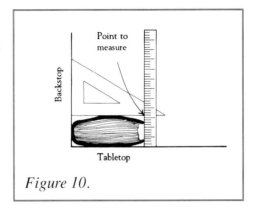

Figure 10.

Now that you have the measurements of the book, you can construct a box yourself, or order one by sending the measurements to a commercial boxmaker.

Acknowledgements

NEDCC gratefully acknowledges the work of Margaret R. Brown in illustrating this leaflet.

Northeast Document
Conservation Center

100 Brickstone Square
Andover, MA 01810-1494
www.nedcc.org
Tel: (978) 470-1010
Fax: (978) 475-6021

CARD STOCK ENCLOSURES
FOR SMALL BOOKS

by Richard Horton
Conservator
Bridgeport National Bindery, Inc.

Many librarians are faced with the problem of boxing large numbers of small, thin, or lightweight books and pamphlets. When drop-spine boxes or phase boxes are not appropriate because of cost or the amount of shelf space they require, folding book boxes or enclosures made of 10- or 20-point lignin-free card stock are a suitable alternative. Several types of enclosures have been made over the years. One frequently used enclosure is known as the *tuxedo box* (Figure 1), which offers adequate protection for books less than 1/2 inch thick; but it is less practical for thicker volumes. It is easily pushed out of alignment and the corners tend to gape on larger volumes, allowing light and dust to enter the box.

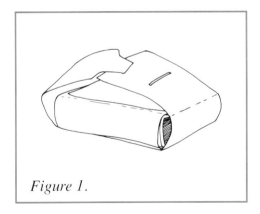

Figure 1.

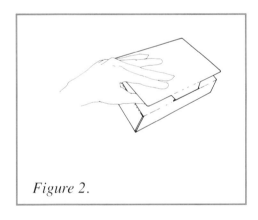

Figure 2.

A one-piece folded enclosure with corner flaps solves both problems while providing additional benefits (Figure 2). The corner flaps block out light and dust, prevent fragments from falling out of the enclosure, add firmness at the corners where most shock occurs, and when the enclosure is closed, lock the end flaps in position. The enclosure with corner flaps does not require taping and adds four thicknesses of card stock to the lateral shelf space taken by the book, rather than the six added by the tuxedo box. Both enclosures are easy to make; student workers or trainees can make either without difficulty in about fifteen minutes.

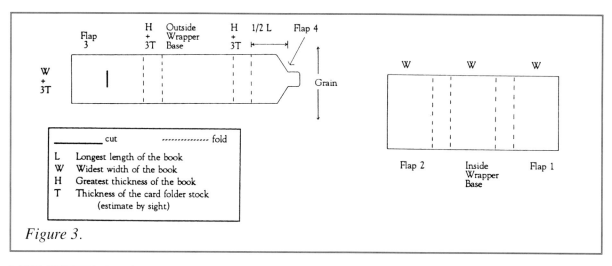

Figure 3.

THE TUXEDO BOX

Materials and Tools Needed

10- or 20-point calendered lignin-free card stock. Small pamphlets will require the lighter weight stock; larger materials will require the heavier weight.
Bone folder
Scissors
Mat knife
Board shear (optional)
Straight-edge
L-shaped ruler, T-square, or large triangle
Self-healing cutting mat, or a piece of mat board or binder's board on which the card stock can be creased
Double-sided tape

Construction

1. Construct a ruler-template by placing the book on a strip of paper or card and making measurement marks for longest length (L), widest width (W), and greatest thickness (H) (Figure 4).

2. Select a sheet of card stock from which the inside and outside wrappers (see Figure 3) can be cut. Determine the grain direction of the sheet, and cut the wrappers so that the grain is parallel to the expected fold lines of the wrappers. The grain is the direction in which most of the fibers of the stock run. A fold made parallel to the grain folds more easily than one made against (at right angles to) the grain. Cuts should be made completely across the sheet of card stock. When using the ruler-template to mark locations of cuts or folds, add card stock thicknesses (T) by sight estimate. For instance, when making a mark H+4T from the previous mark, make a mark four card thicknesses beyond the H mark of the ruler template.

3. Now make marks at all fold locations on both pieces of card stock. When you come to the end of each wrapper, trim off the excess card stock. See Figure 3.

4. Using an L-shaped ruler, T-square or triangle, and a bone folder, make creases and folds across the wrappers at all marks. Using the point of the bone folder on the surface of the card stock, score the card along the edge of the ruler as if you were drawing a line with a pencil. Press the point of the bone folder into the card and pull it along the edge of the ruler, creating a groove. If you are using 10-point card stock, press lightly to avoid tearing the material. The ruler should be held down firmly to prevent slippage. Without releasing the ruler, reinforce the crease by inserting the bone folder under the card and

rubbing it firmly against the ruler to accentuate the crease. See Figure 5.

5. Using your template, measure, mark, and cut the tongue in flap 4 of the outside wrapper. See Figure 3. Cut the slit in flap 3, slightly wider than the tongue, centered, and at a distance of 1/2 L from the nearest fold. Once again, refer to Figure 3.

6. Apply double-sided tape to the outside wrapper base, just inside the folds. Place the inside wrapper base on top of it, aligning the outer edges of the wrappers.

ONE-PIECE ENCLOSURE WITH CORNER FLAPS

Materials and Tools Needed

20-point calendered lignin-free card stock
Bone folder
Scissors
Mat knife
L-shaped ruler, T-square, or large triangle
Self-healing cutting mat, or a piece of book board on which the card stock can be creased

Construction

1. Construct a ruler-template by placing the book on a strip of paper or card and making measurement marks as shown in Figure 4. See Figure 6 for an explanation of the letter symbols.

2. Using your ruler-template, make the appropriate marks on adjoining edges of one of the corners of a large piece of 20-point lignin-free card (Figure 7).

3. Now cut your measured box area off the larger piece of card.

4. Using an L-shaped ruler, T-square or triangle, and a bone folder, make creases across the card at all marks (Figure 8). Make longer creases first and shorter creases second. Refer to step 4 of the tuxedo box construction for use of the bone folder.

5. Now make all peripheral cuts with scissors. Refer to Figure 6 for the appearance of the finished box before folding. Notice that the corner and end flaps are angled slightly.

6. Fold the box and insert the book (Figure 9). You are finished.

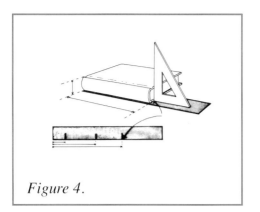

Figure 4.

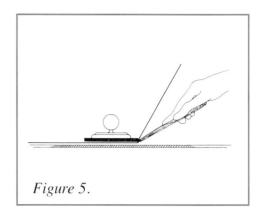

Figure 5.

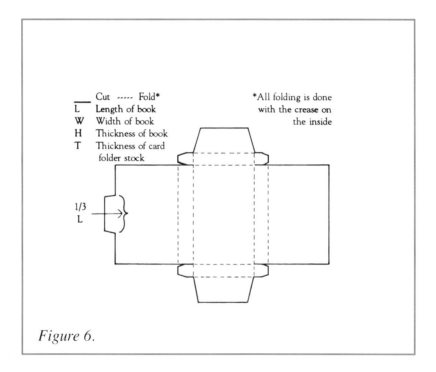

Cut ----- Fold*
L   Length of book
W   Width of book
H   Thickness of book
T   Thickness of card
    folder stock

*All folding is done
with the crease on
the inside

1/3
L

Figure 6.

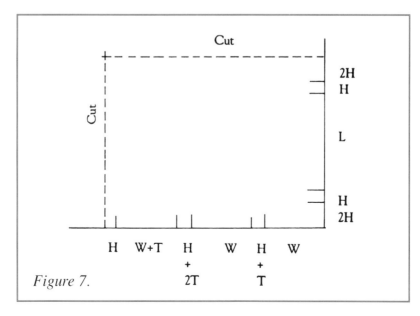

Cut

2H
H

L

H
2H

Cut

H   W+T   H   W   H   W
          +   +
          2T   T

Figure 7.

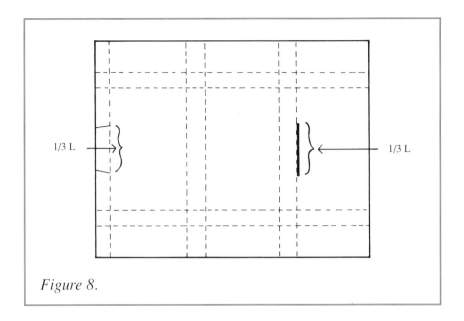

Figure 8.

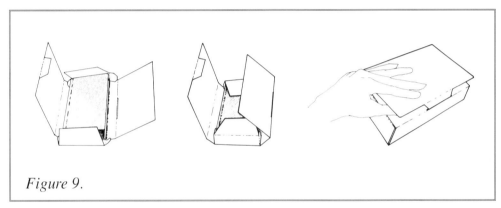

Figure 9.

SOURCES OF SUPPLIES

This list is not exhaustive, nor does it constitute an endorsement of the suppliers listed. We suggest that you obtain information from a number of vendors so that you can make comparisons of cost and assess the full range of available products.

A more complete list of suppliers is available from NEDCC. Consult the Technical Leaflets section of NEDCC's website at www.nedcc.org or contact NEDCC for the most up-to-date version in print.

Bone Folders:
Aiko's Art Materials
3347 North Clark Street
Chicago, IL 60657
Telephone: (312) 404-5600

Bookmakers
6001 66th Avenue
Suite 101
Riverdale, MD 20737
Telephone: (301) 459-3384
Fax: (301) 459-7629

Talas
213 West 35th Street
New York, NY 10001-1996
Telephone: (212) 736-7744
Fax: (212) 465-8722

Card Stock:
Order under the name:
Lig-free
Map/Print Folder Paper
.010" or .020"

Conservation Resources Int.
8000-H Forbes Place
Springfield, VA 22151
Telephone: (703) 321-7730
FAX (703) 321-0629

University Products
517 Main Street
P. O. Box 101
Holyoke, MA 01041
Toll Free: (800) 628-1912
Telephone: (413) 532-3372
Toll Free Fax: (800) 532-9281
Fax: (413) 432-9281
E-mail: info@universityproducts.com
http://www.universityproducts.com

Double-Sided Tape:
Order under the name:
Double Coated
Transparent Film Tape
3M #415
1/4" x 36 yards

Conservation Resources Int.
8000-H Forbes Place
Springfield, VA 22151
Telephone: (703) 321-7730
Fax: (703) 321-0629

Conservator's Emporium
100 Standing Rock Circle
Reno, NV 89511
Telephone: (702) 852-0404
Fax: (702) 852-3737

Light Impressions
439 Monroe Avenue
P.O. Box 940
Rochester, NY 14603-0940
Telephone: (716) 271-8960
Toll Free: (800) 828-6216

Talas
213 West 35th Street
New York, NY 10001-1996
Telephone: (212) 736-7744
Fax: (212) 465-8722

University Products
517 Main Street
P. O. Box 101
Holyoke, MA 01041
Toll Free: (800) 628-1912
Telephone: (413) 532-3372
Toll Free Fax: (800) 532-9281
Fax: (413) 432-9281
E-mail: info@universityproducts.com
http://www.universityproducts.com

Acknowledgements

NEDCC gratefully acknowledges the work of Margaret R. Brown in illustrating this leaflet.

TECHNICAL LEAFLET

Northeast Document
Conservation Center

100 Brickstone Square
Andover, MA 01810-1494
www.nedcc.org
Tel: (978) 470-1010
Fax: (978) 475-6021

STORAGE AND HANDLING

Section 4, Leaflet 7

THE BOOK SHOE: DESCRIPTION AND USES

by Christopher Clarkson
Conservator in Private Practice
Oxford, England and
Sherelyn Ogden,
Head of Conservation
Minnesota Historical Society

Books of all sorts need protection and support. Books may be damaged and need to be held together pending repair or in place of repair; they may be made of particularly vulnerable materials; or they may be of special value. In most libraries these needs can be met by a variety of boxes, folders, and shelf envelopes. Complete enclosure which protects books from light and airborne pollution is by far the best solution. But where books also play a part in the appearance of a fine library room, whether in a historic library or in any other situation where it is important that the books themselves be on open view, the extensive use of boxes will be unacceptable. As a result, these books have largely gone without the protection and support so easily procured for books in closed stacks or in reading rooms that are more functional than elegant. This does not mean, of course, that such books are in any less need of protection and support. The book shoe was developed to supply an almost invisible container that would carry out at least some of the functions of a conventional box. In addition, it is inexpensive and simple to make.

Many occidental binders have never mastered the stress factors set up in the vertically stored book (Figure 1): the drag of the text-block within the boards (A) results in that characteristic flattening at the head of the spine (B) and increased rounding at its tail (C), causing break-up at the head of the joints (D). Such stresses are exacerbated when the closed book is left unsupported and free to expand and partially open (E). Being conscious of this, concerned library personnel try to keep their book shelves packed tightly. But this encourages, during removal, damage to head caps and abrasion to side boards. If a book with tail squares (the part of the board that extends beyond the bottom of the text-block) must be stood vertically, the best method is to encase it entirely in a tailor-made, well constructed book box that includes a text-block support to halt the downward drag of the closed book. If this is not possible because the book must be regarded as a decorative feature, one should at least keep the fore edge tightly closed and provide a tailored text-block support piece (F). Slip cases, which have a closed top, have sometimes been used for this purpose. However, they are now thought of as harmful to bookbindings, particularly ones with fragile or friable exterior surfaces, because of the abrasion caused by the design.

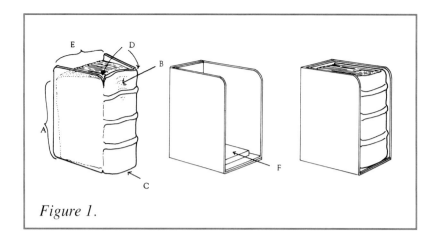

Figure 1.

Sample Standard Sizes:

Height x Width x Depth

S1 270mm x 210mm x 100mm
S2 320mm x 245mm x 100mm
S3 370mm x 285mm x 100mm
S4 500mm x 385mm x 100mm
S5 680mm x 525mm x 100mm

Figure 2.

The book shoe is in essence a slip-case without a top, fitted with a text-block support. The shoe will hold the book closed, and the support will remove much of the strain on the text-block of a vertically standing book.

Book Shoes:

- supply a simple means of text-block support;
- protect the sides of decorated or fragile bindings, such as those covered in textiles, from their neighbors;
- isolate books with metal fittings such as clasps or bosses, and prevent the metalwork from damaging the books on either side (although it is strongly recommended that such bindings be housed in tailored book boxes);
- prevent books with textile or leather ties from having these ties get caught under neighboring books;
- take the wear off the tail edges of binding boards as books are drawn in and out of shelves;
- allow books to be carried without the carrier's hands coming into contact with the binding itself.

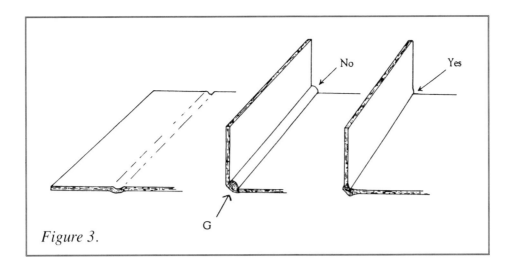

Figure 3.

To minimize abrasion one needs to splay open the top of the shoe slightly as the book is inserted at an angle and is slid down over the text-block support. When all the books on the shelf are in shoes, the temptation may be to leave the shoe in place on the shelf and remove the book from it, but this defeats the purpose, encouraging clawing and abrasion damage—the same in fact as objected to in extracting books from tightly packed shelving or from slip-cases. *Always extract (and insert) the book and its shoe together from a bookshelf.*

One can make elaborately constructed book shoes and cover them in cloth, but the time required will increase the cost, and if too thick, the book shoe may be noticeable on the bookshelf. The following specifications are for the production of simple and economic book shoes to house books by the thousands.

The book shoe should be made of an acid-free, lignin-free board that has good folding quality and mechanical strength for wall stability. One millimeter thickness of board works best, except for books under seven inches high when a slightly thinner board may be substituted. The board should have a smooth surface, minimizing abrasion to delicate book surfaces. A homogeneous hard rolled board, such as a non-layer millboard, works best because it creates minimum piping (G) on the fold (Figure 3.). Board that is one to two millimeters or less thick can be folded in on the creased side (opposite to traditional box creasing) so that 'piping' does not occur on the inside of the shoe. The machine direction of the board in the finished book shoe should run vertically with the book. The color of the exterior of the board should blend unnoticeably with the books when shelved. The text-block support should also be made of an acid-free, lignin-free material and should be obtained in different thicknesses. The adhesive used to fix together the two sides of the shoe should meet conservation standards of chemical stability and have the requisite strength to do the job.

If means of handling large sheets of board are not available, one can get the sheets cut down into standard format sizes and have the creases formed commercially. The standard format sizes required relate to the diversity of dimensions of books in the collection. A sample of format sizes is shown in figure 2; these are useful for general mixed collections. They are a compromise between the sizes required and the board size.

The book shoe is made in two parts, each forming one side of the shoe and overlapping on the fore edge and the bottom (Figure 4). These sides can be cut down to fit the book and then fixed together with a combination of brass staples (placed so they do not catch any part of the book) and/or adhesive. The shoe should be used with a text-block support, which is cut from a separate piece of appropriate thickness. Each side of the shoe is creased twice, with the second crease being at a right angle to the first. Either the corner can be cut out of the board by hand, or a template can be made to cut out the corner by machine.

Shoes are made with a left and right side as you look at them from the front (open side), with flaps which overlap each other at the back (where the fore edge of the book goes) and at the tail edge (bottom). The width and height measurements of the left side must be smaller than those on the right side; the amount smaller should be about 1½ times the thickness of the board from which the shoe is made. The left side should be smaller and fit into the right side so that when stuck together, the head and front edges are exactly level. The board needs to be creased where the flaps are to be folded. This can be done with any one of several creasing devices, which are commercially available, or stamped out by a boxing firm if this is more economical. Top front corners are rounded.

With a well organized set-up and proper equipment, exactly fitting bookshoes can be made in ten to fifteen minutes. Although book shoes do not offer ideal protection and support for volumes, they fulfill many of the functions of a custom-made box and serve as a cost-effective, aesthetically acceptable option for books that must be preserved while being displayed.

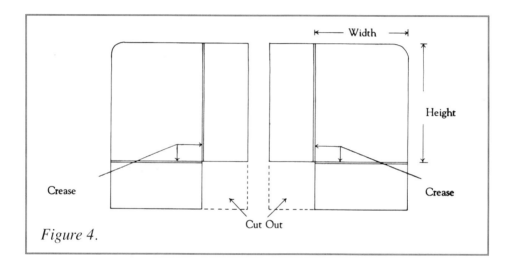

Figure 4.

The book shoe was developed by Nicholas Pickwoad while consultant at the National Trust in England. The commercial design was developed by Christopher Clarkson, then at West Dean College, Chichester, England, and Anthony Cains, Trinity College, Dublin, Ireland.

NOTE

The machine direction is the direction in which most of the fibers run. The board flexes more easily parallel to the machine direction than against (at a right angle to) it.

Acknowledgements

NEDCC gratefully acknowledges the work of Margaret R. Brown in illustrating this leaflet.

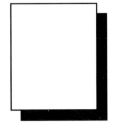
Northeast Document
Conservation Center
100 Brickstone Square
Andover, MA 01810-1494
www.nedcc.org
Tel: (978) 470-1010
Fax: (978) 475-6021

**TECHNICAL
LEAFLET**

**STORAGE AND
HANDLING**

Section 4, Leaflet 8

POLYESTER FILM BOOK JACKET

**by Richard Horton
Conservator
Bridgeport National Bindery, Inc.**

A transparent book jacket made of polyester film offers a number of benefits:

a) A jacket protects the book cover from dirt and from scuffing as the volume is handled and shelved.
b) A jacket contains powdery red-rotted leather and prevents it from rubbing off onto adjacent volumes.
c) The cover and title of the book can be seen through the transparent jacket.
d) Shelf labels can be attached to the jacket's spine rather than directly to the book, avoiding possible damage to the binding from unstable label adhesives.

Not all polyesters are acceptable. Only ones that have been tested and proven to be chemically stable for long periods of time should be used. The polyester film chosen should be free of plasticizers, ultraviolet inhibitors, dyes, and surface coatings so that the film does not interact with the material it is intended to protect and thereby hasten its deterioration. Mylar type D, manufactured by Dupont, and Melinex 516, manufactured by ICI, are acceptable for use on books. Four mil polyester is suitable for most books.

The best known and easiest-to-make polyester jacket is a simple wrap-around (Figure 1). Because it is not fixed in place on the book, a jacket of this design tends to shift out of alignment, especially when used on a large heavy book. This style jacket is sometimes held in place with tape or straps, which can cause other problems. Another disadvantage of the wrap-around jacket is its failure to cover the edges of the book, leaving them exposed and subject to abrasion.

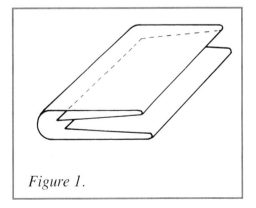

Figure 1.

A slightly more complex polyester jacket avoids these problems. It incorporates flaps which hold the jacket on the book and which cover and thus protect the edges of the book.

INSTRUCTIONS FOR MAKING A POLYESTER JACKET WITH END FLAPS

When constructing polyester jackets, you will need a straight-edge, a bone folder, and either scissors or a mat knife. Cutting and creasing can be done on a self-healing mat or on a large piece of mat board or binder's board.

1. Cut a piece of polyester with a vertical dimension equal to 1 2/3 times the height (H) of the book and a horizontal dimension 4 times the width (W) of the book plus the thickness (T) of the book (Figure 2).

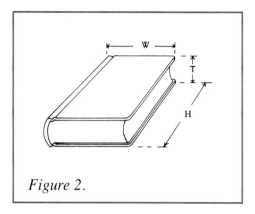

Figure 2.

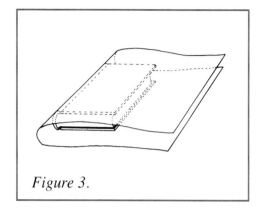

Figure 3.

2. Wrap the polyester around the book so that the edges of the polyester are even with each other and the book is centered between the top and bottom of the polyester (Figure 3). Polyester has a smooth surface and care must be taken to make sure that the book does not shift, especially while being measured.

3. Place the book on a clean work surface and open the polyester flat, being careful not to change the position of the book on the polyester film (Figure 4).

4. Mark the position of the book on the polyester film by making dents with the point of a bone folder at the corners of the book and at both ends of the joint (Figure 4).

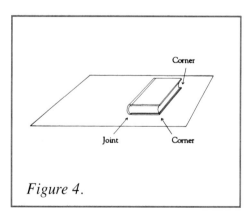

Figure 4.

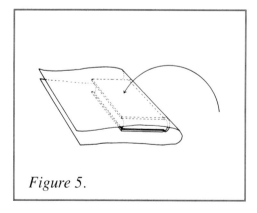

Figure 5.

5. Wrap the polyester over the book again and turn the polyester and book over being careful that the book does not shift on the polyester (Figure 5). Repeat step four.

6. Using a straight-edge and bone folder, crease the polyester straight across connecting the dents as illustrated (Figure 6). Broken lines represent creases.

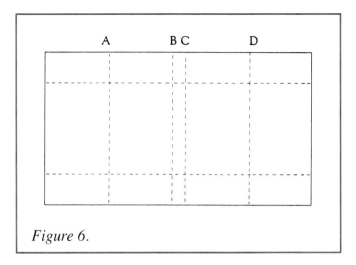

Figure 6.

When creasing the polyester, place the straight-edge on the film with its edge next to, but not covering, the two dents to be used as guides. Create a crease by pressing down on the point of the bone folder while pulling it along the edge of the straight-edge. The straight-edge should be held down firmly to prevent slippage. Without releasing the straight-edge, reinforce the crease by inserting the bone folder under the polyester and rubbing it firmly against the straight-edge (Figure 7).

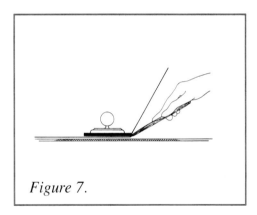

Figure 7.

7. At all "a" locations (Figure 8) make a second crease parallel to the first, outside the first, and at a distance from it equal to the thickness of the book's cover.

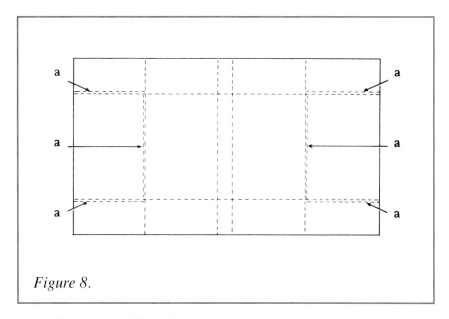

Figure 8.

8. Cut as shown in figure 9. Unbroken lines represent cuts.

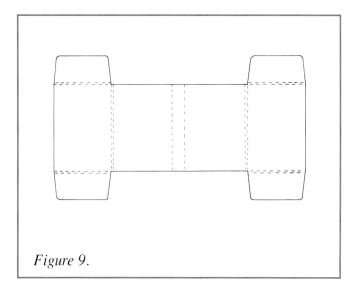

Figure 9.

9. Fold the polyester film at all creases. Make the folds sharp by burnishing them with a bone folder. Remember that closely spaced parallel folds need to be made at all "a" locations. After these have been made, shape them with your fingers until both folds take on a 90° angle (Figure 10). Dampening your finger tips slightly with a moist sponge will make this shaping of the folds easier.

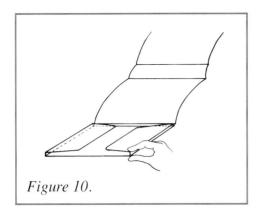

Figure 10.

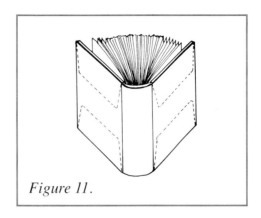

Figure 11.

10. Wrap the polyester film jacket around the book, tucking the end flaps inside the front and back covers. Tuck the top and bottom flaps between the outer surface of the book cover and the polyester film (Figure 11). The top and bottom flaps will be visible through the polyester film jacket.

Polyester film is difficult to work with and you may need a few tries to construct the jacket correctly. Once you have mastered the technique, construction time is about 15 minutes per jacket, excluding set-up time.

Sources of Supplies

This list is not exhaustive, nor does it constitute an endorsement of the suppliers listed. We suggest that you obtain information from a number of vendors so that you can make comparisons of cost and assess the full range of available products.

A more complete list of suppliers is available from NEDCC. Consult the Technical Leaflets section of NEDCC's website at www.nedcc.org or contact NEDCC for the most up-to-date version in print.

Bone folders:

Aiko's Art Materials
3347 North Clark Street
Chicago, IL 60657
Telephone: (773) 404-5600

Bookmakers
6001 66th Avenue, Suite 101
Riverdale, MD 20737
Telephone: (301) 459-3384
Fax: (301) 459-7629

Talas
568 Broadway
New York, NY 10012
Telephone: (212) 736-7744
Fax: (212) 219-0735

Polyester film:

Archivart
7 Caesar Place
P.O. Box 428
Moonachie, NJ 07074
Telephone: (201) 804-8986
Fax: (201) 935-5964

Conservation Resources Int.
8000 H Forbes Place
Springfield, VA 22151
Telephone: (703) 321-7730
Fax: (703) 321-0629

Conservator's Emporium
100 Standing Rock Circle
Reno, NV 89511
Telephone: (702) 852-0404
Fax: (702) 852-3737

Hollinger Corporation
9401 Northeast Drive
P.O. Box 8360
Fredericksburg, VA 22404
Toll Free: (800) 634-0491
Telephone: (540) 898-7300
Toll Free Fax: (800) 947-8814
E-mail: hollingercorp@intersurf.net

Light Impressions
439 Monroe Avenue
P.O. Box 940
Rochester, NY 14603-0940
Toll Free: (800) 828-6216
Telephone: (716) 271-8960
Toll Free Fax: (800) 828-5539
http://www.lightimpressionsdirect.com

University Products
517 Main Street
P. O. Box 101
Holyoke, MA 01041
Toll Free: (800) 628-1912
Telephone: (413) 532-3372
Toll Free Fax: (800) 532-9281
Fax: (413) 432-9281
E-mail: info@universityproducts.com
http://www.universityproducts.com

Mat knife; scissors; self-healing mat; straight-edge; X-acto scalpel:

Local art supply or office supply store

Acknowledgements

NEDCC gratefully acknowledges the work of Margaret R. Brown in illustrating this technical leaflet.

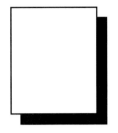

Northeast Document
Conservation Center
100 Brickstone Square
Andover, MA 01810-1494
www.nedcc.org
Tel: (978) 470-1010
Fax: (978) 475-6021

TECHNICAL
LEAFLET

STORAGE AND
HANDLING

Section 4, Leaflet 9

STORAGE SOLUTIONS FOR
OVERSIZED PAPER ARTIFACTS

by Mary Todd Glaser
Director of Paper Conservation
Northeast Document Conservation Center

Maps, posters, large prints, and other oversized objects create storage problems for any institution. Such materials are unwieldy and therefore vulnerable to damage, especially if they are not mounted or backed. It is best to store such objects unrolled and flat in map-case drawers or in large, flat archival boxes. Inside the drawers or boxes objects need the additional protection of folders or other suitable enclosures. Since every collection contains objects larger than the available drawers, other storage solutions must also be found. Some of these are discussed in the final section of this leaflet.

STORAGE FURNITURE

Map Cases (Flat Files)

Map cases or flat files composed of wide, shallow drawers are essential for collections with oversized sheet material. Like all furniture for the storage of works of art or archival materials, map cases should be carefully chosen. Not only must they protect physically, but the cases must be made of chemically stable materials that will not attack paper. Metal cases are much less damaging than wooden ones, but not all metal cases are 100% safe. We now know that steel cases finished with baked enamel, once the furniture of choice, can be problematic. If the enamel has not been baked long enough or at a high enough temperature, it may give off volatiles such as formaldehyde that are potentially damaging to paper. A test is available to determine if your baked enamel steel furniture is safe. However, it requires sophisticated analytical equipment. A simple if less conclusive test is described in the NEDCC leaflet "Storage Furniture: A Brief Review of Current Options."

The metal storage cabinets now recommended have solvent-free powder coatings of finely divided polymers. These appear not to off-gas. Furniture made of anodized aluminum is also excellent. This light-weight metal is strong, and because it has no coating to emit gases, it is non-reactive. For sources of powder-coated steel and anodized aluminum furniture see the NEDCC leaflet on storage furniture cited above.

Wood has always been popular for storage cabinets, including flat files, but wood gives off harmful gases in quantities far greater than improperly baked enamel. Even old wood cabinets are potentially damaging, especially oak ones. If you have wood files and cannot replace them, the drawers should be lined with a barrier material and, if possible, sealed to minimize emissions.

Suitable barriers for lining the insides of wood cabinets include polyester film (Mylar), 4-ply 100% ragboard, or Marvelseal, a laminate of aluminum and inert plastics. Marvelseal is especially recommended since, unlike Mylar or ragboard, it is completely impervious to gases.

All of the above are passive barriers. There are also active barriers, a new class of products, that may provide even better protection. These archival paper materials contain activated carbon and compounds known as zeolites. These are molecular sieves that trap and sequester polluting gases, removing them from the immediate environment. Because these scavenger products are fairly new, little is known about their long-term effectiveness. It is possible the molecular sieves could get used up in time. Such products have great possibilities, however, and bear watching.

Before lining wood file drawers with a barrier material, sealing the wood will give an extra measure of protection. Although no coating or sealant will completely block emissions, polyurethane will seal as well as any. It is important to buy water-based polyurethane, not the more common oil-modified type (oil-based paints and other oil products should be avoided for archival storage). Not all water-based polyurethanes may be safe. Check with a preservation professional for the brands currently being recommended. Or better, test the polyurethane yourself. See the NEDCC leaflet on storage furniture.

After the sealant has been applied, it should be allowed to air for at least three weeks.

Flat file drawers should be no more than two inches deep and should never be filled to the top. You should be able to remove the bottom-most folder easily. The drawers should be equipped with dust covers or rear hoods to prevent objects from being damaged or caught up at the back. Drawers should have ball bearings for smooth gliding and stops to prevent them from dropping out of the cabinet.

It is important to have a clear surface close to the drawers where oversized objects can be examined. Either a large table or the top of the file would serve well for this purpose. In storage areas it is often difficult to keep large areas clear, but doing so is essential for the safety of the collection during retrieval and inspection. Aisles should be wide enough to allow easy removal of items from the drawers.

Boxes

Although vertical storage in office files or in upright Hollinger-type boxes is acceptable for legal-sized or smaller documents, objects larger than 15" x 9" should be stored flat. Sheets smaller than 30" by 40" will fit into archival boxes, which come in various sizes and which are much less expensive than flat files. These should be the buffered, lignin-free boxes available from conservation suppliers.

Boxes come in a variety of sizes and types. The sturdiest is the black Solander box or museum case, which is sturdy enough to hold a group of art works that have been matted. In addition, the thick walls of a Solander box insulate well and give good physical protection. The lids of these boxes have lips that help keep out air-borne materials.

Because Solander boxes are costly, they are used mainly by museums for works of art or important documents. Collections of archival materials are usually housed in the ubiquitous lighter-weight gray or tan boxes.

INSIDE THE DRAWERS OR BOXES: PROTECTIVE ENCLOSURES

Inside drawers or boxes, individual sheets need additional protection from enclosures such as folders, polyester envelopes (encapsulation), or window mats. Folders are the most commonly used enclosure for archival collections, while window mats are often used by museums for works of art on paper. Polyester encapsulation is popular for fragile or much-used oversized objects. Each type of enclosure has certain advantages. Choice depends on the needs of the collection materials, their use, and the resources of the institution.

Folders

Folders are the least expensive type of storage enclosure. Like storage boxes, folders should be archival, that is, made of lignin-free stock. Folders buffered with an alkaline material are recommended for most paper artifacts. However, certain objects such as blueprints are alkali sensitive. For these, some conservators recommend pH-neutral lignin-free folders that have not been buffered. Recent reserach indicates, however, that if the storage environment is maintained at an acceptable relative humidity (30% to 55%), unbuffered folders may not be necessary. Both types are available from conservation suppliers or can be made in-house from archival folder stock. If you buy both kinds of folders, be sure the supplies are clearly labeled and all staff know when to use each type.

Each folder should be somewhat larger than the sheets inside. To keep the contents from slipping out, folders should be cut to the size of the drawer or box. Works of art with delicate surfaces, fragile sheets, or very large objects should have individual folders. Other materials may share a folder. Interleaving with archivally acceptable paper or tissue is recommended, especially if the objects are subject to abrasion. The number of objects per folder and folders per drawer or box should be a matter of common sense, determined by the condition and size of the materials. As a general rule, do not overcrowd. Each object must be stored so that it can be retrieved without risk of damage.

If an oversized object is especially brittle, a folder made from a heavier, more rigid material such as 4-ply archival board provides better support than one made from folder stock. Some recommend that folders be labeled along the fold and positioned in the drawer with the fold side at the front. This way institutional staff must remove the folder from the drawer before it can be opened, a safely measure. If a folder is pulled out spine first, however, there is a risk of leaving sheets behind. The collection manager must decide how to position the folders so that there is least risk. Folders should be clearly labeled in pencil or waterproof ink. To discourage unnecessary rummaging, good finding aids are essential. Self-adhering labels should be avoided. These often bear adhesives that stain invasively and migrate into the folder. In addition, adhesives of this type often fail in time.

Polyester Film Encapsulation

Encapsulation in polyester film, a clear, flexible plastic, is an attractive solution for oversized matcrials, especially if they are brittle or frequently handled. Polyester encapsulation has been used a great deal for posters and maps. The object is sandwiched between two sheets of film slightly larger than the object. The edges of the plastic are sealed either with special welding equipment or with double-sided tape. Polyester film, sold under the brand names Mylar and Melinex, not only protects but reinforces, giving better protection than that offered by a folder.

Encapsulation, however, is not suitable for untreated objects or those with friable media. Because polyester contains a static charge, insecurely bound media such as pastel, charcoal, soft pencil, or gouache can be easily dislodged by this plastic. In addition, research at the Library of Congress has found that acidic papers deteriorate faster within a closed environment such as a polyester envelope. Since most untreated papers are acidic to some extent, objects should be deacidified prior to encapsulation or at least washed to remove acid build-up in the paper. Washing or deacidification must be done by a conservator. When this treatment is not possible, placing a sheet of buffered paper in the polyester envelope behind the object is an acceptable alternative.

For more information and directions see the NEDCC technical leaflet, "Encapsulation in Polyester Film Using Double-Sided Tape."

Window Mats

Mats are much more expensive than folders or polyester envelopes, and they occupy more space. Once matted, however, an object is ready for framing and exhibition. Another advantage is that matted objects can be handled without being touched. Mats also provide more rigid support than folders do.

Mats can be made by a framer or in-house. Making your own mats saves money but requires an investment in a mat cutter, ample space, a solidly supported surface, and a supply of archival-quality board. If making mats will be an ongoing activity, a mat cutter is an excellent investment. Unless you are good with your hands, be sure to buy a good cutter, one costing several hundred dollars. Cutting mats with an inexpensive instrument can be frustrating.

To be rigid enough to support oversized materials, mats should be made of 4-ply or thicker board. The standard museum mat is composed of two sheets: a window and a backboard. These are held together with a strip of cloth tape along one edge, usually the top. The object is attached to the backboard, traditionally by hinges at the upper corners. For hinging, conservators recommend kozo papers and a homemade starch-based paste. Commercial tapes should be avoided as most do not age well and many will stain. Even the "archival tapes" sold by conservation suppliers should not be used with objects of value. These are less damaging than most commercial products but have yet to stand the test of time.

In recent years, some institutions have become reluctant to apply adhesives to artifacts and have experimented with other methods of mounting. Corner supports and edge strips are becoming increasingly popular. For additional information about this and other matting issues, see the NEDCC technical leaflet, "Matting and Framing for Art and Artifacts on Paper."

Folders with Polyester Film Inside Covers

Such folders combine the advantages of a plain folder and polyester encapsulation. They are constructed, as shown in Figure 1, with a sheet of polyester film attached inside the folder. This type of enclosure can be purchased from conservation suppliers or it can be made in-house using double-sided tape to attach the polyester. Such an enclosure is safe for untreated materials for which traditional encapsulation may be inappropriate. The object can be seen without being touched and is held in place by the polyester. Like encapsulation, however, such enclosures cannot be used with friable media.

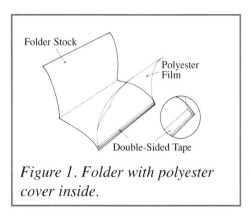

Figure 1. Folder with polyester cover inside.

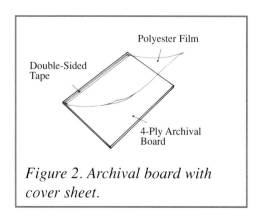

Figure 2. Archival board with cover sheet.

A variation on the above is an enclosure made of 4-ply (or heavier) archival board with a cover sheet of polyester attached at the top with double-sided tape (Figure 2). Because board is more rigid than folder stock, this type of enclosure is especially suitable for oversized materials.

STORAGE OF VERY LARGE SHEETS

Rolling

For objects larger than the available drawers, rolling is a common solution. It is not ideal but may be the only practical means of preventing mechanical damage. Rolling saves space and is satisfactory for materials that are flexible enough to withstand unrolling and rerolling. It is especially suitable for architectural working drawings and other items that are seldom consulted; related items can be rolled together. It is important not to roll too tightly and to support the material. Conservators recommend rolling sheet materials around the outside of a lignin-free tube at least 4" in diameter. The tube should be long enough to extend beyond the edges of the sheets so the edges are protected. Lignin-free tubes of varying diameters are available from conservation suppliers. If these are not immediately available, a temporary solution would be to use a non-archival tube with a barrier sheet of polyester film or buffered paper between it and the material being stored.

Once the object is rolled onto the tube, the assembly should be wrapped in archival paper or given a jacket of polyester film to protect against abrasion, dust, and pollutants. The outer jacket may be secured with Velcro tabs or with ties of undyed fabric tape, white polyester ribbon, or strips of cloth. Ties should be at least 1/2" wide. Tubes should be stored horizontally one layer deep. Shelves should be deep enough so the tubes do not extend into the aisles. They can also be stored by inserting a pole through the tube and resting the ends of the pole on wall brackets. For additional protection some institutions put tubes wrapped with archival materials inside larger tubes.

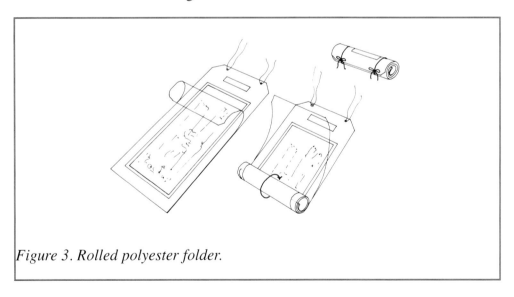

Figure 3. Rolled polyester folder.

A rolled folder made of 4- or 5-mil polyester film provides an alternative storage solution (see Figure 3). Rolled polyester folders, like encapsulation, reinforce and support oversized objects. As with encapsulation, acidic materials should not be placed in polyester rolls unless they are resting against buffered paper. Such folders can be made from a sheet of polyester film folded in half. The object is placed inside and the folder is rolled and secured with ties. The ties can be kept in place by feeding them through holes punched in the end of the roll. A label of archival paper can be attached to the film with double-sided tape (3M brand #415). Labels should face out and not touch the object. The object itself should face in so that it is protected from light exposure.

Many collections contain objects that have been rolled for years and are too brittle to unroll safely. If they are humidified, many of these papers will relax enough to be handled. A conservator can advise on how and when to humidify. Or see the NEDCC leaflet and National Park Service *Conserve-O-Gram* cited below.

If they cannot be flattened right away, rolled objects may be wrapped temporarily in archival paper and stored horizontally in a single layer on shelves wide enough to support them. For better protection, the rolls may be placed inside wide-diameter tubes long enough to cover them or in the long, narrow archival boxes made for such materials. If stored in tubes, the rolls should be wrapped to protect them when they are pulled from the tubes.

Please remember that storing flat is greatly preferred to rolling. Objects should be rolled only if they are too large to fit into drawers.

Folding

Folding damages paper and is not recommended. Some objects, such as newspapers, are meant to be folded once. Such sheets may remain that way but should not be folded a second time.

Hanging

Vertical hanging of paper artifacts is usually not recommended. Wall maps and other objects can be stored this way if they are specifically mounted for hanging, if that mounting is secure and conservationally sound, and if the objects are protected from light and air-borne hazards.

Wall maps were traditionally backed with cloth, attached to rods at the top and bottom edges, and hung on walls with only a coat of varnish to protect their surfaces. These maps are often dark and brittle from long exposure, and their mounts are often failing. These maps, however, can be treated and given new backings and the protection of a polyester envelope. It is safe to store conserved wall maps vertically if they can be kept in the dark much of the time. Plans for an inexpensive rack made of pipes and plumbers' fittings are available from the Northeast Document Conservation Center.

Sectioning

At one time, libraries routinely cut maps into sections for easier storage. Sometimes the sections were mounted together on a single cloth, folded where cut, and put inside a cover in a book format. These interesting examples of early map preservation are found in many libraries. Today maps are never cut. Some, however, can be sectioned without cutting. Many early materials, especially maps, are printed or drawn onto two or more sheets of paper that have been joined together. In the course of conservation treatment these sheets can be separated, treated, and kept separate. Sectioning in such cases is a radical solution but not an irreversible one. The component parts can always be put together for viewing or permanently rejoined at a later time. Whether to section, like so many conservation issues, should be decided on an individual basis, with a consideration of the object's aesthetic importance, its uniqueness, its original function, the amount of handling it will receive, and the feasibility of storage alternatives such as rolling. This is essentially a curatorial issue that must be decided by the collection manager with input from the conservator.

SUGGESTED FURTHER READING

Alper, Diana. "How to Flatten Folded or Rolled Paper Documents." *Conserve-O-Gram* 13.2. Harpers Ferry, WV: National Park Service, rev. 1993, 4 pp.

Rhodes, Barbara, ed. *Hold Everything! A Storage and Housing Information Sourcebook for Libraries and Archives.* New York: Metropolitan Reference and Research Library Agency (Metro), 1990, 63 pp.

Ritzenthaler, Mary Lynn. *Archives and Manuscripts Conservation: A Manual on Physical Care and Management.* Chicago: Society of American Archivists, 1983, 144 pp. SAA Archival Fundamentals Series.

Ritzenthaler, Mary Lynn. *Preserving Archives and Manuscripts.* Chicago: Society of American Archivists, 1993, 225 pp. SAA Archival Fundamentals Series.

Acknowledgements

NEDCC gratefully acknowledges the work of Margaret R. Brown in illustrating this leaflet.

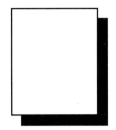

Northeast Document
Conservation Center
100 Brickstone Square
Andover, MA 01810-1494
www.nedcc.org
Tel: (978) 470-1010
Fax: (978) 475-6021

MATTING AND FRAMING FOR ART AND ARTIFACTS ON PAPER

by Mary Todd Glaser
Director of Paper Conservation
Northeast Document Conservation Center

Acid migration from surrounding materials is a common source of damage to paper. Over the years, chemically unstable materials used for storage or framing have taken their toll. These materials include many of the cardboards, tapes, and adhesives used to mount artifacts prior to framing. Framing is intended to protect, but, if not done properly, it will damage instead.

CHOICE OF A FRAMER

Although framers know far more today than they did a few years ago, many are still ignorant of preservation procedures and materials. A paper conservator or a museum can help you find a framer who is familiar with the special requirements of art works or historic artifacts. With any framer, discuss your matting and framing requirements to make certain appropriate materials and mounting procedures will be used.

MATTING

The window mat is the standard mount for a paper artifact that is to be framed. Mats are also used for storage, especially for prints, drawings, and other works of art on paper. Some institutions simplify their framing and storage operations by using mats with standard outer dimensions that fit inside standard-sized storage boxes or frames.

The typical museum mat is composed of a window and a backboard (Figure 1). The two boards are held together with a strip of cloth tape along one edge, usually the top. When an object is matted but not framed, it should have a protective sheet over its face. Clear polyester film, an archival plastic, is often used for the cover sheet because it is chemically neutral, transparent, and dimensionally stable. Polyester, however, carries a static charge and is therefore suitable for secure media only. Archival tissue paper is more appropriate for delicate media such as pastel, charcoal, soft graphite pencil, or opaque watercolor. Acid-free glassine can also be used, but this becomes acidic in time and must be replaced every few years.

The board recommended for preservation matting may be either traditional ragboard, which is usually 100% cotton, or high-quality wood-derived archival board that is free of lignin, a substance that can lead to the formation of acid. Both types are usually buffered with an alkaline material to ensure that they will not be adversely affected by acidic surroundings. Both types are stocked by conservation framers, conservation suppliers, or large art supply stores in several shades of white and in colors.

If wood-derived board is used instead of ragboard, it must be lignin-free. There are always new products coming onto the market, and some may not be appropriate for works of art or historic artifacts. If in doubt about matting or mounting materials, ask a knowledgeable framer or conservator or check the product literature.

The mat window and its backboard should be the same size and fit the frame exactly. The window portion of the mat must be deep enough to ensure that the glazing is not in contact with the object. Four-ply board usually suffices, but thicker mats are required for large sheets, for those that may cockle or ripple, or for works with impasto, seals, or other raised elements. Archival boards thicker than four-ply are available commercially, or they can be made by laminating two or more sheets of four-ply board. Attractive multi-layered stepped mats can be made in one or more colors. With any layered mat, all layers should be made of archival board. If a very deep mat is needed, a sink mat may work best. Sink mats (see Figure 3) are constructed by adhering strips of conservation board (scraps can be used) to the backboard to make a recess or "sink" in which the object is mounted. The walls of the sink are hidden by the window portion of the mat.

The methods and materials for attaching the object to the mount are as important as the mount itself. The object must be mounted on the backboard of the mat, never on the reverse of the window. Under no circumstances should it be glued directly to the backboard. The traditional method is to use paper hinges and an appropriate adhesive. In recent years corner supports or edge strips have become popular since they require that no adhesive be applied to the object. Hinges, corner supports, and edge strips all allow the artifact to be easily removed from the mat if necessary.

Hinges are small rectangles of strong, archival-quality paper, preferably Japanese kozo. Part of the hinge is adhered to the reverse of the object and part to the backboard. Two common types of hinges are shown below. Folded hinges are recommended when the edges of the sheet will be shown.

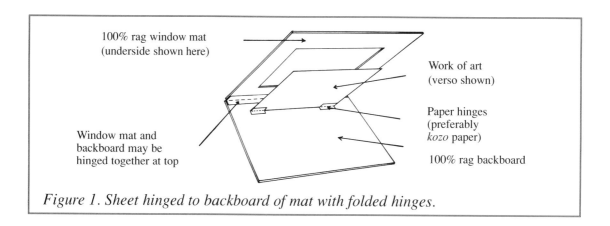

100% rag window mat
(underside shown here)

Work of art
(verso shown)

Paper hinges
(preferably
kozo paper)

Window mat and
backboard may be
hinged together at top

100% rag backboard

Figure 1. Sheet hinged to backboard of mat with folded hinges.

Figure 2. Sheet hinged with tab or pendant hinges.

Acid-free
paper hinge

Tape holding
hinge to
backboard

Part of hinge
adhered to back
of picture

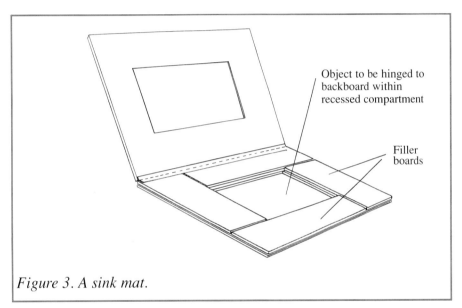

Figure 3. A sink mat.

Object to be hinged to
backboard within
recessed compartment

Filler
boards

Hinges must be attached with an adhesive that is non-staining, permanent, and reversible. Conservators recommend homemade starch-based paste. For more information on the specifics of matting and sources of supply, see the NEDCC leaflet, "How To Do Your Own Matting and Hinging."

Hinges are usually applied to the top corners of the artifact, although with large or heavy sheets, additional hinges may be added at other points along the top edge. If the object is to be "floated" (displayed with edges exposed), additional hinges at the bottom corners or along the other three edges are desirable.

The paper most often recommended for hinging, pure Japanese *kozo*, is sometimes referred to as mulberry paper or, erroneously, as rice paper. Papers made from 100% *kozo* fibers are light in weight, lignin-free, and long-fibered. They age well, remaining strong and flexible for years. Although these papers were once made only by hand, some are now machine made. *Kozo* papers are available from conservation suppliers in different weights and in varying shades of white.

The adhesive preferred by conservators is a home-made starch-based paste. This has the necessary qualities for a conservation adhesive: sufficient strength, good aging properties, no tendency to discolor, and reversibility. Animal glues (mucilage) or rubber cement are not recommended as they darken on aging and stain the object. Synthetic adhesives, such as the ubiquitous white household glue, may not stain but are not recommended because they may become irreversible as they age. The self-adhering "archival" tapes that have come onto the market in recent years have yet to prove themselves. These are non-staining, at least in the short run, but their aging properties are still not known, and they should not be used.

Non-adhesive methods of mounting may be used instead of hinges. One of these methods is to use corner supports, which can be either paper envelopes folded over the corners of the artifact and adhered to the backboard, or strips placed diagonally across the corners. Another method of non-adhesive support uses edge strips, that is, lengths of paper folded over the edges of the artifact. To hold the sheet, these non-adhesive supports must overlap the front of the object. They can be concealed only if covered by a mat, which must also cover a portion of the artifact. Corner supports or edge strips can be made of paper or polyester film. The small corners available commercially for mounting photographs are acceptable for photographs and for small paper objects. Most paper artifacts, however, need larger envelope corners or strips of polyester film (Mylar) across the corners. Strips of finely woven polyester fabric can also be used. Polyester fabric is matte and therefore less visible than polyester film, which is shiny.

MOUNTING WITHOUT A WINDOW MAT

Mats are not always appropriate. Certain contemporary works look odd if matted, and mats are not historically correct for early prints displayed in original frames. When a mat is not used, the object should be hinged to a backing of archival board and framed so that it is not in contact with the glazing. Use of a spacer, which can be at least partially hidden under the frame rabbet, will assure a space between glazing and object. Like all materials inside frames, a spacer must be non-acidic and chemically stable. Strips of ragboard make effective spacers. Ragboard strips can be attached to the glazing under the frame rabbet with archival double-sided tape, such as 3M Scotch brand double-sided tape #415. If painted black, the spacer is less apt to be visible. An acrylic paint should be used. Spacers deeper than 4-ply can be made by laminating two or more strips together with #415 tape. Another option is to ask your framer to construct a frame with a built-in spacer.

GLAZING

With a work on paper, glazing is essential to protect the fragile, porous paper surface from dirt and pollutants. Because moisture can condense on the inside of the picture glazing, the latter should not touch the artifact. The best glazing materials for works of art and historic artifacts are those that are designed to filter out the damaging (UV) component of light. An acrylic sheet, UF-3 Plexiglas, made by Rohm and Haas, has been used by museums for several decades. More recently, other companies have introduced acrylic and glass sheets that filter UV radiation. When choosing glazing, be certain to select a product with a high UV-filtering capacity, at least 90%. Most glass and many acrylics do not block any UV radiation, and others filter only a small percentage.

It should be noted that acrylics carry a static charge and must not be used for pastels, charcoal drawings, or objects with insecure media. UV-filtering glass should be used instead.

Sometimes it is important to retain the original hand-blown glass in an old frame. In such a case, a double glazing system can be used with UV-filtering glazing next to the object (but not touching it) and the old glass on top. The second glazing layer will not be readily discernible to the viewer.

WHAT ELSE GOES INTO A FRAME?

For added protection, the frame should be sealed, and there should be at least one additional layer of sturdy archival board behind that on which the object is mounted. This backing layer, needed for physical and thermal protection, should be an all-paper, lignin-free board. This is preferable to wood or to foam board, which may release chemicals as they age. For even greater protection, a moisture barrier may be inserted between the backing sheets or attached to the back of the frame with 3M double-sided tape #415. Four- or five-mil Mylar can be used as a moisture barrier, although Marvelseal, a laminate of aluminum foil and inert plastics, is even better since it is more impermeable to both moisture and gases.

The frame must be deep enough to accommodate all layers. The contents should not stick out behind the frame and touch the wall. Ideally, all layers are recessed within the frame so there is air space between them and the wall. When ordering new frames, make certain they are deep enough. Existing wood frames can be deepened by building up the back of the frame with wooden strips, screwed or glued into place.

The frame should be as air-tight as possible to keep out dirt and pollutants and to stabilize the interior against short-term fluctuations in temperature and relative humidity. The contents of the frame should be firmly held in place with brads or other metal hardware. The final board layer should be sealed to the frame with special archival tape. An alternative solution is to cover the back of the frame with a "dust sheet" made of sturdy archival paper or of one of the moisture barriers mentioned above. For additional protection, some conservators seal the glazing to the inside of the frame with strips of archival tape. Others make a sandwich of the contents (glazing, mat, object, and backing layers) and seal the edges with tape. The sandwich is then placed in the frame as a unit.

Please note that wood can give off volatile substances that are damaging to paper. This is especially true of freshly cut wood, but even old wooden frames will off-gas. As a precaution, the wood should be an inch or more away from the object. Distance, together with an alkaline buffer in the mat or mounting board, should protect the artifact. When it is necessary to use an original historic frame with a snug fit, the inside of the rabbet should be lined with a barrier material such as polyester film or Marvelseal. The latter is heat sensitive on one side and can be ironed onto the frame rabbet.

FINALLY . . .

Even if ultraviolet-filtering glazing is used, paper objects should be hung in areas of subdued lighting. Because light at any level is potentially damaging, conservators advise that no paper-based work of art be kept on permanent display. In addition, storage and display areas should be cool and dry with minimal fluctuations of temperature and relative humidity. Climatic fluctuations not only weaken paper over time but can cause unsightly rippling or distortion of the sheet. Proper framing will buffer a work of art against minor short-term climate changes but will not protect against seasonal or long periods of high humidity. As is the case with all works of art and historic artifacts on paper, the environment surrounding framed objects is crucial to their preservation.

SUGGESTED FURTHER READING

Clapp, Anne F., *Curatorial Care of Works of Art on Paper*. New York: Nick Lyons Books, 1987.

Glaser, Mary Todd, "How To Do Your Own Matting and Hinging." In *Preservation of Library and Archival Materials: A Manual*, 3rd ed., rev. and expanded; ed. by Sherelyn Ogden. Andover, MA: Northeast Document Conservation Center, 1999.

Phibbs, Hugh, "Building Space Into the Frame," *Picture Framing Magazine*, Feb. 1995.

Phibbs, Hugh, "Preservation Matting for Works of Art on Paper," A Supplement to *Picture Framing Magazine*, Feb. 1997.

Smith, Merrily A., *Matting and Hinging of Works of Art on Paper*. Washington: Library of Congress, 1981.

Acknowledgements

NEDCC gratefully acknowledges the work of Margaret R. Brown in illustrating this technical leaflet.

Northeast Document
Conservation Center
100 Brickstone Square
Andover, MA 01810-1494
www.nedcc.org
Tel: (978) 470-1010
Fax: (978) 475-6021

STORAGE ENCLOSURES FOR PHOTOGRAPHIC MATERIALS

by Gary Albright
Senior Paper/Photograph Conservator
Northeast Document Conservation Center

Storage enclosures for photographic prints and negatives are available in a variety of materials and formats. One must decide between buffered or non-buffered paper, paper or plastic, polyester or other plastics, sleeves or envelopes. Choosing the proper enclosure requires a knowledge of the alternatives. This leaflet reviews the various options, discussing advantages, disadvantages, and special precautions for each. Whatever enclosure is chosen, photographic prints and negatives should not be handled with bare hands. Oils and perspiration can damage emulsions. Lint-free gloves are available from conservation or photographic suppliers.

All enclosures used to house photographs should meet the specifications provided in the American National Standards Institute (ANSI) Standard IT 9.2-1998.[1] The standard provides specifications on enclosure formats, papers, plastics, adhesives, and printing inks, and requires a variety of enclosure tests.

PAPER MATERIALS

The quality of pulp used to make storage paper is important to the preservation of photographs. Groundwood, from which many modern papers are made, contains lignin, which produces acids rapidly. Papers described as lignin-free are produced from cotton or linen (containing little lignin) or from wood fibers that have had the lignin chemically removed. Lignin-free buffered and non-buffered (neutral) paper enclosures are available.

The term *acid-free* is widely used to refer to archival-quality paper materials constructed of either *neutral* or *buffered* paper. A more precise distinction should be made between the two. Neutral enclosures, constructed of paper in the neutral pH range (6.5-7.5), do not contain acids that will damage photos stored in them, but have a limited capacity to neutralize acids from the environment or from paper deterioration. Buffered paper enclosures (pH 7.5-9.5) contain an alkaline material that neutralizes acids as they form. In the past, conservators have recommended the use of neutral paper enclosures for storage of color images, cyanotypes, and albumen prints. It was believed that these processes were sensitive to the alkalinity in buffered papers. Recent research has indicated that buffered storage enclosures are not detrimental to photographs. Therefore whether paper is neutral or buffered is not a major criterion for choosing an enclosure.

Labels such as *acid-free* do not guarantee that a material is safe when used with photographs. Even *archival* papers may be harmful to the photographic image. The only way to be certain of the inertness of the paper is to have materials undergo the Photographic Activity Test (PAT) as specified in ANSI NAPM IT9.16-1993. [2] The PAT has two components: a test to detect image fading resulting from harmful chemicals in enclosures; and a test to detect staining reactions between enclosures and gelatin. Consumers should contact suppliers of archival materials to see if their products comply with ANSI IT9.16-1993, and have passed the Photographic Activity Test. [3]

When PAT test results are not available, purchase materials from suppliers familiar with the special needs of photographs, and choose enclosures that are lignin-free, 100% rag, and not highly colored. Glassine enclosures are not recommended. Glassine paper is made with short, brittle wood pulp fibers, which are prone to rapid decay. Often in the pulp are additives which increase the flexibility and translucency of the paper. Therefore, glassine has three sources of potential harm to photographs: possible impurities from wood pulp, possible harmful additions, and deteriorating paper fiber.

In recent years, MicroChamber and other pro-active storage papers have become available. These scavengers contain activated charcoal and zeolites, which react with polluting gases, trapping them and removing them from the environment. These papers can moderate the destructive effects of pollutant gases. They may be particularly beneficial in an uncontrolled environment, especially if the collection contains color photographs, nitrate film, or early safety film.

Advantages and Disadvantages of Paper

1. Paper enclosures are opaque, protecting the object from light. However, this makes viewing difficult, requiring the removal of the object from the enclosure. This increases damage from handling, abrasion, and fingerprinting, especially in heavily used collections.
2. Paper enclosures are porous, protecting the object from the accumulation of moisture and detrimental gases.
3. Paper enclosures are generally less expensive than plastic enclosures.
4. Paper enclosures are easy to write on.

Seamed Paper Envelopes. An envelope is an enclosure with one open end; it may have a protective top flap. The seams in paper envelopes should be located at the sides and, if unavoidable, across the bottom. Any adhesives used in construction should be non-acidic and unreactive with silver. Most envelopes come with a thumb cut, but those without are preferred. Thumb cuts allow air to touch the photo, and encourage users to grasp the photo and pull it from the sleeve. Rather, to remove a photo, push in slightly on the sides of the envelope, and tap the photo out, handling only the edges. With seamed envelopes, the photograph should be inserted with the emulsion side away from the seam.

Seamless Paper Envelopes. The seamless envelope does not have any adhesive. The envelope is formed with three or four flaps which fold over to produce a pocket. The fourth flap, if present, closes the envelope completely, protecting the object within from dust and dirt. The construction of this envelope encourages the user to place the object on a flat surface to open it, which can be an advantage for brittle or fragile items such as glass-plate negatives. Also, this type of enclosure is constructed so that it can compensate for the thickness of an object.

Paper Folders. A folder is a sheet of paper that is folded in half. It is closed on one side only and must therefore be kept in a properly fitted box to hold the image effectively. If a paper folder is used for vertical storage in files, the photograph stored inside must be well supported to prevent sagging or curling. Folders are simple to make and are most useful for large or mounted items.

PLASTIC MATERIALS

Plastic enclosures of archival quality may be made of polyester, polypropylene, or polyethylene. They should not be coated or contain plasticizers or other additives. Polyester is the most inert, dimensionally stable, and rigid of the three. It can generate static electricity, which attracts dust, and it is expensive. Polyester enclosures should be either DuPont Mylar D or ICI Melinex #516. Polypropylene is almost as rigid as polyester when it is the untreated "oriented" polypropylene used in sleeve formats, but is soft when it is the surface-treated polypropylene used for ring binder storage pages. Because specifications on the surface coatings of the soft polypropylene are proprietary information and not readily available, this material cannot be properly evaluated. Polyethylene is the most easily marred and least rigid of these plastics. High-density polyethylene is a translucent, milky plastic which is naturally slippery. Low-density polyethylene, the clear polyethylene used in ring-binder storage pages, has incorporated antiblock and antislip agents which could be problematic.

Plastic enclosures made from polyvinylchloride (PVC) are unacceptable for archival photographic storage. This plastic, often referred to as "vinyl" by suppliers, is not chemically stable and will cause deterioration of a photograph over time.

Advantages and Disadvantages of Plastic

1. Plastic enclosures have the great advantage of allowing an image to be viewed without being removed from the enclosure. This greatly reduces the chance of abrading, scratching, or fingerprinting the photograph, especially in heavily used collections.

2. Plastic enclosures can abrade and scratch photographs during insertion and removal. Matte or frosted surfaces are not recommended as they are abrasive to emulsions. Low-density polyethylene also can have problems with abrasion. Abrasion can be avoided by minimizing the removal of photographs from enclosures, using properly designed enclosures (such as self-locking sleeves), or using plastics that are naturally slippery (high-density polyethylene).

3. Moisture and sulphides in the environment react with photographs to hasten their deterioration. Plastic enclosures protect the object from the atmosphere.

4. Plastic enclosures can trap moisture and cause ferrotyping (sticking with resulting shiny areas) of the image. This is a particular threat in storage environments with high relative humidity or in the event of a disaster involving water. Those plastics more prone to ferrotyping include surface-treated polypropylene and low-density polyethylene.

5. Plastic enclosures can be difficult to write on.

6. Plastic enclosures can be flimsy and may require additional support, such as archival-quality Bristol board. Any information that should accompany the image can be recorded on this board.

7. Plastic enclosures with low melting points (polyethylene) can melt during a fire, adhering themselves irreversibly to the materials stored inside them.

Plastic Envelopes. Plastic envelopes normally have heat-sealed seams, which eliminate any potential problem with adhesives. Both polyethylene and polyester envelopes are marketed by conservation product suppliers.

Plastic Folders. These may be successfully used in conjunction with paper envelopes, the polyester folder protecting the image from handling whenever it is removed from the paper envelope.

L-Velopes. These are a combination envelope-folder, being an envelope sealed on two adjacent sides. This allows for easy insertion and removal of objects, and provides more support than a folder. This design is particularly useful for smaller-format images.

Plastic Sleeves. Often these sleeves are enclosures open at two opposite sides made from polyester or polypropylene. Usually, these sleeves are a one-piece construction with a self-locking fold on one edge (also called top-flap sleeves). This fold provides for easy insertion and removal of the photograph with no abrasion to the image. However, when these sleeves are stored in groups, the folds can lock onto adjacent sleeves, making retrieval of the photographs difficult.

Polyester Encapsulation. Polyester encapsulation encloses a photograph between two sheets of polyester, sealed on all four sides with either double-sided tape or a special polyester welding machine. Encapsulation provides physical support and protection from the environment. It is useful for storing fragile prints, especially those that are torn. Encapsulation is not recommended for photographs adhered to poor quality mounts or for contemporary color photographs.

Ring-Binder Storage Pages. These pages are made to fit three-ring binders with slipcases. They are available in a wide variety of formats, sizes, and materials, including polyester, polypropylene, and polyethylene. They are an excellent alternative for small, concentrated collections of uniform size.

Polyester Sheet - Matboard Folder. These folders are made of a sheet of polyester and a sheet of matboard of the same size, attached together along one long edge with double-sided tape. The matboard gives needed support and the polyester allows the image to be easily viewed. These folders should be stored flat. They are particularly useful for storage of oversized photographs or photographs on rigid mounts. In time these folders will probably need to be replaced or the double-sided tape will break down, releasing the polyester from the folder and possibly sticking to the object.

Polyester Sheet Within a Paper Folder. This enclosure consists of a paper folder with a polyester sheet attached along an inner edge, opposite the center fold. The attachment is made with double-sided tape. The polyester holds the object in place and protects it from dirt and handling, but allows for easy viewing and removal. The paper folder provides support to the image and protects it from light. These folders are especially useful for small, fragile prints. However, over time the double-sided tape will release, necessitating folder replacement.

SUMMARY

Many of the enclosures available for photographic storage have been described above. Each has been discussed individually, but often two enclosures can be combined to form another format with its own characteristics. An example is the use of polyester folders with seamed paper envelopes. Each of these systems has advantages and disadvantages. The final choice of enclosure will depend upon the particular needs of a collection and the available funds.

NOTES

[1] *American National Standard for Imaging Media—Photographic Processed Films, Plates and Papers—Filing Enclosures and Storage Containers*, ANSI Standard IT9.2-1998. New York: American National Standards Institute, 1998. 1430 Broadway, New York, New York 10018.

[2] *American National Standard for Imaging Media—Photographic Activity Test*, ANSI Standard IT9.16-1993. New York: American National Standards Institute, 1993. 1430 Broadway, New York, New York 10018.

[3] This test can be performed by the Image Permanence Institute, Rochester Institute of Technology/F.E. Gannett Memorial Building, P.O. Box 9887, Rochester, NY 14623-0887.

SOURCES OF SUPPLIES

This list is not exhaustive, nor does it constitute an endorsement of the suppliers listed. We suggest that you obtain information from a number of vendors so that you can make comparisons of cost and assess the full range of available products.

A more complete list of suppliers is available from NEDCC. Consult the Technical Leaflets section of NEDCC's website at www.nedcc.org or contact NEDCC for the most up-to-date version in print.

Archivart
7 Caesar Place
P.O. Box 428
Moonachie, NJ 07074
Telephone: (201) 804-8986
Fax: (201) 935-5964
http://www.members.aol.com/archivart
General conservation supplies

Conservator's Emporium
100 Standing Rock Circle
Reno, NV 89511
Telephone: (702) 852-0404
Fax: (702) 852-3737
General conservation supplies

Conservation Resources International
8000-H Forbes Place
Springfield, VA 22151
Telephone: (703) 321-7730
Fax: (703) 321-0629
Archival storage supplies, MicroChamber boxes

Franklin Distributors Corporation
Box 320
Denville, NJ 07834
Telephone: (973) 267-2710
Fax: (973) 663-1643
Saf-T-Stor slide storage files

Gaylord Brothers
P.O. Box 4901
Syracuse, NY 13221-4901
Toll Free: (800) 448-6160
Toll Free Fax: (800) 272-3412
Toll Free: (800) 428-3631 help line
http://www.gaylord.com
General conservation supplies

Hollinger Corporation
9401 Northeast Drive
P.O. Box 8360
Fredricksburg, VA 22404
Toll Free: (800) 634-0491
Toll Free Fax: (800) 947-8814
E-mail: hollingercorp@intersurf.net
Archival storage supplies

Light Impressions
439 Monroe Avenue
P.O. Box 940
Rochester, NY 14603-0940
Toll Free: (800) 828-6216
Telephone: (716) 271-8960
Fax: (800) 828-5539
http://www.lightimpressionsdirect.com
General conservation supplies, photographic supplies

Russell Norton
P.O. Box 1070
New Haven, CT 06504
Telephone: (203) 562-7800
Polypropylene enclosures

Print File
P.O. Box 4100
Schenectady, NY 12304
Telephone: (518) 374-2334
Plastic sleeves

Talas
568 Broadway
New York, NY 10012
Telephone: (212) 736-7744
Fax: (212) 219-0735
General conservation supplies

University Products
517 Main Street
P.O. Box 101
Holyoke, MA 01041
Toll Free: (800) 628-1912
Telephone: (413) 532-3372
Toll Free Fax: (800) 532-9281
Fax: (413) 432-9281
E-mail: info@universityproducts.com
http://www.universityproducts.com
General conservation supplies, polyester, blotters, small tools

REFORMATTING

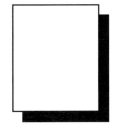

Northeast Document
Conservation Center
100 Brickstone Square
Andover, MA 01810-1494
www.nedcc.org
Tel: (978) 470-1010
Fax: (978) 475-6021

TECHNICAL LEAFLET

REFORMATTING

Section 5, Leaflet 1

MICROFILM AND MICROFICHE

by Steve Dalton
Director of Field Service
Northeast Document Conservation Center

INTRODUCTION

Amidst the bells and whistles of the digital revolution, preservation microfilming quietly maintains its status as a highly valued and widely practiced preservation reformatting strategy. And why not?

The enduring popularity of preservation microfilm is because of its practicality. Unlike its digital counterpart, microfilm is the product of a nearly static, tested technology that is governed by carefully crafted national standards. When created and stored according to these standards, microfilm boasts a life expectancy of 500+ years.[1] It is also worth noting that, while digital data require use of a sophisticated retrieval system to access their treasures, microforms (i.e., microfilm and microfiche) can be read by the naked eye using only light and magnification.

The access potential of microforms admittedly pales in comparison with that of digital technology. Still, microforms can enhance access to information that would otherwise be unavailable because the original item is at a distant site or is vulnerable to damage and/or loss through handling. Also, microforms are relatively inexpensive to produce and to copy.

One key indicator of the continuing relevance of preservation microfilming is its ongoing support at the national level.

THE NATIONAL ENDOWMENT FOR THE HUMANITIES

The National Endowment for the Humanities (NEH) continues to support the preservation microfilming of brittle books and serials through its Division of Preservation & Access.

In 1989, the U.S. Congress authorized NEH to implement a twenty-year initiative to preserve the intellectual content of approximately three million brittle volumes from research collections across the United States. According to George Farr, Director of NEH's Division of Preservation & Access, seventy-two libraries and library consortia, located in forty-two states, have participated in this cooperative effort thus far. When currently funded projects are completed, an estimated 862,418 volumes will have been microfilmed.

FILM BASES

Through the years, microforms have appeared on various film bases, including cellulose nitrate, cellulose acetate, and polyester.

Cellulose nitrate-based microforms, like other cellulose nitrate films, are highly flammable, prone to releasing hazardous gases over time, and subject to natural decomposition. By the early 1950s, commercial production of all formats of cellulose nitrate film had permanently ceased.

Cellulose acetate film, touted as safety base film and non-flammable, will still naturally degrade over time. This degradation process is accelerated when acetate film is not properly stored. Although a great deal of acetate microfilm exists, acetate film is not acceptable as a preservation medium for microforms.

Polyester is the only film base currently recommended for preservation microfilming. Both stable and durable, black-and-white polyester film has a life expectancy of 500+ years under proper storage conditions.

MICROFORM TYPES

Microforms come in a number of formats. The most familiar of these are 16mm or 35mm roll microfilm and microfiche, the latter resembling a plastic file card. Roll microfilm, in either 16mm or 35mm formats, can be cut into short strips and housed in clear "jackets" to produce a microfiche. Three types of film are common in microform collections: silver-gelatin, diazo, and vesicular.

Silver-gelatin (or silver-halide) microfilms

These are based on the familiar technology of black-and-white photography and are the only microform medium appropriate for archival purposes. The image is produced by exposing light-sensitive silver compounds in a film emulsion to light. The resulting image is chemically developed, but potentially harmful chemicals are washed out in processing. The original (master) silver-gelatin microfilm is almost always a negative image, but positive or negative duplicates can be made. The emulsion side of this film is matte, while the non-emulsion side is glossy. Modern silver-gelatin films are long-lived under appropriate storage conditions and normal library use.

Diazo microfilms

These contain diazonium salts in the coating layer that combine with dye couplers to produce strong, dense colors. Exposure to UV radiation causes the salts to decay and to lose this coupling capacity. In the diazo process, film is exposed by contact printing from a master. Acids used in the coating to prevent the coupling reaction are neutralized by exposure to a strong alkali (usually ammonia), and dyes form in unexposed areas of the film. The image duplicates the master directly. Diazo film is available in a variety of colors, including black. It may have an acetate or polyester base, although polyester is increasingly popular because of its stability and resistance to environmental factors. Resistance to fading depends on the choice of salt and dye coupler; black requires a combination of dyes. Processed black diazo resembles silver gelatin film but is glossy on both sides. Diazo film is reasonably stable but eventually fades, even in the dark. Fading is accelerated by prolonged exposure to light (as in a film reader).

Vesicular microfilms

These take advantage of the fact that diazonium salts produce nitrogen as they decompose upon exposure to UV radiation. In vesicular films, diazonium salt coating is sandwiched between two base layers. The film is exposed via contact printing from a master, and the image is developed by heating the film. This momentarily softens the base material and causes expanding nitrogen to form tiny bubbles (or vesicles) that remain when the film is cooled. Typically, residual photosensitive material is then fixed by exposing the film to UV radiation, causing complete decay of the diazonium salts. Incident light passes through the clear areas of the film but is scattered and reflected by the bubbles, causing those areas with vesicles to appear dense. The image will always exhibit slightly raised areas. The film base is always polyester because acetate cannot tolerate the heat used in processing. Vesicular film can easily be damaged by mechanical pressure, which can collapse the bubbles. Another major vulnerability of vesicular film is bubble migration or movement. At high temperatures, the base material softens allowing the gas contained in the bubbles to expand. As the bubbles grow in size, they can rupture, leaving patches of clear film where the image was formerly visible. Vesicular film may suffer damage at temperatures below 167°F, the American National Standards Institute (ANSI) permissible temperature for film readers; so special care is warranted when this film is used in a film reader.

ALTERNATIVE MICROFORM TYPES

In recent years, interest in color and continuous-tone microforms has grown in the preservation community. A brief discussion of these microform types follows.

Color microfilms and microfiche

Though there are many potential applications for color microforms, use of this technology cannot accurately be considered a preservation strategy because the life expectancies of most 35mm color films fall far short of preservation goals. Yet there is one (positive) color transparency film, Ilfochrome, that is considered quite promising for preservation. Unlike other color microfilms, which generate their dye image during processing, this film has color layers built directly into its emulsion. Testing at the Image Permanence Institute (Rochester, NY) suggests that the life expectancy of the dyes is excellent—possibly 300 to 500 years—when the film is not exposed to light. The research also suggests, however, that the film's polyester base may be less resistant to deterioration than some other polyester bases. Even so, the life expectancy of the base may be as much as 200 years or more. No testing of light stability (important to estimate permanence in use) has yet been done.

Continuous-tone microfilms

Quality black-and-white microfilming yields a high-contrast negative with excellent text resolution. Unfortunately, high-contrast microfilm cannot ordinarily capture a broad spectrum of gray tones; thus, what is gained in text resolution is lost in reproducing halftone photographic images and illustrations. Continuous-tone microfilming attempts to maximize gray scale reproduction without sacrificing textual resolution. A variety of methods can be used to create continuous-tone microfilm. For example, one preservation microfilming vendor uses Kodak 2470 direct duplicating silver gelatin microfilm in the camera and exposes the film for a prolonged time (exposure time can vary) under halogen lamps. Another, uses Fuji SuperHR20 film at normal shutter speed and achieves continuous-tone results primarily through processing in a low-contrast developer at a slower than normal processing speed. In either case, a wide range of gray tones can effectively be captured.

MICROFORM STANDARDS

Microforms used for long-term preservation of information require careful production and examination in addition to well controlled storage and handling conditions. Curators and managers of collections that use microforms should establish specifications to insure that vendors provide films to meet their use and preservation needs. ANSI/Association for Information and Image Management (AIIM) standards, as well as specifications developed by the Research Libraries Group (RLG) and by the Library of Congress, are useful guidelines. Each institution's requirements will differ, however, and these requirements should be contractually specified and systematically monitored to protect the collections themselves and the institution's interests.

The AIIM Standards Catalog can be browsed online at: www.aiim.org/industry/standards/97stdcat.htm.

QUALITY CONTROL

In order to ensure that contractual specifications regarding film quality have been achieved, microfilm vendors should thoroughly inspect processed first-generation film, including: a frame-by-frame inspection to detect filming errors (e.g., focus problems, overexposed images, underexposed images, etc.), visible defects (e.g., fingerprints, scratches, etc.), missing pages, and the number of splices on each reel; a resolution test using either the Quality Index or the systems resolution method described in ANSI/AIIM MS23-1998; density readings, interpreted according to the guidelines in the RLG Preservation Microfilming Handbook; and a methylene blue test to detect the presence of residual thiosulfate (see ANSI/NAPM IT9.1-1996). The microfilming vendor should also take density readings on all second- and third-generation duplicates to ensure compliance with specifications, and should subject all duplicates to a lightbox inspection for legibility and contrast. Results of all quality-control inspection done by the vendor should be submitted to the contracting institution on a quality-control report form.

The responsibility for quality control should not rest exclusively with the vendor. The institution should also conduct its own inspection to determine compliance with contractual specifications. A practical guideline can be found in Appendix 18 of the RLG Preservation Microfilming Handbook (listed in the bibliography under "Elkington").

STORAGE ENVIRONMENTS

Temperature and relative humidity

In general, microform requirements resemble those of other photographic materials. Year-round relative humidity lower than 50% is recommended for all film types. An upper limit of 40% is recommended for silver-gelatin films to minimize the likelihood of microscopic blemishes from silver oxidation (sometimes called "measles"). Temperature should not exceed 70°F; cooler temperatures are preferable. Master films should be stored at maximums of 65°F, 35% RH, ±5%. ANSI/NAPM IT9.11-1993 and ANSI/PIMA IT9.2-1998 specify exact conditions for archival storage of film.

If low temperatures are maintained for the storage of collections, and if readers are located outside of the storage areas, a conditioning period is required to allow gradual warming of cold films before they are read. Rapid transfer from a cold to a warm space may cause water condensation on the surface of the films.

Dehumidification systems should be refrigerant based. Desiccant-based systems can generate fine dust particles that may scratch the surface of films. Desiccant-charged storage cabinets are not recommended for use with microform collections; the relative humidity in such a system is difficult to monitor and control, and dust may abrade film surfaces. If humidification is required to stabilize fluctuations in the storage environment, it should be derived from a system with a contaminant-free water source. Corrosion inhibitors used in many large-scale systems can leave reactive deposits on library and archival materials. Film is particularly susceptible to chemical and abrasive damage from this source. Trays of water or chemical solutions should never be used to humidify storage cabinets.

As in the case of paper artifacts, fluctuations in temperature and relative humidity must be controlled for long-term preservation. Relative humidity and temperature for microform collections in use should not vary more than ±5%, and ±3% is preferable. The cooler the storage and the better controlled the relative humidity, the longer the expected life of the films.

Pollution

Particulate air pollutants are an obvious source of scratches and abrasions for microfilm. Silver-gelatin films are particularly vulnerable to such damage. House cleaning, including regular vacuuming, is important in storage and use areas.

Gaseous air contaminants, e.g., oxides of sulfur and nitrogen, paint fumes, ammonia, peroxides, ozone, and formaldehyde, damage film bases and emulsions. These contaminants may produce oxidizing or reducing effects that cause microblemishes on silver-gelatin films; precautions must therefore be taken to reduce the risk of exposure. Microforms should not be stored near photocopiers, which may be a source of ozone. Also, microforms should be removed from any area to be painted; good air circulation should be provided by fans and open windows, and paint should be allowed to cure for three months before films are returned to the space. Wooden shelving or cabinets should not be used in areas where microforms of long-term value are stored.

Diazo, vesicular, and silver-gelatin films should not be rolled on the same spools, sleeved in the same enclosures, or (ideally) stored in the same containers. Space and access problems usually make separate cabinets for different film types impracticable, but separate spools and fiche sleeves should always be used. In addition, older vesicular films may be a source of acidic deterioration products. They should be physically separated from other films and systematically replaced.

MULTIPLE COPIES

While perfectly controlled storage environments are ideal, multiple copies of microforms can provide a pragmatic solution for archival preservation. Most collections with film of enduring value use a three-generation system to allow some flexibility in storage requirements.

Master negative

The first generation film (or master negative) should be a silver-gelatin negative produced from the original artifact and processed according to standards given in ANSI/AIIM MS23-1998. This is the archival copy, which is used to produce a duplicate negative (see below) for the generation of use copies. The master negative should be stored in a different location from secondary copies and under conditions as close as possible to the ideal. There are a number of repositories that rent space for the archival storage of microfilm. These are recommended, but the user should be sure the storage conditions at the chosen facility meet ANSI standards outlined in ANSI/NAPM IT9.11-1993. The only subsequent use of the master negative should be the reproduction of a duplicate negative lost to damage or disaster.

Duplicate negative (or print-master negative)

This copy is almost always silver-gelatin. The duplicate negative is used to generate use copies (see below) for the collection. It should be stored under the best available conditions, since it serves as a working master, to protect the master negative. Ideally, it should be physically separated from use copies.

Use copies (or service copies)

Any of the available media or formats may be acceptable, and images may be positive or negative. Good storage and handling will extend the life of use copies, thus protecting previous generations of microforms.

STORAGE ENCLOSURES

Since it is difficult with available technologies to completely remove gaseous contaminants, it is important to enclose polyester films well. (Older acetate films, however, can off-gas acetic acid and should therefore be well ventilated or sealed with molecular sieves.) If master polyester negatives must be stored in poorly controlled environments, sealed metal cans or inert plastic containers may provide a solution. Kodak publication D-31, *Storage and Preservation of Microfilms* (Eastman Kodak Company, Rochester, New York, 14650) offers valuable guidance for the use of sealed containers. This strategy is not a panacea and must be used judiciously. Cans, to be acceptable, must meet chemical composition requirements. It will be necessary to examine the film periodically to make sure that no deterioration is occurring. Guidelines for inspecting silver-gelatin film are offered in ANSI/AIIM MS45-1990. If no deterioration is evident, the film can then be returned to the conditioned cans. The preferred means of storing master film is in a preservation-quality box and in a temperature- and relative-humidity-controlled facility.

Enclosures should be chosen following established guidelines for archival storage and should all pass the Photographic Activities Test as performed by the Image Permanence Institute. NEDCC recommends that paper enclosures be of high-quality, lignin-free, buffered or neutral paper. MicroChamber storage boxes (produced by Conservation Resources International, Inc., of Springfield, Virginia) are made from a board impregnated with zeolites, which neutralize gaseous pollutants. Use of these boxes appears to increase film life significantly in environments that are heavily polluted with ozone, peroxides, and other compounds that attack microfilm; it may also slow deterioration from chemicals off-gassed by older, non-preservation-quality film.

If the relative humidity of the storage environment is stable and below 50%, buffered enclosures should present few, if any, problems. Where possible, adhesives should be avoided. Safe plastics, such as polyester, polyethylene, or polypropylene, but not polyvinylchloride (PVC) or vinyl, are acceptable. Microfiche should be sleeved with the emulsion side away from the interior enclosure edges to prevent abrasion; this also adds protection from adhesives on sealed edges. Microfilm reels should be individually boxed, with film held in the wound position by a preservation-quality paper tag secured with a string and button tie. Rubber bands contain residual sulfur, a source of film and emulsion damage, and must never be used.

Steel filing cabinets are most desirable for microform storage, but inert plastic containers are acceptable for library shelf use. Microfiche enclosures should fit without buckling into drawers. Dividers and placement guides should be made of pH neutral materials. Do not compress fiche in filing, and use space dividers to prevent curling. As noted, different types of film should be stored in different containers to prevent chemical interactions. Filing systems should be designed to minimize handling, and storage cabinets should facilitate the location and retrieval of information. Wear is inevitable in used collections, but its speed and severity can be controlled.

HANDLING OF FILM

Since acidic oils and fingerprints can damage film, users should always wear gloves when handling master negatives. All films should be handled by the edges or leaders. Only one microform at a time should be removed from its enclosure. Fiche should be resleeved immediately after use; film should be immediately reboxed. In addition, rolled film should never be pulled tight on the reel as this can cause abrasions. Education of staff and users regarding the proper handling of microforms is essential to the longevity of the film.

EQUIPMENT

Ease of use and maintenance should be considered in choosing equipment. Microform readers generate heat; ANSI standards specify an upper limit of 167°F for temperature at the film plane. Some diazo films are damaged at this temperature, and prolonged exposure of small areas of film (e.g., a single frame) should be avoided for this reason. As mentioned above, vesicular film damage can occur at temperatures below the ANSI limit, so special care is warranted. Microform-reading machines should be turned off if the user leaves the equipment.

Reader lens size should take into account the reduction ratios used for filming. In preservation microfilming the image is usually reduced between 8x and 14x, so lens magnification should be in similar ratios. Zoom lenses, which allow for changing magnification, are available.

Equipment should be inspected weekly and maintained daily. Dirty equipment will decrease image quality. A staff member should have assigned responsibility for equipment maintenance and should be trained by the manufacturer's personnel. Dust on the glass flats will be magnified by the optics of the reader. Dust can also be transferred to the microform, where it might obscure details and even damage film. Dust covers should always be used whenever the film reader is not in use. Grime builds up on the edges of glass flats to create another source of film abrasion. For this reason, glass flats and carriers should be cleaned daily. A regular schedule for cleaning lenses, mirrors, and the matte surface of viewing screens should also be established, but this cleaning must be done with extreme care as these items can be easily damaged and/or made to appear smeared or mottled. Instructions for equipment maintenance are beyond the scope of this report. General instructions are given in Francis Spreitzer's *Microforms in Libraries* (see bibliography, below).

DISASTER PLANNING

Disaster planning is critical for microform collections. Microforms are highly susceptible to water damage. They must be protected from flooding or burst pipes. Once wet, this material must not be allowed to dry in rolls or enclosures as it will stick to itself and to the enclosures. Wet microforms must be removed from their enclosures. Rolled film must be unrolled for drying. Air drying is acceptable, but it is most efficient to locate, in advance, a local film processing lab that can provide this service in the event of an emergency. Microfiche can be dried flat, emulsion side up, in single layers or clipped to a line by an edge that bears no image. Diazo is prone to water spotting, and squeegees or lint-free pads should be used to control beading.

Wet microforms should not be frozen or freeze-dried since film layers may separate as a result and handling damage is difficult to prevent. If microforms cannot be air-dried immediately, they must be immersed in clean, cold water and sent to a laboratory for safe washing and drying. Mold growth must be prevented on all film types. Moldy diazo and vesicular films may be cleaned with a slightly moistened lint-free pad; if mold infects silver gelatin-film, seek professional assistance.

CHOOSING A MICROFORM PROVIDER

Commercial microfilmers are often a cost-effective provider for converting books and documents to microform. As stated above, each institution should develop standards for its microfilm, and these standards should be part of the contract for services. It is a good idea to visit the microform provider to make sure that environmental control, fire protection, housekeeping, and security meet the needs of the collections that will be filmed. This is especially important to prevent damage to original materials that will be returned to the collection rather than being discarded.

In some cases, a special-service filmer is appropriate. Many objects are filmed because they have become too fragile to survive handling by researchers. If that is the case, or if the institution wants to retain bound materials in their original form, a special-service filmer should be considered. High-volume commercial microfilmers lack the equipment, time, and expertise to process fragile materials without damage to brittle paper or deteriorated bindings. Costs for special service will be higher, but valuable artifacts or hard-to-film originals (e.g., tightly bound volumes with narrow gutters or documents with fading or inadequate contrast) may require this expense. Contact a preservation professional for advice.

SELECT BIBLIOGRAPHY FOR MICROFORM MANAGERS

American National Standard for Imaging Materials—Ammonia Processed Diazo Film—Specifications for Stability, ANSI/NAPM IT9.5-1996.

American National Standard for Imaging Materials—Processed Silver Gelatin Type Black and White Film—Specifications for Stability, ANSI/NAPM IT9.1-1996.

American National Standard for Imaging Media—Photographic Processed Films, Plates, and Papers—Filing Enclosures and Storage Containers, ANSI/PIMA IT9.2-1998.

American National Standard for Imaging Media—Processed Safety Photographic Films—Storage, ANSI/NAPM IT9.11-1993.*

Association for Information and Image Management. *Practice for Operational Procedures/Inspection and Quality Control of First-Generation, Silver Gelatin Microfilm of Documents,* ANSI/AIIM MS23-1998 Revised.**

Association for Information and Image Management. *Recommended Practice for the Inspection of Stored Silver Gelatin Microforms for Evidence of Deterioration,* ANSI/AIIM MS45-1990.

Borck, Helga. "Preparing Material for Microfilming: A Bibliography." *Microform Review* 14 (Fall 1985): 241-43.

Chace, Myron B. "Preservation Microfiche: A Matter of Standards." *Library Resources & Technical Services* 35.2 (April 1991): 186-90.

Child, Margaret S. "The Future of Cooperative Preservation Microfilming." *Library Resources & Technical Services* 29.1 (Jan.-March 1985): 94-101.

Cox, Richard J. "Selecting Historical Records for Microfilming: Some Suggested Procedures for Repositories." *Library and Archival Security* 9.2 (1989): 21-41.

Diaz, A.J., ed. *Microforms in Libraries: A Reader.* Westport, CT: Microform Review, 1975, 443 pp.

Elkington, Nancy E., ed. *RLG Archives Microfilming Manual.* Mountain View, CA: Research Libraries Group, 1994, 218 pp.

Elkington, Nancy E., ed. *RLG Preservation Microfilming Handbook.* Mountain View, CA: Research Libraries Group, 1992, 203 pp.

Fox, Lisa L., ed. *Preservation Microfilming: A Guide for Librarians and Archivists,* 2nd ed. Chicago: American Library Association, 1996, 394 pp.

Johnson, A.K *A Guide for the Selection and Development of Local Government Records Storage Facilities.* New York: NAGARA, 1989.

Library of Congress. *Specifications for the Microfilming of Manuscripts.* Washington, DC: Library of Congress, 1980, 21 pp.

McKern, Debra, and Sherry Byrne. *ALA Target Packet for Use in Preservation Microfilming.* Chicago: American Library Association, 1991.

Preservation Microfilming: Planning & Production. Papers from the RTSD Preservation Microfilming Institute, New Haven, Conn., April 21-23, 1988. Chicago: Association for Library Collections & Technical Services, ALA, 1989, 72 pp.

RLIN Preservation Masterfile. A CD-ROM listing of microfilmed books and journals. Compiled from the RLIN database and others. Available from Chadwick-Healey, Inc. for $750 a year; updated twice annually.

Recommended Practice for Operational Procedures/Inspection and Quality Control of Duplicate Microforms of Documents and from COM, ANSI/AIIM MS43-1998.

Recordak. Storage and Preservation of Microfilms. Kodak pamphlet no. P-108. Rochester, NY: Eastman Kodak Company, 1985.

Reilly, James, et al. "Stability of Black-and-White Photographic Images, with Special Reference to Microfilm." *Abbey Newsletter* 12.5 (July 1988): 83-87.

Saffady, William. *Micrographic Systems.* Silver Spring, MD: Association for Information and Image Management, 1990.

Spreitzer, Francis, ed. *Microforms in Libraries: A Manual for Evaluation and Management.* Chicago: American Library Association, 1985, 63 pp.

Spreitzer, Francis, ed. *Selecting Microform Readers and Reader-Printers.* Silver Spring, MD: AIIM, 1983.

*American National Standards Institute, Inc., 11 West 42nd Street, New York, NY 10036, (212) 642-4900.

**AIIM International, 1100 Wayne Avenue, Suite 1100, Silver Spring, MD 20910-5603, (Toll Free) (888) 839-3165.

SOURCES OF EQUIPMENT AND SUPPLIES

This list is not exhaustive, nor does it constitute an endorsement of the suppliers listed. We suggest obtaining information from a number of vendors so that you can make cost comparisons and assess the full range of available products.

A more complete list of suppliers is available from NEDCC. Consult the Technical Leaflets section of NEDCC's website at www.nedcc.org or contact NEDCC for the most up-to-date version in print.

Conservation Resources International, Inc.
8000-H Forbes Place
Springfield, VA 22151
Toll Free: (800) 634-6932
storage enclosures, reel tags, etc.

Crowley Micrographics, Inc.
8601 Grovemont Circle
Gaithersburg, MD 20877-4199
Telephone: (301) 330-0555
microfilm cameras, etc.

The Foxx Group
P.O. Box 401
Topsfield, MA 01983
Toll Free: (800) 992-5010
storage enclosures, reels, etc.

Gaylord Bros.
Box 4901
Syracuse, NY 13221-4901
Toll Free: (800) 448-6160
storage enclosures, reel tags, etc.

Gretag Macbeth
617 Little Britain Road
New Windsor, NY 12553
Toll Free: (800) 622-2384
densitometers

Keyan Industries, Inc.
8601 Grovemont Circle
Gaithersburg, MD 20877-4199
Telephone: (301) 330-0476
quality control and inspection equipment

Metric Splicer & Film Company, Inc.
3930 East Miraloma, Unit C
Anaheim, CA 92806
Telephone: (714) 630-2999
ultrasonic splicers

National Microsales Corp.
45 Seymour Street
Stratford, CT 06615
Telephone: (203) 377-0479
microfilming equipment, including cameras, processors, etc.

Neumade Products Corporation
30-40 Pecks Lane
Newtown, CT 06470
Telephone: (203) 270-1100
winders, reels, and flanges

Pohlig Bros., Inc.
8001 Greenpine Road
Richmond, VA 23237
Telephone: (804) 275-9000
storage boxes for microfilm

University Products
517 Main Street
P.O. Box 101
Holyoke, MA 01041-0101
Toll Free: (800) 628-1912
storage enclosures, reel tags, etc.

NOTE

[1] According to further guidelines provided by the Research Libraries Group (RLG).

ACKNOWLEDGEMENTS

The author is grateful for the significant contributions made by Karen Motylewski, who wrote the original technical leaflet updated here, and Robert Mottice of Mottice Micrographics, who served as technical editor for this revised version.

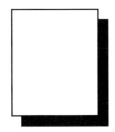

Northeast Document
Conservation Center
100 Brickstone Square
Andover, MA 01810-1494
www.nedcc.org
Tel: (978) 470-1010
Fax: (978) 475-6021

RESOURCES FOR FACSIMILE REPLACEMENT OF OUT-OF-PRINT AND BRITTLE BOOKS

This list is not exhaustive, nor does it constitute an endorsement of the companies listed. We suggest that information be obtained from several companies so that cost comparisons can be made and the range of services assessed.

A more complete list of suppliers is available from NEDCC. Consult the Technical Leaflets section of NEDCC's website at www.nedcc.org or contact NEDCC for the most up-to-date version in print.

Acme Bookbinding Company
100 Cambridge Street
Charlestown, MA 02129-1228
Telephone: (617) 242-1100
Fax: (617) 242-3764
http://www.acmebook.com
Double-sided photocopies on permanent paper; LBI Standard binding; duplication of plates or binding of original.

Bridgeport National Bindery Inc.
662 Silver Street
P.O. Box 289
Agawam, MA 01001-0289
Toll Free: (800) 223-5083
Telephone: (413) 789-1981
Fax: (413) 789-4007
E-mail: info@BNBindery.com
E-mail: JNoyes@BNBindery.com
http://www.bnbindery.com
Double-sided photocopies on permanent paper; LBI Standard binding; duplication of plates or binding of original.

Document Reproduction Services
6204 Corporate Park Drive
Brown Summit, NC 27214
Toll Free: (800) 444-7534
Telephone: (910) 375-1202
Fax: (910) 375-1726
E-mail: 70304.3023@compuserve.com
http://www.webmasters.net/bookbinding
Double-sided photocopies on permanent paper; LBI Standard binding.

Ocker and Trapp Library Bindery
17A Palisade Avenue
P.O. Box 314
Emerson, NJ 07630
Telephone: (201)265-0262
Fax: (201) 265-0588
http://www.ockerandtrapp.com
Double-sided photocopies on permanent paper; LBI Standard binding; duplication of plates or binding of original.

University Microfilms International
300 North Zeeb Rd.
Ann Arbor, MI 48106
ATTN: Out-of-Print Books
Toll Free: (800) 521-0600
Toll Free: (800) 343-5299 (Canada)
Telephone: (313) 761-4700
collect from AK, HI, MI
E-mail: library_sales@umi.com
http://www.umi.com
Double-sided photocopies on permanent paper; over 100,000 out-of-print books; cloth binding available; microfilm author guide.

University of Minnesota
University Bindery
2818 Como Avenue SE
Minneapolis, MN 55414
Telephone: (612) 626-1516
E-mail: flech001@maroon.tc.umn.edu
Double-sided photocopies on permanent paper; LBI Standard binding. Capabilities include duplication of plates or retention of the original in a variety of formats.

2/99

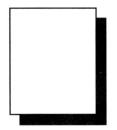

Northeast Document
Conservation Center
100 Brickstone Square
Andover, MA 01810-1494
www.nedcc.org
Tel: (978) 470-1010
Fax: (978) 475-6021

DUPLICATION OF HISTORICAL NEGATIVES

by Gary Albright
Senior Paper/Photograph Conservator
Northeast Document Conservation Center

Photographic negative collections present unique problems to institutions and collectors. Glass-plate negatives can break easily, cellulose nitrate and the various cellulose acetate negatives will self-destruct over time, and negatives are generally difficult to read and to access. The duplication of negatives is one preservation option available to help alleviate the problems. Duplication can preserve a deteriorated image, protect a negative from excessive handling, or improve access to a collection. However, duplication has limitations: each successive generation of an image loses quality and detail. Therefore it is critical that duplicate negatives be printed on stable materials and have the highest quality image reproduction. Duplicate negatives should be on modern polyester film and duplicates should have, as close as possible, the same density range and the same amount of detail as the originals.

Duplication of a negative collection is a complex and expensive process. Many decisions need to be made before a duplication project is undertaken. The information below will provide some guidance for those considering the duplication of historical negatives.

WHAT TO DUPLICATE

- Negatives that show any signs of deterioration. Deterioration includes characteristics such as breakage, flaking, fading, discoloration, warping, bubbling, channeling, or a strong odor.
- Negatives that are particularly susceptible to deterioration.
- Nitrate film negatives. Insurance companies and fire departments often have specific and expensive regulations governing storage of nitrate film. If these regulations cannot be met, duplication and disposal of the film may be necessary.
- Original negatives that are frequently printed or handled.
- Negatives with high intrinsic value.

PREPARATION FOR DUPLICATION

- In a collection, number the negatives and their enclosures consecutively and store them in numerical order.
- Number the original negatives on the base (non-emulsion) side in a non-image border area using a fine-point permanent marker. Once the images are duplicated, the numbers will appear on the duplicates, eliminating the need to spend more time numbering.

- Some nitrate films are edge-marked "nitrate." This identification should be masked out to prevent its duplication onto safety film.

DESCRIPTION OF DUPLICATION OPTIONS

Prints and Copy Negatives

The simplest way to duplicate negatives is to make a print and then to photograph the print using a large-format camera (4" x 5" or larger) to produce a copy negative. The advantages of this method are cost and convenience. Most museum darkrooms or local photo labs should be able to do the work with little or no investment in equipment. Further savings may be achieved by using already existing prints for copying. Where no original negatives exist, copying existing prints is the only available option. The disadvantage of this system is loss of detail in both the print and the copy negative. A print always has detail loss and a compressed tonal range when compared to the original negative, and further detail is lost when the copy negative is made.

Direct Duplicate Negatives

Eastman Kodak Professional Black & White Duplicating Film #SO-339 is designed for directly duplicating negatives. This is a one-step process yielding a negative from a negative. Duplicating film has high resolution, minimizing loss of image detail during copying. Also contrast can be manipulated during duplication to salvage some problem negatives. However, since the film is blue sensitive, minimizing staining can be problematic. This film can be difficult to work with, making accurate tone reproduction hard to achieve. Contact-printed direct duplicate negatives are laterally reversed, therefore the image can mistakenly be printed backwards if the photographer is not aware of the nature of the material.

If the original negatives are disposed of, the duplicate negatives become the masters. This is a major disadvantage since whenever an image is needed the master is used for printing, exposing it to the likelihood of eventual damage.

Interpositive Duplicate Negatives—Contact Duplication

The original negative is contact-printed onto film to produce an interpositive (a positive image on film). The interpositive is then contact-printed onto film to produce the duplicate negative. This process provides the most accurate tone reproductions possible. Problems in original negatives can often be corrected by using selected films and filters to reduce staining during the production of the interpositive. The disadvantages of this system are the higher production costs, the complexity of the procedure, and the added storage space required for the multiple duplicates. However, this method results in two duplicates for relatively little additional cost; the interpositive becomes the master and the duplicate negative becomes the use copy.

Interpositive Duplicate Negatives—Reduced Format, Long Roll Systems

Original negatives are copied onto 5-inch/105mm, 70mm, or 35mm roll film using a camera to produce interpositives (a positive image on film). The interpositive is then contact-printed onto film to produce the duplicate negatives. This system provides accurate tone reproduction. Also, problems in original negatives can often be corrected with the use of selected films and filters to reduce staining during the production of the interpositive. These systems provide easy access to collections. They have high production capabilities and lower production costs, and they require less storage space. However, with reduced-size duplicates there is usually some loss of image detail, proportional to the amount of reduction. As with contact interpositive duplicate negatives, this system results in two copies; the interpositive becomes the master and the duplicate negative the use copy.

Digital Imaging Storage Systems

With these systems images are stored on digital optical disks, which can be read in players that use a laser. Disk players can be interfaced with computers to allow easy cross-referencing between images and information. These systems are great access tools, but are not archival. High-resolution image files provide good quality reproductions but are impractical. They are expensive, they require more space than photographic film, and, because of their large files, they take time to access. Screen-resolution image files or files of lower quality are less expensive and do not have the storage and access time problems; however, their resolution is only fair.

The technology for optical disks is still in flux. Professionals estimate that innovations in disks and computer hardware and the design of new software to use them necessitate replacement of systems every three to five years. Therefore institutional budgets must include funds to continually upgrade the systems with new software and hardware. Also, no standards have yet been developed to insure the translation of information from one generation to another.

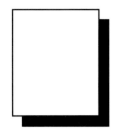

Northeast Document
Conservation Center
100 Brickstone Square
Andover, MA 01810-1494
www.nedcc.org
Tel: (978) 470-1010
Fax: (978) 475-6021

DIGITAL TECHNOLOGY MADE SIMPLER

by Paul Conway
Head, Preservation Department
Yale University Library

Abstract

This leaflet has three purposes. It first defines digital technologies from the perspective of communication and coding. Then it describes the key components of a digital imaging system and the most important steps in the digital imaging process. Finally, it asks some big questions that ought to be considered as libraries and archives move from experimenting with the technology to using it as a tool for transforming the way they do business.

Introduction

We are living in a digital world. The evidence is everywhere. Keyboards outnumber office workers. Everybody has a web page. Nobody carries cash. We are hearing words like "bitslag," "jitterati," "NIMQ," and "CGIJoe" in everyday conversation. Billionaire technologists seem to own all the digital copies of all the art that matters. There seems to be a growing concern in libraries and archives that if we are not going digital, being digital, or dreaming digital, then we are relegating ourselves to the great museum of paper.[1]

And yet, it may be that our biggest challenge may not be embracing digital technology but rather building a common language to describe the transformations that are having such a phenomenal impact on our everyday lives. A shared vocabulary is the key element in the development of a community of practice and a shared vision of the future among those of us who have responsibility to shepherd the nation's cultural resources. Jim Taylor and Watts Wacker note that "Looking backward, the true legacy of Naisbitt's *Megatrends* or Toffler's *Third Wave* may turn out to be not the worldviews but the words." [2] Nowhere have the words mattered more than in our view of the place of preservation in the digital world in which we live.

Fundamental Digital Concepts

At their most fundamental level, digital technologies are an extension of the long history of the way we communicate with each other. The desire to communicate provides the motive and the ultimate rationale for the development of technologies of all sorts. Today's digital world is concerned with creating, sharing, and using information in digital form. Digital information is data that are structured and manipulated, stored and networked, subsidized and sold.

Information takes many forms. One way to think about these forms is to distinguish between symbolic information and coded information. Let us illustrate this by looking at the many ways that the most common letter in the roman alphabet—the "E"—can be represented, beginning with the early symbols of the printed alphabet.

A History Lesson

The period from the time Gutenberg invented in the middle of the fifteenth century through the year 1500 is referred to generally as the period of incunabula. During this time printers and book designers went to great lengths to make their products—type faces, format, and layout—look and function much like the manuscript books of the preceding centuries. Only when a theory of the alphabet and a theory of the book emerged around the time of Geofroy Tory's classic text on the structure of the roman alphabet were book designers able to begin taking full advantage of Gutenberg's technological innovation.[3]

Figure 1 is an illustration of the capital letter "E" from Tory's *Champ Fleury* of 1529, which sought to develop a theory of the alphabet around the proportions of the human body and the basic principles of Euclid. Here the letter "E" is a pattern of ink on paper.[4]

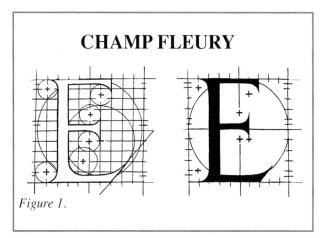

CHAMP FLEURY

Figure 1.

The world defined by strings of 1's and 0's has existed for a long time. The idea of the digital computer originated over 300 years ago in the fertile mind of a German mathematician, Gottfried Wilhelm von Leibnitz. In 1679, Leibnitz imagined a device in which binary numbers were represented by spherical pellets, circulating within a kind of pinball machine controlled by a rudimentary form of punched cards. He described a comprehensive numerical system in which all calculation can be expressed in combinations of 1 and 0—the identical approach that all digital technologies use today.[5]

We are living in an era of digital incunabula—a period marked by furtive efforts to make our digital products look and behave as their analog relatives do. Only when we have developed a theory of digital representation of information will we begin to take full advantage of Leibnitz's mathematical innovation. That theory is emerging today.[6]

Figure 2 is another symbolic pattern—Braille. Here the letter "e" is represented by large and small raised dots in a predictable grid. Note, too, that the same pattern can mean either the letter "E" or the number "5" depending upon the context in which the pattern is located. Context is another idea that is fundamental to the representation of information in digital form. With Braille, if you know the context and understand the pattern, communication is fast and efficient.

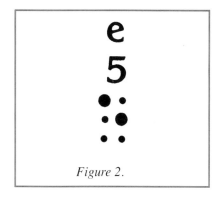

Figure 2.

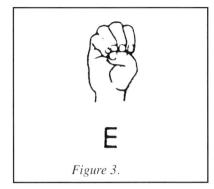

Figure 3.

American Sign Language is symbol as signal. It is a language in which the form and motion of the hands combine to convey meaning. Form without motion is only half of the process. Communication depends upon a shared understanding of the meaning of both components of the language. Figure 3 is a static representation of the letter "E"

With semaphore, however, the pattern of motion *is* the symbol. The transformation from one formation of flags and arms to another establishes the communication link. Figure 4 is yet another static representation of the letter "E." Emerging theories of digital communication have yet to account fully for the multiple senses that we routinely use to communicate directly—the subtleties of body language, gesture, and inflection. As sophisticated as digital communication has become, its dependence on machines is seriously limiting.

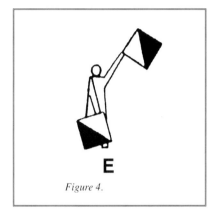

Figure 4.

Some of the earliest modern forms of direct communication over long distances, however, have been digital in character. Figure 5 is an illustration of Lord George Murray's Visual Telegraph that operated for a time from London to Deal beginning in 1794.[7] The system consisted of raised platforms placed horizon to horizon. On each platform a large board had six large circular holes that could be closed by wooden shutters—strikingly familiar to the patterns of Braille—manipulated by a trained operator. Reports indicate that a message could reach along the chain of fifteen stations in a few minutes. But just think about the administrative overhead!

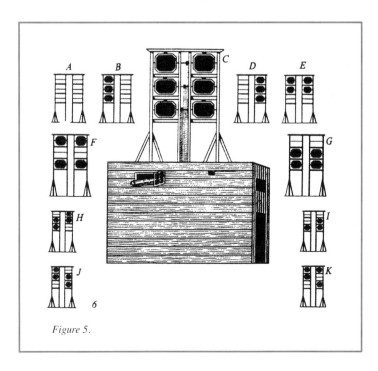

Figure 5.

The route from the Visual Telegraph to modern digital communication is marked by successive transformations from symbol to code. Samuel F.B. Morse invented his digital code of dots and dashes as the language of his telegraph. The origins of radio—or wireless telegraphy—lie in the desire to extend the digital communication of Morse where wires could not reach. An early application of the analog technology of continuous waves was the transmittal of Morse's dots and dashes to ships at sea. The modern coding of the letter "E" as the ASCII code 01100101 owes its lineage to the theories of Leibnitz and the practical technology of Samuel Morse rather than to the technology of radio and television.

Code as Numbers—Some Building Blocks

A **digital** system uses numbers to represent a concrete object or an abstract idea. **Digitization** is the process of transforming the object or idea into a numerical code. The baseline of digital technology is a coding system with only two numbers—1 and 0—hence the term **binary**. Each numerical place in the system is a **bit**. In the digital world bits are things; they take up space; they take time to move from one place to another. A collection of bits can be described and counted, much like anything.[8] The most common way to count the bits in a system is by **"byte"** or eight bits, even though computer technology abandoned the byte as a discrete object decades ago.

- Digital: using numbers to represent variables
- Digitalize: to treat with ditigalis, a heart medication
- Digitize: to translate an analog measurement into a numerical description
- Binary: a number system in which each number is expressed in powers of two by using only two digits, specifically 0 and 1
- Bit: binary digit
- Byte: eight bits

A **bit-mapped image** is a digital picture made up of row after row of bits in a grid. In a digital image, a bit is commonly referred to as a pixel, short for "picture element." As objects, digital images are described in terms of three characteristics: resolution, dynamic range, and pixel size.

More recently, a fourth term, tonal value, has been applied to describe the characteristics of a "digital image," confusing terminology about a digital representation of an image, such as a photograph. A bitmap is a digitally coded pattern, not a digitally coded symbol such as text we recognize through an alphabet.

- Resolution: number of pixels (in both height and width) making up an image
- Dynamic Range: number of possible colors or shades of gray that can be included in a particular image
- Pixel Size: the proportion of the pixel grid that can be detected and coded by a scanner
- Tone: the degree to which an image conveys the luminance ranges of an original scene

---

Resolution is the number of pixels (or dots) used to code a linear inch of surface horizontally and/or vertically. Visualize a piece of graph paper. The number of small blocks in a running inch up or down the paper is the resolution. The more pixels per inch the higher the resolution and the more accurately the patterns visible on a given surface can be represented digitally. The description of an image as 300 dots per inch (dpi) means that 300 pixels are used to represent each inch across the horizontal surface. It is sometimes (mistakenly) assumed that an image with 300 pixels horizontally will also be represented by 300 lines vertically. The actual structure of the digital grid depends on the capabilities of the scanning device.

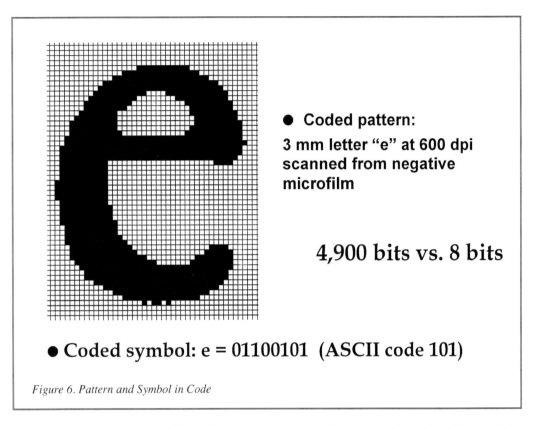

● **Coded pattern:**

3 mm letter "e" at 600 dpi scanned from negative microfilm

4,900 bits vs. 8 bits

● Coded symbol: e = 01100101 (ASCII code 101)

Figure 6. Pattern and Symbol in Code

Figure 6 is a 3 mm letter "e" at 600 dpi resolution scanned from negative microfilm at Yale University Library. Note that the digitally coded pattern occupies some 4,900 bits in the computer system compared to the eight bits required for the digitally coded symbolism of ASCII code.

Dynamic range refers to the number of possible colors or shades of gray that can be included in a particular image. Dynamic range is sometimes called "depth" and is commonly represented as bits per pixel. In bitonal scanning, the sampled image level for each pixel is rounded to 0 (black) or 1 (white). One bit of information is required to code the value of the pixel. In 8-bit gray scanning, the sampled image level for each pixel is rounded to one of 256 values, each representing successively lighter shades of gray. Eight bits of information are required to represent each pixel. In full-color scanning, the three hues of the color system are represented by one of 256 possible shades and encoded as a total of 24 bits (8 bits per hue). The two predominant color systems are Red/Green/Blue for monitor projection and Cyan/Magenta/Yellow for digital printing.

Pixel size is an important measure of the capability of a given piece of scanning hardware to represent the patterns of a surface completely. The "real resolution" of a scanner is the proportion of the surface that is detected. The "addressable resolution" of a scanner is number of pixels in a running inch of an array without optical correction. Greater real resolution depends upon the quality of the electrical and mechanical engineering of a given device. Scanner manufacturers sometimes use software solutions (synthetic resolution) to compensate for limited real resolution. It is important to be wary of scanner manufacturer claims and to undertake rigorous testing and benchmarking before committing to the purchase of scanning equipment. [10]

Tone reproduction refers to the degree to which an image conveys the luminance ranges of an original scene (or of an image to be reproduced in the case of digital imaging). According to Reilly and Frey, tone "is the single most important aspect of image quality." Tone reproduction is the matching, modifying, or enhancing of output tones relative to the tones of the original document. Because all of the varied components of an imaging system contribute to tone reproduction, it is often difficult to control. [11]

Resolution, dynamic range, real resolution, and tone reproduction combine to endow an image with quality. When defined and measured carefully, the terms can be used to describe the characteristics of an image, to compare quality characteristics of two or more collections of images, and to compare the digital image with its original source. The resolution and dynamic range values of a given image can also be combined to describe the size of an image in terms of the amount of data that is required to represent the image in digital form.

Describing digital objects. The description of an image or collection of images in terms of quality and quantity is but half the story of a digital image product. Equally important is the digital data that describe the digital object itself. In modern imaging systems, such descriptive data exist as a linkage of at least three components. The first are the technical data (often called the image header) that describe the format of the digital image and the ways in which the raw digital data are compressed to save storage space and transmission time.

The second component is data describing the characteristics of the digital object (which may consist of one or more digital images). Metadata is data about data and as such is fundamentally linked to the accessibility of an object. As mere bitmaps, digital images are stupid and cannot be found or understood without some level of metadata.

The third descriptive component is information that describes the relationships between or among digital objects. Structural indexes are a crucial component to any digital imaging system where the content is hierarchical in nature (such as archival collections, books, scrapbooks, classified photograph collections, and the like). It is a rare digital object whose accessibility cannot be enhanced through the use of structural indexes. Structural information may reside as separate data (e.g., an encoded finding aid) or be built into the metadata system itself (e.g., controlled subject headings in a bibliographic record).

In summary, at the heart of the digital world is communication, which cannot happen without a shared vocabulary and a shared system of symbols. Digital imaging is representation by numbers of the world we can sense (see, touch, hear, smell, and taste). Images as bitmaps are pictures without intelligence. All meaning embedded in the digital technology system derives from layer upon layer of numerical coding, most of which must be done by people rather than machines. In the end, then, digital imaging is more profoundly about us than about the tools we use.

Digital Imaging Process and Product

We shall now turn our attention to the digital imaging processes and products by examining two general models.

Imaging Process Model

At its most elementary, the conversion of a book, a manuscript, a photographic negative, or a reel of microfilm is straightforward and linear. **Source** objects appropriate for conversion are selected and prepared for scanning; **conversion** occurs via scanning technology that transforms reflected light signals to digital data; **access** to the digital data is through display of the stored digital data. This apparent simplicity masks great complexity at all phases of the process.

- **Source:** Archives and libraries are legion for the complexity and variety of the collections eligible for digital conversion. Sources vary in size, format, medium, and condition; they may be text based; they may contain illustrations that themselves may vary wildly in character. Sources may have significant color content.

  Not all digital conversion takes place from the original source. Film intermediates play an increasingly large role in a digital imaging system. Intermediates range in type from 35 mm color slides and high-contrast microfilm to full-frame microfiche and large-format negatives. Michael Ester has underscored the importance of understanding the characteristics of film intermediates. "The digital image will only be as good as its photographic source; if visual detail or subtlety is not in the photographic medium, neither will it appear in the digital image." [12]

- **Conversion:** The conversion of source materials is—in equal parts—people and machinery. Equipment configurations are complex and rapidly evolving in capability. They consist of hardware, software, firmware (chip-based software), and storage systems. Imaging systems vary in their engineering sophistication, the quality of their sensory devices, the character of the software that is brought to bear to streamline the process, and the speed with which the system can carry out the conversion of a given source or collection of sources. It is crucial to "test drive" equipment configurations before purchasing or leasing them. A visit to other libraries, archives, service bureaus, and other organizations that have similar operational systems is a good way to learn how conversion systems work.

  The digital conversion process is intensely labor intensive. At present, the quality and accessibility of the digital product largely depends upon the skills and talents that people bring to bear on the process of inspection, scanning, indexing, and data-file management. With enough effort, these skills can be obtained and maintained in-house. Today, it is more feasible than in the past to contract with companies that specialize in high-quality image conversion services.

- **Access:** At some level of abstraction, a digital product exists only if it can be found and viewed. Access systems for digital products are at least as complex as the systems that support conversion. Platforms (PC, Unix, Mac) vary in their capabilities; the adequacy of a network architecture can make or break an access system. Similarly, display technology (screens and printers) are vital to the ultimate use of the digital product.

Display technology is one of the main weak links in the entire system. Conversion technology is capable of generating far more data than can be usefully displayed by most of today's computer monitors.

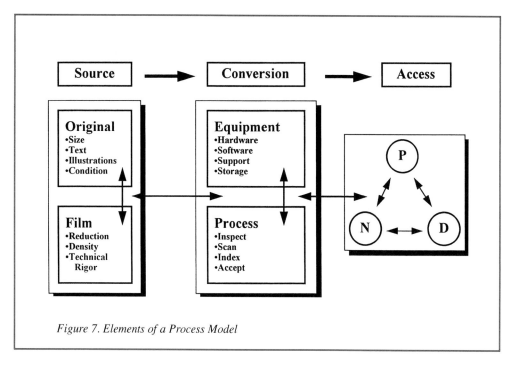

Figure 7. Elements of a Process Model

Figure 7 is a schematic illustrating the elements of the process model. It is important to recognize that the complexity of a digital imaging system is only in part related to the complexity of the individual components. The elements of the process interact with each other to add complexity.

Imaging Product Model

The digital imaging process results in a product with its own characteristics that are distinct from the characteristics of the original sources. The biggest challenge in building an image product is to balance three issues: the characteristics of the source; the capabilities of the technologies of digital conversion; and the purposes or expected uses of the end product.

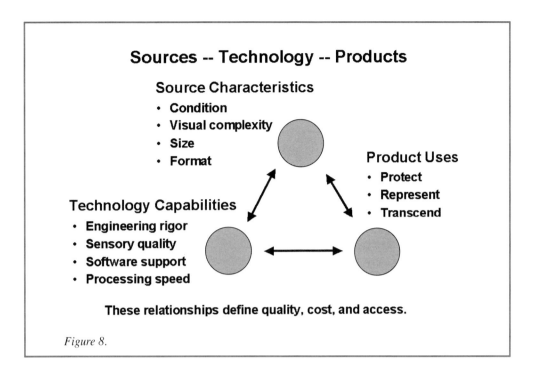

Sources -- Technology -- Products

Source Characteristics
- **Condition**
- **Visual complexity**
- **Size**
- **Format**

Product Uses
- **Protect**
- **Represent**
- **Transcend**

Technology Capabilities
- **Engineering rigor**
- **Sensory quality**
- **Software support**
- **Processing speed**

These relationships define quality, cost, and access.

Figure 8.

Figure 8 is a schematic defining the issues and suggesting a set of relationships that must be managed to produce an image product with sufficient value built in that it will be worth the cost and effort of ensuring its long-term preservation.

Of the three sets of issues (source, technology, uses) in the model, the concept of varying product uses is perhaps the least generally understood. A number of researchers in the field[13] have begun to suggest that the quality of the end product can in some way be established through reference to one of three possible purposes that the product may serve for end users.

- **Protect Originals.** The most basic application of digital technologies in an archives or library is to create digital copies of sufficient quality that they can be used for ready reference in lieu of casual browsing through the original sources. Examples include image reference files of photographs, clippings, or vertical files that permit the identification of individual items requiring closer study. Preservation goals are met because the original documents can be protected by limiting access to them.

- **Represent Originals.** A digital system could be built that represents the information content of the original sources in such detail that the system can be used to fulfill most, if not all, of the research and learning potential of the original documents. High-resolution systems that strive for comprehensive and complete content and seek to obtain "full information capture" based on emerging standards and best practices, fit this definition. Systems of this intermediate level of quality open new avenues of research and use and have the capability to have a transformative effect on the service missions of those who create the products.

- **Transcend Originals.** In a small number of applications, digital imaging holds the promise to generate a product that can be used for purposes that are impossible to achieve with the original sources. This category includes imaging that uses special lighting to draw out details obscured by aging, use, and environmental damage; imaging that makes use of specialized photographic intermediates; or imaging of such high resolution that the study of artifactual characteristics is possible.

Each of these applications places separate, but increasingly rigorous demands on digital technologies. In each case, the use of an intermediate film or paper copy to facilitate the scanning process may be necessary or advisable. Finally, the disposition of original sources (including undertaking preservation treatments before or after conversion) is a separate matter. Ultimately, the purpose of the digital product is driven by access goals, while preservation of original source documents should be determined by the preservation needs of the original sources.

Food for Thought

This leaflet has already suggested a number of issues with which librarians and archivists must wrestle if their digital initiatives will have lasting value. Here are five questions that transcend the specifics of digital imaging technology.

- **Technology. Is digital imaging the tail or the dog?**
  Those who market digital imaging technology prefer to use the term "solution" to describe the value of the their products. This term implies that the customer defines the problem and buys a technology solution. Digital technologies are a set of tools that offer many choices and few solutions. It may be more appropriate to distinguish between imaging projects that experiment with the capabilities of the technology (and result in institutional learning) from those that transform the very nature of our information management strategies.

- **Control. Is it a four letter word?**
  Fundamental digital technology is stable. The digital imaging market place, however, is large, complex, and in a constant state of flux. Libraries and archives hold a small share of this market place. It is imperative that we seek to identify which elements of digital technology we can control, where our expertise is one of many important influences, and when we must accept the processes and products of the world in which we live.[14]

- **Selection. Are our digital collections useful and usable?**
  Choice is at the heart of digital technology applications; the choice of technology is just the beginning. The choice of content is equally important. Unlike traditional library and archives collection development strategies that result in one decision to acquire and a separate decision to preserve many years later, selection in the digital world is an ongoing process of assessment and evaluation. Few digital collections will warrant the costs involved in maintaining access over time without factoring in the value and the character of ongoing use.[15]

- **Quality. Are you willing to pay for it and will our readers?**
  In the past five years, librarians and archivists have made significant progress in defining their expectations for the quality of digital image products built from a variety of source materials. Quality is value that we add to our digital image products. Although important issues of quality measurement remain, the barriers to achieving quality do not appear to reside in the technology itself. Rather, the cost of creating and maintaining digital objects remains high; uncertainties persist about whether the overall costs of creating a product are declining.

- **Preservation. Is any digital program NOT about preservation?**
  Costs are high; so is the risk of loss. Preservation in the digital world is knowing how to adapt preservation concepts to manage risk in the midst of rapid technological change.

Digital imaging technology is more than another reformatting option. Imaging involves transforming the very concept of format, rather than creating an accurate picture of a book, document, photograph, or map on a different medium. Just as the invention of the vacuum tube created an entirely new form of mass communication—radio— instead of simply making point-to-point messaging possible without wires, digital imaging technologies create an entirely new form of information.

NOTES

[1] This leaflet is based upon a presentation at the School for Scanning, an ongoing sequence of conferences developed by the Northeast Document Conservation Center. The author wishes to thank Steve Dalton for his continuing support and encouragement.

[2] Jim Taylor and Watts Wacker, *The 500 Year Delta: What Happens After What Comes Next* (New York: Harper Business, 1997).

[3] S.H. Steinberg, *Five Hundred Years of Printing*, new ed., rev. by John Trevitt (London: British Library, 1996).

[4] Geofroy Tory, *Champ Fleury*, Translated into English and annotated by George B. Ives (New York: The Grolier Club, 1927).

[5] George B. Dyson, *Darwin Among the Machines: The Evolution of Global Intelligence*, (Reading, MA: Addison-Wesley, 1997), 37.

[6] Margaret Hedstrom, "Understanding Electronic Incunabula: A Framework for Research on Electronic Records," in *American Archivist* 54 (Summer 1991): 334-54.

[7] *From Semaphore to Satellite* (Geneva: International Telecommunication Union, 1965), 13-14.

[8] Michael K. Buckland, "Information as Thing," in J*ournal of the American Society for Information Science* 42 (June 1991): 351-60.

[9] An excellent glossary is included in: Howard Besser and Jennifer Trant, *Introduction to Imaging: Issues in Constructing an Image Database* (Santa Monica: Getty Art History Information Program, 1995), http://www.gii.getty.edu/intro_imaging/.

[10] Don R. Williams, "Data Conversion: A Tutorial on Electronic Document Imaging," in *Preserving Digital Information: Report of the Task Force on Archiving of Digital Information* (Washington, D.C.: Commission on Preservation and Access and Research Libraries Group, May 1996), 59-79.

[11] James M. Reilly and Franziska A. Frey, *Recommendations for the Evaluation of Digital Images Produced from Photographic, Microphotographic, and Various Paper Formats*, Report to the Library of Congress National Digital Library Project. Rochester, NY: Image Permanence Institute, May 1996 20. http://memory.loc.gov/ammem/ipirpt.html

[12] Michael Ester, *Digital Image Collections: Issues and Practice* (Washington, D.C.: Commission on Preservation and Access, December 1996).

[13] For three examples of this trend, see: Franziska Frey, "Digital Imaging for Photographic Collections: Foundations for Technical Standards," in RLG *DigiNews* 1 (December 15, 1997), http://www.rlg.org/preserv/diginews/diginews3.html#com/; Picture Elements, Inc. [Louis Sharpe], *Guidelines for Electronic Preservation of Visual Materials*, Part 1, 2 March 1995; Kenney, Anne R. and Stephen Chapman, *Digital Imaging for Libraries and Archives* (Ithaca: Cornell University Library, 1996), 45-46.

[14] Paul Conway, *Preservation in the Digital World* (Washington, D.C.: Commission on Preservation and Access, March 1996), http://www.clir.org/cpa/reports/conway2/.

[15] Don Waters and John Garrett, *Preserving Digital Information: Report of the Task Force on Archiving of Digital Information* (Washington, D.C.: Commission on Preservation and Access and Research Libraries Group, 1996), http://www.rlg.org/ArchTF/.

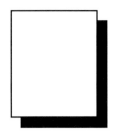

Northeast Document
Conservation Center
100 Brickstone Square
Andover, MA 01810-1494
www.nedcc.org
Tel: (978) 470-1010
Fax: (978) 475-6021

THE RELEVANCE OF
PRESERVATION IN A DIGITAL WORLD

**by Paul Conway
Head, Preservation Department
Yale University Library**

Abstract

Preservation remains an ill-defined concept when applied to the development of digital library projects and collections. This technical leaflet suggests a framework for understanding preservation in the digital context by creating a bridge from the five core principles of traditional preservation practice: longevity, choice, quality, integrity, and access. The essay describes how the purposes that preservation serves have broadened. It describes the transformation of preservation principles and outlines a perspective that reaffirms the relevance of preservation in the digital world. The leaflet is derived from two sources: the author's report *Preservation in the Digital World* and his presentations at a sequence of NEDCC's *School for Scanning* from 1996 to 1999. [1]

Introduction

Preservation is not just for the world of paper. We know that digital imaging technology, in and of itself, provides no easy answers to the preservation question. Indeed, simply defining what preservation means in the digital imaging environment is a challenge; responding to the insight that such a definition might provide is harder still. [2] The digital world poses significant challenges to, but does not eliminate the need for responsible, effective preservation activity.

When a library, archives, historical society, museum, or any other cultural institution with a preservation mandate stops experimenting with digital technology and decides to use it to improve services or transform operations, then that institution has embarked down the preservation path. Digital imaging technologies entail a tremendous investment of resources in an environment of flat budgets. The risk of loss is high—far higher than in most other preservation functions. The nearly constant swirl of product development that fuels our perceptions of change raises the stakes yet higher. Understanding where the risk lies and making an institutional commitment to lessen it is precisely what preservation in a digital world is all about.

Transforming the Purpose of Preservation

The term "preservation" is an umbrella under which most librarians and archivists cluster all of the policies and options for action, including conservation treatments. It has long been the responsibility of librarians and archivists—and the clerks and scribes who went before them—to assemble and organize documentation of human activity in places where it can be protected and used. The ethic of preservation as coordinated and conscious action to increase the likelihood that evidence about how we live, how we think, and what we have accomplished will survive, however, is a recent phenomenon. Traditional preservation as "responsible custody" is successful when the value of the evidence exceeds the cost of keeping it, when this evidence has a physical form, and when the roles of evidence creators, evidence keepers, and evidence users are mutually reinforcing.

The essence of preservation management is resource allocation. People, money, and materials must be acquired, organized, and put to work to prevent deterioration or renew the usability of selected groups of materials. Preservation is concerned largely with the evidence embedded in a nearly endless variety of forms and formats. Things are preserved so that they can be used for all kinds of purposes, scholarly and otherwise. People with the responsibility to do so have determined that some small portion of the vast sea of information, structured as collections of documents, books, collections, and other "things," has research value as evidence well beyond the time and the intentions of those who created or published it.[3] This distinction between the value of the content (usually text and illustration) and the value of the evidence embedded in the object is at the heart of a decision-making process that is itself central to effective management of traditional and digital library materials.

It is possible to distinguish among three distinct but not mutually exclusive preservation applications of digital technologies, defined in part by the possible purposes that the product may serve for end users.[4]

- *Protect Originals.* The most common application of digital technologies in an archive or library is to create digital copies of sufficient quality that they can be used for ready reference in lieu of casual browsing through the original sources. Preservation goals are met because the original documents can be protected by limiting access to them. Examples include image reference files of photograph, clipping, or vertical files which permit the identification of individual items requiring closer study. The original order of the collection, or a book, is "frozen" much like microfilm sets images in a linear array. This preservation use of the technology has become a compelling force motivating archives and libraries to experiment with hardware and software capabilities.

- *Represent Originals.* A digital system could be built that represents the information content of the original sources in such detail that the system can be used to fulfil most, if not all, of the research and learning potential of the original documents. High-resolution systems that strive for comprehensive and complete content and seek to obtain "full information capture" based on emerging standards and best practices, fit this definition. Systems of this intermediate level of quality open new avenues of research and use and have the capability to have a transformative effect on the service missions of those who create the products.

- *Transcend Originals.* In a very small number of applications, digital imaging promises to generate a product that can be used for purposes that are impossible to achieve with the original sources. This category includes imaging that uses special lighting to draw out details obscured by aging, use, and environmental damage; imaging that makes use of specialized photographic intermediates; or imaging of such high resolution that the study of artifactual characteristics is possible.

Each of these applications places separate, but increasingly rigorous, demands on digital technologies. In each case, the use of an intermediate film or paper copy to facilitate the scanning process may or may not be necessary or advisable. Finally, the disposition of original sources (including undertaking preservation treatments before or after conversion) is a matter quite separate from the decision to undertake digital conversion. Ultimately, the purpose of the digital image product is driven by the uses to which it will be put, while preservation of original source documents should be determined by the preservation needs of the original sources.

Leadership in Transforming Preservation

Preservation in the digital world is one of the central leadership issues of our day. Some librarians and archivists seem to think that leadership on technological issues is a matter of establishing control through the application of standards and procedural guidelines. Others have argued that the rapid pace of technological change and the sheer complexity of the technology render librarians and archivists helpless in influencing the technological developments. Both perspectives are misleading. Those who hope to exercise control over the use of digital imaging technology in libraries and archives assume that moral persuasion can prevail in the absence of a significant market share. Those who prefer to "wait and see" how digital imaging technology shakes out, before making the administrative commitments necessary to ensure long-term preservation, shirk their responsibility to define the terms of the debate.

Preservation in the digital world must be the shared goal that leaders and followers elicit together. It is the responsibility of many people in many institutions fulfilling many roles. An understanding of the impact of this role differentiation on digital preservation action is crucial to identifying which of the many facets of digital technology we can control, which trends we may only influence, and which aspects we must relinquish any vain expectation for either control or influence.

In the past two decades, a consensus has emerged within a community of practitioners about a set of fundamental preservation principles that should govern the management of available resources in a mature preservation program. The fundamental principles of preservation in the digital world are the same as those of the analog world and, in essence, define the priorities for extending the useful life of information resources. These fundamental concepts are longevity, choice, quality, integrity, and access.

The Transformation of Longevity

The central concern in traditional preservation practice is the media upon which information is stored. The top priority is extending the life of paper, film, and magnetic tape by stabilizing their structures and limiting the ability of internal and external factors to cause deterioration. The focus on *external* factors led to specifications for proper environmental controls, care and handling guidelines, and disaster recovery procedures. Progress on efforts to control or mitigate the *internal* factors of deterioration has resulted in alkaline paper standards, archival quality microfilm, mass deacidification, and more rugged magnetic media. And yet, now that archivists and librarians have defined the issues surrounding the life expectancy of media, the very concept of longevity itself is fading as a meaningful intellectual construct for preservation.

Digital preservation has little concern for the longevity of optical disks and newer, more fragile storage media. The viability of digital image files is much more dependent on the life expectancy of the access system — a chain only as strong as its weakest component. Today's optical media most likely will far outlast the capability of systems to retrieve and interpret the data stored on them. Since we can never know for certain when a system cannot be maintained or supported by a vendor, libraries must be prepared to migrate valuable image data, indexes, and software to future generations of the technology.

Librarians can exercise control over the longevity of digital image data through the careful selection, handling, and storage of rugged, well-tested storage media. They can influence the life expectancy of the information by making sure that local budgetary commitments are made consistently at an appropriate level. Ultimately, we have no control over the evolution of the imaging marketplace, especially corporate research and development activities that have a tremendous impact on the life expectancy of the digital files we are creating today.

The Transformation of Choice

Preservation adds value through selection. Selection is choice and choice involves defining value, recognizing it in something, and then deciding to address its preservation needs in the way most appropriate to that value. Over decades the act of preservation has evolved from saving material from oblivion and assembling it in secure buildings to more sophisticated condition and value assessments on the already-collected. Preservation selection in libraries has largely been dictated by the need to stretch limited resources in as wise a fashion as possible, resulting in the dictum that "no item shall be preserved twice." The net result is a growing "virtual" special collection of items preserved with a variety of techniques, most notably by reformatting on microfilm. Selection is perhaps the most difficult of undertakings precisely because it is static and conceived by practitioners as either completely divorced from present use or completely driven by demand.

Selection in the digital world is not a choice made "once and for all" near the end of an item's life cycle, but rather is an ongoing process intimately connected to the active use of the digital files. The value judgments applied when making a decision to convert documents from paper or film to digital images are valid only within the context of the original system. It is a rare collection of digital files, indeed, that can justify the cost of a comprehensive migration strategy. Without factoring in the larger intellectual context of related digital files stored elsewhere and their combined uses for teaching and learning, preservation decision making cannot take place.

Even while recognizing that selection decisions cannot be made in a vacuum, librarians and archivists CAN choose which books, articles, photographs, film, and other materials are converted from paper or film into digital image form. Influence over the continuing value of digital image files is largely vested in the right to decide, in close coordination with the many parties interested in the decision, when it is time to migrate image data to future storage and access systems and when a digital file has outlived its usefulness to the institution charged with preserving it. What we cannot control is the impact of these ongoing value judgments on the abilities of our patrons to find and use information in digital form.

The Transformation of Quality

Maximizing the quality of all work performed is such an important maxim in the preservation field that few people state this fundamental principle directly. Instead, the preservation literature dictates high quality outcomes by specifying standards for treatment options, reformatting processes, and preventive measures. The commitment to quality standards—do it once, do it right—permeates all preservation activity, including library binding standards, archival microfilm creation guidelines, conservation treatment procedures, the choice of supplies and materials, and a low tolerance for error. The evolution of preservation microfilming as a central strategy for the bulk of brittle library materials has placed the quality of the medium and the quality of the visual image on an equal plane. In the pursuit of quality microfilm, compromise on visual truth and archival stability is dictated only by the characteristics of the item chosen for preservation.

Quality in the digital world is conditioned significantly by the limitations of capture-and-display technology. Digital conversion places less emphasis on obtaining a faithful reproduction in favor of finding the best representation of the original in digital form. Mechanisms and techniques for judging quality of digital reproductions are different and more sophisticated than those for assessing microfilm or photocopy reproductions.[5] Additionally, the primary goal of preservation quality is to capture as much intellectual and visual content as is technically possible and then present that content to readers in ways most appropriate to their needs.

The image market has transformed the principle of maintaining the highest possible quality over time to one of finding the minimal level of quality acceptable to today's system users. We must reclaim image quality as the heart and soul of digital preservation. This means maximizing the amount of data captured in the digital scanning process, documenting image enhancement techniques, and specifying file compression routines that do not result in the loss of data during telecommunication. We can control standards of digital quality, just as we have done for microfilm. We can only influence the development of standards for data compression, communication, display, and output. Out of our hands are improvements in the technical capabilities of image conversion hardware and software. We risk hastening obsolescence by prematurely setting overly rigorous equipment specifications.

The Transformation of Integrity

The concept of integrity has two dimensions in the traditional preservation context—physical and intellectual—both of which concern the nature of the evidence. Physical integrity largely concerns the item as artifact and plays out most directly in the conservation studio, where skilled bench staff use water-soluble glues, age-old hand-binding techniques, and high quality materials to protect historical evidence of use, past conservation treatments, and intended or unintended changes to the structure of the item. The preservation of intellectual integrity is also based upon concern for evidence of a different sort. The authenticity, or truthfulness, of the information content of an item, maintained through documentation of both provenance—the chain of ownership—and treatment, where appropriate, is at the heart of intellectual integrity. Beyond the history of an item is concern for protecting and documenting the relationships among items in a collection. In traditional preservation practice, the concepts of quality and integrity reinforce each other.

In the digital world, a commitment to maintaining the physical integrity of a digital image file has far less to do with the media upon which the data are stored than with the loss of information when a file is created originally and then compressed mathematically or sent across a network. In the domain of intellectual integrity, structural indexes and data descriptions traditionally published with an item as tables of contents or prepared as discrete finding aids or bibliographic records must be inextricably linked and preserved along with the digital image files themselves. Preserving intellectual integrity also involves authentication procedures, like audit trails, to make sure files are not altered intentionally or accidentally.[6] Ultimately, the digital world transforms traditional preservation principles from guaranteeing the physical integrity of the object to specifying the creation of the object whose intellectual integrity is its primary characteristic.

Librarians and archivists can control the integrity of digital image files by authenticating access procedures and documenting successive modifications to a given digital record. We can also create and maintain structural indexes and bibliographic linkages within well developed and well understood database standards. We also have a role to play in influencing the development of metadata interchange standards—including the tools and techniques that will allow structured, documented, and standardized information about data files and databases to be shared across platforms, systems, and international boundaries. It is vain to think, however, that librarians and archivists are anything but bystanders observing the rapid development of network protocols, bandwidth, or data security techniques

The Transformation of Access

In spite of decades of claims to the contrary, increased access is largely a coincidental byproduct of traditional preservation practice, not its central focus. Indeed, the preservation and access responsibilities of an archive or library are more often in constant tension. "While preservation is a primary goal or responsibility, an equally compelling mandate—access and use—sets up a classic conflict that must be arbitrated by the custodians and caretakers of archival records," states the fundamental textbook in the field.[7] The mechanism for ensuring access to a preserved item or collection is a bibliographic record located in local online catalogs or national bibliographic databases. In traditional preservation, access mechanisms, such as bibliographic records and archival finding aids, simply provide a notice of availability and are not an integral part of the object.

In the fifty years that preservation has been emerging as a professional speciality in libraries and archives, the intimate relationship between the concepts of preservation and access has undergone a sequence of transformations that mirror the changes in the technological environment in which cultural institutions have functioned. In the digital world, access is transformed from a convenient byproduct of the preservation process to its central motif.

Control over the access requirements of digital preservation, especially, the capability to migrate digital image files to future generations of the technology, can be exercised in part through prudent purchases of only non-proprietary hardware and software components. In the present environment, true "plug-and-play" components are becoming more widely available and our (limited) checkbooks provide the only incentive we can provide to vendors to adopt open system architectures or at least provide better documentation on the inner workings of their systems. Additionally, librarians and archivists can influence vendors and manufacturers to provide new equipment that is "backwardly compatible" with existing systems. This capability assists image file system migration in the same way that today's word processing software allows access to documents created with earlier versions. Much as we might wish otherwise, the life expectancy of a given digital image system and the requirement to abandon that system are profoundly important matters over which we have little or no control. Perversely, it seems, the commitment of a vendor to support and maintain an old system is inversely related to that vendor's ability to market a new system.

The Transformation of Preservation AND Access

- *Preservation OR Access:* In the early years of modern archival agencies—prior to World War II—preservation simply meant collecting. The sheer act of pulling a collection of manuscripts from a barn, a basement, or a parking garage and placing it intact in a dry building with locks on the door fulfilled the fundamental preservation mandate of the institution. In this regard preservation and access are mutually exclusive activities. Use exposes a collection to risk of theft, damage, or misuse of either content or object. The safest way to ensure that a book lasts for a long time is to lock it up or make a copy for use.

- *Preservation AND Access:* Modern preservation management strategies posit that preservation and access are mutually reinforcing ideas. Preservation action is taken on an item so that it may be used. In this view, creating a preservation copy on microfilm of a deteriorated book without making it possible to find the film is a waste of money. In the world of preservation AND access, however, it is theoretically possible to fulfill a preservation need without solving access problems. Conversely, access to scholarly materials can be guaranteed for a very long period, indeed, without taking any concrete preservation action on them.

- *Preservation IS Access:* Librarians and archivists concerned about the preservation of electronic records sometimes view the two concepts as interchangeable nouns. The act of preserving makes access possible. Equating preservation with access, however, implies that preservation is defined by availability, when indeed this construct may be getting it backwards. Preservation is no more access than access is preservation. Simply re-focusing the preservation issue on access oversimplifies the preservation issues by suggesting that access is the engine of preservation without addressing the nature of the "thing" being preserved.

- *Preservation OF Access:* In the digital world, preservation is the action and access is the thing—the act of preserving access. A more accurate construct simply states "preserve access." When transformed in this way, a whole new series of complexities arises. Preserve access to WHAT? The answer suggested in this report is a high quality, high value, well-protected, and fully integrated version of an original document. The content, structure, and integrity of the information object assume center stage—and the ability of a machine to transport and display this information object becomes an assumed end result of the preservation action rather than its primary goal.

A New Mandate for Digital Technology

It is impossible to come to terms with the responsibilities inherent in digital preservation without distinguishing between "acquiring" digital imaging technology to solve a particular problem and "adopting" it as an information management option. Acquiring an imaging system to enhance access to library and archive materials is now almost as simple as choosing the combination of off-the-shelf scanners, computers, and monitors that meets immediate specifications. Hundreds of libraries and archives have already invested in or are planning to purchase digital image conversion systems and experiment with their capabilities. Innumerable pilot projects demonstrate how much more challenging it is to digitize scholarly resources than the modern office correspondence and case files that drove the technology a decade ago. In time, most of these small-scale, stand-alone applications will fade away quietly—and the initial investment will be lost—as the costs of maintaining these systems become apparent, as vendors go out of business, and as patrons become more accustomed to remote-access image databases and the latest bells and whistles.

The process of converting library materials to an electronic form—a process which in many aspects is similar to the one used to create preservation microfilm—is distinct from any particular medium upon which the images may be stored at a particular point in time. This distinction allows for a continuing commitment to creating and maintaining digitized information while entertaining the possibility that other, more advanced storage media may render optical media obsolete.

Administrators who have responsibility for selecting systems for converting materials with long-term value also bear responsibility for providing long-term access. This commitment is a continuing one — decisions about digital preservation cannot be deferred in the hope that technological solutions will emerge like a Medieval knight in shining armor. An appraisal of the present value of books, manuscript collections, or a series of photographs in their original format is the necessary point of departure for judging the preservation of the digital image version. The mere potential of increased access to a digitized collection does not add value to an underused collection. Similarly, the powerful capabilities of a relational index cannot compensate for a collection of documents whose structure, relationships, and intellectual content are poorly understood. Random access is not a magic potion for effective collection management.

Conclusion: The Preservation Uses of Digital Technology

If libraries, archives, and museums expect to adopt digital imaging technology for purposes of transforming the way they serve their patrons and each other, then they must move beyond the experimental stage. Digital image conversion, in an operational environment, requires a deep and long-standing institutional commitment to preservation, the full integration of the technology into information management procedures and processes, and significant leadership in developing appropriate definitions and standards for digital preservation.

In the past three years, significant progress has been made to define the terms and outline a research agenda for preserving digital information that was either "born digital" or transformed to digital from traditional sources. "Digital preservation refers to the various methods of keeping digital materials alive into the future," according to a recent report from the Council on Library and Information Resources.[8] Digital preservation typically centers on the choice of interim storage media, the life expectancy of a digital imaging system, and the expectation of migrating the digital files to future systems while maintaining full functionality and the integrity of the original digital system. PBS recently aired the film, "Into the Future," which graphically portrayed the problem of digital information and speculated on the consequences of inaction, all the while offering precious few ideas of what to do about the dilemma.

It may be premature for most of us to worry about preserving digital objects until we have figured out how to make digital products that are worth preserving. Digital imaging technologies create an entirely new form of information. Digital imaging technology is not simply another reformatting option in the preservation tool kit. Digital imaging involves transforming the very concept of format, not simply creating a faithful reproduction of a book, document, photograph, or map on a different medium. The power of digital enhancement, the possibilities for structured indexes, and the mathematics of compression and communication together alter the concept of preservation in the digital world. These transformations, along with the new possibilities they place on us, in turn, as information professionals, force us in turn to transform our library and archival services and programs.

NOTES

[1] Paul Conway, *Preservation in the Digital World* (Washington, D.C.: Commission on Preservation and Access, 1996), http://www.clir.org/cpa/reports/conway2/.

[2] Donald Waters and John Garrett, *Preserving Digital Information: Report of the Task Force on Archiving Digital Information* (Washington, D.C.: Commission on Preservation and Access and Research Libraries Group, 1996).

[3] Michael K. Buckland, "Information as Thing," in *Journal of the American Society for Information Science* 42 (June 1991): 351-60.

[4] For three examples of this trend, see: Franziska Frey, "Digital Imaging for Photographic Collections: Foundations for Technical Standard," in RLG *DigiNews* 1 (December 15, 1997), http://www.rlg.org/preserv/diginews/diginews3.html#com/; Picture Elements, Inc. [Louis Sharpe], in *Guidelines for Electronic Preservation of Visual Materials, Part 1*, (2 March 1995); Anne R. Kenney and Stephen Chapman, in *Digital Imaging for Libraries and Archives* (Ithaca: Cornell University Library, 1996), 45-46.

[5] Anne R. Kenney and Stephen Chapman, *Digital Resolution Requirements for Replacing Text-Based Material: Methods for Benchmarking Image Quality* (Washington, D.C.: Commission on Preservation and Access, 1995).

[6] Clifford A. Lynch, "The Integrity of Digital Information: Mechanics and Definitional Issues," in *Journal of the American Society for Information Science* 45 (December 1994): 737-44.

[7] Mary Lynn Ritzenthaler, *Preserving Archives and Manuscripts* (Chicago: Society of American Archivists, 1993), 1.

[8] Donald J. Waters, "Digital Preservation?" in *CLIR Issues* (November/December 1998): 1, http://www.clir.org/pubs/issues/issues.html.

Selected Readings

Besser, Howard and Jennifer Trant. *Introduction to Imaging: Issues in Constructing an Image Database.* Santa Monica: Getty Art History Information Program, 1995. http://www.gii.getty.edu/intro_imaging/

Coleman, James and Don Willis. *SGML as a Framework for Digital Preservation and Access.* Washington, D.C.: Commission on Preservation and Access, 1997.

Conway, Paul. "Selecting Microfilm for Digital Preservation." *Library Resources & Technical Services* 40 (January 1996): 67-77.

Conway, Paul. *Preservation in the Digital World.* Washington, D.C.: Commission on Preservation and Access, March 1996. http://www.clir.org/cpa/reports/conway2/

Digital Imaging Technology for Preservation. Proceedings from an RLG Symposium Held March 17 and 18, 1994. Edited by Nancy E. Elkington. Mountain View, CA: Research Libraries Group, 1994.

Dollar, Charles M. *Archival Theory and Information Technologies: The Impact of Information Technologies on Archival Principles and Methods.* Macerata: University of Macerata Press, 1992.

Ester, Michael. *Digital Image Collections: Issues and Practice.* Washington, D.C.: Commission on Preservation and Access, 1996.

Fox, Edward A., et al. "Digital Libraries: Introduction," *Communications of the ACM* 38 (April 1995): 23-24.

Frey, Franziska. "Digital Imaging for Photographic Collections: Foundations for Technical Standards." *RLG DigiNews* 1 (3), December 15, 1997. http://www.rlg.org/preserv/diginews/diginews3.html#com

Gertz, Janet. *Oversize Color Images Project, 1994-1995: Final Report of Phase I.* Washington, D.C.: Commission on Preservation and Access, 1995.

Graham, Peter S. "Requirements for the Digital Research Library." *College & Research Libraries* 56 (July 1995): 331-39.

Hazen, Dan, Jeffrey Horrell, Jan Merrill-Oldham. *Selecting Research Collections for Digitization.* Washington, D.C.: Council on Library and Information Resources, 1998. http://www.clir.org/pubs/reports/hazen/pub74.html

Kenney, Anne R. and Stephen Chapman. Digital Resolution Requirements for Replacing Text-Based Material: Methods for Benchmarking Image Quality. Washington, D.C.: Commission on Preservation and Access, 1995.

Kenney, Anne R. and Stephen Chapman. *Digital Imaging for Libraries and Archives.* Ithaca, NY: Dept. of Preservation and Conservation, Cornell University Library, 1996.

Levy, David M. and Catherine C. Marshall. "Going Digital: A Look at Assumptions Underlying Digital Libraries." *Communications of the ACM* 38 (April 1995): 77-84.

Lynch, Clifford. "The Integrity of Digital Information: Mechanics and Definitional Issues." *Journal of the American Society for Information Science* 45 (December 1994): 737-44.

McClung, Patricia A. *Digital Collections Inventory Report.* Washington, D.C.: Commission on Preservation and Access, February 1996.

Mohlhenrich, Janice. *Preservation of Electronic Formats: Electronic Formats for Preservation.* Fort Atkinson, Wisc.: Highsmith, 1993.

Ostrow, Stephen E. *Digitizing Historical Pictorial Collections for the Internet.* Washington, D.C.: Council on Library and Information Resources, 1998. http://www.clir.org/pubs/reports/ostrow/pub71.html

Reilly, James M. and Franziska A. Frey. *Recommendations for the Evaluation of Digital Images Produced from Photographic, Microphotographic, and Various Paper Formats. Report* to the Library of Congress National Digital Library Project. Rochester, NY: Image Permanance Institute, May 1996. http://memory.loc.gov/ammem/ipirpt.html

Robinson, Peter. *The Digitization of Primary Textual Sources.* Office for Humanities Communication Publication, no. 4. Oxford: Oxford University Computing Services, 1993.

Rothenberg, Jeff. "Ensuring the Longevity of Digital Documents." *Scientific American* 272 (January 1995): 42-47.

Van Bogart, John W. *Magnetic Tape Storage and Handling: A Guide for Libraries and Archives.* Washington, D.C.: Commission on Preservation and Access, 1995.

Waters, Donald and John Garrett. *Preserving Digital Information: Report of the Task Force on Archiving of Digital Information.* Washington, D.C.: Research Libraries Group and Commission on Preservation and Access, May 1996. http://www.rlg.org/ArchTF/

CONSERVATION PROCEDURES

Northeast Document
Conservation Center
100 Brickstone Square
Andover, MA 01810-1494
www.nedcc.org
Tel: (978) 470-1010
Fax: (978) 475-6021

GUIDELINES FOR LIBRARY BINDING

by Sherelyn Ogden
Head of Conservation
Minnesota Historical Society

Because books differ in value and in the way they are used, it is important to select an appropriate type of rebinding when they become damaged. Library binding, one type of rebinding, is probably chosen for more books than any other type. Library binding is a good choice where economy and durability are the objectives. It is appropriate for books that are significant primarily for the information they contain and that do not have value as objects. Books that have artifactual or associational significance in addition to informational value should be sent to a professional conservator for treatment.

The goals of library binding have changed over the years. In the past, library binders strove to produce sturdy, economical, serviceable bindings. As librarians and users began to take a fresh look at the physical quality of library materials, however, and became concerned with the openability of a book and photocopying problems associated with oversewing, the goals of library binding broadened. In 1984 Jan Merrill-Oldham identified the following desirable characteristics of a library binding: 1) The binding should be as conservative as possible, altering the text block minimally; 2) the binding should be as non-damaging to the text block as possible and should not shorten its useful life; 3) the bound volume should open easily to a 180° position to facilitate non-damaging photocopying; and 4) the bound volume should stay open when resting face up on a flat surface so the reader has both hands free and can take notes easily.[1] Today good openability and minimal intervention, as well as durability and low cost, are the primary goals of library binding.

The result of this broadening of goals was the development of a revised edition of the *Library Binding Institute Standard for Library Binding*. This eighth edition of the *Standard* includes changes in technical and materials specifications that reflect a heightened awareness of the importance of using archival-quality materials, and of legitimizing and perfecting a variety of binding methods. An updated version of this standard is in the process of being developed jointly by the National Information Standards Organization and the Library Binding Institute. It is not expected to differ significantly from the eighth edition of the *Standard*. The eighth edition is based on the assumption that the reader is knowledgeable of the materials, processes, machinery, and terminology used in library binding and is able to select the most appropriate option out of several that may be available.[2] Its audience is mainly library binders. In response to the librarian's need for explanation, discussion, and historical context, *A Guide to the Library Binding Institute Standard for Library Binding* was prepared. This Guide is intended to enable readers to use the Standard to its fullest advantage.[3] Both the *Standard* and the *Guide* should be followed when contracting for library binding. Contracts with library binders should specify methods and materials appropriate for the range of materials in a library's collections. They should be as detailed as necessary. Two sample contracts are reproduced in the resource guide, *Managing a Library Binding Program*.[4]

Even though the *Standard* and *Guide* should be consulted no matter how limited the amount of binding being contracted, sometimes this is not possible. In very small institutions where the amount of binding being done is minimal, staff time is severely restricted, and staff members' knowledge of binding is limited. Such institutions include small museums, historical societies, and historic sites.

The following guidelines were drawn up with the needs of these institutions in mind. They are intended to assist library staff members in specifying binding so that basic standards of quality will be met and inadvertent damage avoided. It is important to remember that there are exceptions to every rule and that there will be books for which these guidelines are not appropriate.

These guidelines may in some cases cause the cost of rebinding to be higher than usual because of the extra time, handling, and special attention that they necessitate. This higher price, however, is usually not prohibitive for institutions doing a small amount of rebinding.

When questioned informally, several library binders indicated that their firms would take measures such as these if requested to do so. You may need to search for a binder who is interested in this type of work. In selecting a binder, choose one who is certified by the Library Binding Institute. That way you will be sure the binder is familiar with these procedures as well as with current trends and new techniques.

- The binder should not trim the edges of the book unless they are damaged or pages are uncut. The preservation of margins is important, and a no-trim policy insures that folded plates as well as images and text that bleed to the edges of pages will not be trimmed.

- Original signatures and sewing should be preserved in all fragile and special volumes. Ask that these volumes be "recased" whenever possible. Where original sewing is badly deteriorated in an important book, ask to have the book resewn through the folds using the original sewing stations if possible. This is an expensive option. Another is to have a box made for the book instead. Books that cannot be recased or resewn through the folds should almost always be double-fan adhesive bound rather than oversewn. The binder may be given the authority to decide when oversewing is necessary (usually because of extreme thickness or heaviness of a text block). The technique, however, should be used only very rarely. If it is used more often than that, seek advice from a consultant who can evaluate the binder's decisions.

- For paper repairs, a paper-based pressure-sensitive tape with acrylic adhesive should be used rather than a household-type plastic-based tape. Although use of Japanese paper and starch paste repairs is a standard conservation procedure, the need for such repairs, which require a high degree of skill, signals the need for conservation binding rather than library binding. Ask the binder what materials will be used in repair work and, if you are unsure of the quality, ask a conservator if these materials are appropriate. Remember that repair tape is not suitable for books that have artifactual or associational significance, but only for books valuable solely for the information they contain.

- Materials that are durable and chemically stable should be used throughout the binding process. Of greatest concern are the endpapers, which come in direct contact with the first and last pages of the book. Endpapers should be alkaline and meet ANSI Standard Z-39.48-1992. Ask the binder to return old labels, bookplates, and anything else that may be of special interest.

- Urge the binder to call you whenever questions arise regarding materials or procedures.

Each bound volume returned by the library binder should be inspected to insure that the quality of the work is acceptable and specifications have been met. This is of critical importance in maintaining a high quality product. Guidelines for inspecting bound volumes appear in *A Guide to the Library Binding Institute Standard for Library Binding.*

NOTES

[1] Jan Merrill-Oldham, "Binding for Research Libraries," *The New Library Scene* (August 1984): 1, 4-6.

[2] Paul A. Parisi and Jan Merrill-Oldham, eds., *Library Binding Institute Standard for Library Binding,* 8th ed. (Rochester, NY: Library Binding Institute, 1986). Foreword.

[3] Jan Merrill-Oldham and Paul Parisi, *Guide to the Library Binding Institute Standard for Library Binding,* (Chicago and London: American Library Association, 1990), vii.

[4] Jan Merrill-Oldham, *Managing a Library Binding Program,* Jutta Reed-Scott, Series ed. (Washington, DC: Association of Research Libraries, Preservation Planning Program, 1993).

Acknowledgements

The author gratefully acknowledges the assistance of Jan Merrill-Oldham, Paul Parisi, and Robert deCandido in the preparation of this technical leaflet.

Northeast Document
Conservation Center
100 Brickstone Square
Andover, MA 01810-1494
www.nedcc.org
Tel: (978) 470-1010
Fax: (978) 475-6021

SURFACE CLEANING OF PAPER

by Sherelyn Ogden
Head of Conservation
Minnesota Historical Society

WHEN TO CLEAN

Although it is neither necessary nor desirable to remove all dirt or discoloration from old papers, some cleaning will often improve the appearance of an artifact. Cleaning can also remove substances that could eventually be detrimental to the paper.

The term *cleaning* refers to a variety of conservation procedures. The simplest of these is surface or dry cleaning, which is done with a soft brush or an erasing compound. If the dirt is superficial, a dry surface treatment may provide all the cleaning that is necessary. Paper may also be cleaned with water. Placing an artifact in a bath is the most common way of cleaning with water, but there are other aqueous methods that do not require immersion. The most complex cleaning procedures involve chemicals. The two principal types use bleaching agents or organic solvents. These methods, especially bleaching, are most appropriate when the appearance of the artifact is of great importance. Surface or dry cleaning can be safely carried out by a novice. If more thorough cleaning is required, it should be done only by a conservator. Surface cleaning should precede wet cleaning and mending. If artifacts are not dry cleaned before washing, surface dirt may become ingrained in the paper. Adhesives used in mending can also set surface dirt in place.

The surface cleaning technique described here may be used on book pages, manuscripts, maps, and other documents. It should not be used on brittle newspapers, bookbindings, book edges, photographs, or intaglio prints (those with raised lines such as engravings, etchings, etc.). Neither should it be used on pastels, pencil, charcoal, watercolors, or other media that are not firmly bound to the paper or that may be lifted or erased by abrasives. Artifacts with hand-applied coloring should not be treated because coloring may smear. Cleaning all such objects should be left to a professional conservator.

SUPPLIES AND EQUIPMENT

Materials needed for dry cleaning are a soft brush (a drafting brush is excellent) and an erasing compound. Different types and commercial brands of erasing compounds are available. These vary in composition and are sold as granules and also as block erasers. Most granules are potentially damaging to paper if not properly removed after cleaning. Some have the additional problem of being too abrasive for especially fragile paper. Block erasers may also leave a damaging residue, so care should be taken to remove all traces of this erasing compound as well. Non-colored vinyl block erasers, such as the Eberhard-Faber Magic Rub

Eraser and the Staedtler Mars Plastic Eraser, are believed to have minimal potential for damage to paper. Many conservators prefer to use these erasers ground into granules, which are now available commercially from conservation suppliers.

HOW TO CLEAN

To start work, clear an area that has a large, clean, smooth surface. Begin the cleaning by gently brushing the surface of the object with a soft brush to remove loose dirt and dust. Use up-and-down strokes and work across the paper. Be careful to avoid enlarging tears by working towards the tears and in the direction of the tear. With books, be sure to brush the dirt out of the gutter.

If, as is usually the case, dirt is well attached to the paper, an erasing compound is more effective than a brush. But use a brush first to remove the loose dirt. Because residues of the erasing compound may be left behind on the paper regardless of how carefully the paper is brushed after cleaning, an erasing compound should be used only when necessary. If the erasing compound does not appear to be removing dirt, do not use it.

Test first in an inconspicuous spot to make certain that no damage to the media will occur. Steady the paper with one hand and test by gently rubbing the granules with a finger over one small area. Once you are certain that the media will not be lifted or erased, begin cleaning. Sprinkle granules over the artifact to be cleaned. Using your fingers, gently rub the granules over the surface of the object moving in small circles to avoid streaking. Start from the middle and work towards the edges. When cleaning near the edges, do not use a circular motion, but rub from the middle towards the edges using a straight movement. This will prevent tearing the edges, which are often fragile. Be careful going over inks that have eaten through or weakened the paper. Avoid areas of color or pencil notations that may be archivally significant.

Granules and loosened dirt produced during the cleaning process should be brushed away frequently. Keep a careful eye on your work at all times to make sure that you are not smearing the medium or producing any tears and that you are not erasing or lifting anything but surface dirt. If the granules appear to have a color other than that of dirt, check to make sure that ink or color is not being lifted from the document.

It is essential that all granules be removed from the artifact following cleaning. Brush both sides of the object thoroughly and give special attention to the gutters of books, where granules may accumulate. Remove treated objects from the work area. It is most important to keep the work area free of the erasing granules produced by cleaning. If granules remain on the working surface and the artifact to be cleaned is placed over them and rubbed, holes may be created in the artifact. Working on large sheets of brown kraft paper may help you to dispose of the granules.

While granules will remove most surface dirt, block erasers may remove even more. It is not necessary, or even desirable, to remove all surface dirt from old papers. Erasers can abrade soft papers and are best used by persons experienced in surface cleaning. If it is necessary to use an abrasive harsher than granules, a block eraser is comparatively safe. Proceed with caution, trying an inconspicuous spot first. Rub gently in a single direction or in small circles. Take care not to create light erased areas, which will contrast with the general surface color. Do not rub erasers over pencil, color, or inks.

Dry cleaning sponges made of vulcanized rubber, which were intended originally for soot removal following a fire, are now being used increasingly for surface cleaing dirt on artifacts. These sponges are reported to leave no damaging residues on paper, nor do they appear to be abrasive. They degrade upon exposure to light and with age, so they need to be stored in an air-tight container and in the dark. As the surface of the eraser becomes dirty with use, it can be sliced off and discarded. The precautions listed above for the use of granules and block erasers should be followed when using sponges as well.

SOURCES OF SUPPLIES

This list is not exhaustive, nor does it constitute an endorsement of the suppliers listed. We suggest that you obtain information from a number of vendors so that you can make comparisons of cost and assess the full range of available products.

A more complete list of suppliers is available from NEDCC. Consult the Technical Leaflets section of NEDCC's website at www.nedcc.org or contact NEDCC for the most up-to-date version in print.

Surface cleaning supplies:

Bookmakers
6001 66th Avenue
Suite 101
Riverdale, MD 20737
Telephone: (301) 459-3384
Fax: (301) 459-7629

Charrette Corporation
31 Olympia Avenue
P.O. Box 4010
Woburn, MA 01888
Toll Free: (800) 626-7889
Telephone: (781) 935-6000
Fax: (617) 935-4387
E-mail: custser@charette.com

Talas
568 Broadway
New York, NY 10012
Telephone: (212) 736-7744
Fax: (212) 219-0735

University Products
517 Main Street
P. O. Box 101
Holyoke, MA 01041
Toll Free: (800) 628-1912
Telephone: (413) 532-3372
Toll Free Fax: (800) 532-9281
Fax: (413) 432-9281
E-mail: info@universityproducts.com
http://www.universityproducts.com

Acknowledgements

The author gratefully acknowledges the contributions made by NEDCC staff over the years in the development of this technical leaflet.

2/99

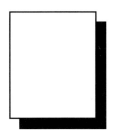

Northeast Document
Conservation Center

100 Brickstone Square
Andover, MA 01810-1494
www.nedcc.org
Tel: (978) 470-1010
Fax: (978) 475-6021

REPAIRING PAPER ARTIFACTS

by Sherelyn Ogden
Head of Conservation
Minnesota Historical Society

The generally accepted method of repairing torn paper or reinforcing weak areas in a sheet uses strips of strong, almost transparent, acid-free paper, adhered with a strong, colorless water-based adhesive that is acid-free and easily reversed. The following materials are recommended for repair of documents, book pages, and other paper objects.

PAPERS

The preferred repair papers are made in Japan from kozo fibers. These papers (often erroneously called rice papers) exist in different weights with names such as *Sekishu, Tengujo, Kizukishi,* and *Usumino.* The fiber content of Japanese papers differs, with some papers containing fibers that are not of conservation quality. To be safe, only papers that contain 100% *kozo, mitsumata,* or *gampi* fibers, or a combination of these, should be used. These Japanese papers are ideal for repairs because they do not discolor or become brittle over time, and they have long, strong, flexible fibers, which produce a lasting repair. The lighter-weight papers are especially well suited to the repair of documents since they are translucent and unobtrusive and will not obscure the text of a document. Most conservators use strips of paper with torn rather than cut edges because a frayed edge makes a less visible, softer repair.

ADHESIVES

Use of a proper adhesive is essential. Any adhesive used for mending paper objects must have the following properties:

Sufficient strength: it should hold the object for an indefinite length of time.

No tendency to discolor: it should not yellow, darken, or stain.

Reversibility: it should allow the repair paper to be easily removed with minimal effort and no damage to the object, even after many years.

Few commercially available adhesives meet all these criteria. Commercial library and wallpaper pastes may lose hold as they age and often contain harmful additives. Rubber cement and animal glues usually darken or stain. Several synthetic adhesives, such as white "glues," are very difficult if not impossible to remove once they have begun to age.

Pressure-sensitive (self-adhering) tapes should be avoided. Most of the adhesives on these tapes cause staining over time and require toxic solvents and technical expertise for removal.

In recent years pressure-sensitive tapes that are advertised as archival have been introduced. These are probably more stable than other similar tapes but because their aging properties are not yet known, their use should be avoided for objects of value. The adhesives on commercial gummed tapes, which require wetting, are less damaging, but most stain in time, and these tapes also should be avoided for objects of value.

Commercial products in general should be avoided even if they are reputed to be safe because commercial products are subject to alteration by the manufacturer. This year's non-staining tape may have an adhesive with a different formula next year.

Starch-Based Paste

For many years conservators have favored homemade starch-based pastes. These are made most often from either rice starch or wheat starch (not flour, but the starch that has been extracted from the flour). There are many recipes for these pastes. One recipe for wheat starch paste follows:

1. Place one part of wheat starch and four parts of distilled water in a saucepan or the top of a very clean double boiler.

2. Mix well and let stand at least 20 minutes.

3. If a double boiler is used, fill the bottom part with a small amount of water making sure that the upper section does not touch the water.

4. Place on medium high heat and cook, stirring constantly with a clean wire whisk.

5. When the paste begins to thicken (this may happen right away), reduce heat and continue stirring.

   Stir for about half an hour; then remove from the stove. The paste should be thick and translucent. As it cooks and thickens, it will become more difficult to stir. To aid instirring, a wooden spoon may be substituted for the wire whisk, but the spoon should be one that has not been used for the preparation of food.

6. When cooked, the paste should be transferred to a clean container for storage. It should be allowed to cool before use. Prior to use the paste should be strained. A Japanese paste strainer works well for this.

Quick Wheat Paste

University Products, a supplier of conservation materials, has published a quick recipe for wheat starch paste.[1] The advantage of this recipe is that small quantities of paste can be easily prepared. If necessary strain the paste prior to use.

Place 1 tablespoon wheat starch in a microwave-safe container, add 5 tablespoons distilled water and place in microwave unit. Microwave on high setting 20 to 30 seconds. Remove paste and stir. Place back in unit and microwave another 20 to 30 seconds. Remove and stir again. Continue this process several times until the paste is stiff and translucent. If larger quantities are made in the microwave oven, increase the cooking time between stirrings. Paste should cool before use.

Diluting and Storing Paste

Different consistencies of paste are required, depending upon the particular mending task at hand. A consistency similar to heavy cream is adequate for most mending. Pastes should be diluted with distilled water to achieve the consistency required.

Starch paste should not be refrigerated; cover and store in a cool, dry place. It will keep for only a week or less. Some conservators recommend adding a preservative. The preservatives used, however, are toxic. It is preferable to make paste in small quantities when it is needed rather than add a preservative and store it for long periods. If paste discolors, grows mold, or develops a sour smell, discard it immediately. Discard it if dark flecks appear in the paste since they may indicate mold or bacterial growth.

Methyl Cellulose

Starch pastes require time to make and thus are not practical if they are to be used only occasionally. A simpler adhesive can be made from methyl cellulose, which comes in powdered form and is sold by viscosity (in general, the higher the viscosity the more stable the methyl cellulose). Mix one rounded tablespoon of methyl cellulose with 1/2 cup of distilled water. Let it stand for several hours before use. It will thicken on standing but can be thinned to the appropriate consistency with water. Methyl cellulose is not as strong as starch paste but should hold adequately if the document is not to be handled extensively or if it is to be encapsulated in polyester film. Methyl cellulose keeps well for several weeks and does not require a preservative.

MENDING PROCEDURES

Tearing Mending Strips

It is desirable for mends to have a soft edge, both to increase the strength of the bond and to prevent paper from breaking where it bends against the edge of the mend. To tear mending strips, draw parallel lines of clean water on the Japanese paper using a small, soft artist's brush, a ruling pen filled with water (instead of ink), or a small cotton swab. Tease the mending paper apart along the wet lines. Make the strips different widths to conform to different tears; 1/4", 1/2", and 3/4" will be most useful. If many mends are to be made, it is helpful to tear a supply of strips in advance.

Applying the Mending Strips

Using a flat piece of glass or plastic as a pasting surface, apply starch paste or methyl cellulose to a strip of Japanese paper with a flat brush (about 1/4" wide). Include the exposed fibers on the edges of the strip. Then lift the strip with tweezers and place it over the tear. If the document is one sided, place the mend on the reverse, with the pasted side against the document. Lighter-weight papers tend to pull apart when wet with paste. For this reason it is easiest to use strips not more than two inches long. For longer tears, several short strips may be used, placed end to end. It will take practice to manipulate the thin, wet repair strips. Once the mending strip is in place, lay a sheet of silicone release paper or nonwoven polyester (Reemay, Hollytex) over the repair. Tap the repair lightly.

Drying the Mended Sheet

If possible, weight the repair while it dries. Weighting insures good adhesion and prevents cockling of the paper. Repairs may be weighted as follows: first place small pieces of release paper or nonwoven polyester over and under the area to be dried. Sandwich these and the mend between pieces of blotter. Lay a piece of glass on top of the sandwich and put a weight (about one pound) on top of the glass. The weights may be small bags of lead shot or pieces of lead covered with cloth. One pound fishing weights from sporting good stores make excellent weights provided they have at least one flat side to prevent rolling. Repairs should be weighted for one hour or longer. A photographer's tacking iron, placed on a low to medium setting, can be used to speed up the drying process. The tacking iron should not be applied directly to the document. Place a piece of nonwoven polyester between the iron and the document. Iron until dry (10 to 20 seconds) then place a weight on top for a few minutes to flatten.

NOTES

[1] Paste prepared in a microwave oven has been used by many paper conservators when only small quantities are required. This particular recipe was developed by Nancy Heugh, Heugh-Edmonson Conservation Services, Kansas City, MO.

SOURCES OF SUPPLIES

This list is not exhaustive, nor does it constitute an endorsement of the suppliers listed. We suggest that you obtain information from a number of vendors so that you can make comparisons of cost and assess the full range of available products.

A more complete list of suppliers is available from NEDCC. Consult the Technical Leaflets section of NEDCC's website at www.nedcc.org or contact NEDCC for the most up-to-date version in print.

Bookmakers
6001 66th Ave., Suite 101
Riverdale, MD 20737
Telephone: (301) 459-3384
Fax: (301) 459-7629
Paste, Reemay, Hollytex, silicone release, methyl cellulose, tacking iron, polyester film, Japanese papers

Gaylord Brothers
P. O. Box 4901
Syracuse, NY 13221-4901
Toll Free: (800) 428-3631 (Help Line)
Toll Free: (800) 448-6160 - ordering
Toll Free Fax: (800) 272-3412
http://www.gaylord.com
Paste, Reemay, silicone release, methyl cellulose, tacking iron, polyester film, Japanese papers

Hiromi Paper International
2525 Michigan Avenue, Unite G9
Santa Monica, CA 90404
Telephone: (310) 998-0098
Fax: (310) 998-0028
Japanese Papers

Paper Nao
4-37-28 Hakusan
Bunkyo-Ku
Tokyo 112-0001
Japan
Telephone: 03-3944-4470
Fax: 03-3944-4699

Japanese papers

Talas
568 Broadway
New York, NY 10012
Telephone: (212) 736-7744
Fax: (212) 219-0735
Paste, paste strainer, Reemay, Hollytex, silicone release, methyl cellulose, tacking iron, polyester film, Japanese papers

University Products
517 Main Street
P. O. Box 101
Holyoke, MA 01041
Toll Free: (800) 628-1912
Telephone: (413) 532-3372
Toll Free Fax: (800) 532-9281
Fax: (413) 432-9281
E-mail: info@universityproducts.com
http://www.universityproducts.com
Paste, Reemay, silicone release, methyl cellulose, tacking iron, polyester film, Japanese papers

Hardware Store, Grocery Store
Double boiler, wooden spoon, whisk, distilled water

Acknowlegements

The author gratefully acknowledges the contributions made by NEDCC staff over the years in the development of this technical leaflet.

Northeast Document
Conservation Center

100 Brickstone Square
Andover, MA 01810-1494
www.nedcc.org
Tel: (978) 470-1010
Fax: (978) 475-6021

RELAXING AND FLATTENING
PAPER BY HUMIDIFICATION

**by Mary Todd Glaser
Director of Paper Conservation
Northeast Document Conservation Center**

Paper objects such as maps, posters, and documents can be difficult to access if they have been rolled or folded for many years. Some papers remain flexible and can be easily and safely unrolled, but others become stiff and brittle as they age. Unrolling or unfolding brittle papers can be hazardous, especially if those papers are torn or damaged. If brittle papers are humidified, they relax and become more flexible, at least temporarily, and unrolling is less risky. Humidification is also helpful for flattening documents that are not brittle but resistant to unfolding or unrolling.

The safest way to relax a paper artifact is to leave it for several hours in an environment where the relative humidity approaches 100%. Although exposing paper to high humidity for prolonged periods is definitely not recommended, a few hours will do no harm if the artifact is allowed to dry soon after it has been unrolled.

The most practical way to humidify paper is to use a simple homemade humidification chamber. Before doing so, however, some preparatory work is necessary. The steps involved in relaxing and flattening paper are: selection of appropriate artifacts, cleaning, humidification, and flattening under pressure.

Selecting Artifacts for Humidification

Each object should be examined for the presence of water-soluble media that may bleed or feather during the humidification process. Such media include most felt-tip pen inks, certain writing inks, and some hand-applied colors. These materials should be tested for water sensitivity by placing a very small water droplet on each color or ink. Although you can test only the media on the outside of the roll, they are usually representative of the media inside. After a few seconds, press each water drop gently with a small white blotter or other absorbent paper. If color comes up on the blotter, the medium is sensitive to water and the object should not be humidified by an inexperienced person.

Other objects best left to professional conservators include:

- works of art or artifacts of great value;

- objects with delicate media such as pastel, charcoal, gouache, or soft pencil;

- coated or varnished papers because these may become sticky, or the varnish may bloom (turn cloudy);

- heavily soiled papers;

- parchment because the drying of this material is complex, and humidification can cause permanent damage.

Although most photographs can be safely humidified, photographic emulsions may soften slightly. Some conservators recommend that nothing touch the emulsion during the drying and flattening phase and that weight be applied only to the edges of the photograph.

Cleaning

Once testing has determined that no water-soluble media are present, make certain the document is as clean as possible. Cleaning is important because moisture can "muddy" surface dirt and cause it to become more firmly attached to the paper. Although overall cleaning may not be possible with rolled materials, the exposed part of the artifact can be swept with a soft brush. If it has been rolled or folded for many years, most of the dirt will be on the outside of the roll. Do not attempt to humidify heavily soiled papers.

Humidification

The safest way to add moisture to paper is to leave it for several hours in a tightly closed space with a source of humidity. There are several ways to make a humidification chamber. The one described below is inexpensive, and the components are easy to find. More elaborate chambers are described in the excellent publication by the National Park Service cited at the end of this leaflet. If you plan to do a great deal of humidification, you should read this article.

Necessary Supplies

- A large plastic trash can with a tight-fitting lid. Get the tallest can available. If the rolled objects are too long to fit the largest can, a taller chamber can be made by using two large cans of the same size. The second can is inverted and placed on top of the first, replacing the lid. Strips of tape or clamps can be used to hold the cans together.

- A tall plastic waste basket to fit inside the trash can.

- Sheets of clean blotting paper.

- Materials for weighting (see below).

Begin the humidification process early in the day. It may take several hours, and objects should not be left in the chamber over night.

Procedure

- Remove the waste basket from the garbage can.

- Pour about two inches of water (preferably hot) into the garbage can.

- Place one or more rolled objects on end inside the waste basket. The more material placed in the chamber, the longer the process will take.

- Set the waste basket inside the trash can as shown in Figure 1. The waste basket will be sitting in water. The water should not be so deep that the basket becomes buoyant. Be careful not to get water on the artifacts or inside the waste basket.

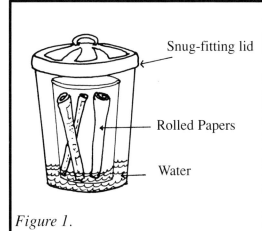

Snug-fitting lid

Rolled Papers

Water

Figure 1.

- Place sheets of blotting paper on edge in the space between the can and the basket. The blotter layer should be as high as the waste basket and should surround it. The water will evaporate and raise the level of humidity in the chamber. Some of the water will wick into the blotting paper, speeding the rate of evaporation. Hot water works faster, as will wetting the blotters before putting them in the can.

- Cover the trash can and wait three to four hours. Check to see if the materials are relaxed enough to unroll. They should be limp, not necessarily damp. If any object is not relaxed, return it to the chamber and wait a while longer.

A Smaller Chamber

Small rolled or folded objects can be humidified in a plastic or stainless steel tray containing alternating layers of damp and dry blotters. Trays for developing photographs come in several sizes and are ideal for this purpose. Place a damp blotter in the bottom of the tray with a dry blotter on top of it and a sheet of plastic window screen on top of the dry blotter. Put the artifact or artifacts on the screen, which will protect them from direct contact with moisture that might wick into the dry blotter. Place another screen over the artifacts, then a dry blotter, and finally, on top, a slightly damp blotter. Cover the tray as tightly as possible. A sheet of glass or rigid acrylic with weights on top should work well. Sheets of spun polyester such as Holly-Tex or Reemay can be used instead of plastic window screening. If available, a sheet of Gore-Tex between the damp blotter and the artifact will allow humidity to come through while keeping out the moisture.

Remember that paper can grow mold in moist conditions. Do not leave objects in a humidity chamber for more than eight hours. Some heavy or non-absorbent papers may not relax in that time. If they are still stiff and resistant, artifacts should not be unrolled or unfolded. Allow them to dry completely in their rolled state, then wrap and store them until a conservator can flatten them.

Fungicides such as thymol have been used by conservators inside humidification chambers to discourage mold. Fungicides, however, are a health hazard. They should not be used by untrained persons or without respiratory protection.

Unrolling and Flattening

Remove the relaxed objects one at a time, place them on dry blotting paper, and unroll them. Handle carefully since damp paper can be fragile. If the object is torn, one must be especially careful. During unrolling, it may be advisable to place weights along the entire outside edge so that tears are not aggravated. Cloth snakes filled with sand or lead shot are one solution. Another is a two-by-four-inch board covered with undyed fabric such as muslin. Pieces of blotting paper inserted between the weights and the object will help protect the moist paper.

- As each artifact is unrolled, place it between two or more sheets of blotting paper. The blotters should be larger than the artifact. Put a weight the same size as the blotters on top of this sandwich. If available, sheets of heavy plate glass work well as weights. Glass 1/2 inch thick is ideal as are 1/2 inch acrylic panels (Plexiglas or Lucite). Other less heavy materials can be used with additional weight on top. These include ordinary glass (with polished or taped edges to prevent injury) or wood composites such as plywood or Masonite. If wood products are used, the panels must be flat and smooth without
any warping.

- Change the blotter sheets after 15 to 20 minutes and leave the object weighted until it is dry. Several artifacts can be dried in a stack with blotters between each.

This process will probably not remove all distortion from the paper. Do not expect the artifacts to turn out perfectly flat. The goal of this treatment is to make them just flat enough for storage purposes.

SUGGESTED FURTHER READING

Alper, Diana. "How to Flatten Folded or Rolled Paper Documents." *Conserve-O-Gram* 13.2. Harpers Ferry, WV: National Park Service, rev. 1993, 4 pp.

Acknowledgements

Northeast Document
Conservation Center
100 Brickstone Square
Andover, MA 01810-1494
www.nedcc.org
Tel: (978) 470-1010
Fax: (978) 475-6021

ENCAPSULATION IN POLYESTER FILM USING DOUBLE-SIDED TAPE

by Sherelyn Ogden
Head of Conservation
Minnesota Historical Society

Encapsulation is a simple technique designed to protect documents from physical wear and tear and from grime. The document is enclosed between two sheets of clear polyester film, the edges of which are sealed with double-sided pressure-sensitive tape. After encapsulation, even a brittle document can usually be safely handled. The process is easily reversed by carefully cutting the film envelope along the edges in the space between the tape and the document.

Polyester film can also be sealed using equipment that forms either an ultrasonic or heat-activated weld. Double-sided tape, however, is the most practical method when a limited amount of encapsulation is done because of the cost of the equipment needed for ultrasonic or heat welding.

Encapsulated documents are held in place in the film envelope by static electricity. The static also helps to hold torn paper together, reducing the need to repair small tears before encapsulation. However, the static can also lift loosely bound media from the paper. For this reason the technique is inappropriate for documents with media that are not firmly bound to paper, such as pastel, charcoal, and some pencil. If in doubt, test: if the media lift off on a tiny swab rubbed gently in an inconspicuous spot, the document should not be encapsulated.

Research by the Library of Congress demonstrates that acidic papers may age much faster after encapsulation. It further shows that leaving an air space at the corners of the film package does not slow this aging as was once speculated. Documents should be alkalized (deacidified) by a qualified person before encapsulation. If this is not feasible, encapsulation may still be desirable to protect very fragile or heavily handled material. The Library of Congress finds that, in such a case, including a sheet of buffered paper the same size and shape as the document to back it in the enclosure can slow the rate of deterioration.

Documents that are not alkalized before encapsulation should be labelled for future custodians. A label typed onto buffered paper and inserted in the envelope is more secure than one attached to the outside of the envelope. If a buffered backing sheet is used, it can be labelled.

It is important to remember that encapsulation, like any conservation technique, should not be used for every document. The decision to use this strategy to preserve documents should be a matter of informed judgment, weighing the need to support or protect the document against the possibility that chemical deterioration may occur at an increased rate.

MATERIALS

Polyester is strong, flexible, and relatively inert. If free from plasticizers, UV-inhibitors, dyes, and surface coatings, it will not interact with documents. Mylar Type D and Melinex 516 are polyesters safe for use on valuable materials. These are widely available in 3-, 4-, and 5-mil thicknesses. The thickness of the film should be chosen for its ability to support the surface area of the object being encapsulated; large objects require thicker film.

Testing at the Library of Congress found 3M Scotch Brand double-sided tape no. 415 the only acceptable tape for encapsulation. It is sufficiently stable to minimize problems from creeping or deteriorating adhesive, although creeping does sometimes occur.

Materials Needed:

Scalpel, knife, or good scissors
Lint-free cloth (cheesecloth)
1 weight
1 window-cleaning squeegee (Figure 1a)
1 hard rubber brayer (optional) (Figure 1b)
Polyester film (Mylar Type D, Melinex 516) pre-cut or in rolls;
3-4 mil for small and medium-sized documents,
5 mil for large documents.
3M Scotch Brand double-sided tape no. 415,
1/4" or 1/2" wide, depending on size of document.

A work surface can be prepared by taping 1/4" graph paper to the underside of a sheet of glass or Plexiglas (optional). The lines on the graph paper assist in laying the tape straight (Figure 2).

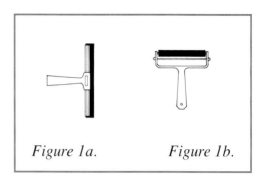

Figure 1a.   *Figure 1b.*

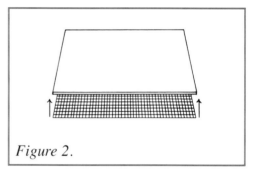

Figure 2.

INSTRUCTIONS

1. If you are using a backing sheet of buffered paper, cut the sheet to the dimensions of your document.

2. Cut two sheets of polyester film at least two inches larger than the document in each dimension.

3. Place one sheet of film on a clean, flat, work surface. Wipe the surface of the film with a lint-free cloth to remove dust and improve the static charge, which will adhere the film to the work surface.

4. Center the backing sheet, if one is used, on the film and place the document on top of it. If a backing sheet is not used, center the document on the film.

5. Place a weight on the center of the document to hold it in position (Figure 3).

6. Apply the tape to the film along the edge of the document, leaving a space of 1/8" to 1/4" between the edge of the document and the edge

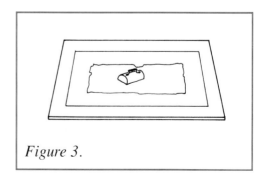

Figure 3.

of the tape (Figure 4). The ends of the tape should be cut square and butted on three corners with no overlap (Figure 5a). Alternatively the tape edges can be cut on the diagonal to make a more elegant joint (Figure 5b). Leave a gap of at least 1/16" at the fourth corner to allow air to escape. Leave the brown protective paper on the tape.

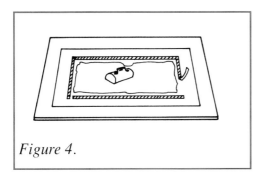

Figure 4.

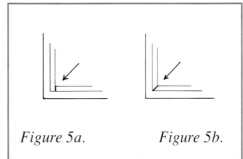

Figure 5a.   Figure 5b.

7. Wipe the second sheet of film with a lint-free cloth.

8. Remove the weight from the document and center the second sheet of film over the assembly, cleaned side down.

9. Replace the weight on the center of the top sheet of film.

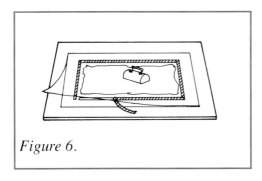

Figure 6.

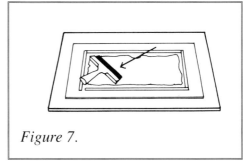

Figure 7.

10. Lift one corner of the top sheet of film. Carefully peel the protective paper from the tape along one edge of the document. Lower the corner of the film and rub the film over the tape to adhere it (Figure 6). Repeat for the other three edges.

11. To remove air from between the sheets of film, slide the squeegee across the envelope towards the air gap left in one corner of the envelope (Figure 7).

12. Roll the brayer or squeegee over the tape to bond it firmly to the polyester, or run your finger over the tape to secure the bond.

13. Trim the envelope, leaving a 1/8" to 1/4" margin of polyester outside the tape on all four edges. Rounding the corners of the envelope will help prevent scratching or cutting other materials during handling.

Good encapsulation takes practice. Expect to try this several times before you are satisfied with the result. Do not give up; you will quickly gain proficiency.

SOURCES OF SUPPLIES

This list is not exhaustive, nor does it constitute an endorsement of the suppliers listed. We suggest that you obtain information from a number of vendors so that you can make comparisons of cost and assess the full range of available products.

A more complete list of suppliers is available from NEDCC. Consult the Technical Leaflets section of NEDCC's website at www.nedcc.org or contact NEDCC for the most up-to-date version in print.

Double-sided Tape:

Conservation Resources International
8000-H Forbes Place
Springfield, VA 22151
Telephone: (703) 321-7730
Fax: (703) 321-0629

Gaylord Brothers
P.O. Box 4901
Syracuse, NY 13221-4901
Toll Free: (800) 448-6160
Toll Free: (800) 428-3631 (Help Line)
Toll Free Fax: (800) 272-3412
http://www.gaylord.com

Light Impressions
439 Monroe Avenue
P.O. Box 940
Rochester, NY 14603-0940
Telephone: (716) 271-8960
Toll Free: (800) 828-6216
http://www.lightimpressionsdirect.com

Talas
568 Broadway
New York, NY 10012
Telephone: (212) 736-7744
Fax: (212) 219-0735

University Products
517 Main Street
P.O. Box 101
Holyoke, MA 01041
Toll Free: (800) 628-1912
Telephone: (413) 532-3372
Toll Free Fax: (800) 532-9281
Fax: (413) 432-9281
E-mail: info@universityproducts.com
http://www.universityproducts.com

Lint-free Cloth (cheesecloth):

Grocery or Fabric Store

Polyester Film:

Bookmakers
6001 66th Avenue
Suite 101
Riverdale, MD 20737
Telephone: (301) 459-3384
Fax: (301) 459-7629

Conservation Resources Int.
8000-H Forbes Place
Springfield, VA 22151
Telephone: (703) 321-7730
Fax: (703) 321-0629

Gaylord Brothers
P.O. Box 4901
Syracuse, NY 13221-4901
Toll Free: (800) 448-6160
Toll Free: (800) 428-3631 (Help Line)
Toll Free Fax: (800) 272-3412
http://www.gaylord.com

Light Impressions
439 Monroe Avenue
P.O. Box 940
Rochester, NY 14603-0940
Toll Free: (800) 828-6216
Telephone: (716) 271-8960
Toll Free Fax: (800) 828-5539
http://www.lightimpressions.com

Talas
568 Broadway
New York, NY 10012
Telephone: (212) 736-7744
Fax: (212) 219-0735

University Products
517 Main Street
P.O. Box 101
Holyoke, MA 01041
Toll Free: (800) 628-1912
Telephone: (413) 532-3372
Toll Free Fax: (800) 532-9281
Fax: (413) 432-9281
E-mail: info@universityproducts.com
http://www.universityproducts.com

Scalpel, Knife:

Bookmakers
6001 66th Avenue
Suite 101
Riverdale, MD 20737
Telephone: (301) 459-3384
Fax: (301) 459-7629

Talas
568 Broadway
New York, NY 10012
Telephone: (212) 736-7744
Fax: (212) 219-0735

University Products
517 Main Street
P.O. Box 101
Holyoke, MA 01041
Toll Free: (800) 628-1912
Telephone: (413) 532-3372
Toll Free Fax: (800) 532-9281
Fax: (413) 432-9281
E-mail: info@universityproducts.com
http://www.universityproducts.com

Scissors:

Hardware Store; Office Supplier

Squeegee:

Hardware Store

Gaylord Brothers
P.O. Box 4901
Syracuse, NY 13221-4901
Toll Free: (800) 448-6160
Toll Free: (800) 428-3631 (Help Line)
Toll Free Fax: (800) 272-3412
http://www.gaylord.com

University Products
517 Main Street
P.O. Box 101
Holyoke, MA 01041
Toll Free: (800) 628-1912
Telephone: (413) 532-3372
Toll Free Fax: (800) 532-9281
Fax: (413) 432-9281
E-mail: info@universityproducts.com
http://www.universityproducts.com

Weight:

Make from covered brick, lead shot, fishing weights.

Acknowledgements

The author gratefully acknowledges the contributions made by NEDCC staff over the years in the development of this technical leaflet.

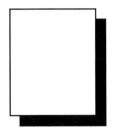

Northeast Document
Conservation Center

100 Brickstone Square
Andover, MA 01810-1494
www.nedcc.org
Tel: (978) 470-1010
Fax: (978) 475-6021

HOW TO DO YOUR OWN MATTING AND HINGING

by Mary Todd Glaser
Director of Paper Conservation
Northeast Document Conservation Center

When matting paper artifacts, using the right materials is essential. Cardboards for mounting must be chemically stable with good aging properties. These are the so-called archival-quality or acid-free boards sold by conservation suppliers. They are free of lignin and are pH neutral or, more often, slightly alkaline. The methods and materials for attaching the artifact to the mount are also important. The traditional method is to hinge the object with Japanese paper and a starch paste. More recently, corner supports or edge strips have come into favor since these can be used without applying adhesives to the object.

WINDOW MATS

A window mat is the traditional mount for a work of art or valuable artifact on paper. A mat is composed of a top sheet with a window and a backboard (see figure 1). The two boards are held together with a strip of cloth tape along one edge, usually the top. The function of the window is to permit the object to be seen while the mat protects it from handling and isolates it from surrounding materials.

Mats for works of art were traditionally made of rag fibers, that is, cotton or linen. Today ragboard is still favored by museums, but lignin-free wood-derived boards are now accepted by the preservation community. Matting boards of either type are usually buffered with an alkaline material to neutralize any acids they may absorb as they age. It is important to confirm the quality of the board by asking the supplier and by reading descriptive material provided by the manufacturer.

Four-ply board is the thickness most often used for matting. Larger works of art or those with raised elements such as seals may require a thicker board for the window portion of the mat. Boards heavier than four-ply are available from conservation suppliers, or they can be made by laminating two or more four-ply boards. Sink mats may also be used (see figure 3). These are constructed by adhering strips (often scraps) of conservation board to the backboard to make a recess or "sink" in which the object is mounted. The sink construction is hidden by the window portion of the mat.

Mats can be ordered from any framer, but making them yourself will save money. The tricky part is learning to make a clean-looking window opening, which is usually beveled (cut on a slant). With practice, a skilled person can make a beveled window with a simple utility knife, but using a mat cutting device greatly simplifies the procedure. There are a number of mat cutters on the market. The best of these are the easiest for an inexperienced person to use. Such mat cutters are expensive but will pay for themselves if cutting mats is to be an ongoing activity.

HINGING

Hinging is the traditional way to mount an object in a window mat. The work of art is hinged, usually with Japanese paper and starch paste, to the backboard of the mat, never to the reverse of the window. As shown in figures 1 and 2, part of the hinge is attached to the object and part to the backboard. Hinges allow the artwork to be removed easily from the board if that becomes necessary. Under no circumstances should the object be adhered directly to the mount. Alternatives to hinging are discussed toward the end of this leaflet.

PAPERS FOR HINGING

High quality Japanese papers, sometimes referred to as mulberry papers, make effective hinges because they are strong without being bulky and do not discolor or weaken with age. Traditionally these papers were made by hand, but now Japan exports machine-made papers of suitable quality. They are available in different weights and under a variety of names. The names are not specific and do not guarantee the fiber content of the paper. Some Japanese papers contain wood pulp and are not appropriate for conservation purposes. To be safe, use sheets made of 100% kozo fibers and buy them from conservation suppliers, not general art or paper suppliers.

Hinges may be cut or torn. Some conservators believe a fibrous torn edge holds better. A torn edge will create a less visible attachment on thin or transparent papers.

TYPES OF HINGES

Figures 1 and 2 show two common types of hinges. Folded hinges (figure 1) are tucked out of sight under the object. They must be used when the object is floated, i.e., when the edges of the work of art are exposed. Pendant or tab hinges (figure 2) use two pieces of paper that form a "T." The bottom of the "T" is adhered to the reverse of the object. The top is attached to the backboard, usually with a cross piece. Because the cross piece does not touch the object, Japanese paper and paste do not have to be used. A commercial tape is acceptable, but it is best to use an "archival" product sold by conservation suppliers.

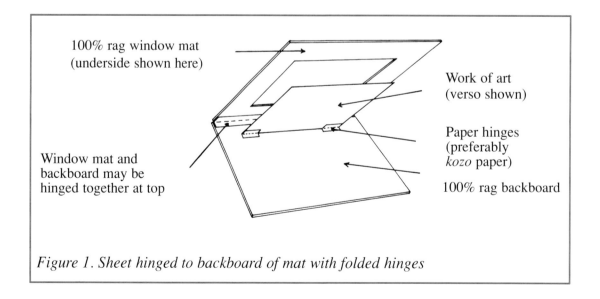

100% rag window mat
(underside shown here)

Work of art
(verso shown)

Paper hinges
(preferably
kozo paper)

Window mat and
backboard may be
hinged together at top

100% rag backboard

Figure 1. Sheet hinged to backboard of mat with folded hinges

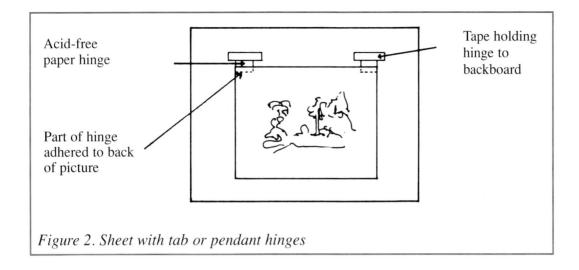

Figure 2. Sheet with tab or pendant hinges

Acid-free paper hinge

Tape holding hinge to backboard

Part of hinge adhered to back of picture

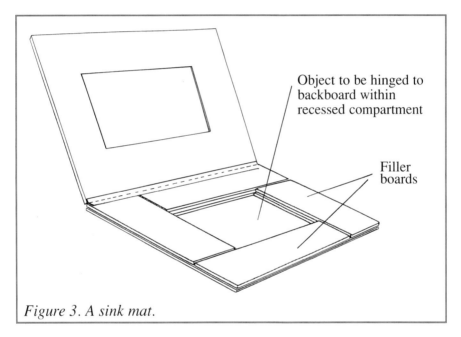

Figure 3. A sink mat.

Object to be hinged to backboard within recessed compartment

Filler boards

PLACEMENT, SIZE, AND NUMBER OF HINGES

Hinges are usually placed at the top edge of the work of art. If the object is small, a hinge at each upper corner will provide adequate support. Larger objects or those on heavy paper will require one or more additional hinges evenly spaced along the top edge. If the object is to be floated (shown with the edges exposed), additional hinges at the bottom corners or along the edges are desirable. Large sheets that tend to ripple may require several small hinges on each edge if they are floated.

The number and size of the hinges as well as the weight of the hinge paper depend on the weight and size of the object being mounted. If the mat covers the edges of the object, thereby helping to hold it in place, fewer hinges are needed. Hinges should be small, less than three inches across. The part of the hinge that is adhered to the object should be less than 1/2 inch wide. Use several small hinges rather then a few large ones. Large hinges or a strip across the top edge may restrict the natural movement of the paper and encourage rippling.

ADHESIVES FOR HINGING

Adhesives for hinging must have three qualities that remain constant over time:

- Sufficient strength: The adhesive must hold for an indefinite period.

- No tendency to discolor: It should not yellow or darken.

- Reversibility: It must remain readily water soluble so that the hinge can be easily removed with a minimal amount of moisture, even after several years.

Few if any commercially available adhesives meet all these criteria. Staining from self-adhering tapes and from adhesives such as rubber cement and animal glue is frequently seen by conservators. There are commercial adhesives that do not stain, but these may not be permanent or easily reversible. The archival tapes introduced in recent years and sold by conservation suppliers are probably more stable than other commercial products. However, because their aging properties are not yet known, their use is not recommended at this time for objects of value.

Conservators recommend paste that is homemade from pure starch extracted from flour, usually wheat or rice flour. This starch is available from conservation suppliers in powdered form. A recipe for starch paste follows, as well as directions for making paste in a microwave oven.

STARCH PASTE

Note: All utensils used for paste making must be spotlessly clean. They should not be used for other purposes, least of all food preparation.

1. Place one part wheat or rice starch and four parts of distilled water in a sauce pan or the top of a double boiler. The cooking vessel should be enamel-coated, stainless steel, or Teflon lined, not aluminum.

2. Mix well. Some allow the mixture to stand for 20 minutes before cooking.

3. Cook on medium high heat, stirring constantly with a clean wire whisk. If a double boiler is used, the upper section should not touch the water in the lower section.

4. When the paste begins to thicken (this may or may not happen right away), reduce heat and continue stirring. As it thickens, the paste will become stiffer and more difficult to stir. When that occurs, a wooden spoon may be substituted for the wire whisk. The spoon and whisk should not have been used with food.

5. Stir until the paste is thick and translucent and runs off the spoon in sheets. It usually takes about half an hour to reach this stage.

6. Transfer the paste to a clean jar or covered glass container and allow it to cool. Paste must be cool before it can be strained and used.

7. Straining and thinning is necessary because the paste becomes hard and rubbery when cool. Strain as much as you will need just before using. A plastic strainer, cheesecloth, or a Japanese paste strainer (available from conservation suppliers) can be used.

8. Mix distilled water into the paste a little at a time until the paste reaches the consistency of mayonnaise.

If a small amount of paste is needed, a Cook 'n' Stir may be used. Once made by Tefal, this appliance has become difficult to find in stores. If you use a Cook 'n' Stir, set it on high and cook the starch and water mixture for about half an hour. Caution: use the Cook 'n' Stir only for very small amounts. Too much may cause the machine to break when the paste thickens.

Because refrigeration may cause the paste to lose its tack, keep it at room temperature. It is best to make small batches, since the paste does not usually keep for more than a week. A preservative can be added, but these are toxic and not recommended for home use.

MICROWAVE WHEAT PASTE

University Products, a supplier of conservation materials, publishes a quick, easy paste recipe in its catalogue. This is ideal if paste is used only occasionally and in small quantities. If necessary, strain the paste prior to use.

Place 1 tablespoon of wheat starch in a microwave-safe container, add 5 tablespoons of distilled water, stir and place the mixture in a microwave oven. The oven must be very clean. Microwave on a high setting 20 to 30 seconds, remove the paste, and stir. Place it back in the unit and microwave it another 20 to 30 seconds. Remove it and stir again. Repeat this process several times until the paste is stiff and translucent. If larger quantities are made in the microwave oven, increase the cooking time between stirrings. Paste should cool before it is used.

ANOTHER SIMPLE PASTE: METHYL CELLULOSE

Methyl cellulose, the main ingredient in most commercial wallpaper pastes, is acceptable for conservation purposes if used in its pure form. It is available from conservation suppliers as a white powder and does not need to be cooked. Add one rounded tablespoon of methyl cellulose powder to 1/2 cup distilled water (not the other way around), stir, and let stand for several hours. Thin to the consistency of mayonnaise with distilled water. Methyl cellulose is not as strong as starch paste but should give adequate support for objects of moderate size. Methyl cellulose paste keeps for several weeks and does not require refrigeration.

THE HINGING PROCEDURE

Before hinging, assemble the following:

- The finished window mat.

- Hinging paper (Japanese kozo) torn or cut in strips.

- Starch paste in a small dish, thinned to the consistency of mayonnaise.

- A stiff bristle brush, ideally 3/8 to 1/2 inch wide.

- Pieces of clean white blotter, about 2 by 3 inches.

- A larger blotter for pasting on.

- Small pieces of silicon release paper, wax paper or spun polyester (Hollytex or Reemay), the same size as the blotter pieces. Release paper and spun polyester are available from conservation suppliers.

- Several weights, at least one pound each (two pounds is better). Lead weights with a flat surface can be custom made and covered with cloth so they do not leave marks. Fishing weights or bags of lead shot can also be used on top of small pieces of glass or rigid acrylic.

- Archival tape for securing the top of the hinge to the backboard (for example, Lineco Framing/Hinging Gummed Paper Tape).

- Optional: tweezers for handling wet hinges.

Attaching the Hinges

1. Make the mat first. Attach the window portion of the mat to the backboard with a strip of cloth tape so that the window and backboard are aligned.

2. Place the object face up on the mat backboard and check that it is centered in the window. Weight the object so it does not move. To protect the face of the object, put a blotter under the weight. Lightly mark the backboard with pencil to indicate the location of the upper corners.

3. Remove the object from the mat and place it face down on a clean surface.

4. If pendant hinges are being used, brush starch paste on one edge of the tab and apply the tab to the reverse of the object at each upper corner. Once the hinges are in place, tamp them lightly with blotting paper or other absorbent material to remove excess moisture and paste. Place a small blotter and weight over each hinge and leave until the hinge is completely dry. Because the blotter may stick to the hinge initially, it should be changed after about a minute. Inserting a piece of release paper or nonwoven polyester (Hollytex or Reemay) between the blotter and the hinge will prevent sticking. Household wax paper may also be used for this purpose, although this tends to wrinkle. Allow at least an hour for hinges to dry. Frequent blotter changes will speed the process as will drying the blotters for a few seconds in a microwave oven before using them.

5. When the hinge is dry, reposition the object in the mat and attach the top of the hinge to the backboard as shown in figure 2. This step can be done before the hinges are completely dry as long as the hinges are weighted while they are drying.

Folded hinges can be attached to the reverse of an object in the same way. After drying, they are folded under the object, pasted to the backboard as shown in figure 1, and weighted once again. Folded hinges may stick together as they dry unless release paper or nonwoven polyester is inserted between the two parts of the hinge.

It may take time before hinging comes easily, but persistence and practice will pay off.

MOUNTING WITHOUT HINGES

In recent years some institutions have been reluctant to apply adhesives to artifacts, especially if they are valuable. Mounting without adhesives can be done with corner supports or edge strips.

Small corners of chemically stable plastic (polyester film) or archival paper are commercially available for mounting photographs. Although photo corners work well for many photographs and for very small works on paper, they are too small to support most objects. Larger envelope corners (made from folded paper) or strips across the corners give better support, but they cannot be hidden under the mat unless much of the object is also concealed. Strips of polyester film placed diagonally across the corners are transparent and therefore less obtrusive than paper supports, but still they are shiny. Using strips of very fine, translucent, woven polyester is an alternative. This is matte and therefore less obtrusive than polyester film.

Hugh Phibbs, Coordinator of Matting and Framing Services at the National Gallery of Art in Washington, D.C., has developed innovative ways of mounting without adhesives. He gives workshops periodically, and his ideas appear in a monthly column in *Picture Framing Magazine*. Some of these articles are cited below.

SUGGESTED FURTHER READING

Munro, Susan Nash. "Window Mats for Paper Objects." Washington: National Park Service *Conserve O Gram* 13/1, 1993.

Phibbs, Hugh. "Preservation Matting for Works of Art on Paper." A Supplement to *Picture Framing Magazine* (Feb. 1997).

Phibbs, Hugh. "Reinforcements for Support Strips." *Picture Framing Magazine* (Jan. 1998).

Phibbs, Hugh. "Stable Support for Overmatted Artwork." *Picture Framing Magazine* (Dec. 1997).

Smith, Merrily A. *Matting and Hinging of Works of Art on Paper*. Washington: Library of Congress, 1981.

SOURCES OF SUPPLIES

This list is not exhaustive, nor does it constitute an endorsement of the suppliers listed. We suggest that you obtain information from a number of vendors so that you can make comparisons of cost and assess the full range of available products.

A more complete list of suppliers is available from NEDCC. Consult the Technical Leaflets section of NEDCC's website at www.nedcc.org or contact NEDCC for the most up-to-date version in print.

Mat Board:

Archivart
7 Caesar Place
P.O. Box 428
Moonachie, NJ 07074
Telephone: (201) 804-8986
Fax: (201) 935-5964

University Products
517 Main Street
P. O. Box 101
Holyoke, MA 01041
Toll Free: (800) 628-1912
Telephone: (413) 532-3372
Toll Free Fax: (800) 532-9281
Fax: (413) 432-9281
E-mail: info@universityproducts.com
http://www.universityproducts.com

Japanese Kozo Paper:

A&W Crestwood
205 Chubb Avenue
Lyndhurst, NJ 07071
Telephone: (201) 438-6869
Fax: (201) 804-8320

Hiromi Paper International
2525 Michigan Avenue, Unit G9
Santa Monica, CA 90404
Telephone: (310) 998-0098
Fax: (310) 998-0028

Paper Nao
4-37-28 Hakusan
Bunkyo-Ku
Tokyo 112-0001
JAPAN
Telephone: 03-3944-4470
Fax: 03-3944-4699

Miscellaneous Conservation Supplies [starch for paste, methyl cellulose powder, spun (non-woven) polyester, and silicon release paper]:

Gaylord Bros.
P. O. Box 4901
Syracuse, NY 13221-4901
Toll Free: (800) 448-6160
Toll Free: (800) 428-3631 (Help Line)
Toll Free Fax: (800) 272-3412
http://www.gaylord.com

Light Impressions
439 Monroe Avenue
P.O. Box 940
Rochester, NY 14603-0940
Toll Free: (800) 828-6216
Telephone: (716) 271-8960
Fax: (800) 828-5539
http://www.lightimpressionsdirect.com

Talas
568 Broadway
New York, NY 10012
Telephone: (212) 736-7744
Fax: (212) 219-0735

University Products
517 Main Street
P. O. Box 101
Holyoke, MA 01041
Toll Free: (800) 628-1912
Telephone: (413) 532-3372
Toll Free Fax: (800) 532-9281
Fax: (413) 432-9281
E-mail: info@universityproducts.com
http://www.universityproducts.com

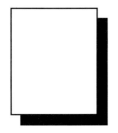

Northeast Document
Conservation Center
100 Brickstone Square
Andover, MA 01810-1494
www.nedcc.org
Tel: (978) 470-1010
Fax: (978) 475-6021

CONSERVATION TREATMENT FOR WORKS OF ART AND UNBOUND ARTIFACTS ON PAPER

by Mary Todd Glaser
Director of Paper Conservation
Northeast Document Conservation Center

Most of the following procedures should be performed by a professional conservator who specializes in the treatment of paper collections. This leaflet will explain many of the operations done by paper conservators. The treatment chosen for any artifact or collection should be the outcome of communication between a conservator and the client or custodian after the conservator has examined the artifact. There are many variations and different levels of treatment, and the conservator may offer choices. The procedures ultimately chosen will depend on several factors. These include the condition of the artifact, its future use, its aesthetic importance, what the media will allow, and, inevitably, the client's financial resources. The client should feel free to discuss the treatment with the conservator and ask questions.

EXAMINATION AND INITIAL REPORT

Treatment is always preceded by a careful examination of each object. Before beginning work, the conservator will provide a written report outlining the treatment and estimating its cost. Magnification aids such as a binocular microscope are used as necessary during the examination. The solubility of all media is tested prior to water or solvent treatment.

DOCUMENTATION

During the course of treatment the conservator keeps written notes on all procedures, carefully noting any chemicals that are used. Photographs (often color slides) are taken of each object before, occasionally during, and after treatment. Following treatment, a written report is given to the client with copies of the photographic record.

SURFACE CLEANING

Superficial grime, dirt, and soot are removed with a soft brush or with non-abrasive erasing compounds such as powdered vinyl or soft block erasers. Accretions including insect specks and mold residues are removed mechanically with an appropriate tool.

REMOVAL OF MOLD AND INSECT RESIDUES

Mold and insect deposits are best removed individually by mechanical means. A small vacuum aspirator is recommended for lifting mold. It is not always possible to eliminate all traces of mold, since the mycelium may be well rooted in the paper. Fumigation, once a standard treatment for mold and insects, is now seldom done because chemical fumigants can have adverse effects both on personnel and on the artifacts.

CONSOLIDATION AND FIXING

When absolutely necessary, flaking or friable media are consolidated with an appropriate natural or synthetic material. Fixatives are not used on pastels, however, because color change can result. When it is desirable to wash a paper artifact, small areas of water-soluble color can sometimes be fixed with brush applications of a dilute synthetic resin. This treatment is practical only for isolated areas of soluble media.

REMOVAL OF BACKINGS

If the object has been backed with a material that is not part of its original structure and the backing is destructive or inadequate, it should be removed. Sometimes backing removal can be done in a water bath. If the object cannot be put in water, dry removal by mechanical means is necessary. Use of steam or local application of moisture can assist with mechanical backing removal. Removing fragile paper from a solid backing can be time consuming and therefore costly. It is often difficult for a conservator to know in advance how long a backing removal will take or how much it will cost.

REMOVAL OF OLD REPAIRS OR TAPES

In the past, repairs were often made with materials harmful to paper, such as commercial tapes or adhesives that stain. Repairs made with water-based adhesives such as animal glue are removed in a water bath, by local application of moisture, or with steam. Synthetic adhesives and pressure-sensitive (self-adhering) tapes usually have to be dissolved in or softened with an organic solvent before they can be removed.

WASHING

Water washing is often beneficial to paper. Washing not only removes dirt and aids in stain reduction, but it can wash out acidic compounds that have built up in the paper. Washing can also relax brittle or distorted paper. For these reasons artifacts that are not discolored or dirty may still be washed. Beforehand, all media are carefully tested for water sensitivity. Where the materials permit, objects are immersed in filtered water. On occasion, a carefully controlled amount of an alkaline material such as ammonium hydroxide is added to the water to raise the pH to about 8.0; this assists in the cleaning process. Artifacts with soluble media may be partially washed, float washed, or washed on a suction table.

ALKALIZATION (DEACIDIFICATION)

Although simple water washing is often enough to reduce acidity, the addition of an alkaline buffer to the paper is sometimes recommended. This is appropriate for papers that will be subject to acid attack even after washing or acidic papers that cannot be washed. Where possible, alkalization is achieved by immersion in an aqueous solution of an alkaline substance such as magnesium bicarbonate or calcium hydroxide. If water-soluble media are present, the artifact may be treated nonaqueously with an alkaline salt dissolved in organic solvents. Non-aqueous solutions are usually applied by spraying. While the addition of an alkaline buffer is often beneficial, such chemicals may cause alteration or even damage to certain components of a work of art. Some colors, for example, may change if subjected to alkaline conditions. This change may be immediate or may occur over time. For this reason alkalization is not recommended for all materials. Like all conservation procedures, the decision to alkalize must be made on a case by case basis in consultation with a conservator.

MENDING

Tears are carefully aligned, then repaired, usually on the reverse, with narrow strips of torn Japanese tissue. The strips are adhered with a permanent, non-staining adhesive such as starch-based paste. Fine, transparent tissue is used to avoid build-up and to allow writing on the reverse to be seen.

FILLING AREAS OF PAPER LOSS

Holes or paper losses may be filled individually with Japanese paper (the least expensive method), with paper pulp, or with a paper carefully chosen to match the original in weight, texture, and color. The latter is the most time-consuming option, usually reserved for objects of aesthetic value. If the conservator has the necessary equipment, multiple pulp fills on a single sheet can be achieved in a single operation by leafcasting the sheet. With archival objects that are not of great aesthetic importance, conservators may simply back the materials (see below) and allow the backing sheet to visually fill the lost areas.

BACKING (LINING)

Especially weak or brittle sheets may be reinforced by backing them with another sheet of paper or tissue. The backing should be somewhat lighter in weight than the original. Japanese paper, either handmade or machine-made of high-quality cellulose fibers (kozo), is the usual lining material, although western paper is occasionally used. The backing is usually adhered with a dilute starch-based paste.

Historically, artifacts, especially oversized objects such as maps, were backed with woven fabrics like linen or muslin. Woven materials respond differently to climatic changes and are therefore not as compatible with artifacts as paper. Occasionally fabric is used with very large objects that will not otherwise remain flat or with historic wallpaper that may have to be removed from the wall in the future. In such cases the object is lined first with paper, which isolates the object from the fabric.

Please note that a protective enclosure such as a mat or polyester encapsulation can sometimes be substituted for backing (see below).

INPAINTING (RETOUCHING)

This is done by judicious application of watercolor, acrylic, gouache, or pastel to filled areas or to minor surface losses such as scratches, small abrasions, or media losses along tears. Care is taken to confine the retouching to the area of loss.

BLEACHING

Bleaching is time-consuming and tricky. It is warranted only when staining or discoloration compromises the aesthetic value of a work of art. Bleaching may be undertaken by exposure to artificial light or to sunlight or it can be done with chemicals. Bleaching with light is often preferred by conservators because it is gentle and not harmful to cellulose. Some stains, however, require use of chemicals.

Chemical bleaching of paper must be done under carefully controlled conditions with a bleach that is known to be safe for both the paper and the media. The bleach must be removed from the paper after treatment. Chemical bleaching is always followed by a thorough water rinsing of the treated area. Whenever possible, the chemical is confined to the area of stain, but sheets with extensive staining or discoloration may have to be bleached overall. Such objects may be immersed in a bath, or the solution may be brushed or sprayed on.

FLATTENING

Flattening is always necessary following aqueous treatment. It is usually done between blotters or felts under moderate pressure. Objects that have been lined are often dried and flattened by stretching on a Japanese *kari-bari* screen or on a chemically inert surface such as an acrylic panel.

HOUSING

Once an object has been treated, it must be properly stored in an archival folder or other enclosure. Special housings such as matting, framing, and polyester film encapsulation give extra protection to objects. In some instances these enclosures can be used in place of more invasive reinforcement procedures such as lining.

Polyester film encapsulation

This method of protection and reinforcement is most appropriate for archival materials. Encapsulation is done by sandwiching the object between two sheets of polyester film (Mylar;), usually 4 or 5 mil thick, and sealing the film at all edges. Some conservation laboratories have special equipment for sealing the film ultrasonically or with heat. Double-sided tape (3M Scotch; brand #415 tape) can also be used. Because polyester carries a static charge, encapsulation is not recommended for materials with loose, flaking, or friable media, nor should it be used for papers that are acidic.

Matting

Although many museums use mats routinely for storage of prints and drawings, this type of housing is especially suited to works of art or artifacts intended for framing. Mats are usually composed of a window and backboard of 4-ply 100% ragboard or lignin-free archival board. The object is attached to the backboard with hinges of Japanese paper and starch paste or with corner supports.

Framing

Once matted, an object can be safely sent to a framer for a new frame or it can be put into an existing frame. If an existing frame is reused, it may need alteration to make it acceptable from a conservation point of view. For example, if the frame fits so tightly that the edges of the object come in contact with the wood, the frame rabbet should be enlarged and/or lined with a barrier material. Some frames will need to be deepened to accommodate a mat, the glazing, and the backing layers needed to protect the artifact. Frames can be made deeper by building up the back of the frame with strips of wood screwed in place. Ultraviolet-filtering acrylic or glass is recommended as a glazing. Please note that acrylics such as UF-3 Plexiglas carry a static charge so are not appropriate for pastels or objects with insecure or friable media.

For further information about these enclosures, see the NEDCC technical leaflets "Matting and Framing Art and Artifacts on Paper" and "Encapsulation in Polyester Film using Double-Sided Tape."

2/99

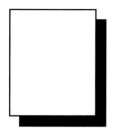

Northeast Document
Conservation Center

100 Brickstone Square
Andover, MA 01810-1494
www.nedcc.org
Tel: (978) 470-1010
Fax: (978) 475-6021`

CONSERVATION TREATMENT FOR BOUND MATERIALS OF VALUE

by Sherelyn Ogden
Head of Conservation
Minnesota Historical Society

Many conservation procedures are available for bound materials, several of which are briefly described here. Books of value should be examined individually, and the most appropriate treatment should be chosen based on use, condition, and the nature of the value of the book. Although some procedures seem straightforward, they are not and require the judgment and technical expertise of a conservator to avoid harming a book. A conservator may recommend one or more of the following.

SURFACE CLEANING OF BOOK PAGES

Superficial grime, dirt, and soot disfigure and abrade book pages. They can be removed with a soft brush or with a powdered eraser or a soft block eraser. Accretions like insect specks and mold residue may have to be removed mechanically with a small sharp tool like a spatula or, in the case of mold, with an aspirator, which vacuums the mold.

REMOVAL OF OLD REPAIRS AND TAPE ON BOOK PAGES

Past repairs may have been made with materials now known to be harmful, such as rubber cement and most tapes, and should be removed. Repairs that were made using water-based adhesives can be removed in a water bath, with moisture, or with steam. Many synthetic adhesives and pressure-sensitive tapes require use of an organic solvent for removal.

WASHING BOOK PAGES

Immersion of pages in water helps to remove dirt and lessen stains. It also helps to reduce acidity, which is one of the major causes of paper deterioration. Prior to washing the pages, every ink and color must be carefully tested for solubility to make sure media are stable and will not fade or blur during the washing process. Occasionally a carefully controlled amount of alkaline material may be added to the water to assist in the cleaning process.

DEACIDIFICATION OF BOOK PAGES

Deacidification and alkalization of acidic paper, usually referred to simply as deacidification, is a generally accepted conservation practice, which can be carried out aqueously or nonaqueously. The purpose of the treatment is to neutralize acids and to deposit in paper a buffer that will protect it from the formation of acid in the future. Even though the effectiveness of deacidification is questioned in certain instances, such as in the treatment of degraded ground wood pulp paper, it is generally believed to be beneficial. A few materials, however, may be altered by deacidification and should not be treated. Certain colors, for example, may change under alkaline conditions, either immediately or over time. For this reason pages with colors are often not deacidified. Also, some papers may not require deacidification because of the high-quality fibers from which they are made, such as linen or cotton rag papers, or because they have been stored well and are in good condition. Washing followed by aqueous deacidification is a more thorough treatment than nonaqueous deacidification. However, aqueous treatment requires that a volume be disbound. If the volume should not be disbound or if inks are soluble in water, nonaqueous deacidification is an acceptable alternative.

MENDING, FILLING AND GUARDING BOOK PAGES

Tears in leaves can be carefully aligned and repaired with thin strips of Japanese paper and a starch paste or other adhesive of conservation quality. Holes or losses can be filled with inlays of Japanese paper pulp (leaf-casting). Another option is inlaying with a paper similar to the original in weight, texture, and color. This is extremely time consuming and is reserved for books of significant value. The folds (Figure 1) through which folios are sewn together when a book is bound often require reinforcement prior to rebinding. In this procedure, referred to as guarding, strips of Japanese tissue are adhered to the folds with a starch paste.

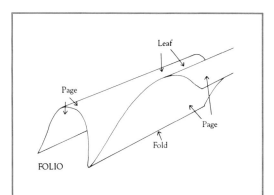

Figure 1. Folio: a folded peice of paper
Leaf: one half of a folio
Page: one side of a leaf

SEWING BOOK PAGES

This refers to the fastening together of the leaves of a book by means of thread. Several techniques are used in conservation binding. Sewing is often accomplished by grouping several folios together, one inside another, to form sections. The sections are then sewn to each other with thread (Figure 2). Often sections are sewn to sewing supports such as tapes or cords. Unbleached linen is the type of thread most frequently selected by conservators. The original sewing in a volume should be retained if this is possible; it can be reinforced using new linen thread and sewing supports.

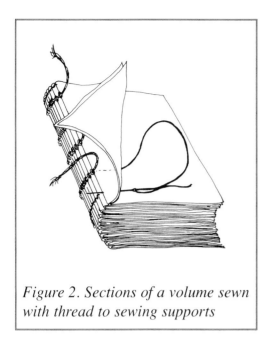

Figure 2. Sections of a volume sewn with thread to sewing supports

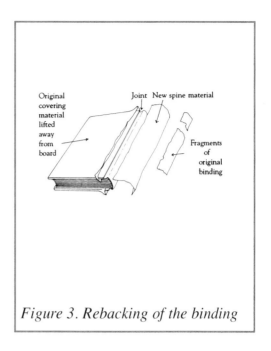

Figure 3. Rebacking of the binding

LEATHER, CLOTH AND PAPER REBACKING OF THE BINDING

This procedure is appropriate for those books that have partially or completely detached boards (covers) and/or spines (Figure 3). Original boards are reattached to the sewn pages using new leather, cloth or paper dyed to blend with the original covering material. The new material is worked under the original at the joints, and the fragments of the spine covering of the original binding are adhered to the surface of the new spine material.

REBINDING USING A LACED-IN STRUCTURE

If the existing binding is too deteriorated to retain, the book may be rebound in a binding made of new materials of conservation quality. A laced-in structure (Figure 4) is often chosen by conservators for books that are to be bound in leather. When properly constructed this is a strong yet flexible structure, which provides adequate support for a book while allowing it to open fully and be easily read. The term *laced-in* refers to the way the boards are attached to the text block: they are laced to the text block by the sewing supports to which the sections are sewn. Although this structure can be used on books of any size, it is often chosen for large, heavy books because of the structural support it provides. This is a durable structure and, if made of good quality materials, will last a long time.

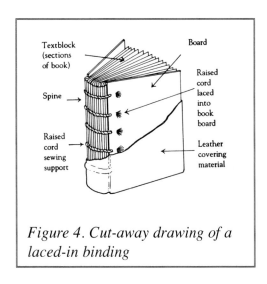

Figure 4. Cut-away drawing of a laced-in binding

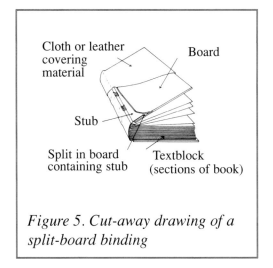

Figure 5. Cut-away drawing of a split-board binding

REBINDING USING A SPLIT-BOARD STRUCTURE

An alternative to a leather-covered laced-in structure is a split-board structure (Figure 5). The term split-board also refers to the way the boards are attached to the textblock: stubs, which are sewn to the text block, are slipped into a split in each board and adhered in place. This structure is most often chosen for medium to large books because it provides adequate support for them. This structure can be covered in leather or cloth. When cloth is used it is a good alternative to a leather laced-in structure for some medium to large books because it provides adequate support and costs less to construct due to savings in time and materials.

REBINDING USING A CASE STRUCTURE

For lightweight books a case structure (Figure 6) is adequate. In this type of binding the case (cover) is made separate from the text block and is attached to it by being adhered to the endpapers, either directly or by means of a hinge. This structure is not as strong as a laced-in or split-board structure and should be limited to light- to medium-weight books. The case is most frequently covered in cloth, although it can be covered in paper or leather as well. This structure takes less time to produce than a laced-in or split-board structure and thus costs less.

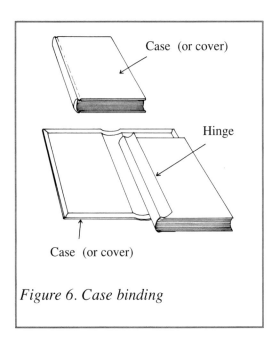

Figure 6. Case binding

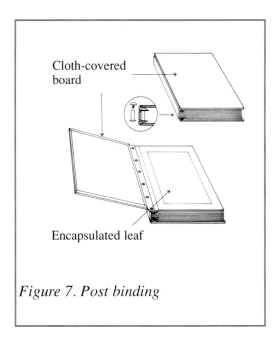

Figure 7. Post binding

ENCAPSULATION IN POLYESTER FILM AND BINDING USING A POST-BINDING STRUCTURE

When all the leaves in a book are extremely weak and/or brittle and require overall support, encapsulation in polyester film and post-binding may be appropriate (Figure 7). Polyester film is a clear, inert plastic that provides excellent support for fragile paper. Each leaf of the book is placed between two sheets of polyester film, and the film is sealed along all four edges. Ultrasonic welding is the preferred method of sealing the film. If the leaves of a book are still in folio form, the folios will usually need to be cut along the fold to facilitate encapsulation. However, paper requiring encapsulation is usually so fragile that any folds that once existed have already broken. Polyester film has an electrostatic charge. For this reason encapsulation is not recommended for leaves that have loose, flaking, or friable media because the electrostatic charge may loosen media even more. The encapsulated leaves can be bound together in what is referred to as a post-binding. Boards (covers) are attached to the encapsulated leaves by means of screw posts, which pass through the covers and polyester film to produce an album-style binding. Although the boards can be covered in almost any material, they are usually covered in cloth.

DOCUMENTATION OF TREATMENT

Preparation of written and photographic records is a requirement of responsible conservation treatment for materials of value. The purpose of documentation is to record the appearance and condition of a book prior to treatment, describe the treatment that was done, and specify the materials that were used in the treatment. The purpose is also to identify a book that has been treated and to provide information helpful to conservators who may in the future treat that book further, especially as new improved techniques and materials become available. Documentation includes a written description of the condition prior to treatment, a listing of the procedures and specific materials used in treatment, and a statement of where and when the treatment was done. Written records are supplemented by photographs taken before, after, and sometimes during treatment. These records should be retained permanently.

COLLATION OF BOOK PAGES

Collation is an important part of documentation. In the context of the conservation treatment, this procedure includes careful checking of each page of a book to document the number and order of pages, plates, maps, etc.; to check for missing pages; and to note serious tears, stains, or other types of damage or irregularity.

MINIMAL TREATMENT (BASIC STABILIZATION)

This refers to the minimal amount of treatment required to slow deterioration of a book. It excludes all cosmetic treatments and many structural repairs as well. For example, a book with detached boards and fragile paper may only be microfilmed, nonaqueously deacidified, and boxed. This level of treatment is most often chosen for books of limited value or for those that receive little use.

EXTENSIVE TREATMENT

This refers to full treatment of both pages and binding. It includes structural repairs and often cosmetic treatment as well. It frequently involves disbinding, surface cleaning, washing, aqueous deacidification, mending and guarding of pages, resewing, repairing the original covers and reattaching them to the text. If the original covers are too deteriorated to reuse, the book is rebound in one of a variety of binding styles (case, splitboard, or laced-in structure) and titled. This level of treatment is usually reserved for books of high value.

BOXING

Boxing is crucial to the preservation of many books. Boxes provide both structural support for a book and protection from dust, dirt, light, and mechanical damage. Books with bindings of historic or aesthetic value, which should be retained as much as possible in their present condition, should be boxed. Damaged books, which are rarely used and do not warrant treatment or repair of the binding, should also be boxed. Boxes should be constructed of durable materials of conservation quality and should be custom made to fit a book's dimensions exactly. Both drop-spine (Figure 8) and phase boxes (Figure 9) are acceptable. Drop-spine boxes are preferable because they provide better support and keep books cleaner; however they are more expensive. Both types of boxes are available from commercial suppliers.

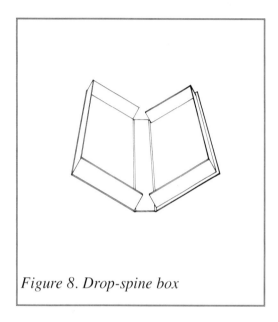

Figure 8. Drop-spine box

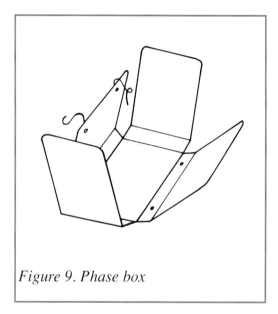

Figure 9. Phase box

PHOTODUPLICATION

Microfilming and other types of photoduplication are a cost-effective alternative for preserving information when extensive treatment of the original is not practical. Copying also has advantages when combined with treatment; by eliminating the need to handle fragile materials, copying makes minimal treatment adequate for many books that would otherwise require extensive treatment. Copying allows added security through off-site storage and also provides researchers with greater access to unique information.

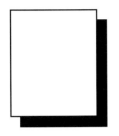

Northeast Document
Conservation Center
100 Brickstone Square
Andover, MA 01810-1494
www.nedcc.org
Tel: (978) 470-1010
Fax: (978) 475-60213

CHOOSING AND WORKING WITH A CONSERVATOR

**by Jan Paris
Conservator
University of North Carolina at Chapel Hill**

"The preserver, restorer, conserver is the indispensable,
the primary living link in the human chain that connects
yesterday's accomplishments with tomorrow's possibilities."

James H. Billington, Librarian of Congress,
The Moral Imperative of Conservation

INTRODUCTION

Collections in our libraries, archives, and historical societies consist of diverse records
materials that differ in type, size, and format. They are stored under varying environmental
conditions, housed in a variety of boxes and enclosures, and used for various purposes and to
different extents. The net result is that the records in our collections range in condition from
pristine to severely deteriorated. Some of these items need conservation attention, and
institutions without a conservator on staff must entrust precious materials to the care of an
individual outside the institution. Choosing a conservator is an important step in providing
responsible conservation.

To assist in that process, this publication explores some of the issues related to selecting a
conservator. It addresses the nature of conservation, the qualifications and background of a
conservator, and how to find, work with, and what to expect from, the conservator. The focus
is on factors relevant to conservation treatment of special collections materials—that is, those
materials that are significant as artifacts because of their age, rarity, beauty, monetary value,
or historical or bibliographic importance.[1] These factors are also relevant for those items
whose physical features (e.g., color illustrations, folding maps, or charts) necessitate
preservation of the physical artifact. That is, even if the item's intrinsic value may not
demand conservation, treatment may be the option of choice if the physical features
preclude reformatting or other alternatives.

CONSERVATION AND THE PROFESSIONAL CONSERVATOR

Certain items in a collection are so significant that they warrant conservation attention.
Conservation of such items is especially appropriate when the materials cannot withstand
use—even careful use—without being damaged, when they are physically or chemically unstable,
or when they have received inappropriate treatment in the past.[2]

Conservation treatment is the application of techniques and materials to chemically stabilize and physically strengthen items in the collection. The aim of conservation treatment for materials with artifactual value is to assure the item's longevity and continued availability for use, while altering their physical characteristics as little as possible. Conservation also includes the decisions involved in identifying items needing treatment and determining appropriate treatments.

Conservation treatment of special collections materials requires the judgment and experience of a qualified conservator. A professional conservator is a highly trained individual with a broad theoretical and practical knowledge in the following areas:

- the history, science, and aesthetics of the materials and techniques of records materials;
- the causes of deterioration or damage to these materials;
- the range of methods and materials that can be used in conservation treatment; and,
- the implications of any proposed treatment.

A conservator also demonstrates throughout every aspect of work a commitment to high standards of practice.

Conservation is a relatively new field that over the last ten years has experienced a period of rapid growth and increasing specialization, especially in the areas of library and archives conservation. As yet, however, the field has no educational accreditation system, professional certification process, or national professional standards.

As a result, it may sometimes be difficult to locate and choose a conservator who is trained and qualified to provide the treatment services required. In evaluating prospective conservators, consider the individual's conservation training, length and extent of practical experience, and professional affiliations. In addition, contact client and peer references to insure that you are making the best, informed choice.

Conservator Training

Competent conservators are trained in one of two ways: through completion of an academic graduate program that leads to a master's degree or through a lengthy apprenticeship. The six graduate training programs in North America offer two to three years of academic course work covering the history and science of records materials, the cultural context of their production, and conservation treatment practices.[3] A final year is spent obtaining intensive practical experience under the direction of a respected conservator in an established conservation laboratory. Graduates often undertake an additional year of advanced internship or pursue further study or research opportunities through existing fellowship programs.

Some individuals choose not to attend a graduate training program because of the program's cost, because its focus does not match their own interests, or for other reasons. Training through apprenticeship offers an alternative for such people. The success of any apprenticeship program relies on the resourcefulness of the individual to obtain broad theoretical and practical knowledge through sustained internships in respected conservation laboratories; attendance at workshops, seminars, and selected academic courses; and independent reading and study. Apprenticeship training is especially common in and can provide very good preparation for book conservation, where formal academic training opportunities are extremely limited. Since apprenticeship training strategies differ considerably from one another and may vary in quality as a result, it becomes very important to evaluate each individual carefully.

A trained bookbinder is not necessarily a book conservator. While he or she may possess many of the necessary manual skills, a bookbinder may not have the broader knowledge required to evaluate, propose, and carry out the most appropriate treatment from a conservation standpoint. Similarly, professional framing studios may include "paper restoration" in their list of services, but framers may not have the knowledge required to make conservation decisions.

Regardless of their educational training, all conservators specialize in treatment of particular types of materials and can provide only general advice about storage, housing, or maintenance of other materials. For example, a responsible book conservator will not provide technical consultation or treatment for works of art or furniture since they are outside the realm of his or her expertise.

Professional Organizations for Conservators

Membership and active involvement in one of the field's professional organizations indicates a conservator's interest in keeping abreast of technical and scientific developments, in exchanging information, and in strengthening professional contacts. To achieve these goals, many professional conservators belong to organizations such as the American Institute for Conservation (AIC), the International Institute for Conservation (IIC), and regional conservation guilds. While not a guarantee of a conservator's knowledge, competence, or ethics, membership in a professional organization is an important indicator of professional involvement, without which it is almost impossible to keep up with developments in the field.

Categories of membership may provide some indication of the conservator's experience. In particular, "Fellow" or "Professional Associate" membership in AIC is conferred after a specified number of years in the field, based on a peer review process. These membership categories indicate that the conservator has agreed to abide by the AIC Code of Ethics and Standards of Practice. The AIC Code and Standards are designed to "guide the conservator in the ethical practice of his profession" and call for "unswerving respect for the aesthetic, historical, and physical integrity of the object." [4]

HOW TO FIND A CONSERVATOR

Finding a qualified conservator may require ingenuity and perseverance, since conservation expertise (especially in book conservation) is not available in all areas of the country and many conservators do not advertise.

Begin by developing a list of potential conservators. Contact conservation departments in nearby libraries, museums, and archives. The staff is often a good source of general information and advice. They may be able to recommend conservators in private practice in a nearby area or regional centers that offer treatment and broader preservation services. In some cases, conservators employed by an institution may accept private work outside of their institutional commitments.

In addition, contact people who work in the special collections departments of libraries, state archives, large historical societies, and major museums to obtain the names of conservators who have worked for them on a regular basis. In all cases, find out whether the recommendation is based on direct experience with the conservator or on secondary information.

Also, call or write to the American Institute for Conservation for additional referrals. The Conservation Services Referral System of the Foundation of the American Institute for Conservation (FAIC) will provide the names of professionals who practice in your area or who specialize in the treatment of particular types of artifacts. The FAIC does not endorse individual conservators or the quality of their work, but the Referral System does provide some general information to explain what a consumer of conservation services should expect from the conservator.

These contacts should provide the names of several potential conservators. However, these referrals are not necessarily an indicator of quality. Comparison shopping is always a sound principle, even when seeking conservation services. A series of informed questions, outlined in the following sections, can provide a framework for evaluating a conservator's capabilities.

You may also find that some of the conservators on your list are not able to provide the kind of treatment you require because a particular problem lies outside their expertise or because they are unable to accommodate your artifacts in their lab. Others may have a large backlog of work and may not be able to treat your item as quickly as you would like.

Be wary of a conservator who too casually offers to do a quick and inexpensive job for you. Conservation treatment is usually time consuming and expensive. A waiting period and the expense of competent services are small prices to pay when compared to the risk that an artifact may be irreparably lost or damaged through inadequate or inappropriate treatment.

If you are located in an area of the country with few conservators, do not hesitate to obtain referrals from a broad geographic area. Many conservators are accustomed to dealing with clients located at a great distance and can offer guidance for safely packing and transporting fragile materials. They should also be able to provide you with information about shipping and courier services that can provide insurance, special handling, and security for valuable materials during transit.

If you want to do a collection survey to help you evaluate your overall conservation needs, consider retaining a conservation consultant. A collection survey is designed to assess the overall conditions of a collection and the environment in which it is housed. The survey results in recommendations that can help an institution develop a long-range plan for the care of its collections. Such recommendations might include suggestions for environmental improvements, procedural changes, staff education, rehousing projects, and the conservation treatment of selected materials. This approach is especially useful for institutions that do not have adequate expertise or experience in assessing conservation needs. The referral strategy outlined above will help you identify those who may be qualified to do a conservation survey. Several of the organizations listed in the "Information Resources" and "Regional Conservation Centers" sections also provide consultation and survey services.

CONTACTING A CONSERVATOR

What the Conservator Will Ask You

To ensure that your collections receive appropriate treatment, it is essential to develop a collaborative working relationship with a conservator from the beginning, so that treatment decisions reflect a balance between curatorial and conservation priorities. When you have obtained the name of a conservator, call and arrange a time and location to discuss your conservation needs. Some conservators will come to an institution, while others will request that you bring the item to them. If you are located at a great distance, arrangements will need to be made for shipping the item for examination, after preliminary discussion by telephone.

To facilitate this interaction at the outset, be prepared to provide the conservator with the following:

- the nature of the item (e.g., book, manuscript, art on paper)
- the component materials (e.g., paper, leather, parchment)
- the media (e.g., writing, typing, printing ink)

- the nature of the problem (e.g., tears, physical distortion, brittleness, a combination of factors)
- the type and extent of anticipated use (e.g., extensive or limited research use, exhibition)
- environmental conditions (e.g., winter heating only, stable conditions with temperature and humidity control)
- housing systems (e.g., upright or flat shelving, boxes or other protective enclosures)
- the desired outcome of treatment (e.g., basic stabilization or protection, improved appearance, prevention of loss of information).

This information is critical for the conservator to judge whether or not he or she can work on the item. It is also critical information if the conservator is to develop a treatment proposal that adequately addresses both the condition of the item and your institutional requirements.

Also, decide in advance when you would like the work completed and determine if there are any deadlines that must be met. Finally, know the amount of money that is available, as this may dictate the level of treatment you can afford. Valuable time and effort will be saved if you are clear with the conservator from the outset.

At this point, a conservator may make general suggestions about different treatment approaches and techniques that might be suitable for your items. However, do not expect the conservator to offer concrete treatment proposals or cost estimates until he or she has had a chance to examine the items fully.

What You Should Ask the Conservator

From the outset, ask questions that will help you evaluate a conservator's qualifications and ability to treat the items in your collection. Bearing in mind the discussion above concerning the education, training, and professional development of conservators, your questions should address:

- training
- length of practice
- scope of practice
- membership in professional organizations
- references
- whether a portfolio of work or treatment reports is available.

Determine how the conservator estimates costs (by the hour, day, or project), and whether or not the cost estimate is binding if treatment requires more or less time than had been projected. Ask if there are separate fees for the preliminary examination and estimate — a time consuming but vital part of conservation treatment. It is not unusual for a conservator to charge at an hourly rate, with a flat fee for the preliminary examination and estimate, payable whether or not the client decides to proceed with treatment. At this point, clarify any questions about fees for insurance, shipping, or other separate charges that may be part of the final bill. Costs will vary from one area of the country to another and may also depend upon the nature of a particular conservator's practice specialty.

Contact the conservator's references and, if possible, speak to the person who worked directly with the conservator. Ask each reference if the treatment was completed satisfactorily, in accord with the signed agreement, and on time. Inquire about the adequacy of photographic and written documentation (see "Course of Treatment" below). Ask if the conservator maintained communication as necessary during treatment — whether, for example, unexpected developments and proposed changes in treatment were adequately discussed.

Remember that different clients contract for treatment services for different reasons, and therefore may have different standards or criteria for judging the work that was done. Bear in mind that a client may not always be able to determine if a treatment is technically flawed, especially when the client must base that evaluation simply on appearance.

Evaluate all the information that you receive from former or current clients as well as from the conservator. Listen carefully to what the conservator says and to the kinds of questions that he or she asks. For example, did he or she ask about the kind and level of anticipated use, or about the environment in which the item will be stored? These and other questions may reveal the way the conservator thinks about the broader issues and implications of conservation treatment.

THE COURSE OF TREATMENT: WHAT TO EXPECT

Preliminary Examination and Treatment Proposal

Once you have chosen a conservator and have established that he or she is available to work with you, you should expect to interact at several different points. Although the conservator may have provided preliminary recommendations in the initial contact, more detailed examination must now take place. The item should be taken or sent to the conservator, who will examine it and prepare a written condition report describing these features:

- materials, structure, and method of fabrication of the item
- location and extent of physical damage, chemical deterioration, or previous repairs.

Along with this report, the conservator prepares a treatment proposal containing these elements:

- where appropriate, different options for correcting the conservation problems
- for each option, an outline of the procedures to be used and a description of the condition(s) they are intended to correct
- an estimate of the time required to complete the treatment
- an estimate of the cost.

The proposal should reflect clearly the conservator's intention to retain the original character of the item to the greatest extent possible. All proposed procedures should be designed to allow, insofar as possible, subsequent removal of materials added during treatment. When more than one treatment option is included in the proposal, the conservator should explain the benefits and implications of each.

Read the treatment proposal carefully, and do not hesitate to ask questions if you need clarification on technical aspects of the proposal. Consider suggestions that the conservator may offer for a less involved treatment than you originally envisioned. For example, when proposing treatment for a book with an early original binding that has become weak but is still serviceable, a conservator may recommend that the book be placed in a box rather than treated with more elaborate procedures. This recommendation may be based on the desire to retain intact as much of the original binding as possible. Boxing is especially appropriate if the volume receives limited use.

Once you agree to a specific proposed treatment, the conservator will ask you to sign the proposal and return it before any treatment begins. During the course of treatment, the conservator may discover that the proposed treatment must be changed, for any of a variety of reasons. In that event, he or she should contact you to discuss the revision.

Treatment Report and Evaluation

After the treatment is complete, the conservator should prepare and submit a final report to you. Treatment reports vary in format and length, but all reports should include descriptions of the following:

- techniques used during the course of treatment
- exact materials used in correcting conservation problems
- photographs documenting the condition before and after treatment, with dates
- any photographs or diagrams necessary to clarify procedures that were used.

The conservator may also make recommendations for special handling or use of the item, when this information is essential to its continued maintenance.

It is important that the institution retain the treatment report permanently, for it may be needed in the future by bibliographic scholars or conservators doing additional work on the item. The report may be kept with the item itself (perhaps housed with it) or easily accessible with other records concerning items in the collection.

When reviewing completed work, keep in mind that it is difficult to evaluate technical aspects of a treatment. A good rule of thumb is that all repairs should be discernable to a trained eye, but should not clash aesthetically or historically with the item. No attempt should be made to obscure the treatment. This is important so that people consulting the materials in the future will not be misled. Remember that the nature and severity of damage or deterioration will influence the degree to which the item can be stabilized, strengthened, and aesthetically improved through treatment.

SUMMARY

Selecting a conservator is a serious proposition, but it need not be daunting. It is important to exercise caution and not rashly entrust our cultural treasures to a person whose judgment and skills are not commensurate with the task.

By asking careful questions, contacting references, and working with the conservator before and during treatment, you can obtain competent conservation services. In this way, the sometimes delicate chain linking the past and the future will not be broken, and these important cultural resources will remain available to researchers now and in the future.

NOTES

[1] For an overview of this concept, see Paul Banks' *The Preservation of Library Materials* and Barclay Ogden's *On the Preservation of Books and Documents in Original Form*, both cited in the "Further Readings" section.

[2] Some examples of inappropriate treatments include the use of poorly designed and acidic pamphlet binders that cause damage and discoloration to the leaves of the pamphlet, and the use of pressure-sensitive tapes that become yellow or brittle, cause bleeding of inks, or leave a damaging and disfiguring adhesive residue on the paper.

[3] Training program addresses can be found in the "Conservation Training Programs" section. Only the program at the University of Texas at Austin currently offers training specifically oriented to collections in libraries and archives.

[4] "Code of Ethics and Guidelines for Practice," *The American Institute for Conservation of Historic and Artistic Works Directory*, 1998, or most current. Available from the AIC, whose address is provided in the "Information Resources" section.

FURTHER READINGS

American Institute for Conservation. *Guidelines for Selecting a Conservator.* Washington, DC: AIC, 1991, 6 pp.

Banks, Paul N. "The Preservation of Library Materials." Chicago: The Newberry Library, 1978. Reprinted from the *Encyclopedia of Library and Information Science* 23 (1969): 180-222.

Clarkson, Christopher. "The Conservation of Early Books in Codex Form: A Personal Approach." *The Paper Conservator 3* (1978): 33-50.

Cullison, Bonnie Jo, and Jean Donaldson. "Conservators and Curators: A Cooperative Approach to Treatment Specifications." *Library Trends* 36.1 (Summer 1987): 229-39.

Dachs, Karl. "Conservation: The Curator's Point of View." *Restaurator* 6 (1984): 118-26.

Foot, Mirjam. "The Binding Historian and the Book Conservator." *The Paper Conservator* 8 (1984): 77-83.

Henderson, Cathy. "Curator or Conservator: Who Decides on What Treatment?" *Rare Books & Manuscripts Librarianship*. 2.2 (Fall 1987): 103-07.

Ogden, Barclay. *On the Preservation of Books and Documents in Original Form.* Washington, DC: The Commission on Preservation and Access, 1989. Reprinted in *The Abbey Newsletter* 14.4 (July 1990): 62-64.

Pillette, Roberta, and Carolyn Harris. "It Takes Two to Tango: A Conservator's View of Curator/Conservator Relations." *Rare Books & Manuscripts Librarianship* 4.2 (Fall 1989): 103-11.

Roberts, Matt T., and Don Etherington. *Bookbinding and the Conservation of Books: A Dictionary of Descriptive Terminology.* Washington, DC: Preservation Office, Library of Congress, 1982, 296 pp.

ACKNOWLEDGEMENTS

SOLINET and the author are grateful to the following individuals who reviewed early drafts of this work:

- Paul Banks, Columbia University
- Karen Garlick, National Museum of American History
- Walter Henry, Stanford University
- Lyn Koehnline, Ackland Art Museum
- Ellen McCrady, Abbey Publications
- Sandra Nyberg, SOLINET

Partial funding for this publication was provided by a grant from the National Endowment for the Humanities Office of Preservation, whose support is gratefully acknowledged.

INFORMATION RESOURCES

The American Institute for Conservation of Historic and Artistic Works (AIC)
1717 K St., NW, Ste. 301
Washington, DC 20006
Telephone: (202) 452-9545
Fax: (202) 452-9328
E-mail: InfoAIC@aol.com

Institute of Museum and Library Services (IMLS)
1100 Pennsylvania Avenue, NW
Room 609
Washington, DC 20506
Telephone: (202) 606-8539
Fax: (202) 606-8591
E-mail: imsinfo@ims.fed.us

The International Institute for Conservation of Historic and Artistic Works (IIC)
6 Buckingham Street
London WC2N 6BA, England
Telephone: 01-839-5975
E-mail: iicon@compuserve.com

National Institute for Conservation of Cultural Property (NIC)
3299 K Street, NW, Suite 602
Washington, DC 20007
Telephone: (202) 625-1495
Fax: (202) 625-1485
E-mail: lreger@nic.org

SOLINET Preservation Program
1438 West Peachtree St., NW, Ste. 200
Atlanta, GA 30309-2955
Toll Free: (800) 999-8558 Telephone: (404) 892-0943
Fax: (404) 892-7879
E-mail: solinet_information@solinet.net

CONSERVATION TRAINING PROGRAMS

Buffalo State College
Art Conservation Department
230 Rockwell Hall
1300 Elmwood Avenue
Buffalo, NY 14222-1095
Telephone: (716) 878-5025
E-mail: tahkfc@buffalostate.edu

Strauss Center for Conservation
Harvard University Art Museums
32 Quincy Street
Cambridge, MA 02138
Telephone: (617) 495-2392
Fax: (617) 495-9936
E-mail:

Conservation Center of the Institute of Fine Arts
New York University
14 East 78th Street
New York, NY 10021
Telephone: (212) 772-5800
E-mail: conservation.program@nyu.edu

Queen's University
Art Conservation Programme
Kingston, Ontario K7L 3N6
Canada
Telephone: (613) 545-2156
Fax: (613) 545-6300
E-mail: amz6@qucdn.queensu.cos

University of Texas at Austin
Preservation and Conservation Studies
Graduate School of Library & Information Sciences
EDB #564
Austin, TX 78712-1276
Telephone: (512) 471-8290
Fax: (512) 471-8285 E-mail: glabs@utxdp.dp.utexas.edu

University of Delaware/Winterthur
Art Conservation Department
303 Old College
University of Delaware
Newark, DE 19716-2515
Telephone: (302) 831-2479
Fax: (302) 831-4330
E-mail: debra.norris@mvs.udel.edu

REGIONAL CONSERVATION CENTERS

Balboa Art Conservation Center
P.O. Box 3755
San Diego, CA 92163
Telephone: (619) 236-9702
Fax: (619) 236-0141

Services: Conservation of paintings polychrome sculpture, and selected artifacts. Surveys, educational prog and disaster assistance.

Conservation Center for Art and Historic Artifacts
264 South 23rd Street
Philadelphia, PA 19103
Telephone: (215) 545-0613
Fax: (215) 735-9313
E-mail: ccaha@shrsys.hslc.org

Services: Conservation of paper, photographs, and library and archive materials. Surveys, educational programs and disaster assistance.

Intermuseum Conservation Association
Allen Art Building
83 North Main Street
Oberlin, OH 44074-1192
Telephone: (216) 775-7331
Fax: (216) 774-3431

Services: Conservation of paintings furniture, and decorative art objects Surveys and educational programs.

New York State Conservation Consultancy
c/o Textile Conservation Workshop
3 Main Street
South Salem, NY 10590
Telephone: (914) 763-5805

Services: Conservation information surveys (general, environmental, storage exhibit, treatment) for libraries, archives and historical societies.

Northeast Document Conservation Center
100 Brickstone Square
Andover, MA 01810-1494
Telephone: (978) 470-1010
Fax: (978) 475-6021
E-mail: nedcc@nedcc.org
http://www.nedcc.org

Services: Conservation of library and archival materials, paper, and photographs. Surveys, educational programs, and disaster assistance.

Rocky Mountain Regional Conservation Center
University of Denver
2420 South University Boulevard
Denver, CO 80208
Telephone: (303) 733-2712
Fax: (303) 733-2508
E-mail: lmellon@du.edu

Services: Conservation of paintings, paper, objects, and textiles. Surveys and educational programs.

Strauss Center for Conservation
Harvard University Art Museum
32 Quincy Street
Cambridge, MA 02138
Telephone: (617) 495-2392
Fax: (617) 495-9936
E-mail: lie@fas.harvard.edu

Services: Conservation of paintings, paper, objects, and sculpture. Surveys and educational programs.

Textile Conservation Center
American Textile History Museum
491 Dutton Street
Lowell, MA 01854
Telephone: (978) 441-1198
Fax: (978) 441-1412

Services: Conservation of textiles and costumes. Surveys, educational programs and disaster assistance.

Textile Conservation Workshop
3 Main Street
South Salem, NY 10590
Telephone: (914) 763-5805

Services: Conservation of textiles and costumes Surveys and educational programs.

Upper Midwest Conservation Association
c/o The Minneapolis Institute of Arts
2400 Third Avenue South
Minneapolis, MN 55404
Telephone: (612) 870-3120
Fax: (612) 870-3118

Services: Conservation of pictorial art, paintings, paper, sculpture, and objects. Surveys and educational programs.

Williamstown Art Conservation Center
225 South Street
Williamstown, MA 01267
Telephone: (413) 458-5741
Fax: (413) 458-2314

Services: Conservation of paintings, paper, furniture, objects, and sculpture. Surveys and educational programs.

Acknowledgements

Reprinted with permission from *Choosing and Working with A Conservator*, by Jan Paris, copyright ©1990, Southeastern Library Network, Inc. (SOLINET), Atlanta, GA. Copies of the original publication are available from SOLINET, 1438 West Peachtree St., NW., Suite 200, Atlanta, GA 30309-2955. NEDCC gratefully acknowledges permission by SOLINET to reprint this publication.